Hana-Kimi

For You in Full Blossom

4

story and art by
HISAYA NAKAJO

HANA-KIMI
For You In Full Blossom
VOLUME 4

STORY & ART BY HISAYA NAKAJO

Translation/David Ury
English Adaptation/Gerard Jones
Touch-Up Art & Lettering/Gabe Crate
Design/Izumi Evers
Editor/Jason Thompson

Editor in Chief, Books/Alvin Lu
Editor in Chief, Magazines/Marc Weidenbaum
VP, Publishing Licensing/Rika Inouye
VP, Sales & Product Marketing/Gonzalo Ferreyra
VP, Creative/Linda Espinosa
Publisher/Hyoe Narita

Printed in the U.S.A.

Published by VIZ Media, LLC, P.O. Box 77010, San Francisco, CA 94107

Shôjo Edition
10 9 8 7 6 5

First printing, December 2004
Fifth printing, October 2008

www.viz.com
store.viz.com

CONTENTS

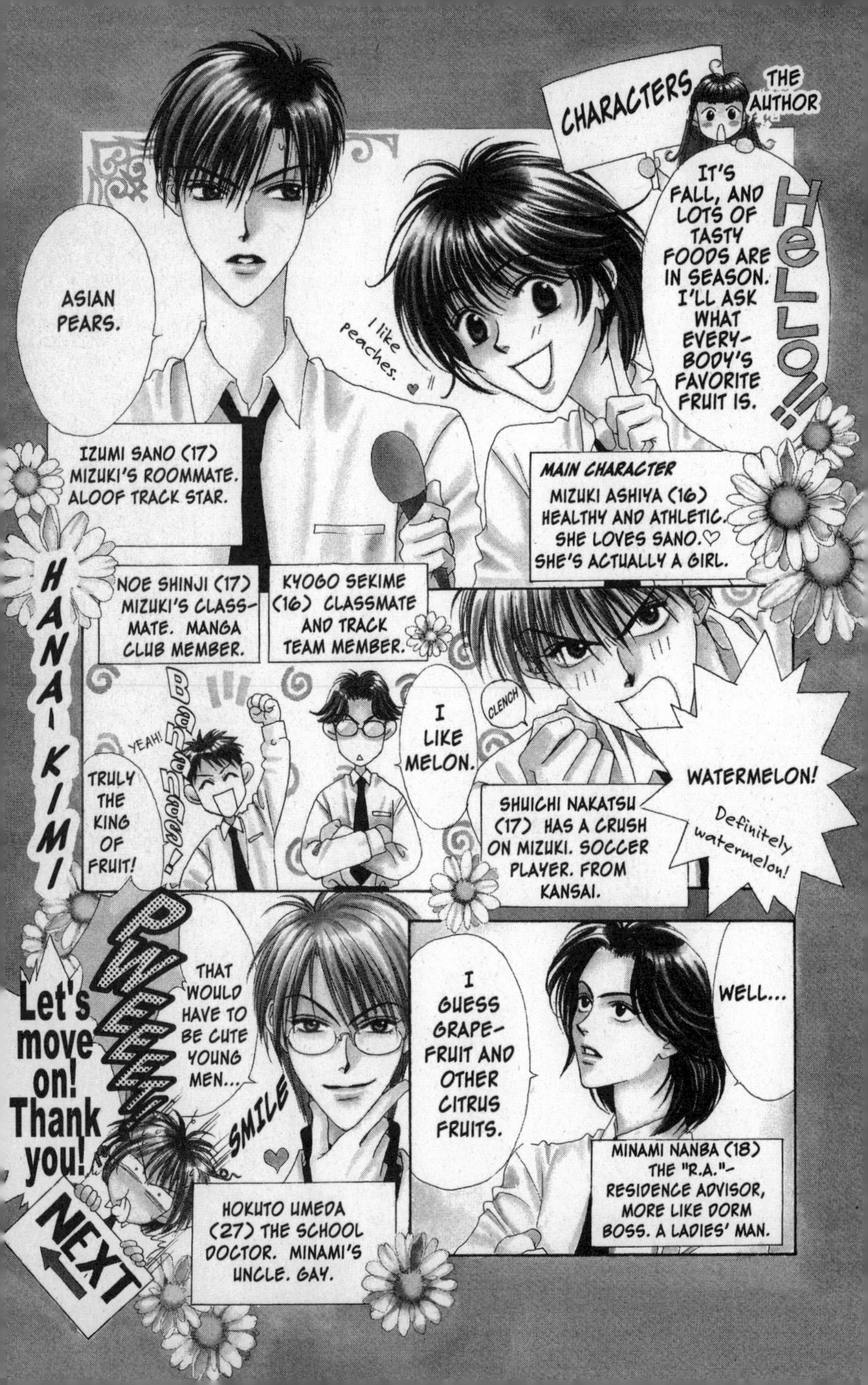

CHARACTERS
THE AUTHOR
HELLO!!
IT'S FALL, AND LOTS OF TASTY FOODS ARE IN SEASON. I'LL ASK WHAT EVERYBODY'S FAVORITE FRUIT IS.
MAIN CHARACTER
MIZUKI ASHIYA (16) HEALTHY AND ATHLETIC. SHE LOVES SANO.♡ SHE'S ACTUALLY A GIRL.
I like peaches. ♥
ASIAN PEARS.
IZUMI SANO (17) MIZUKI'S ROOMMATE. ALOOF TRACK STAR.
CLENCH
WATERMELON!
Definitely watermelon!
SHUICHI NAKATSU (17) HAS A CRUSH ON MIZUKI. SOCCER PLAYER. FROM KANSAI.
KYOGO SEKIME (16) CLASSMATE AND TRACK TEAM MEMBER.
NOE SHINJI (17) MIZUKI'S CLASSMATE. MANGA CLUB MEMBER.
I LIKE MELON.
BANANAAA!
YEAH!
TRULY THE KING OF FRUIT!
HANA-KIMI
WELL...
I GUESS GRAPEFRUIT AND OTHER CITRUS FRUITS.
MINAMI NANBA (18) THE "R.A."- RESIDENCE ADVISOR, MORE LIKE DORM BOSS. A LADIES' MAN.
THAT WOULD HAVE TO BE CUTE YOUNG MEN...
SMILE
HOKUTO UMEDA (27) THE SCHOOL DOCTOR. MINAMI'S UNCLE. GAY.
Let's move on! Thank you!
NEXT

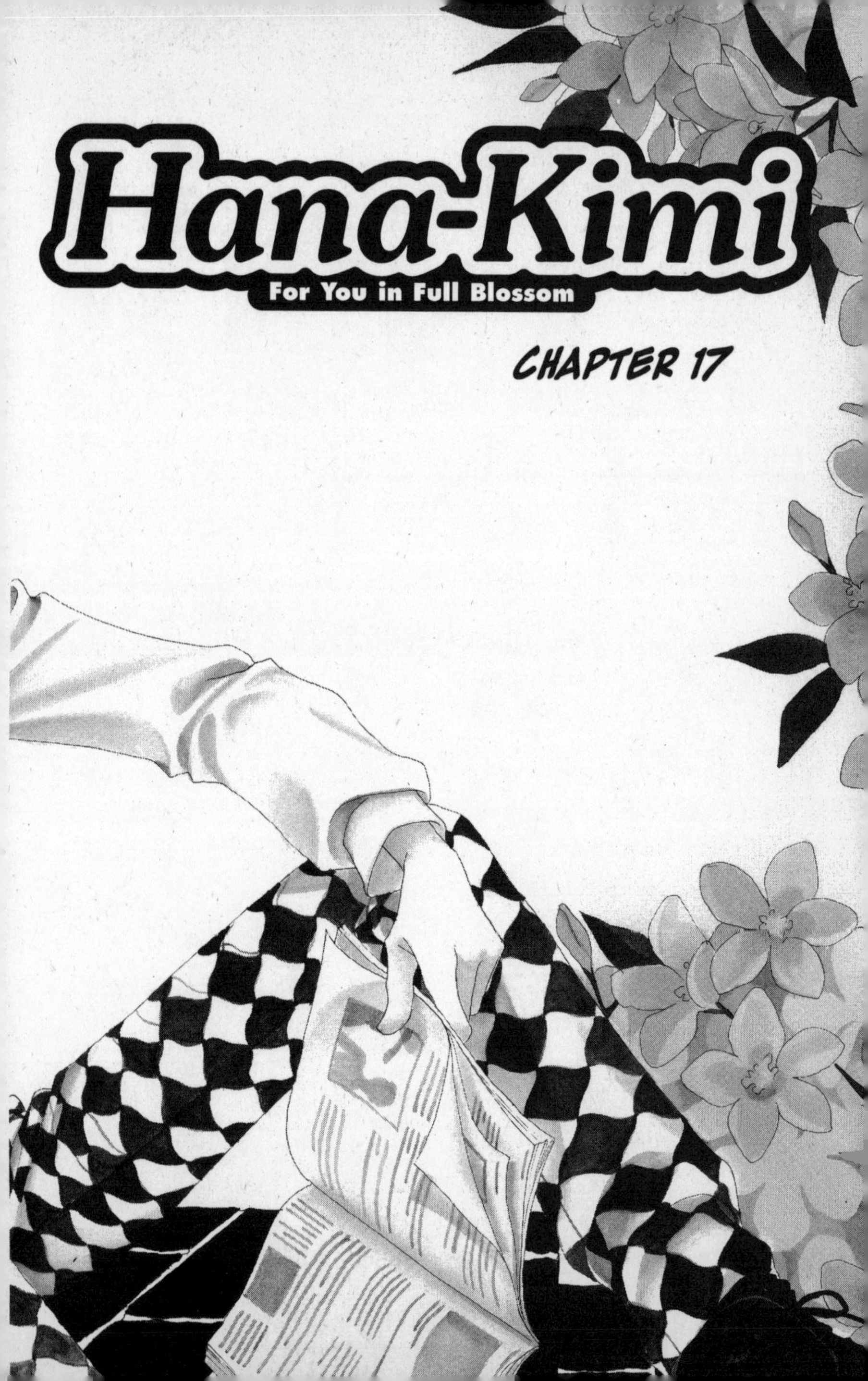
Hana-Kimi
For You in Full Blossom
CHAPTER 17

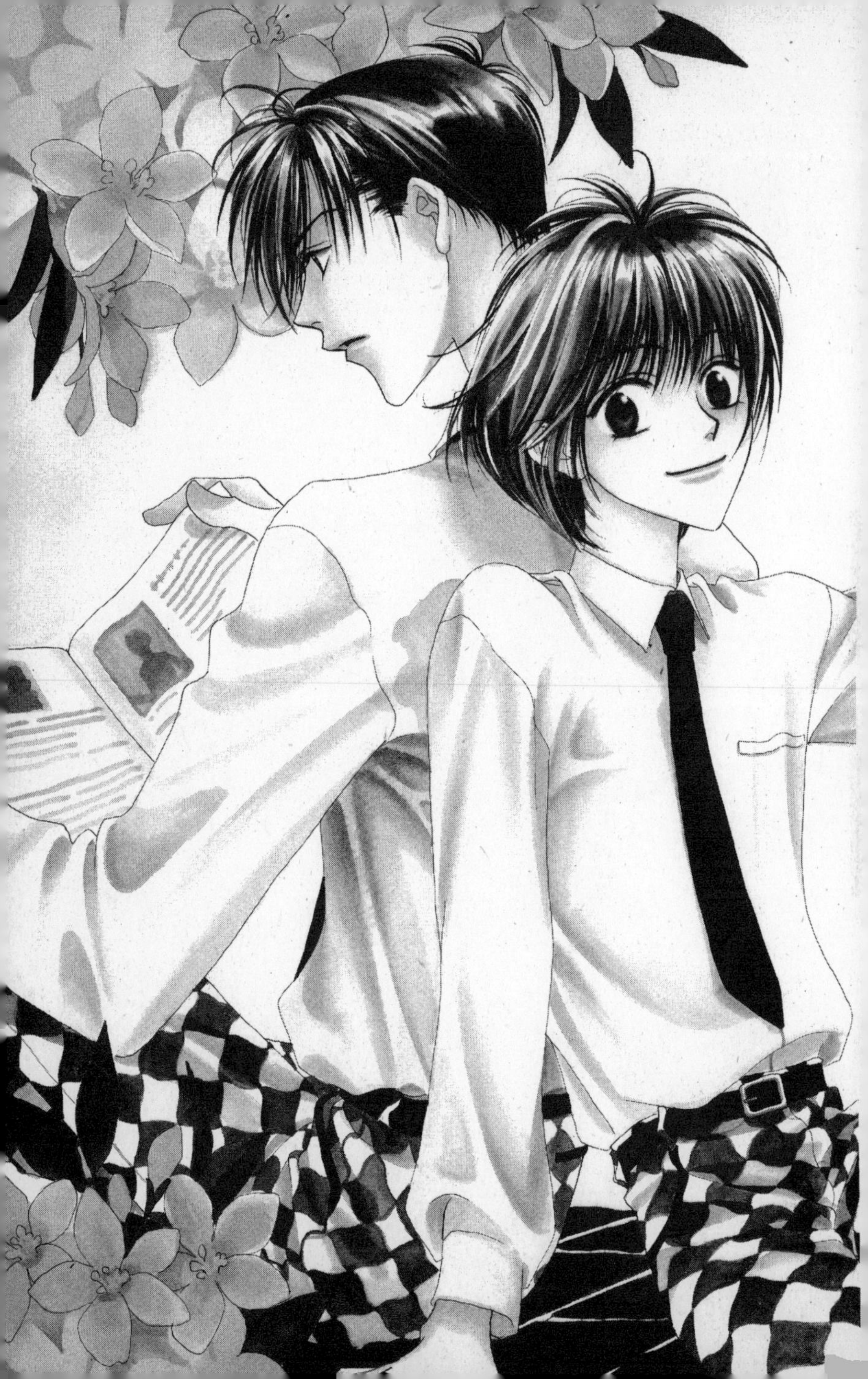

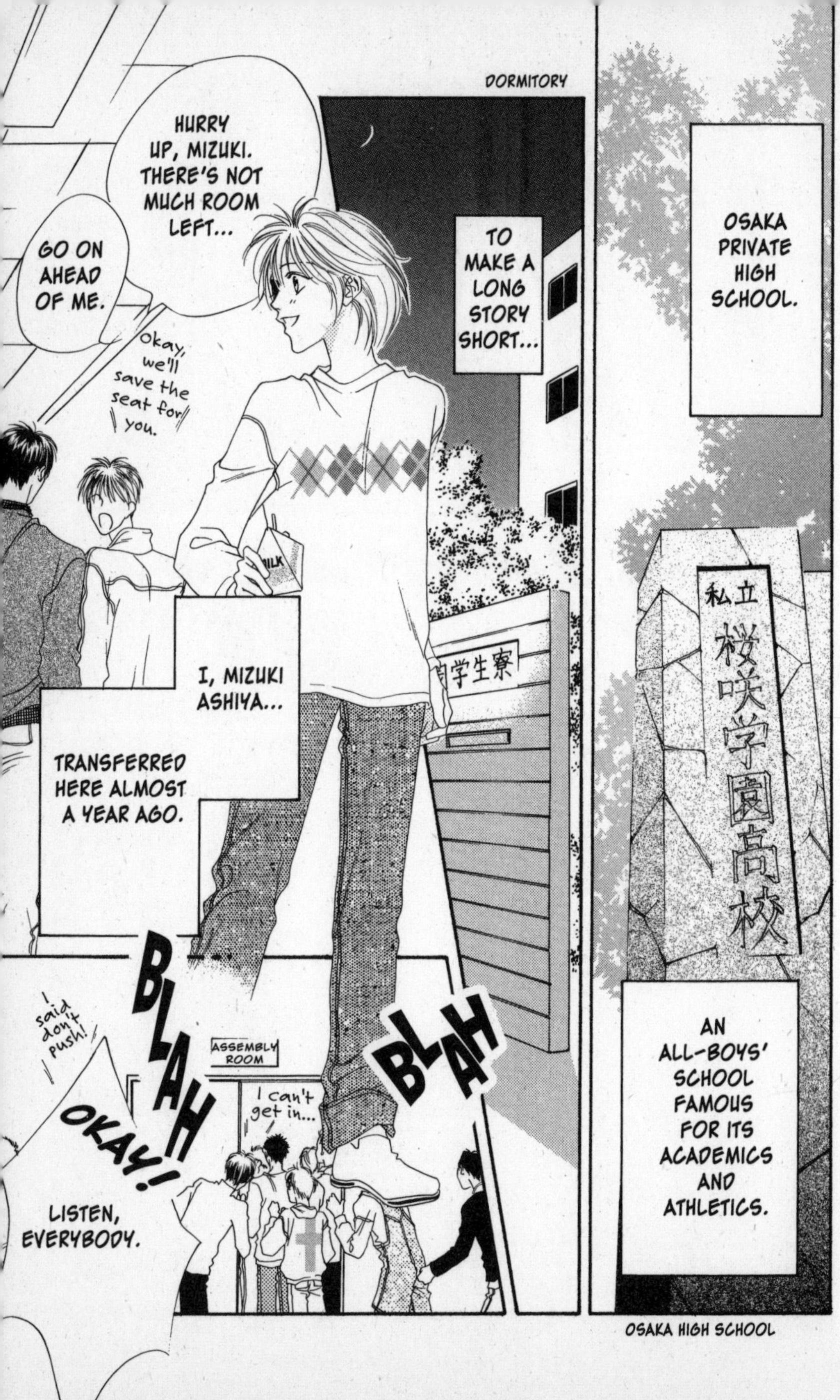
OSAKA PRIVATE HIGH SCHOOL.
私立
桜咲学園高校
AN ALL-BOYS' SCHOOL FAMOUS FOR ITS ACADEMICS AND ATHLETICS.
OSAKA HIGH SCHOOL
DORMITORY
TO MAKE A LONG STORY SHORT...
HURRY UP, MIZUKI. THERE'S NOT MUCH ROOM LEFT...
GO ON AHEAD OF ME.
okay, we'll save the seat for you.
学生寮
I, MIZUKI ASHIYA...
TRANSFERRED HERE ALMOST A YEAR AGO.
BLAH
BLAH
ASSEMBLY ROOM
I can't get in...
I said don't push!
OKAY!
LISTEN, EVERYBODY.

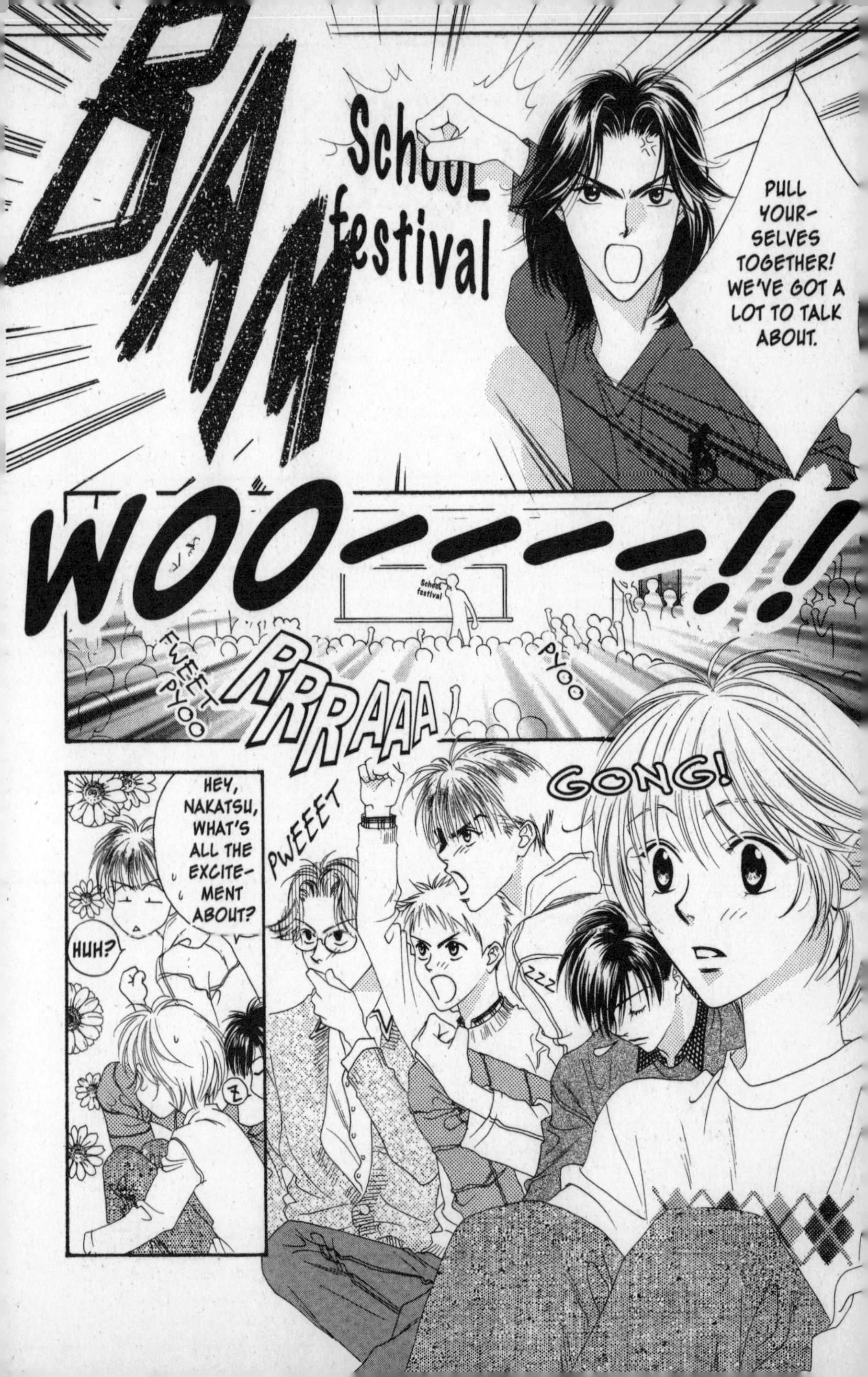
PULL YOURSELVES TOGETHER! WE'VE GOT A LOT TO TALK ABOUT.
School festival
BAM
WOO----!!
School festival
PYOO
RRRAAA
FWEEET PYOO
GONG!
PWEEET
ZZZ
HEY, NAKATSU, WHAT'S ALL THE EXCITEMENT ABOUT?
HUH?
Z

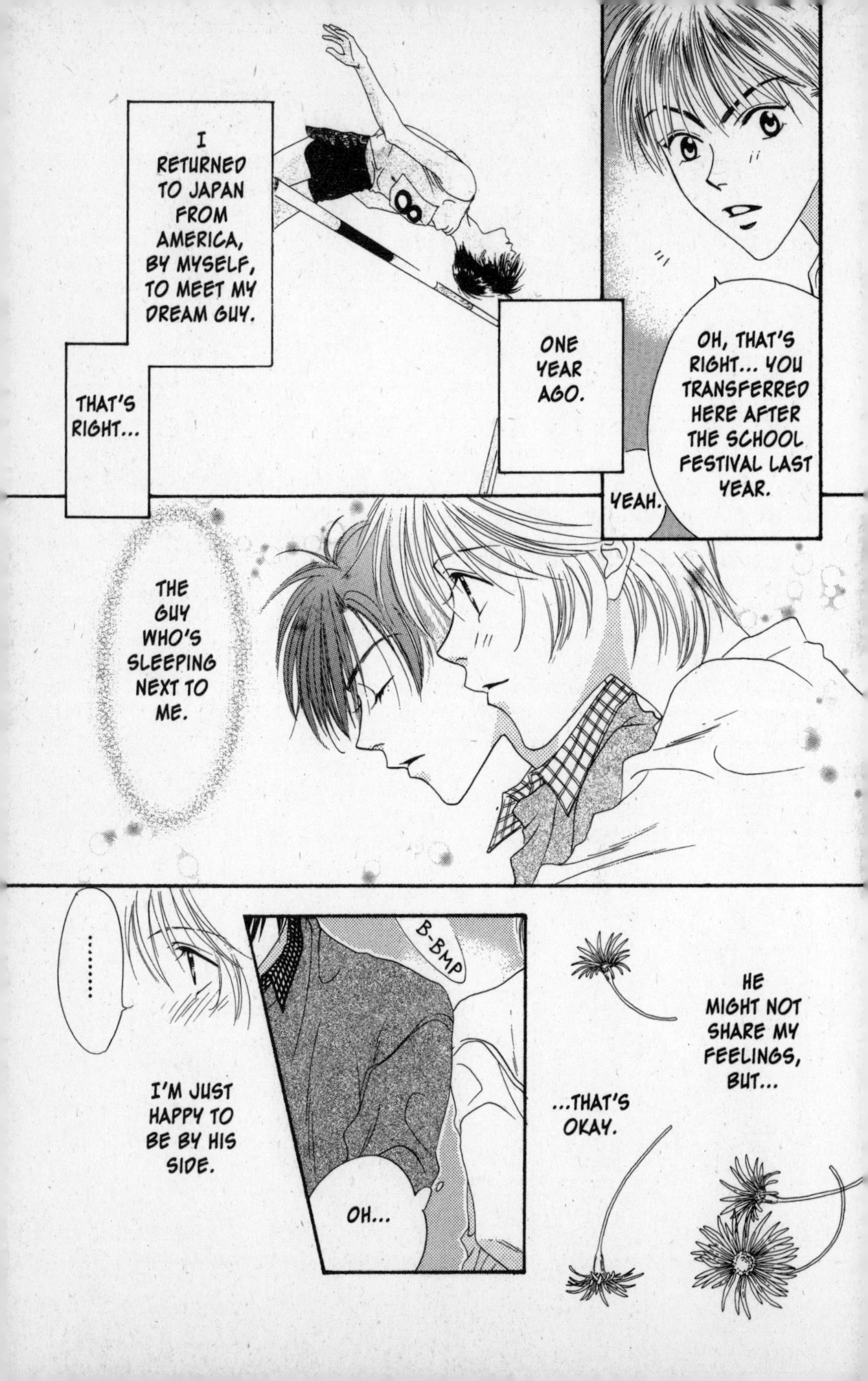
OH, THAT'S RIGHT... YOU TRANSFERRED HERE AFTER THE SCHOOL FESTIVAL LAST YEAR.
YEAH.
ONE YEAR AGO.
I RETURNED TO JAPAN FROM AMERICA, BY MYSELF, TO MEET MY DREAM GUY.
THAT'S RIGHT...
THE GUY WHO'S SLEEPING NEXT TO ME.
HE MIGHT NOT SHARE MY FEELINGS, BUT...
...THAT'S OKAY.
B-BMP
OH...
......
I'M JUST HAPPY TO BE BY HIS SIDE.

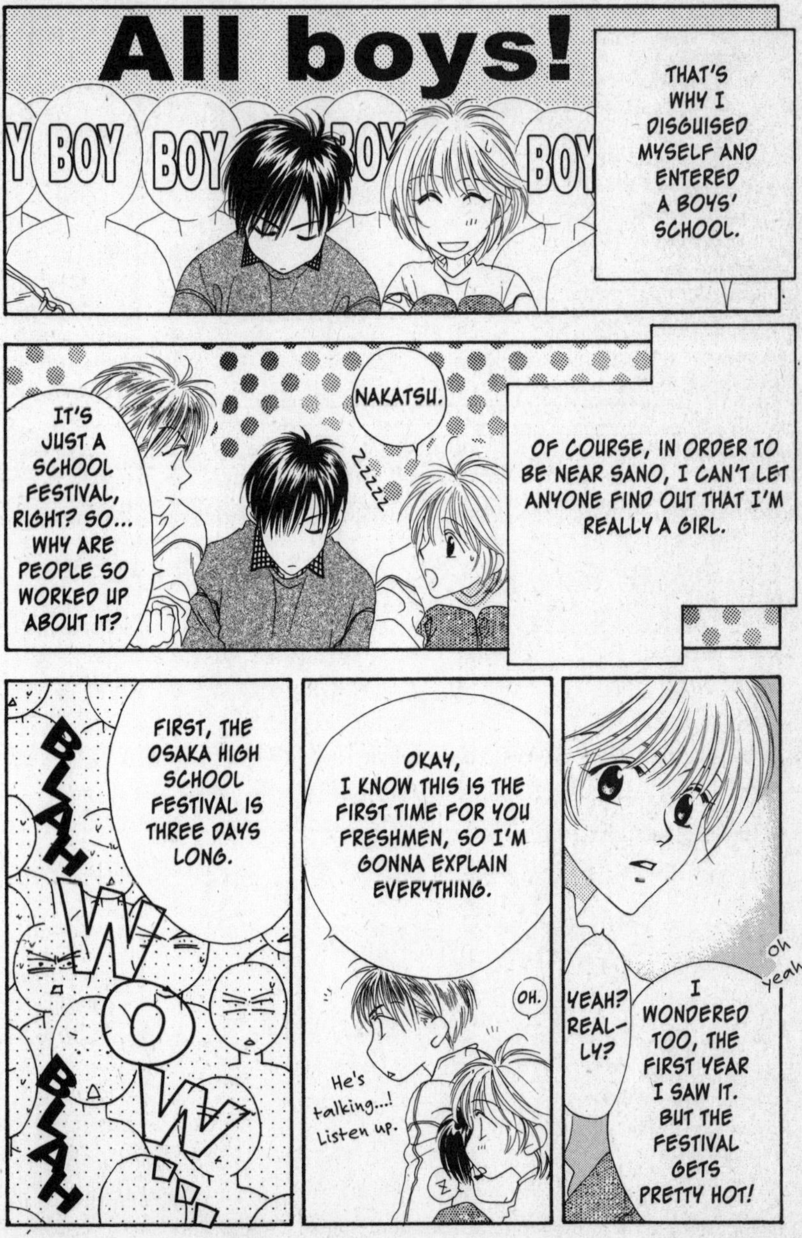
THAT'S WHY I DISGUISED MYSELF AND ENTERED A BOYS' SCHOOL.
All boys!
BOY
BOY
BOY
BOY
OF COURSE, IN ORDER TO BE NEAR SANO, I CAN'T LET ANYONE FIND OUT THAT I'M REALLY A GIRL.
NAKATSU.
ZZZZZ
IT'S JUST A SCHOOL FESTIVAL, RIGHT? SO... WHY ARE PEOPLE SO WORKED UP ABOUT IT?
Oh yeah...
I WONDERED TOO, THE FIRST YEAR I SAW IT. BUT THE FESTIVAL GETS PRETTY HOT!
YEAH? REAL-LY?
OKAY, I KNOW THIS IS THE FIRST TIME FOR YOU FRESHMEN, SO I'M GONNA EXPLAIN EVERYTHING.
OH.
He's talking...! Listen up.
FIRST, THE OSAKA HIGH SCHOOL FESTIVAL IS THREE DAYS LONG.
BLAH
WOW
BLAH

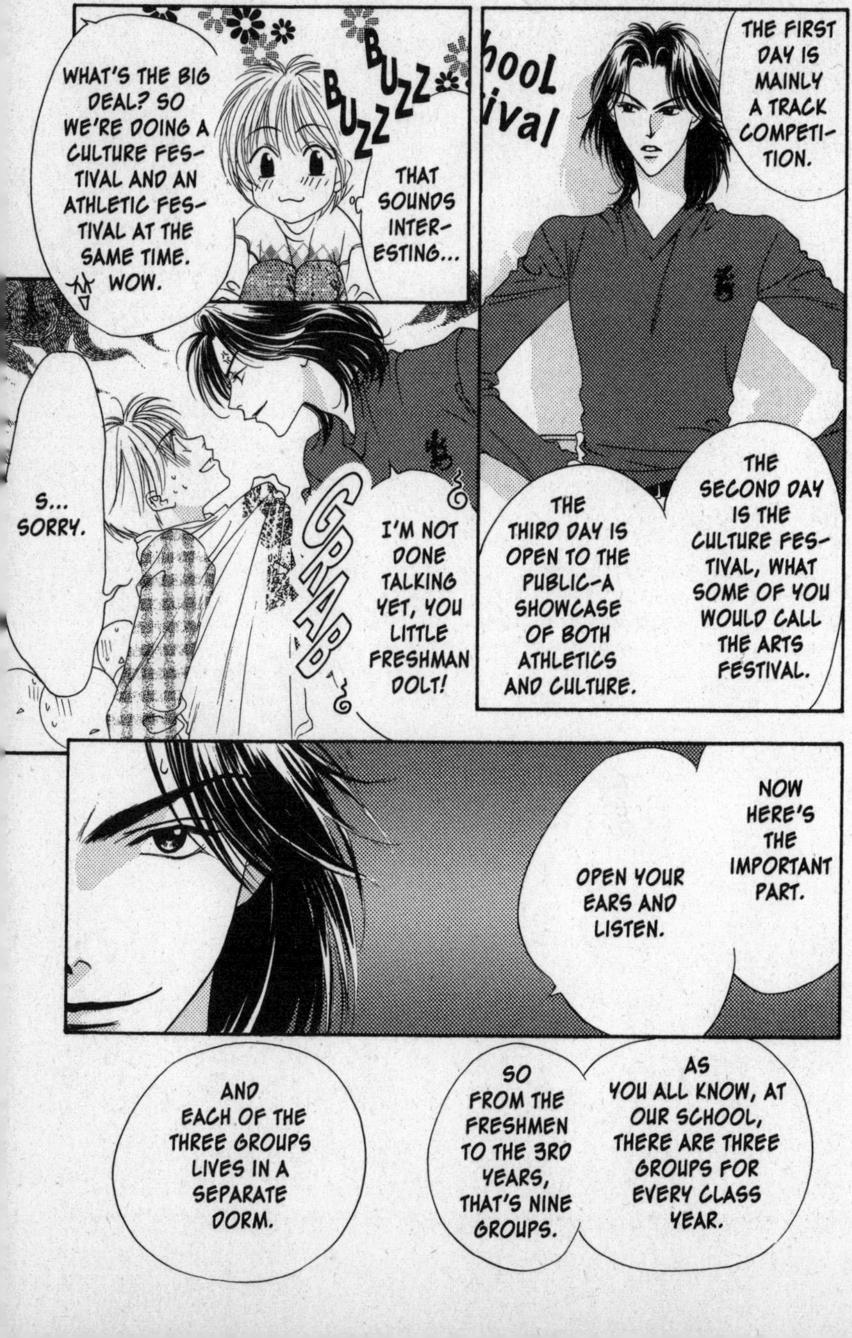
THE FIRST DAY IS MAINLY A TRACK COMPETITION.
THE SECOND DAY IS THE CULTURE FESTIVAL, WHAT SOME OF YOU WOULD CALL THE ARTS FESTIVAL.
THE THIRD DAY IS OPEN TO THE PUBLIC-A SHOWCASE OF BOTH ATHLETICS AND CULTURE.
BUZZ BUZZ
THAT SOUNDS INTERESTING...
WHAT'S THE BIG DEAL? SO WE'RE DOING A CULTURE FESTIVAL AND AN ATHLETIC FESTIVAL AT THE SAME TIME. WOW.
GRAB
I'M NOT DONE TALKING YET, YOU LITTLE FRESHMAN DOLT!
S... SORRY.
NOW HERE'S THE IMPORTANT PART.
OPEN YOUR EARS AND LISTEN.
AS YOU ALL KNOW, AT OUR SCHOOL, THERE ARE THREE GROUPS FOR EVERY CLASS YEAR.
SO FROM THE FRESHMEN TO THE 3RD YEARS, THAT'S NINE GROUPS.
AND EACH OF THE THREE GROUPS LIVES IN A SEPARATE DORM.

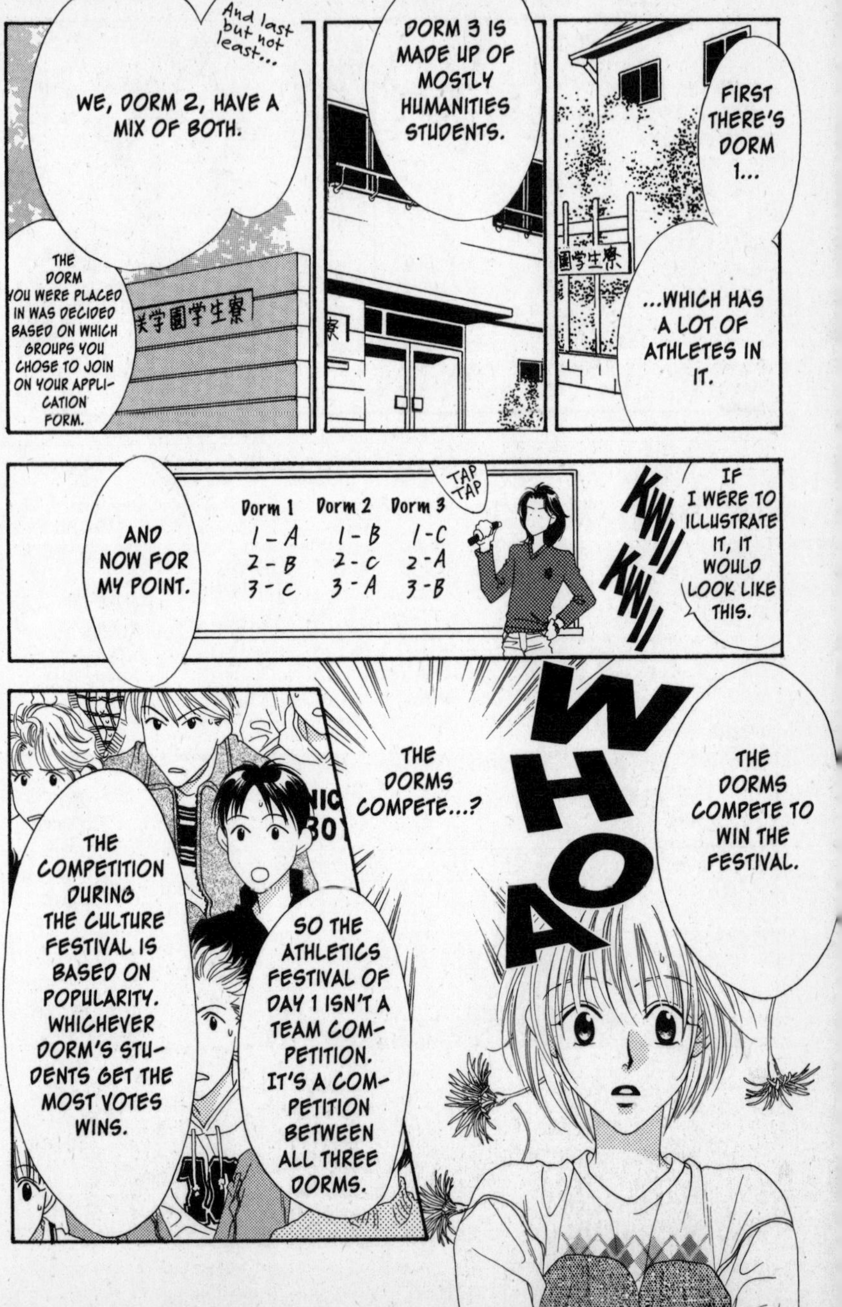
FIRST THERE'S DORM 1...
...WHICH HAS A LOT OF ATHLETES IN IT.
DORM 3 IS MADE UP OF MOSTLY HUMANITIES STUDENTS.
And last but not least...
WE, DORM 2, HAVE A MIX OF BOTH.
THE DORM YOU WERE PLACED IN WAS DECIDED BASED ON WHICH GROUPS YOU CHOSE TO JOIN ON YOUR APPLI-CATION FORM.
IF I WERE TO ILLUSTRATE IT, IT WOULD LOOK LIKE THIS.
KWII KWII
TAP TAP
Dorm 1 Dorm 2 Dorm 3
1-A 1-B 1-C
2-B 2-C 2-A
3-C 3-A 3-B
AND NOW FOR MY POINT.
THE DORMS COMPETE TO WIN THE FESTIVAL.
WHOA
THE DORMS COMPETE...?
SO THE ATHLETICS FESTIVAL OF DAY 1 ISN'T A TEAM COM-PETITION. IT'S A COM-PETITION BETWEEN ALL THREE DORMS.
THE COMPETITION DURING THE CULTURE FESTIVAL IS BASED ON POPULARITY. WHICHEVER DORM'S STU-DENTS GET THE MOST VOTES WINS.

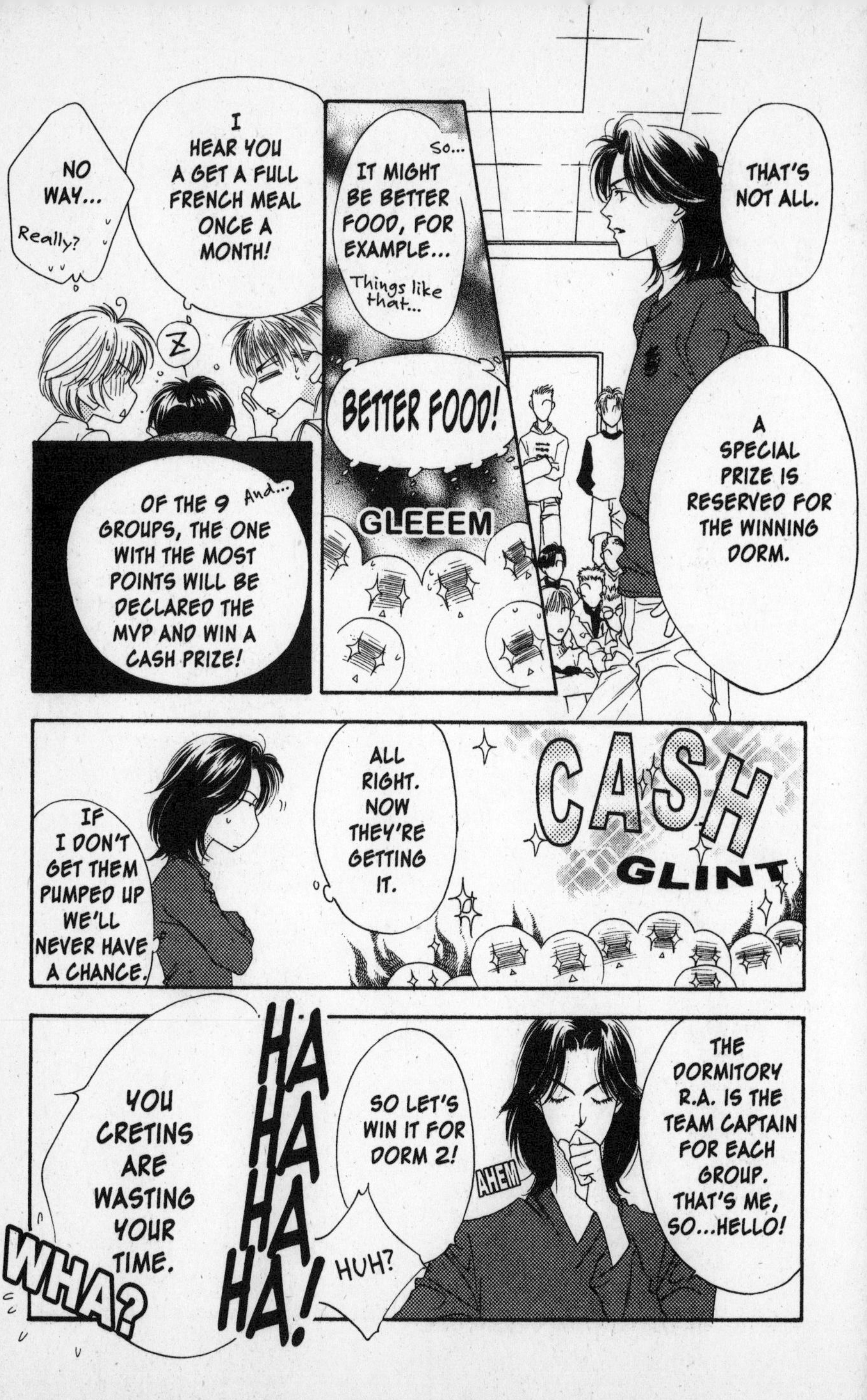
THAT'S NOT ALL.
A SPECIAL PRIZE IS RESERVED FOR THE WINNING DORM.
So... IT MIGHT BE BETTER FOOD, FOR EXAMPLE...
Things like that...
BETTER FOOD!
GLEEEM
I HEAR YOU A GET A FULL FRENCH MEAL ONCE A MONTH!
NO WAY...
Really?
Z
And... OF THE 9 GROUPS, THE ONE WITH THE MOST POINTS WILL BE DECLARED THE MVP AND WIN A CASH PRIZE!
CASH
GLINT
ALL RIGHT. NOW THEY'RE GETTING IT.
IF I DON'T GET THEM PUMPED UP WE'LL NEVER HAVE A CHANCE.
THE DORMITORY R.A. IS THE TEAM CAPTAIN FOR EACH GROUP. THAT'S ME, SO...HELLO!
AHEM
SO LET'S WIN IT FOR DORM 2!
HUH?
HAHAHAHA!
YOU CRETINS ARE WASTING YOUR TIME.
WHA?

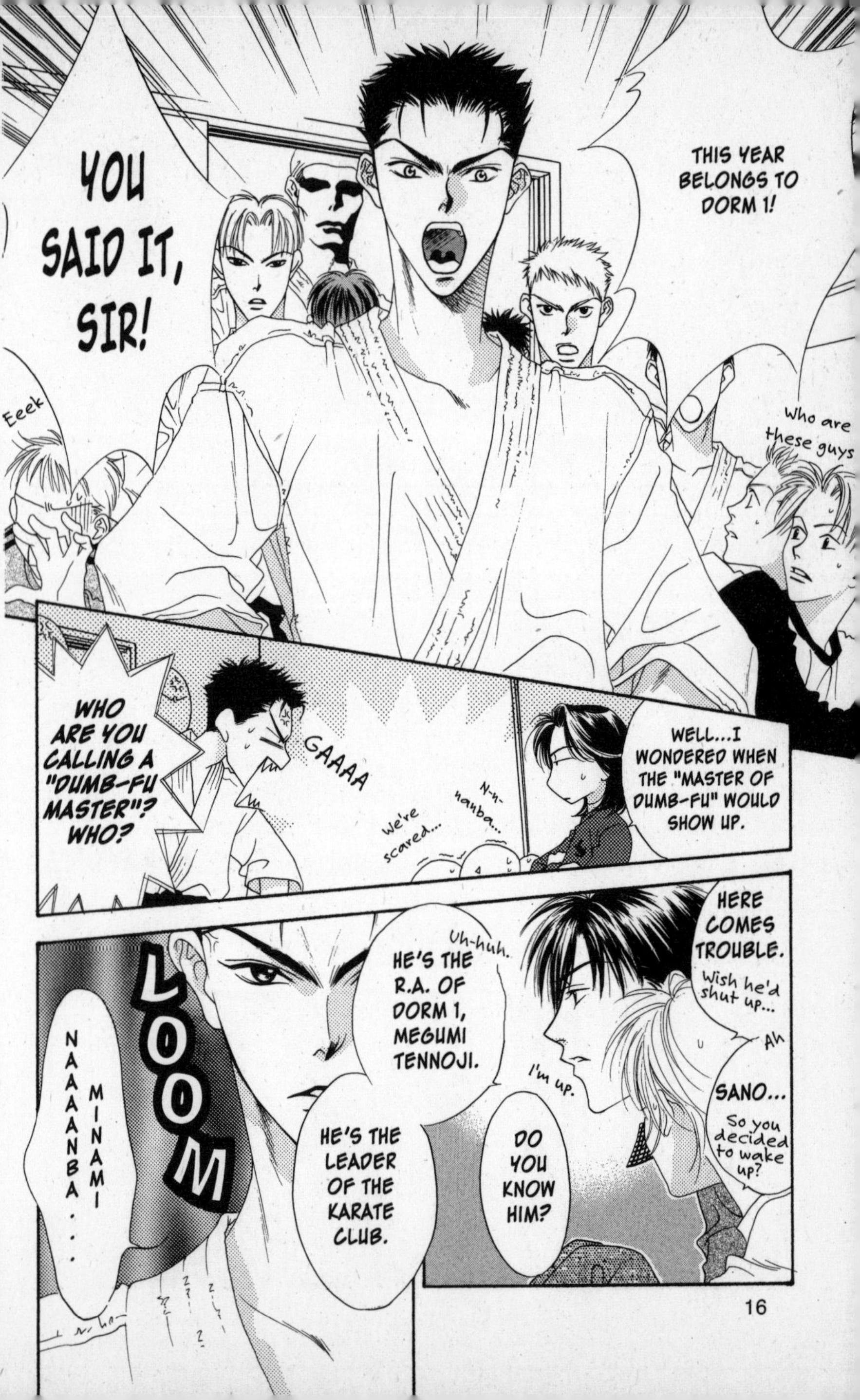
THIS YEAR BELONGS TO DORM 1!
Who are these guys
YOU SAID IT, SIR!
Eeek
WELL...I WONDERED WHEN THE "MASTER OF DUMB-FU" WOULD SHOW UP.
WHO ARE YOU CALLING A "DUMB-FU MASTER"? WHO?
GAAAA
N-n-nanba...
We're scared...
HERE COMES TROUBLE.
Wish he'd shut up...
Ah
SANO...
So you decided to wake up?
I'm up.
DO YOU KNOW HIM?
Uh-huh.
HE'S THE R.A. OF DORM 1, MEGUMI TENNOJI.
HE'S THE LEADER OF THE KARATE CLUB.
LOOM
MINAMI NAAAANBA...

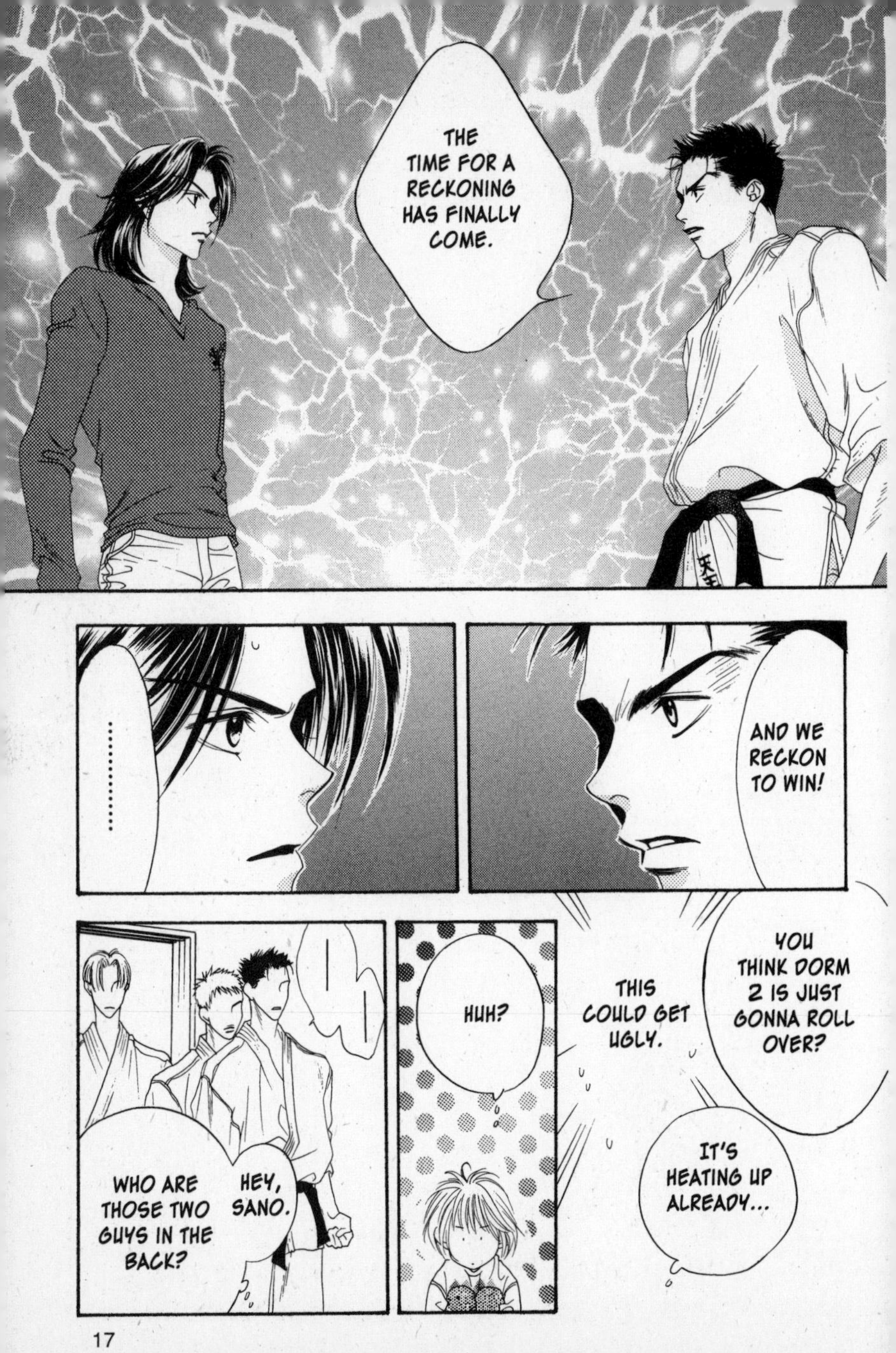
THE TIME FOR A RECKONING HAS FINALLY COME.
AND WE RECKON TO WIN!
......
YOU THINK DORM 2 IS JUST GONNA ROLL OVER?
THIS COULD GET UGLY.
IT'S HEATING UP ALREADY...
HUH?
HEY, SANO.
WHO ARE THOSE TWO GUYS IN THE BACK?

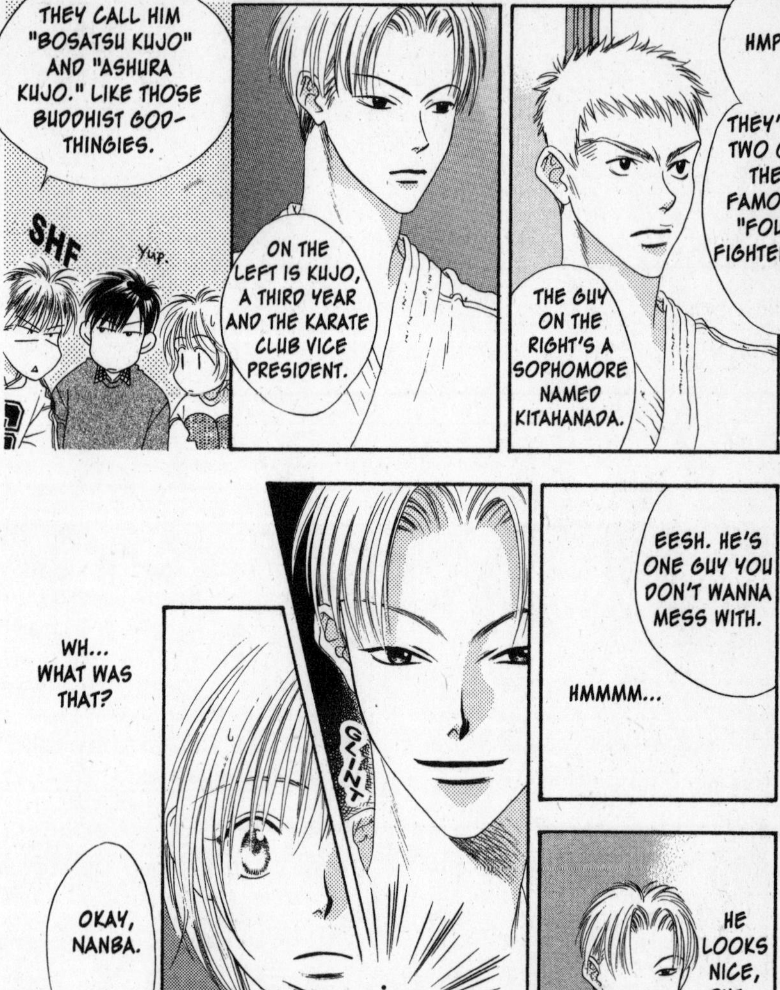
HMPH.
THEY'RE TWO OF THE FAMOUS "FOUR FIGHTERS."
THE GUY ON THE RIGHT'S A SOPHOMORE NAMED KITAHANADA.
ON THE LEFT IS KUJO, A THIRD YEAR AND THE KARATE CLUB VICE PRESIDENT.
THEY CALL HIM "BOSATSU KUJO" AND "ASHURA KUJO." LIKE THOSE BUDDHIST GOD-THINGIES.
SHF
Yup.
EESH. HE'S ONE GUY YOU DON'T WANNA MESS WITH.
HMMMM...
HE LOOKS NICE, BUT...
GLINT
OKAY, NANBA.
JUST REMEMBER THIS.
......!?
WH... WHAT WAS THAT?

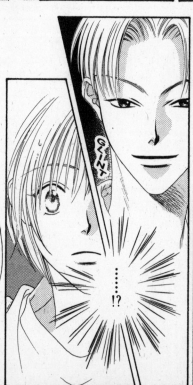

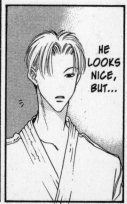

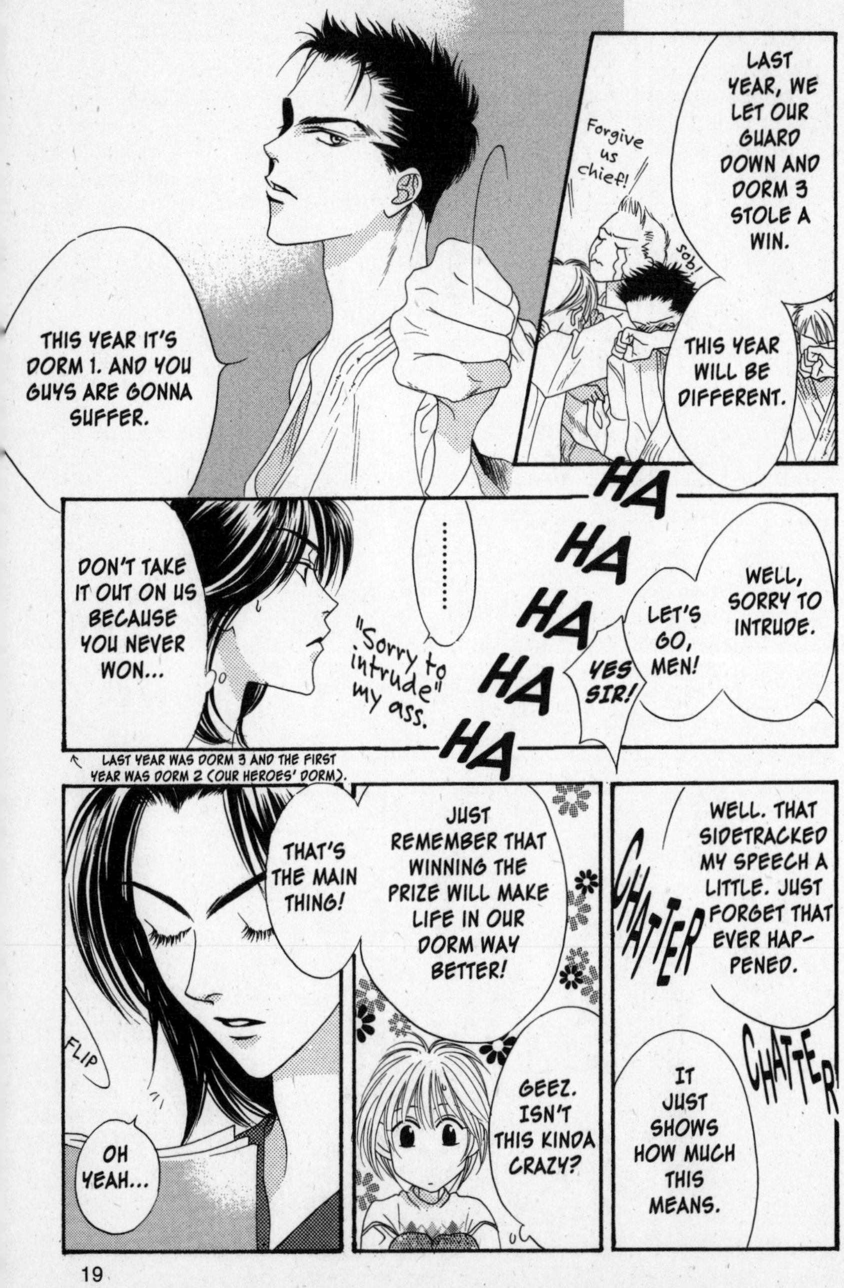
LAST YEAR, WE LET OUR GUARD DOWN AND DORM 3 STOLE A WIN.
Forgive us chief!
Sob!
THIS YEAR WILL BE DIFFERENT.
THIS YEAR IT'S DORM 1. AND YOU GUYS ARE GONNA SUFFER.
WELL, SORRY TO INTRUDE.
LET'S GO, MEN!
YES SIR!
HA HA HA HA HA
......
"Sorry to intrude" my ass.
DON'T TAKE IT OUT ON US BECAUSE YOU NEVER WON...
↖ LAST YEAR WAS DORM 3 AND THE FIRST YEAR WAS DORM 2 (OUR HEROES' DORM).
WELL. THAT SIDETRACKED MY SPEECH A LITTLE. JUST FORGET THAT EVER HAP-PENED.
CHATTER
CHATTER
IT JUST SHOWS HOW MUCH THIS MEANS.
JUST REMEMBER THAT WINNING THE PRIZE WILL MAKE LIFE IN OUR DORM WAY BETTER!
GEEZ. ISN'T THIS KINDA CRAZY?
THAT'S THE MAIN THING!
FLIP
OH YEAH...

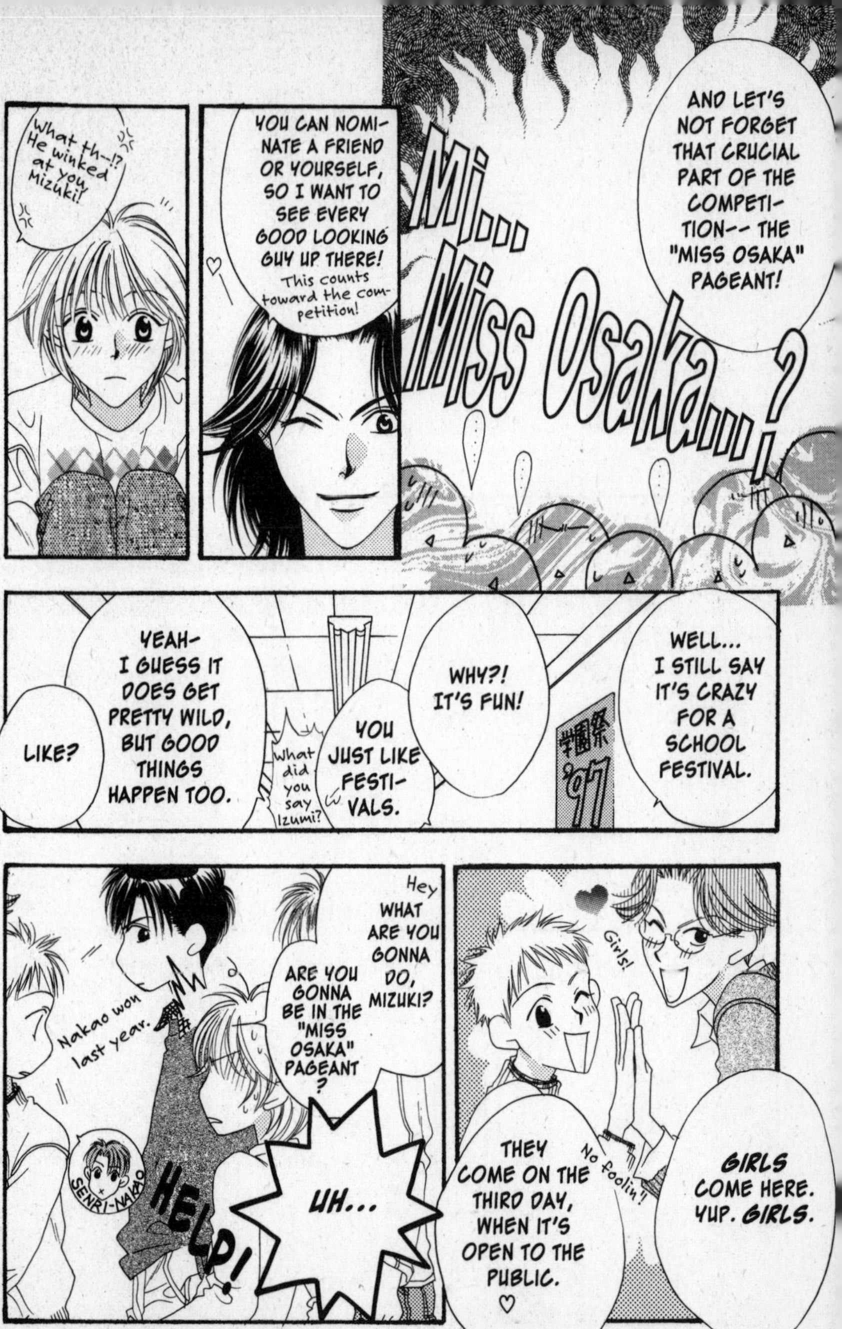
AND LET'S NOT FORGET THAT CRUCIAL PART OF THE COMPETITION-- THE "MISS OSAKA" PAGEANT!
Mi... Miss Osaka...?
YOU CAN NOMINATE A FRIEND OR YOURSELF, SO I WANT TO SEE EVERY GOOD LOOKING GUY UP THERE!
This counts toward the competition!
What th--!? He winked at you Mizuki!
WELL... I STILL SAY IT'S CRAZY FOR A SCHOOL FESTIVAL.
学園祭 '97
WHY?! IT'S FUN!
YOU JUST LIKE FESTIVALS.
What did you say Izumi?
YEAH- I GUESS IT DOES GET PRETTY WILD, BUT GOOD THINGS HAPPEN TOO.
LIKE?
Girls!
GIRLS COME HERE. YUP. GIRLS.
THEY COME ON THE THIRD DAY, WHEN IT'S OPEN TO THE PUBLIC. ♡
No foolin'!
Hey WHAT ARE YOU GONNA DO, MIZUKI?
ARE YOU GONNA BE IN THE "MISS OSAKA" PAGEANT?
UH...
HELP!
Nakao won last year.
SENRI-NAKAO

Greetings!

THIS IS THE 4TH "HANA-KIMI" BOOK!! YAY! IT'S THE SCHOOL FESTIVAL STORY I'VE ALWAYS WANTED TO WRITE. THERE ARE THREE DORMS IN OSAKA HIGH SCHOOL, BUT I REALLY WANTED TO MAKE IT FOUR DORMS. AND LISTEN TO THE NAMES I THOUGHT OF-- "SEIRYU, BYAKKO, GENBU, AND SUZAKU"! (HA HA HA HA... PLEASE LAUGH.) HIMEJIMA WOULD BE IN THE SEIRYU DORM, KUJO IN THE BYAKKO DORM, TENNOJI IN THE GENBU DORM, AND NANBA IN THE SUZAKU DORM. BUT I THOUGHT THAT WOULD BE TOO MUCH, SO I STOPPED.

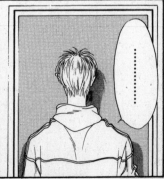

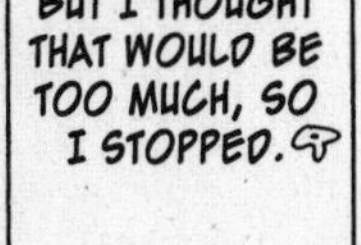
How embarrassing.
PHONE
You think?
She's talking to her friend.

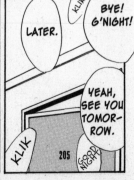

THE GODS WHO WATCH OVER THE FOUR COMPASS DIRECTIONS (NORTH, SOUTH, EAST AND WEST).

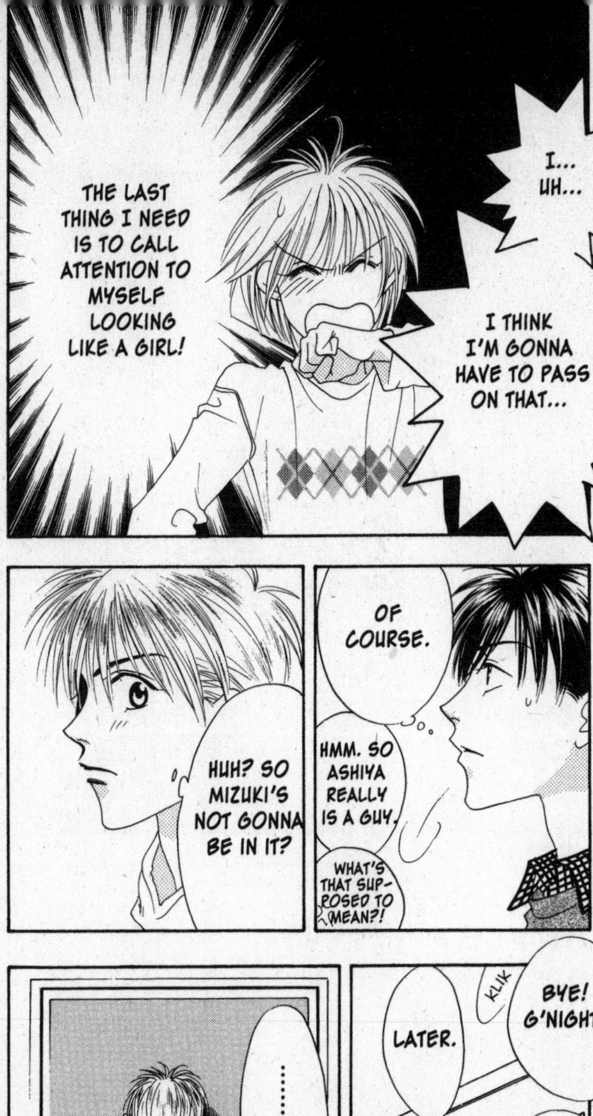
I... UH...
I THINK I'M GONNA HAVE TO PASS ON THAT...
THE LAST THING I NEED IS TO CALL ATTENTION TO MYSELF LOOKING LIKE A GIRL!
OF COURSE.
HMM. SO ASHIYA REALLY IS A GUY.
WHAT'S THAT SUPPOSED TO MEAN?!
HUH? SO MIZUKI'S NOT GONNA BE IN IT?
KLIK
BYE! G'NIGHT!
LATER.
YEAH, SEE YOU TOMORROW.
KLIK
GOOD NIGHT
205
......

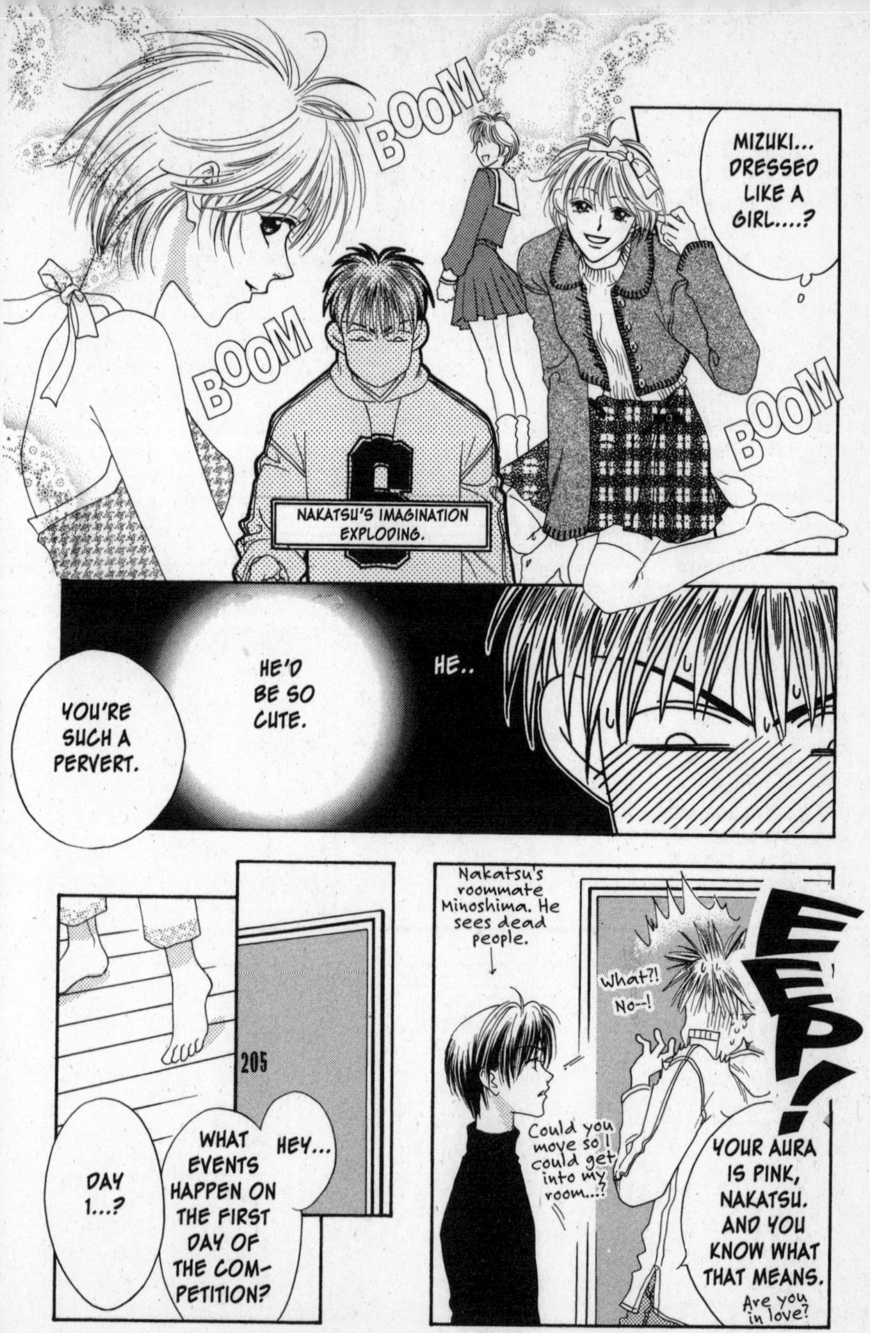
MIZUKI... DRESSED LIKE A GIRL....?
BOOM
BOOM
BOOM
NAKATSU'S IMAGINATION EXPLODING.
HE..
HE'D BE SO CUTE.
YOU'RE SUCH A PERVERT.
Nakatsu's roommate Minoshima. He sees dead people.
EEP!
What?! No--!
Could you move so I could get into my room...?
YOUR AURA IS PINK, NAKATSU. AND YOU KNOW WHAT THAT MEANS.
Are you in love?
205
HEY...
WHAT EVENTS HAPPEN ON THE FIRST DAY OF THE COMPETITION?
DAY 1...?

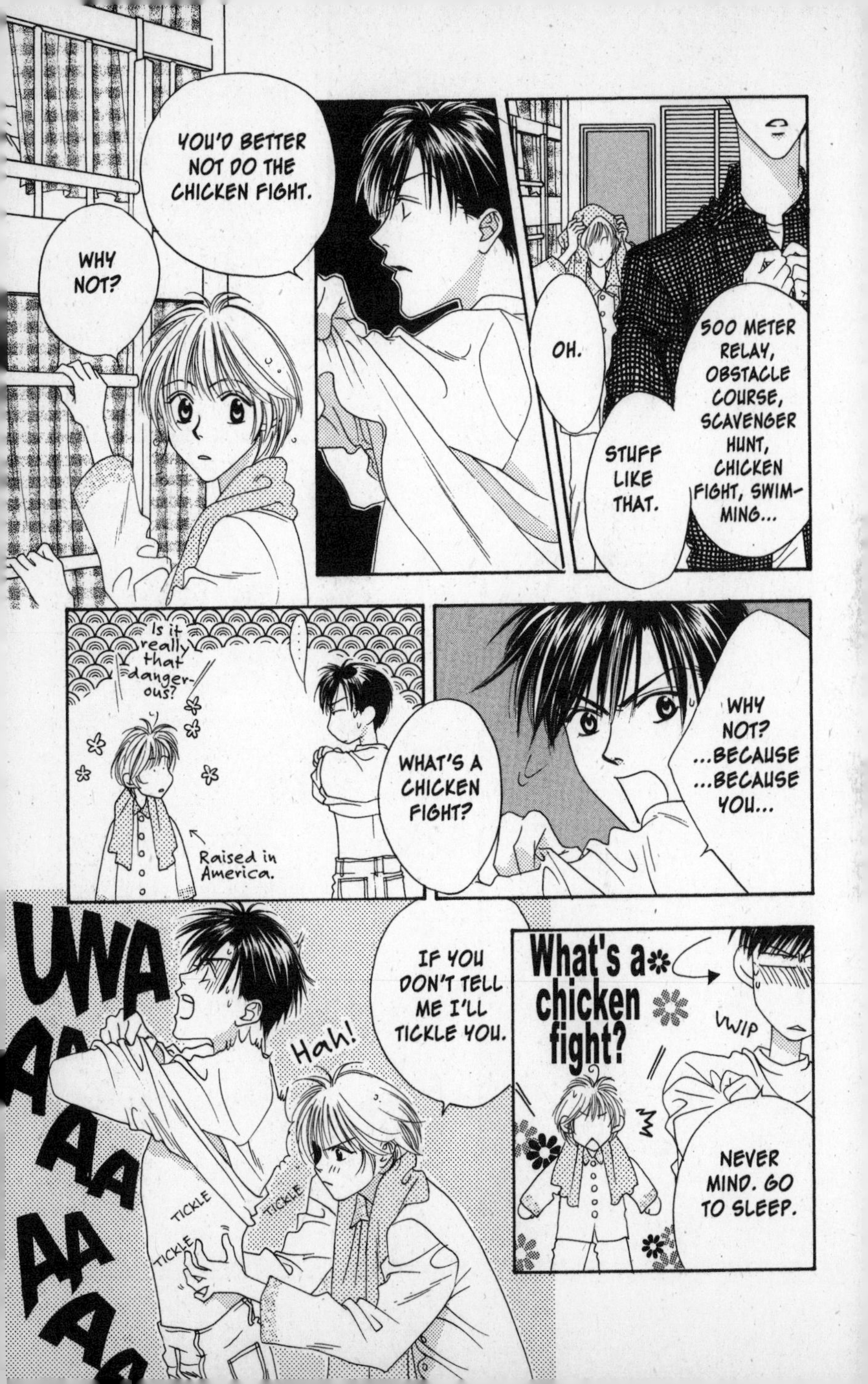

500 METER RELAY, OBSTACLE COURSE, SCAVENGER HUNT, CHICKEN FIGHT, SWIMMING...
OH.
STUFF LIKE THAT.
YOU'D BETTER NOT DO THE CHICKEN FIGHT.
WHY NOT?
WHY NOT? ...BECAUSE ...BECAUSE YOU...
WHAT'S A CHICKEN FIGHT?
Is it really that dangerous?
Raised in America.
What's a chicken fight?
VWIP
NEVER MIND. GO TO SLEEP.
IF YOU DON'T TELL ME I'LL TICKLE YOU.
Hah!
TICKLE
TICKLE
TICKLE
UWAAAAAAAAA

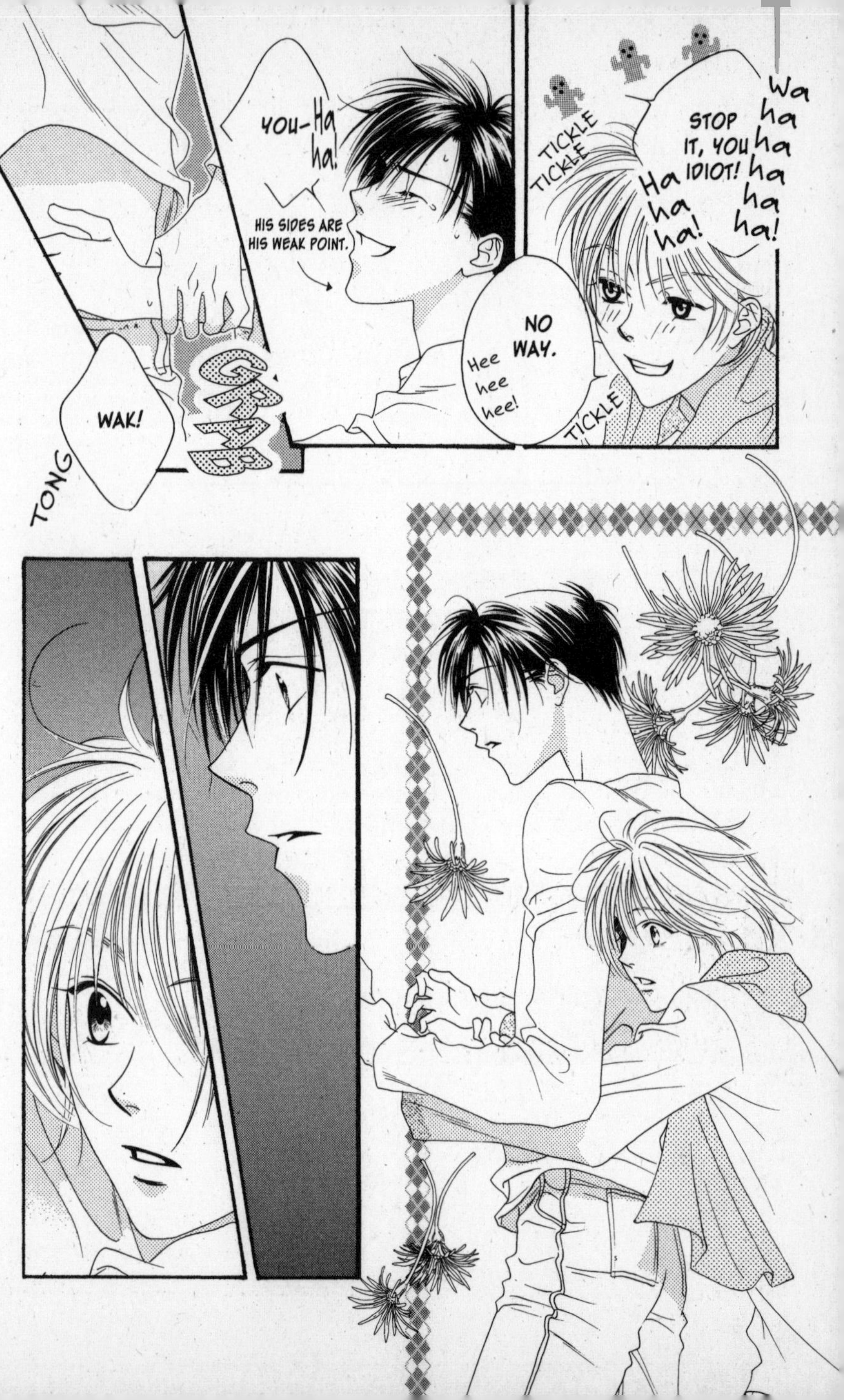
Wa ha ha ha ha ha!
STOP IT, YOU IDIOT!
Ha ha ha!
TICKLE TICKLE
NO WAY.
Hee hee hee!
TICKLE
YOU- Ha ha!
HIS SIDES ARE HIS WEAK POINT.
GRAB
WAK!
TONG

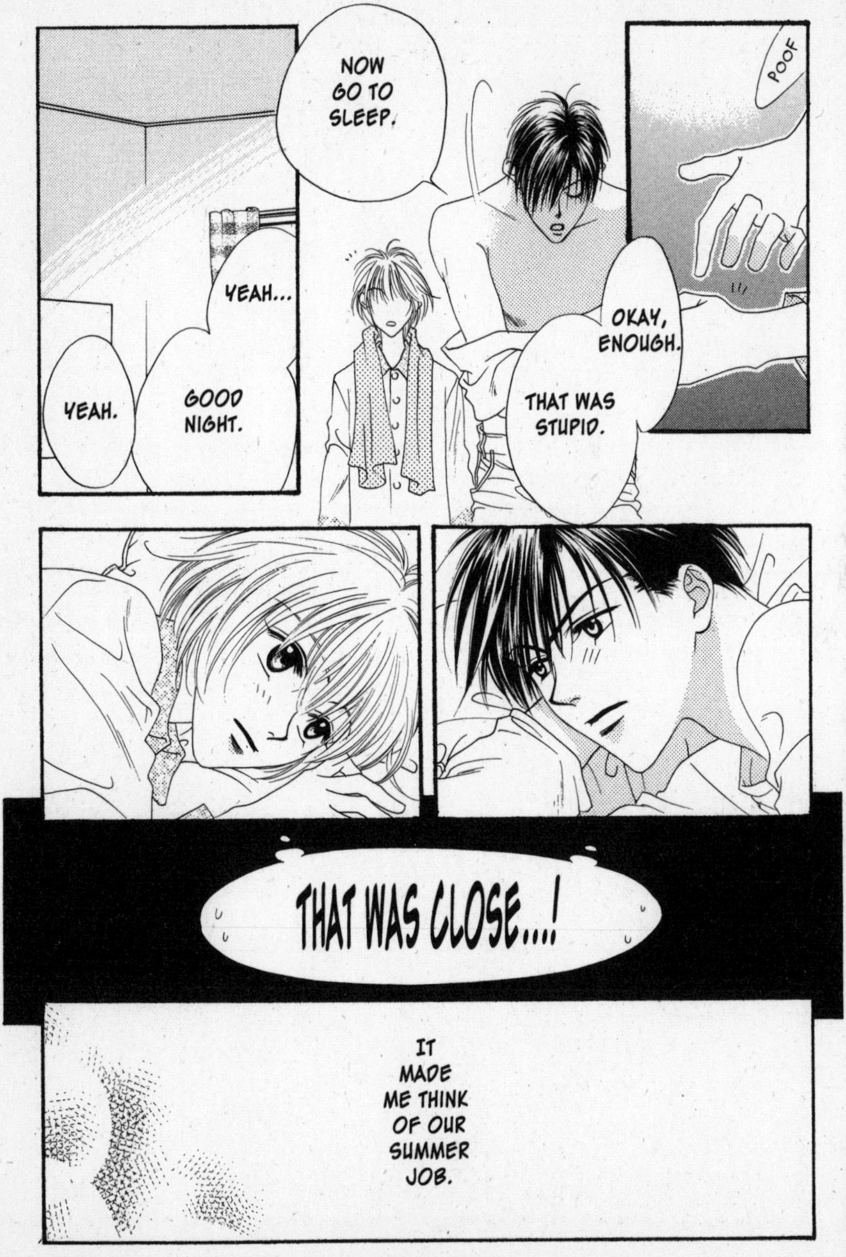
POOF
OKAY, ENOUGH.
THAT WAS STUPID.
NOW GO TO SLEEP.
YEAH...
GOOD NIGHT.
YEAH.
THAT WAS CLOSE...!
IT MADE ME THINK OF OUR SUMMER JOB.

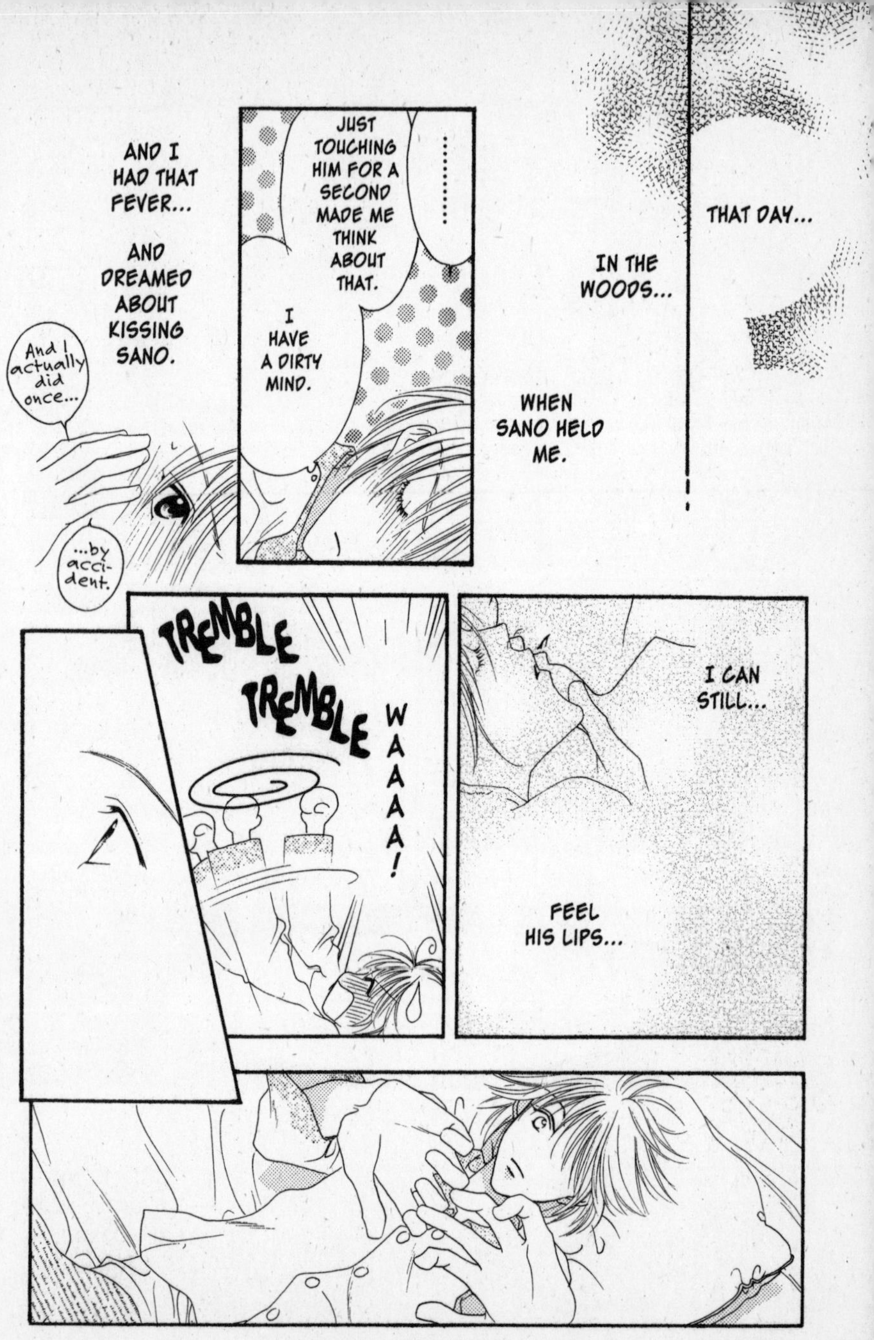
THAT DAY...
IN THE WOODS...
WHEN SANO HELD ME.
......
JUST TOUCHING HIM FOR A SECOND MADE ME THINK ABOUT THAT.
I HAVE A DIRTY MIND.
AND I HAD THAT FEVER...
AND DREAMED ABOUT KISSING SANO.
And I actually did once...
...by acci-dent.
I CAN STILL...
FEEL HIS LIPS...
TREMBLE
TREMBLE
WAAAAA!

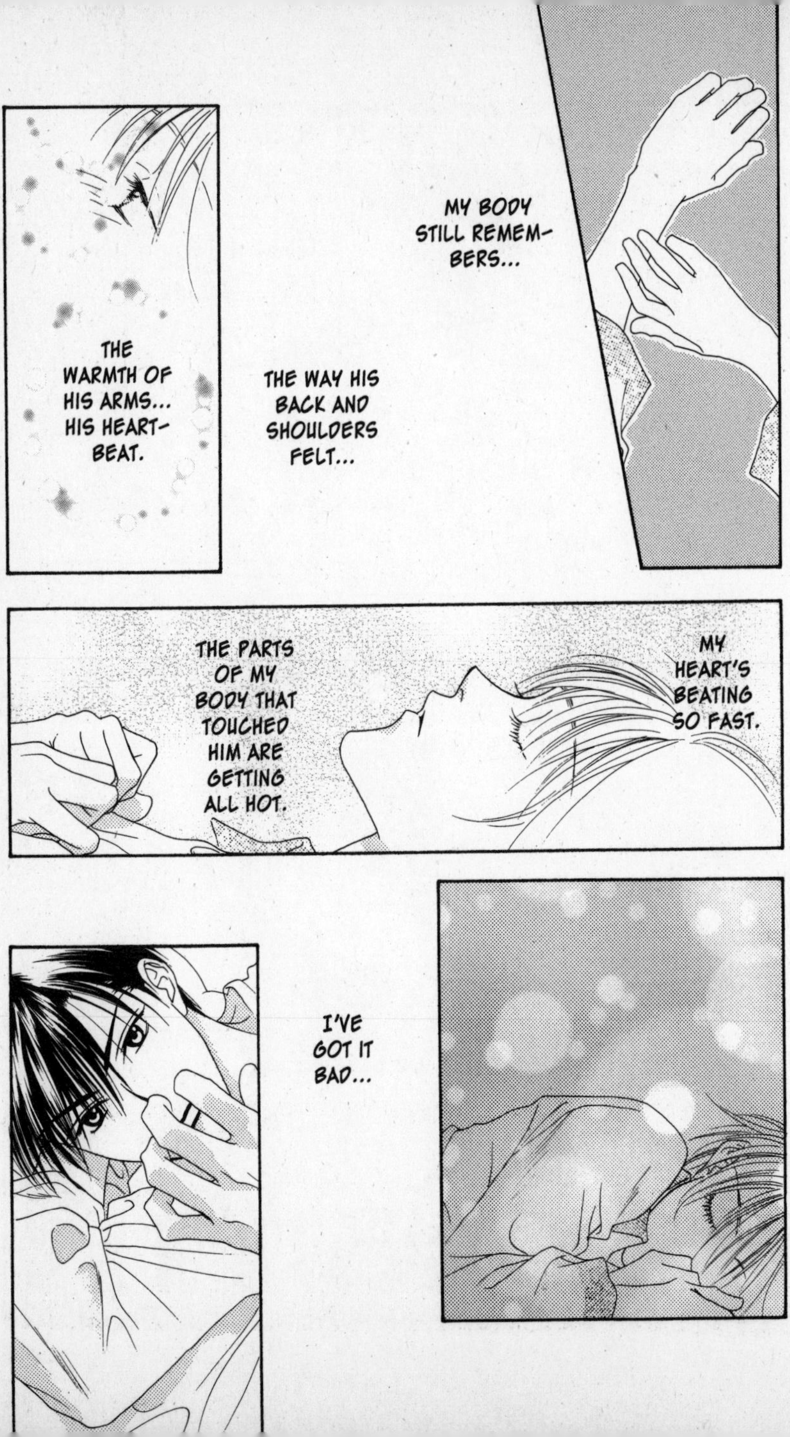
MY BODY STILL REMEMBERS...
THE WAY HIS BACK AND SHOULDERS FELT...
THE WARMTH OF HIS ARMS... HIS HEARTBEAT.
MY HEART'S BEATING SO FAST.
THE PARTS OF MY BODY THAT TOUCHED HIM ARE GETTING ALL HOT.
I'VE GOT IT BAD...

IS THAT WHAT I WANT? TO BE WITH HER...?

I...

RRRING RRRING

EVERYBODY SHOULD PARTICIPATE IN AT LEAST ONE EVENT.

Woo-hoo!

October 16th
00m relay, Obstacle course
Scavenger hunt, Chicken fight
ball push, Daruma

Swimming
Dodge Ball

All right, all the events have been decided!

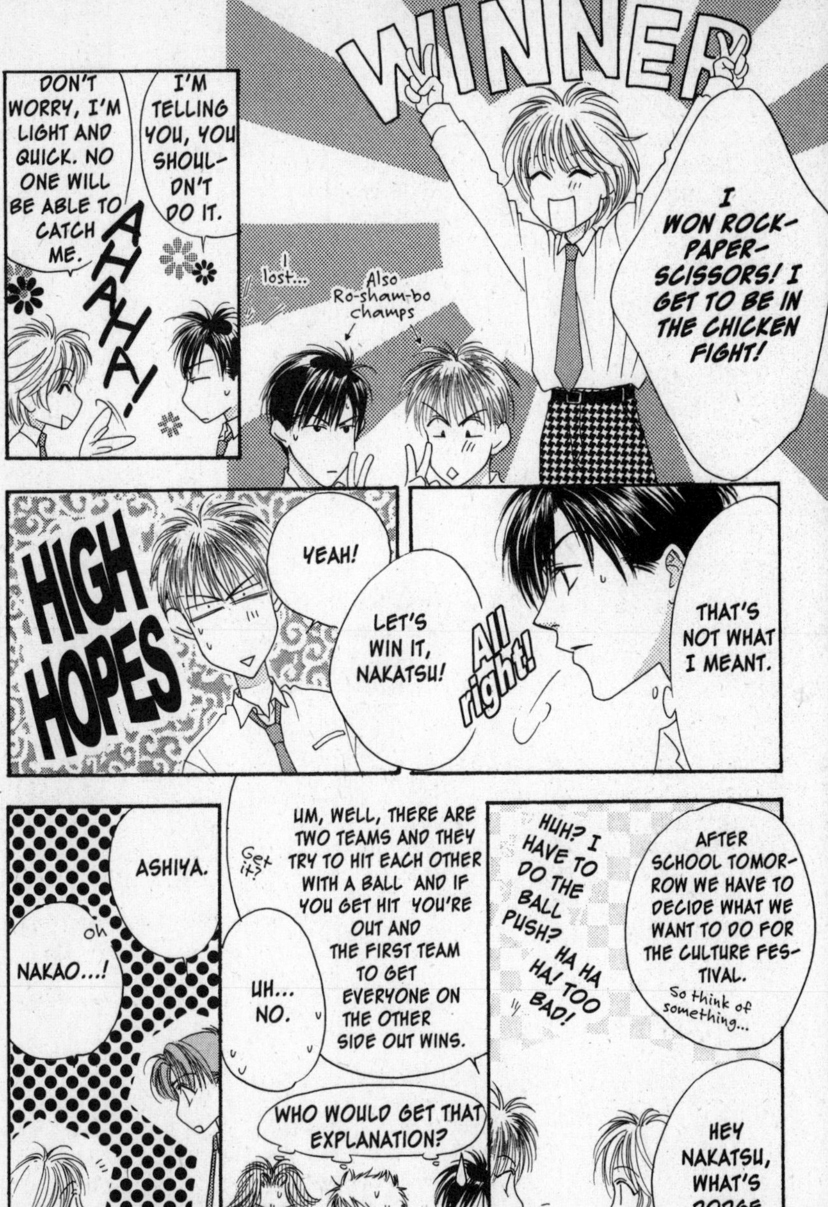
WINNER
I WON ROCK-PAPER-SCISSORS! I GET TO BE IN THE CHICKEN FIGHT!
I lost...
Also Ro-sham-bo champs
I'M TELLING YOU, YOU SHOULDN'T DO IT.
DON'T WORRY, I'M LIGHT AND QUICK. NO ONE WILL BE ABLE TO CATCH ME.
AHAHA!
THAT'S NOT WHAT I MEANT.
All right!
YEAH!
LET'S WIN IT, NAKATSU!
HIGH HOPES
AFTER SCHOOL TOMORROW WE HAVE TO DECIDE WHAT WE WANT TO DO FOR THE CULTURE FESTIVAL.
So think of something...
HUH? I HAVE TO DO THE BALL PUSH? HA HA HA! TOO BAD!
HEY NAKATSU, WHAT'S DODGE BALL?
UM, WELL, THERE ARE TWO TEAMS AND THEY TRY TO HIT EACH OTHER WITH A BALL AND IF YOU GET HIT YOU'RE OUT AND THE FIRST TEAM TO GET EVERYONE ON THE OTHER SIDE OUT WINS.
Get it?
UH... NO.
WHO WOULD GET THAT EXPLANATION?
Um...
ASHIYA.
oh
NAKAO...!

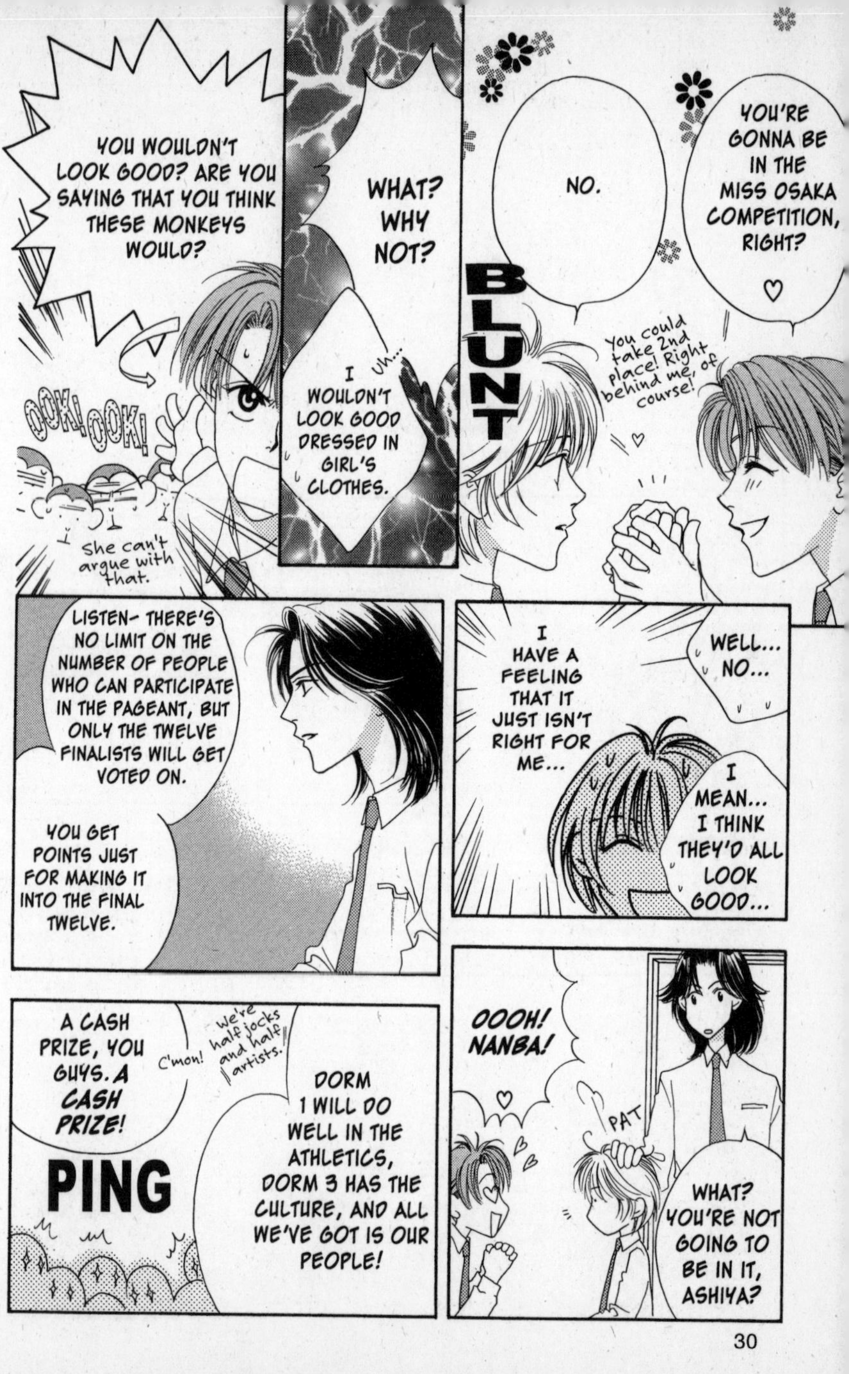
YOU'RE GONNA BE IN THE MISS OSAKA COMPETITION, RIGHT? ♡
NO.
BLUNT
You could take 2nd place! Right behind me, of course!
WHAT? WHY NOT?
Uh...
I WOULDN'T LOOK GOOD DRESSED IN GIRL'S CLOTHES.
YOU WOULDN'T LOOK GOOD? ARE YOU SAYING THAT YOU THINK THESE MONKEYS WOULD?
OOK! OOK!
She can't argue with that.
WELL... NO...
I MEAN... I THINK THEY'D ALL LOOK GOOD...
I HAVE A FEELING THAT IT JUST ISN'T RIGHT FOR ME...
LISTEN- THERE'S NO LIMIT ON THE NUMBER OF PEOPLE WHO CAN PARTICIPATE IN THE PAGEANT, BUT ONLY THE TWELVE FINALISTS WILL GET VOTED ON.
YOU GET POINTS JUST FOR MAKING IT INTO THE FINAL TWELVE.
WHAT? YOU'RE NOT GOING TO BE IN IT, ASHIYA?
PAT
OOOH! NANBA!
DORM 1 WILL DO WELL IN THE ATHLETICS, DORM 3 HAS THE CULTURE, AND ALL WE'VE GOT IS OUR PEOPLE!
We're half jocks and half artists.
C'mon!
A CASH PRIZE, YOU GUYS. A CASH PRIZE!
PING

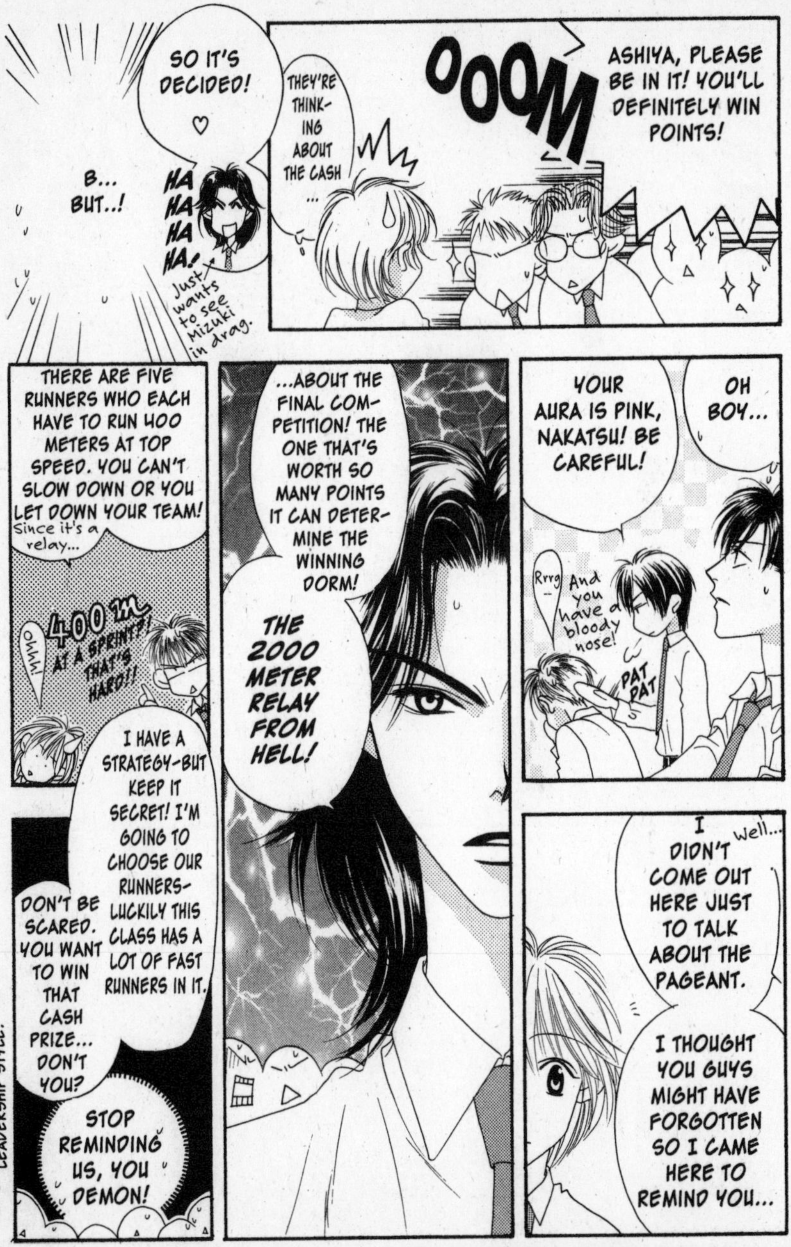

ASHIYA, PLEASE BE IN IT! YOU'LL DEFINITELY WIN POINTS!
OOOM
THEY'RE THINK-ING ABOUT THE CASH ...
SO IT'S DECIDED! ♡
HA HA HA HA!
Just wants to see Mizuki in drag.
B... BUT..!
OH BOY...
YOUR AURA IS PINK, NAKATSU! BE CAREFUL!
Rrrg --
And you have a bloody nose!
PAT PAT
Well...
I DIDN'T COME OUT HERE JUST TO TALK ABOUT THE PAGEANT.
I THOUGHT YOU GUYS MIGHT HAVE FORGOTTEN SO I CAME HERE TO REMIND YOU...
...ABOUT THE FINAL COM-PETITION! THE ONE THAT'S WORTH SO MANY POINTS IT CAN DETER-MINE THE WINNING DORM!
THE 2000 METER RELAY FROM HELL!
THERE ARE FIVE RUNNERS WHO EACH HAVE TO RUN 400 METERS AT TOP SPEED. YOU CAN'T SLOW DOWN OR YOU LET DOWN YOUR TEAM!
Since it's a relay...
OHHH
400 m AT A SPRINT?! THAT'S HARD!!
I HAVE A STRATEGY-BUT KEEP IT SECRET! I'M GOING TO CHOOSE OUR RUNNERS-LUCKILY THIS CLASS HAS A LOT OF FAST RUNNERS IN IT.
DON'T BE SCARED. YOU WANT TO WIN THAT CASH PRIZE... DON'T YOU?
STOP REMINDING US, YOU DEMON!

SWEET AND SOUR-- NANBA'S LEADERSHIP STYLE.

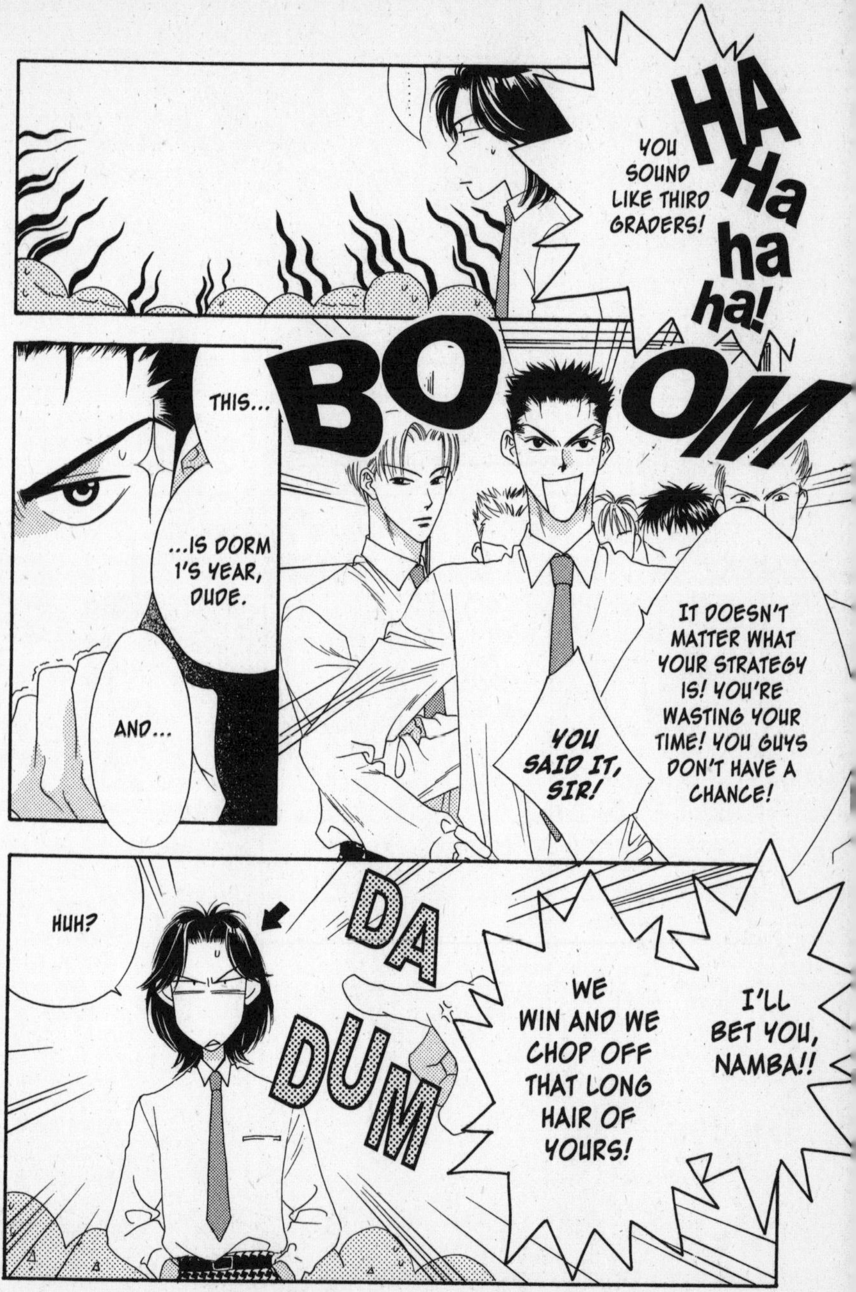
HA Ha ha ha!
YOU SOUND LIKE THIRD GRADERS!
BOOM
IT DOESN'T MATTER WHAT YOUR STRATEGY IS! YOU'RE WASTING YOUR TIME! YOU GUYS DON'T HAVE A CHANCE!
YOU SAID IT, SIR!
THIS...
...IS DORM 1'S YEAR, DUDE.
AND...
I'LL BET YOU, NAMBA!!
WE WIN AND WE CHOP OFF THAT LONG HAIR OF YOURS!
DA DUM
HUH?

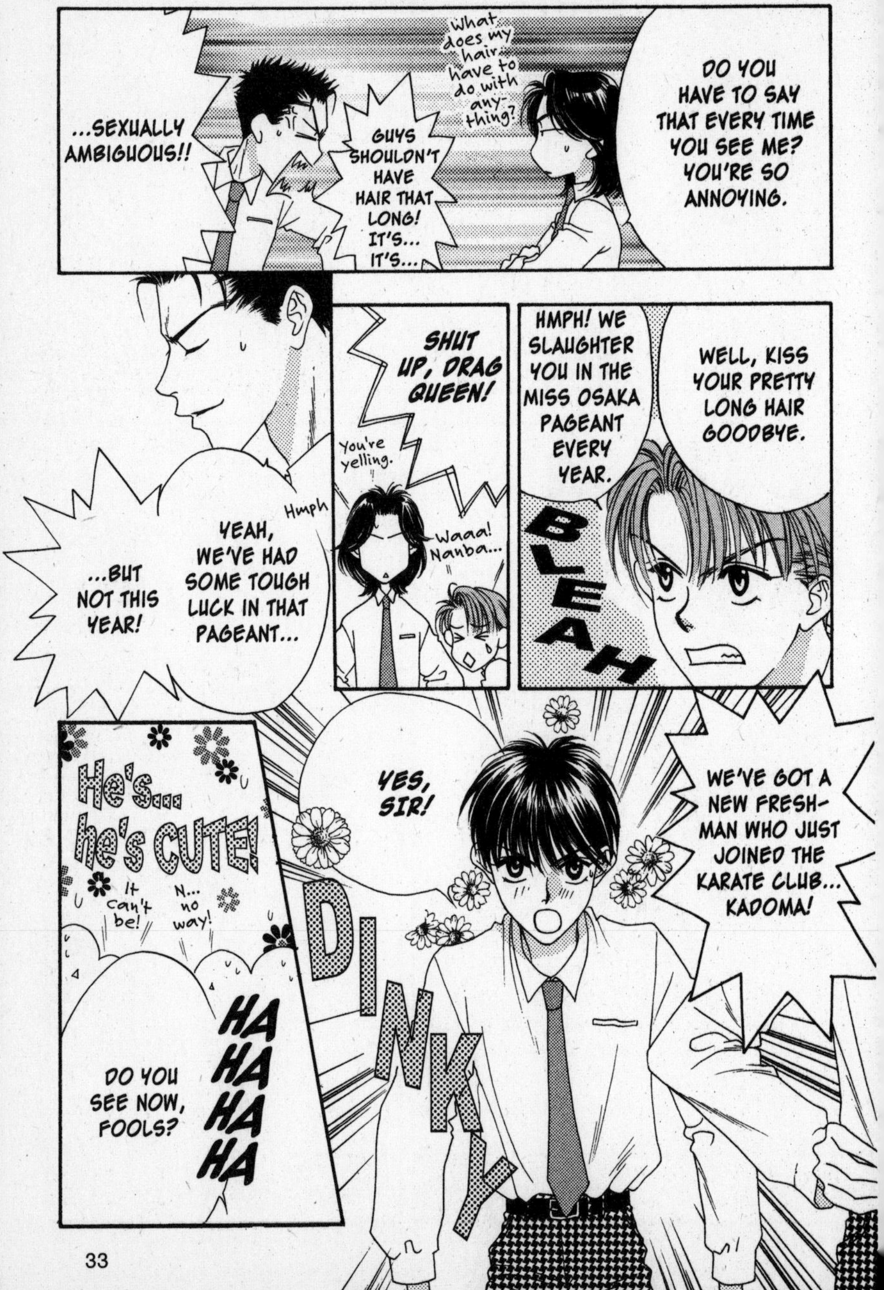
DO YOU HAVE TO SAY THAT EVERY TIME YOU SEE ME? YOU'RE SO ANNOYING.
What does my hair have to do with any-thing?
GUYS SHOULDN'T HAVE HAIR THAT LONG! IT'S... IT'S...
...SEXUALLY AMBIGUOUS!!
WELL, KISS YOUR PRETTY LONG HAIR GOODBYE.
HMPH! WE SLAUGHTER YOU IN THE MISS OSAKA PAGEANT EVERY YEAR.
BLEAH
SHUT UP, DRAG QUEEN!
You're yelling.
Waaa! Nanba...
Hmph
YEAH, WE'VE HAD SOME TOUGH LUCK IN THAT PAGEANT...
...BUT NOT THIS YEAR!
WE'VE GOT A NEW FRESH-MAN WHO JUST JOINED THE KARATE CLUB... KADOMA!
YES, SIR!
DINKY
He's... he's CUTE!
It can't be!
N... no way!
DO YOU SEE NOW, FOOLS?
HA HA HA HA HA HA

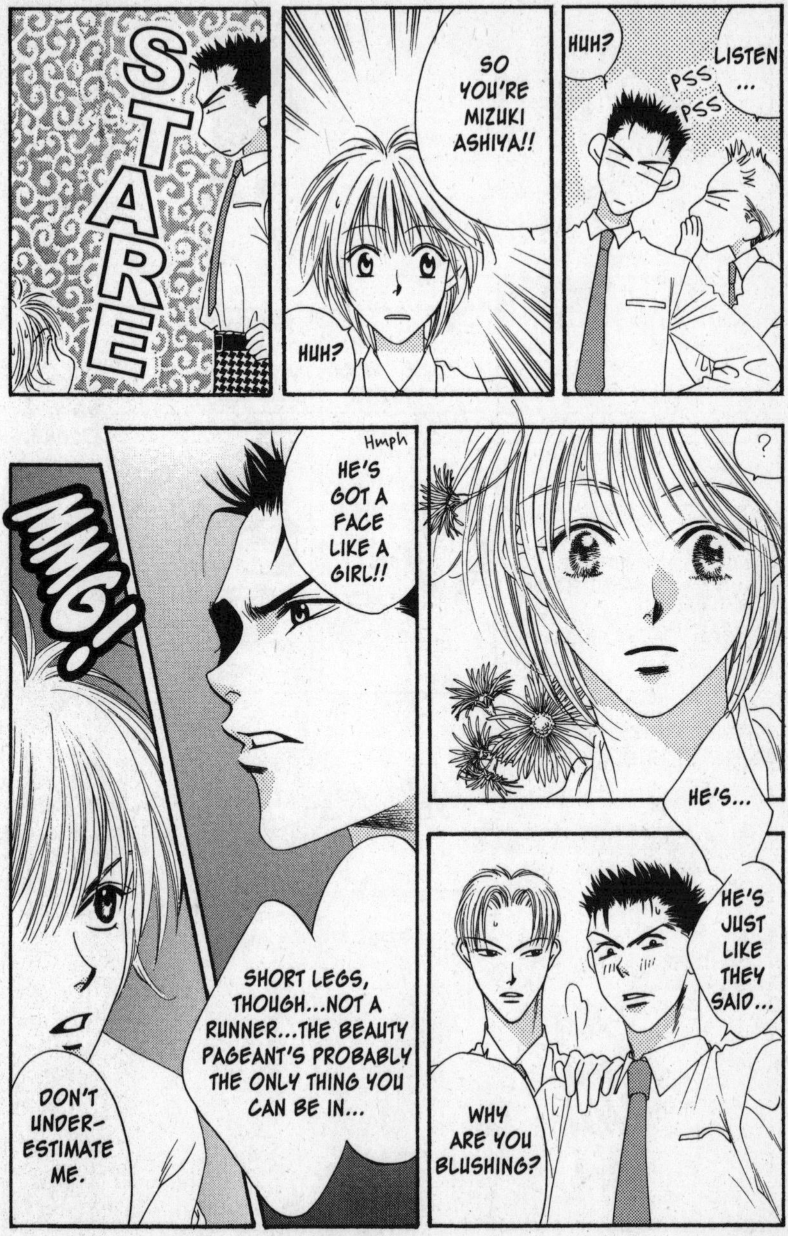
LISTEN ...
PSS PSS
HUH?
SO YOU'RE MIZUKI ASHIYA!!
HUH?
STARE
?
HE'S...
HE'S JUST LIKE THEY SAID...
WHY ARE YOU BLUSHING?
Hmph
HE'S GOT A FACE LIKE A GIRL!!
MMG!
SHORT LEGS, THOUGH...NOT A RUNNER...THE BEAUTY PAGEANT'S PROBABLY THE ONLY THING YOU CAN BE IN...
DON'T UNDER-ESTIMATE ME.

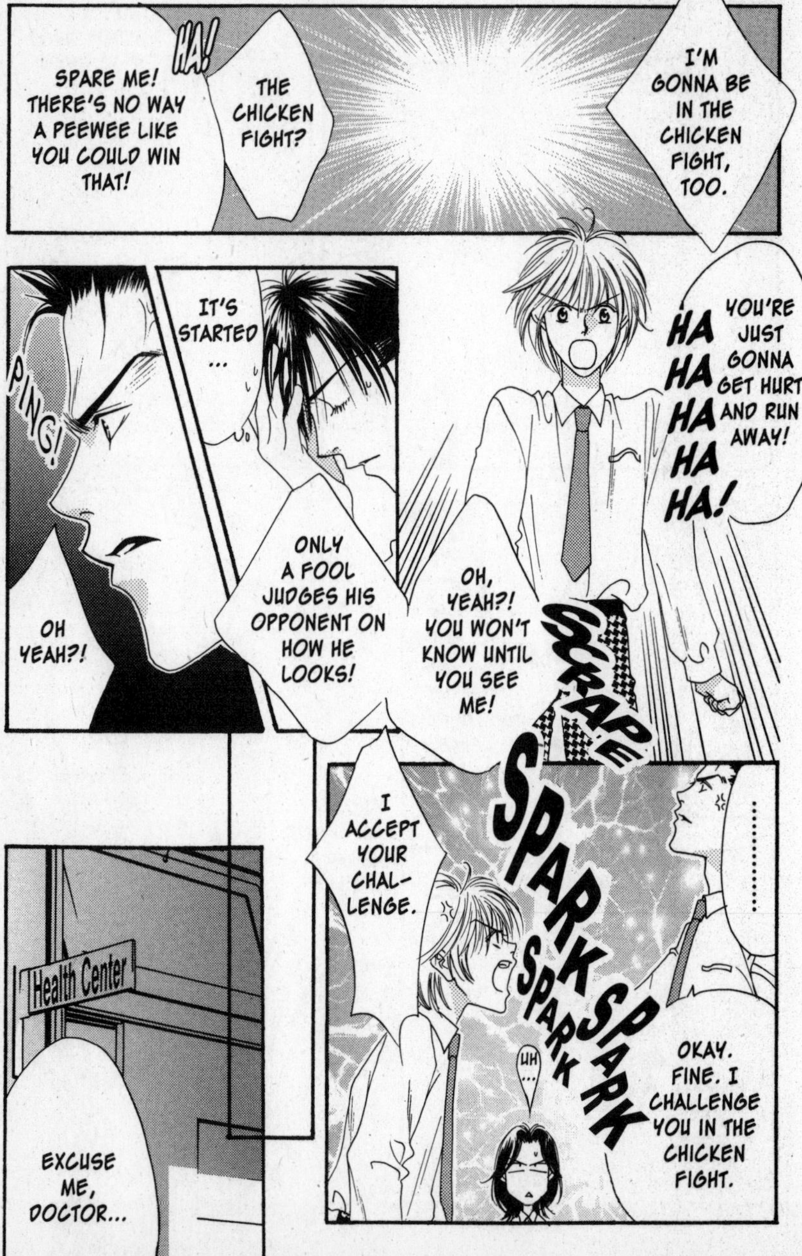
I'M GONNA BE IN THE CHICKEN FIGHT, TOO.
THE CHICKEN FIGHT?
HA!
SPARE ME! THERE'S NO WAY A PEEWEE LIKE YOU COULD WIN THAT!
YOU'RE JUST GONNA GET HURT AND RUN AWAY!
HA HA HA HA HA!
OH, YEAH?! YOU WON'T KNOW UNTIL YOU SEE ME!
SCRAPE
IT'S STARTED ...
ONLY A FOOL JUDGES HIS OPPONENT ON HOW HE LOOKS!
PING!
OH YEAH?!
....
OKAY. FINE. I CHALLENGE YOU IN THE CHICKEN FIGHT.
SPARK SPARK SPARK SPARK
I ACCEPT YOUR CHAL-LENGE.
UH ...
Health Center
EXCUSE ME, DOCTOR...

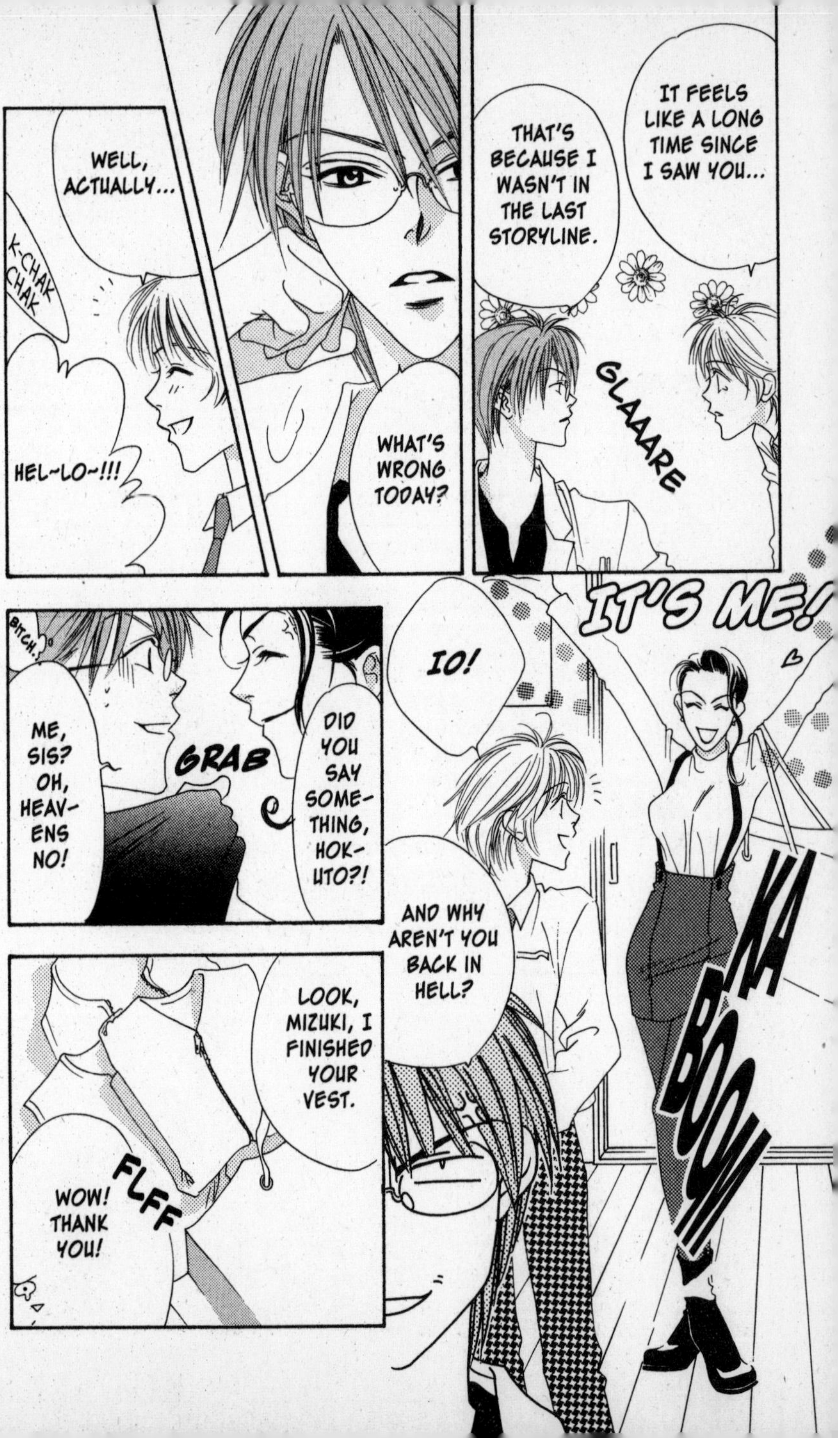
IT FEELS LIKE A LONG TIME SINCE I SAW YOU...
THAT'S BECAUSE I WASN'T IN THE LAST STORYLINE.
GLAAARE
WHAT'S WRONG TODAY?
WELL, ACTUALLY...
K-CHAK CHAK
HEL~LO~!!!
IT'S ME!
IO!
AND WHY AREN'T YOU BACK IN HELL?
KA BOOM
BITCH...
DID YOU SAY SOMETHING, HOKUTO?!
GRAB
ME, SIS? OH, HEAVENS NO!
LOOK, MIZUKI, I FINISHED YOUR VEST.
FLFF
WOW! THANK YOU!

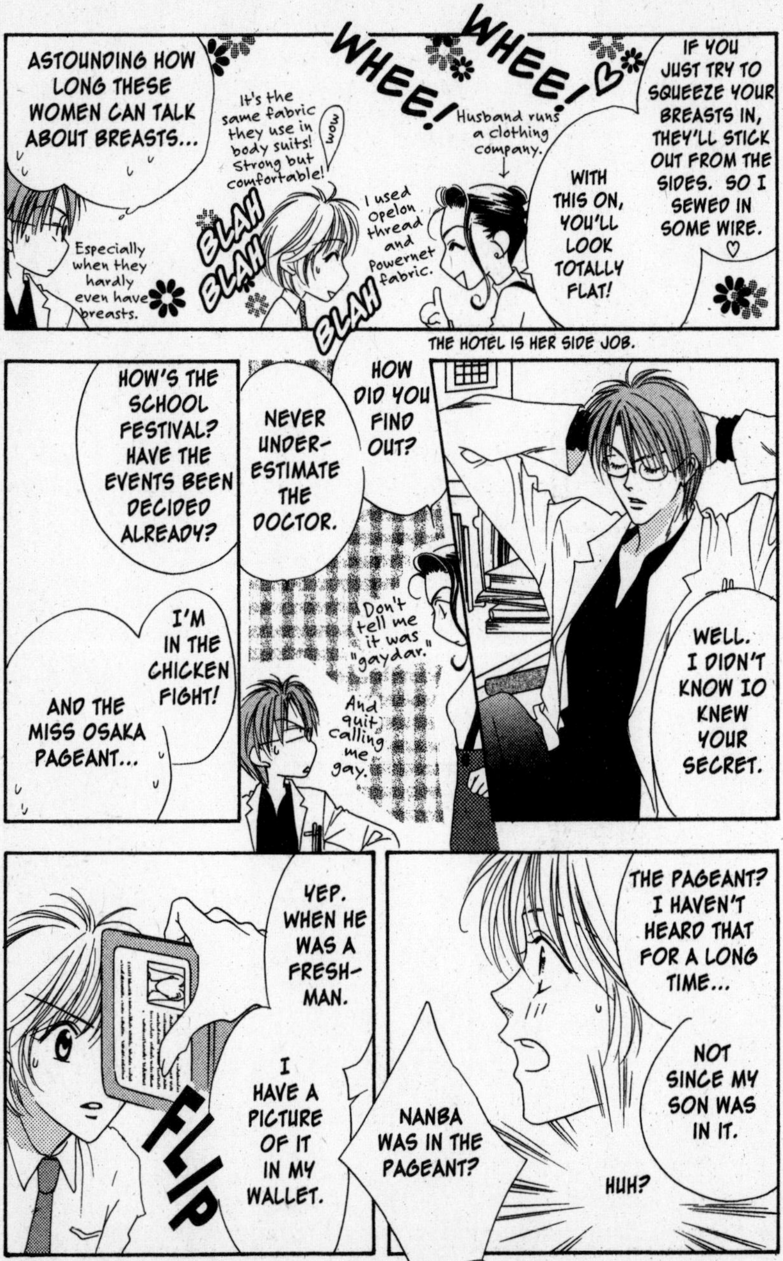
IF YOU JUST TRY TO SQUEEZE YOUR BREASTS IN, THEY'LL STICK OUT FROM THE SIDES. SO I SEWED IN SOME WIRE. ♡
WITH THIS ON, YOU'LL LOOK TOTALLY FLAT!
WHEE! WHEE! ♡
Husband runs a clothing company.
I used Opelon thread and Powernet fabric.
BLAH BLAH BLAH
It's the same fabric they use in body suits! Strong but comfortable!
wow
ASTOUNDING HOW LONG THESE WOMEN CAN TALK ABOUT BREASTS...
Especially when they hardly even have breasts.
THE HOTEL IS HER SIDE JOB.
WELL. I DIDN'T KNOW IO KNEW YOUR SECRET.
HOW DID YOU FIND OUT?
NEVER UNDER-ESTIMATE THE DOCTOR.
Don't tell me it was "gaydar."
And quit calling me gay.
HOW'S THE SCHOOL FESTIVAL? HAVE THE EVENTS BEEN DECIDED ALREADY?
I'M IN THE CHICKEN FIGHT!
AND THE MISS OSAKA PAGEANT...
THE PAGEANT? I HAVEN'T HEARD THAT FOR A LONG TIME...
NOT SINCE MY SON WAS IN IT.
HUH?
NANBA WAS IN THE PAGEANT?
YEP. WHEN HE WAS A FRESHMAN.
I HAVE A PICTURE OF IT IN MY WALLET.
FLIP

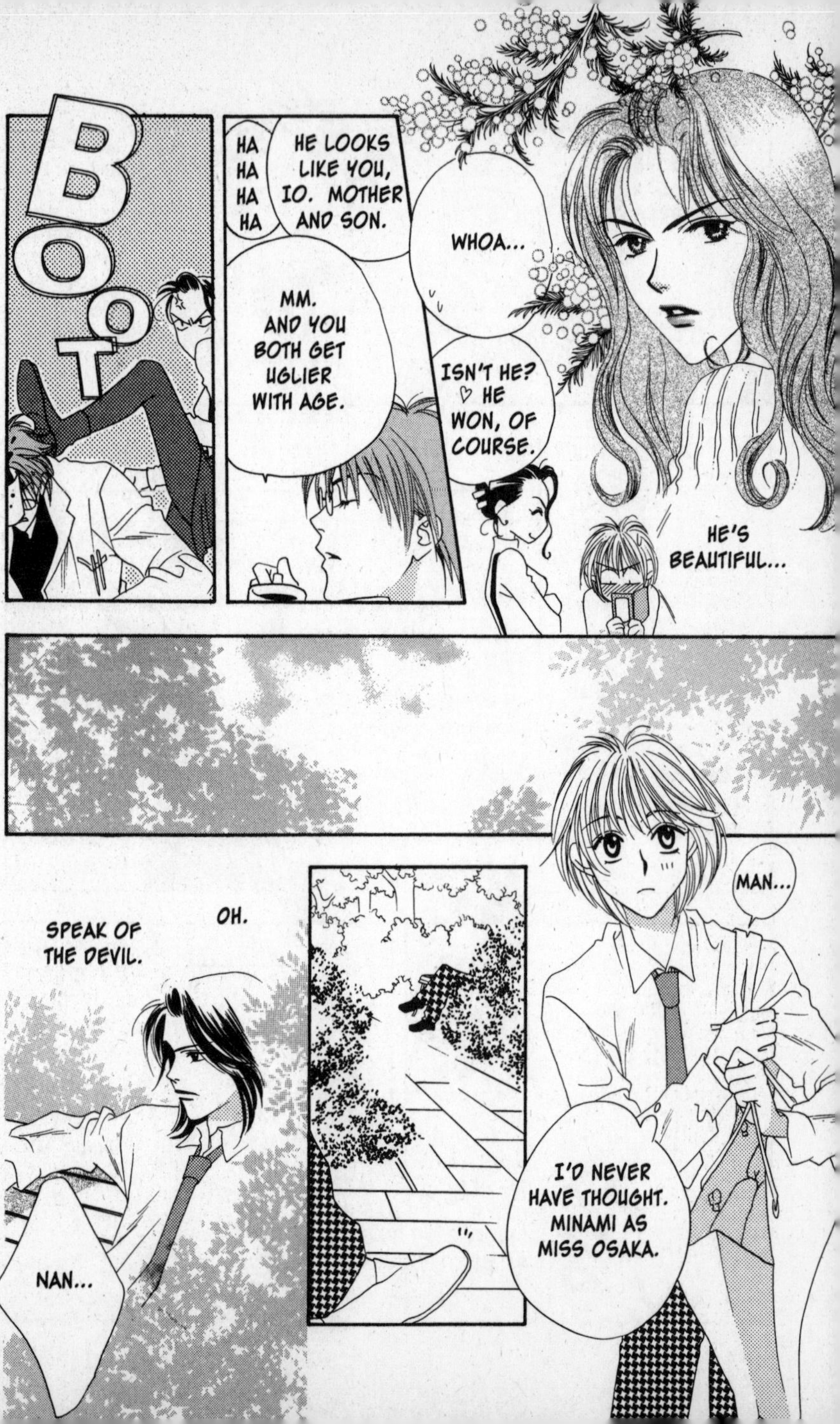
WHOA...
ISN'T HE? ♡ HE WON, OF COURSE.
HE'S BEAUTIFUL...
HE LOOKS LIKE YOU, IO. MOTHER AND SON.
HA HA HA HA
MM. AND YOU BOTH GET UGLIER WITH AGE.
BOOT
MAN...
I'D NEVER HAVE THOUGHT. MINAMI AS MISS OSAKA.
OH.
SPEAK OF THE DEVIL.
NAN...

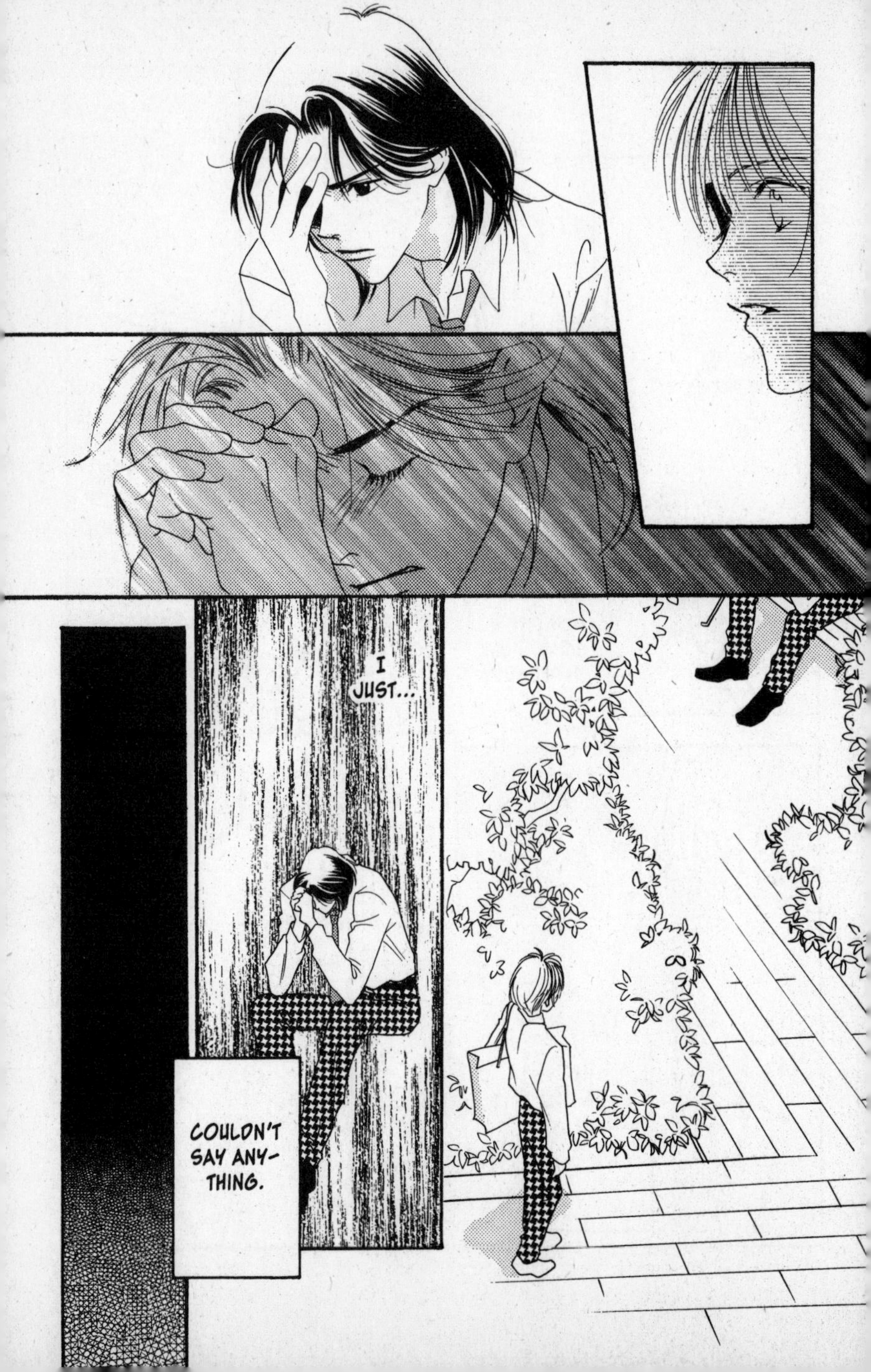

I JUST...
COULDN'T SAY ANY-THING.

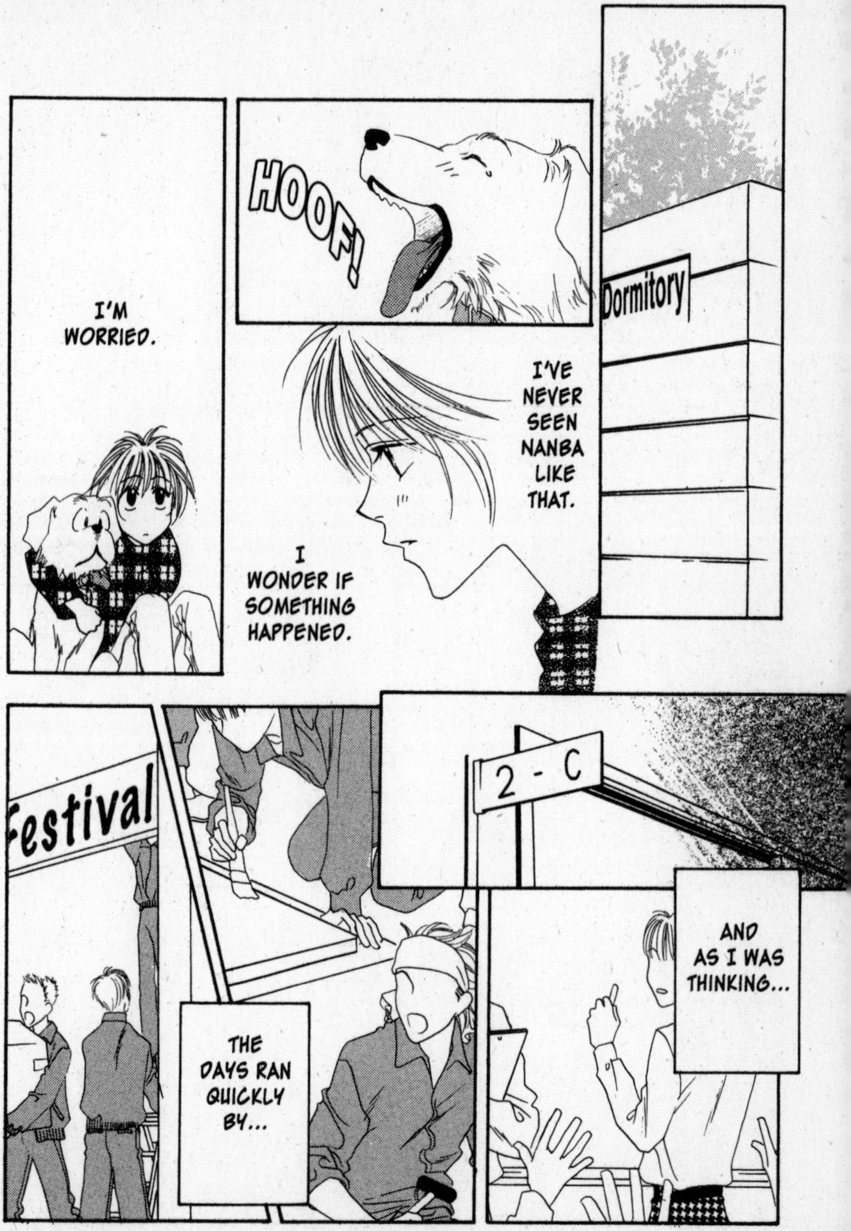
Dormitory
HOOF!
I'VE NEVER SEEN NANBA LIKE THAT.
I WONDER IF SOMETHING HAPPENED.
I'M WORRIED.
2 - C
AND AS I WAS THINKING...
THE DAYS RAN QUICKLY BY...
Festival

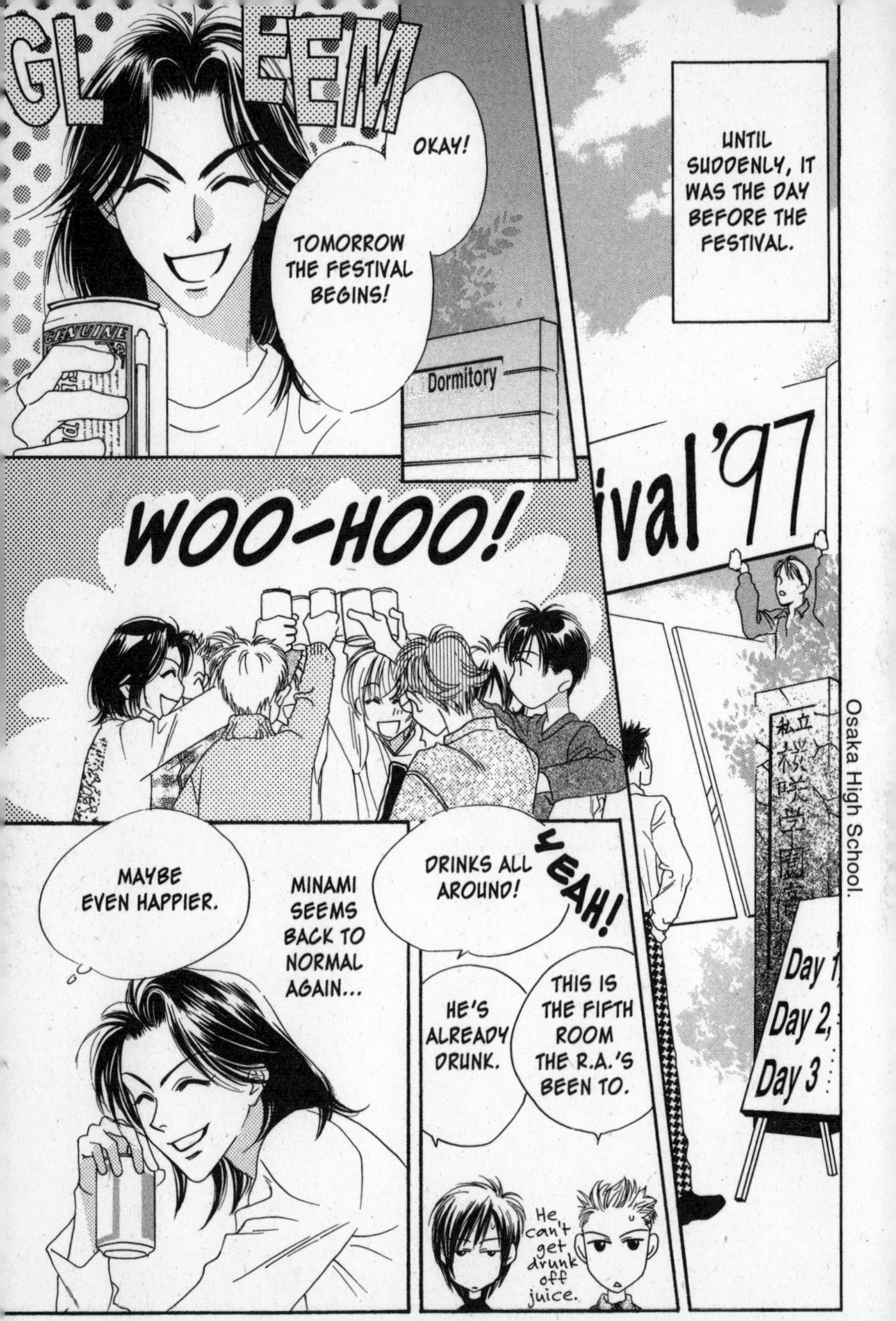

UNTIL SUDDENLY, IT WAS THE DAY BEFORE THE FESTIVAL.
Dormitory
ival'97
Osaka High School.
私立
Day 1,
Day 2,
Day 3 . . .
GL EEM
OKAY!
TOMORROW THE FESTIVAL BEGINS!
GENUINE
WOO-HOO!
DRINKS ALL AROUND!
YEAH!
THIS IS THE FIFTH ROOM THE R.A.'S BEEN TO.
HE'S ALREADY DRUNK.
He can't get drunk off juice.
MINAMI SEEMS BACK TO NORMAL AGAIN...
MAYBE EVEN HAPPIER.

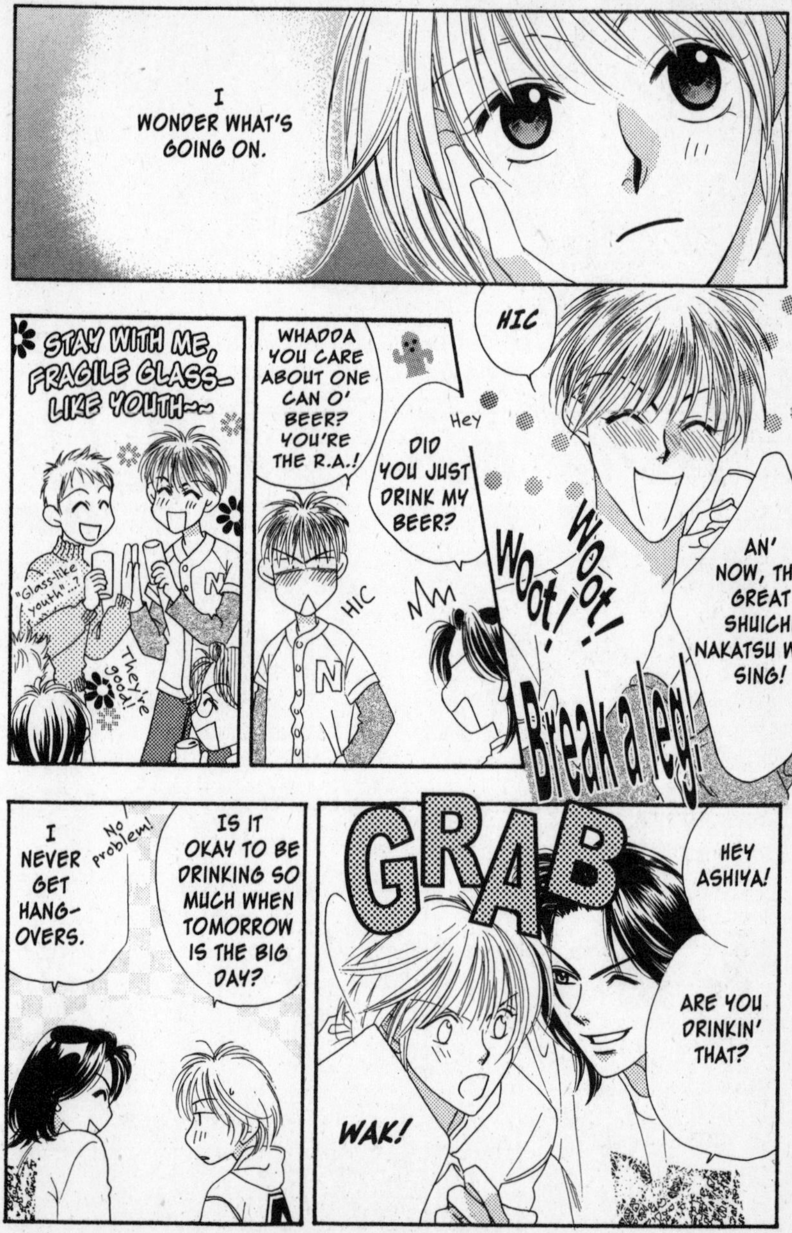
I WONDER WHAT'S GOING ON.
HIC
AN' NOW, THE GREAT SHUICHI NAKATSU WILL SING!
Woot! Woot!
Break a leg!
Hey
DID YOU JUST DRINK MY BEER?
WHADDA YOU CARE ABOUT ONE CAN O' BEER? YOU'RE THE R.A.!
HIC
STAY WITH ME, FRAGILE GLASS-LIKE YOUTH~~
"Glass-like youth"...?
They're good!
GRAB
HEY ASHIYA!
ARE YOU DRINKIN' THAT?
WAK!
IS IT OKAY TO BE DRINKING SO MUCH WHEN TOMORROW IS THE BIG DAY?
I NEVER GET HANG-OVERS.
No problem!

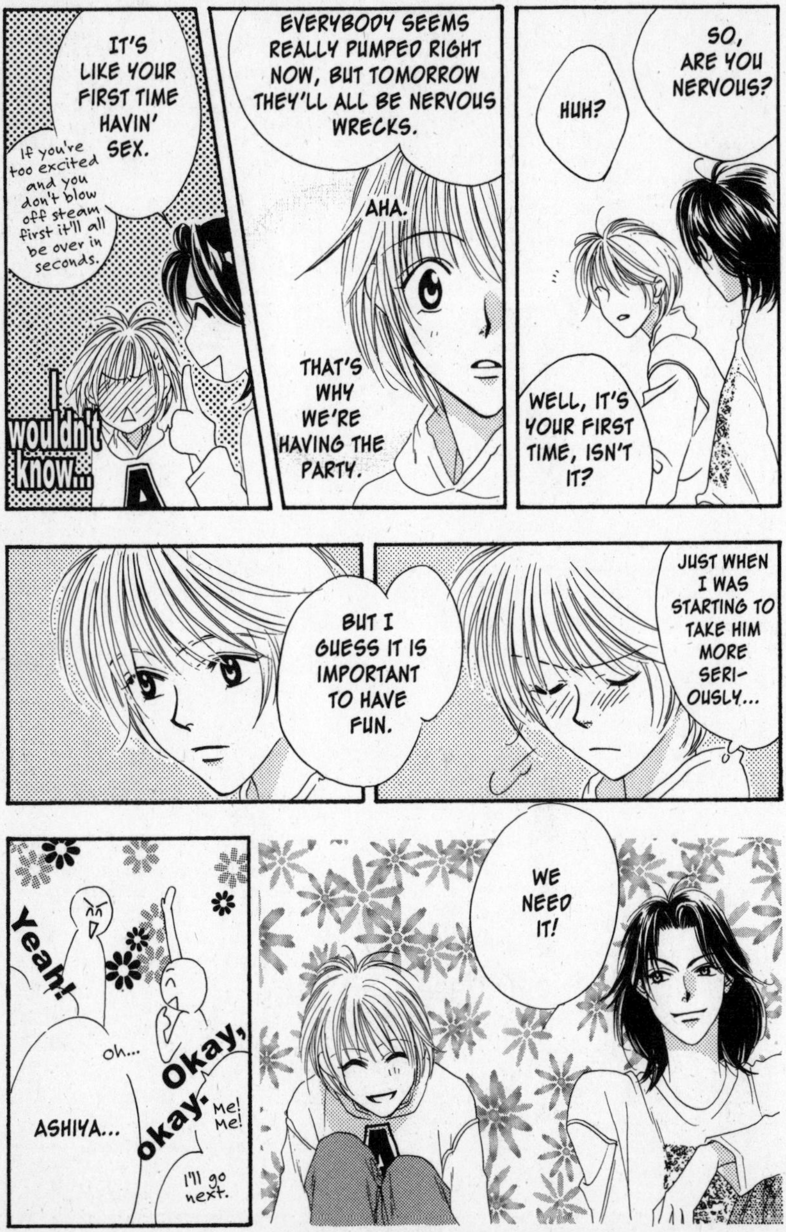
SO, ARE YOU NERVOUS?
HUH?
WELL, IT'S YOUR FIRST TIME, ISN'T IT?
EVERYBODY SEEMS REALLY PUMPED RIGHT NOW, BUT TOMORROW THEY'LL ALL BE NERVOUS WRECKS.
AHA.
THAT'S WHY WE'RE HAVING THE PARTY.
IT'S LIKE YOUR FIRST TIME HAVIN' SEX.
If you're too excited and you don't blow off steam first it'll all be over in seconds.
I wouldn't know...
JUST WHEN I WAS STARTING TO TAKE HIM MORE SERI-OUSLY...
BUT I GUESS IT IS IMPORTANT TO HAVE FUN.
WE NEED IT!
Yeah!
oh...
Okay, okay.
Me! Me!
ASHIYA...
I'll go next.

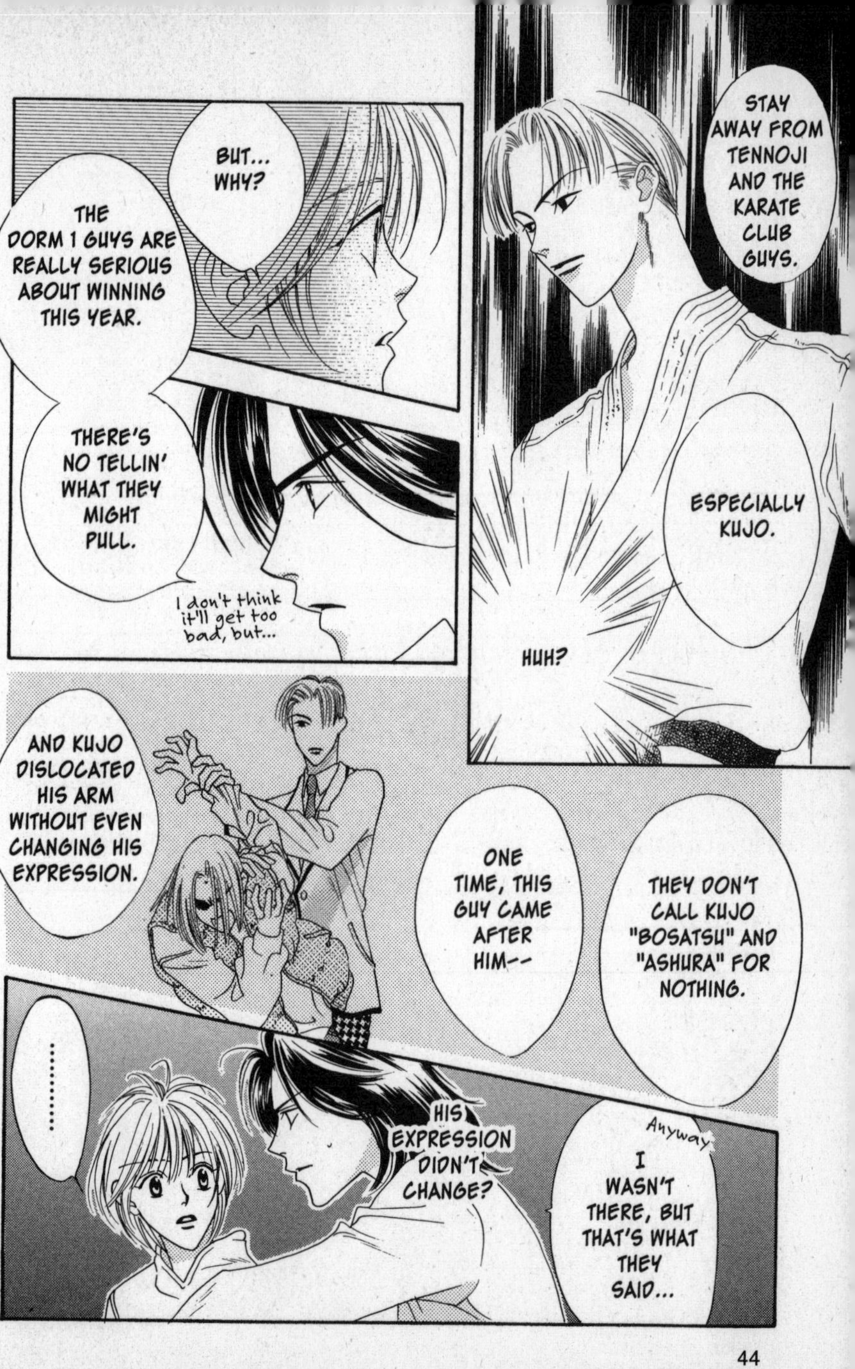
STAY AWAY FROM TENNOJI AND THE KARATE CLUB GUYS.
ESPECIALLY KUJO.
HUH?
BUT... WHY?
THE DORM 1 GUYS ARE REALLY SERIOUS ABOUT WINNING THIS YEAR.
THERE'S NO TELLIN' WHAT THEY MIGHT PULL.
I don't think it'll get too bad, but...
THEY DON'T CALL KUJO "BOSATSU" AND "ASHURA" FOR NOTHING.
ONE TIME, THIS GUY CAME AFTER HIM--
AND KUJO DISLOCATED HIS ARM WITHOUT EVEN CHANGING HIS EXPRESSION.
Anyway
I WASN'T THERE, BUT THAT'S WHAT THEY SAID...
HIS EXPRESSION DIDN'T CHANGE?
....

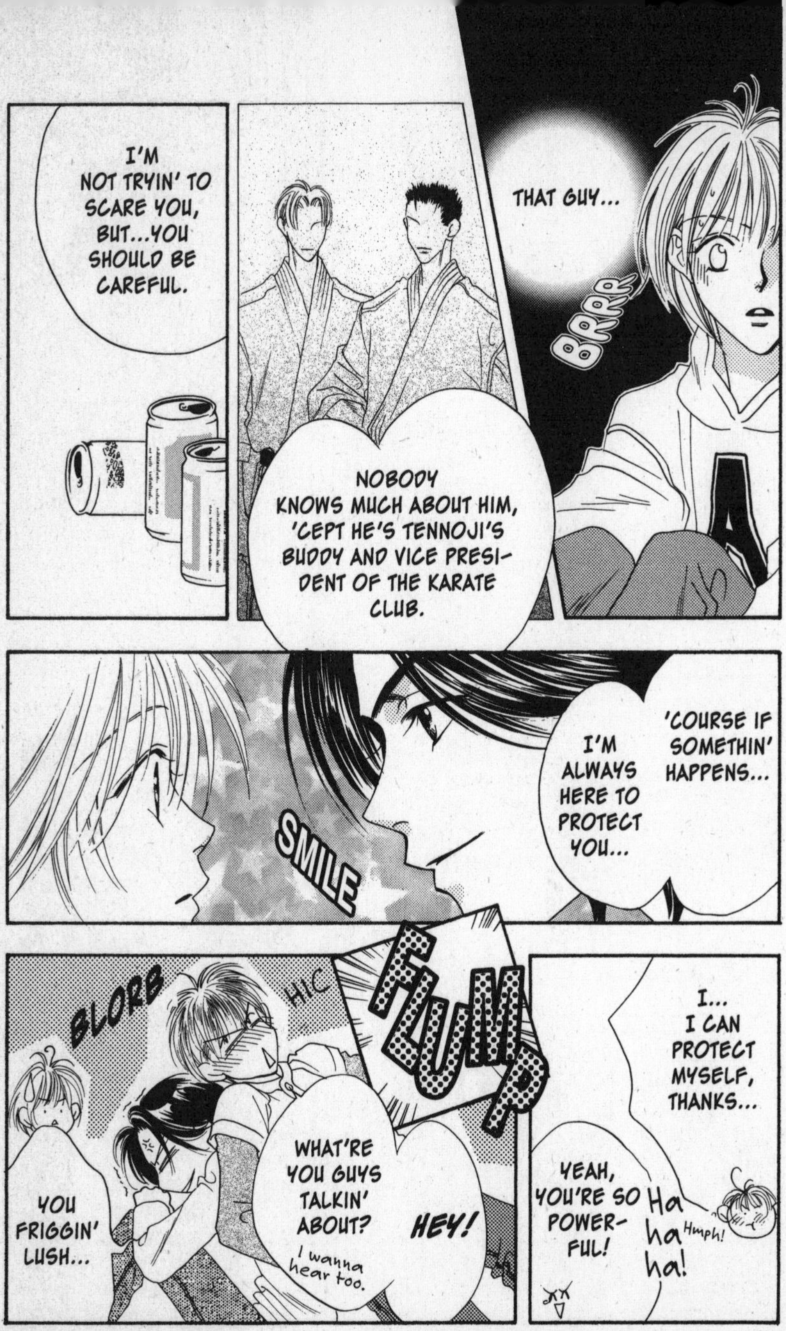
THAT GUY...
BRRR
NOBODY KNOWS MUCH ABOUT HIM, 'CEPT HE'S TENNOJI'S BUDDY AND VICE PRESIDENT OF THE KARATE CLUB.
I'M NOT TRYIN' TO SCARE YOU, BUT...YOU SHOULD BE CAREFUL.
'COURSE IF SOMETHIN' HAPPENS...
I'M ALWAYS HERE TO PROTECT YOU...
SMILE
I... I CAN PROTECT MYSELF, THANKS...
YEAH, YOU'RE SO POWERFUL!
Ha ha ha!
Hmph!
FLUMP
HIC
HEY!
WHAT'RE YOU GUYS TALKIN' ABOUT?
I wanna hear too.
BLORB
YOU FRIGGIN' LUSH...

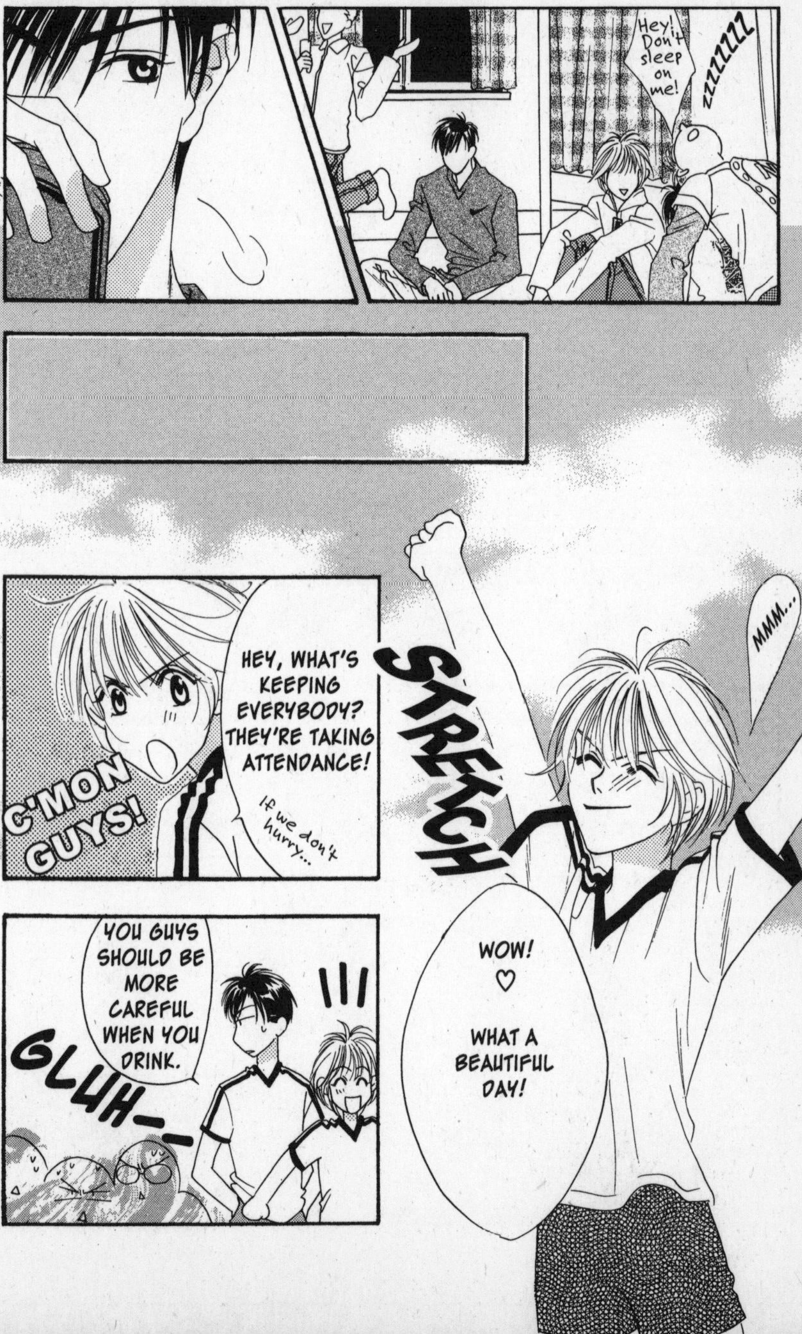
ZZZZZZZZ
Hey! Don't sleep on me!
MMM...
STRETCH
WOW! ♡ WHAT A BEAUTIFUL DAY!
HEY, WHAT'S KEEPING EVERYBODY? THEY'RE TAKING ATTENDANCE!
If we don't hurry...
C'MON GUYS!
YOU GUYS SHOULD BE MORE CAREFUL WHEN YOU DRINK.
GLUH--

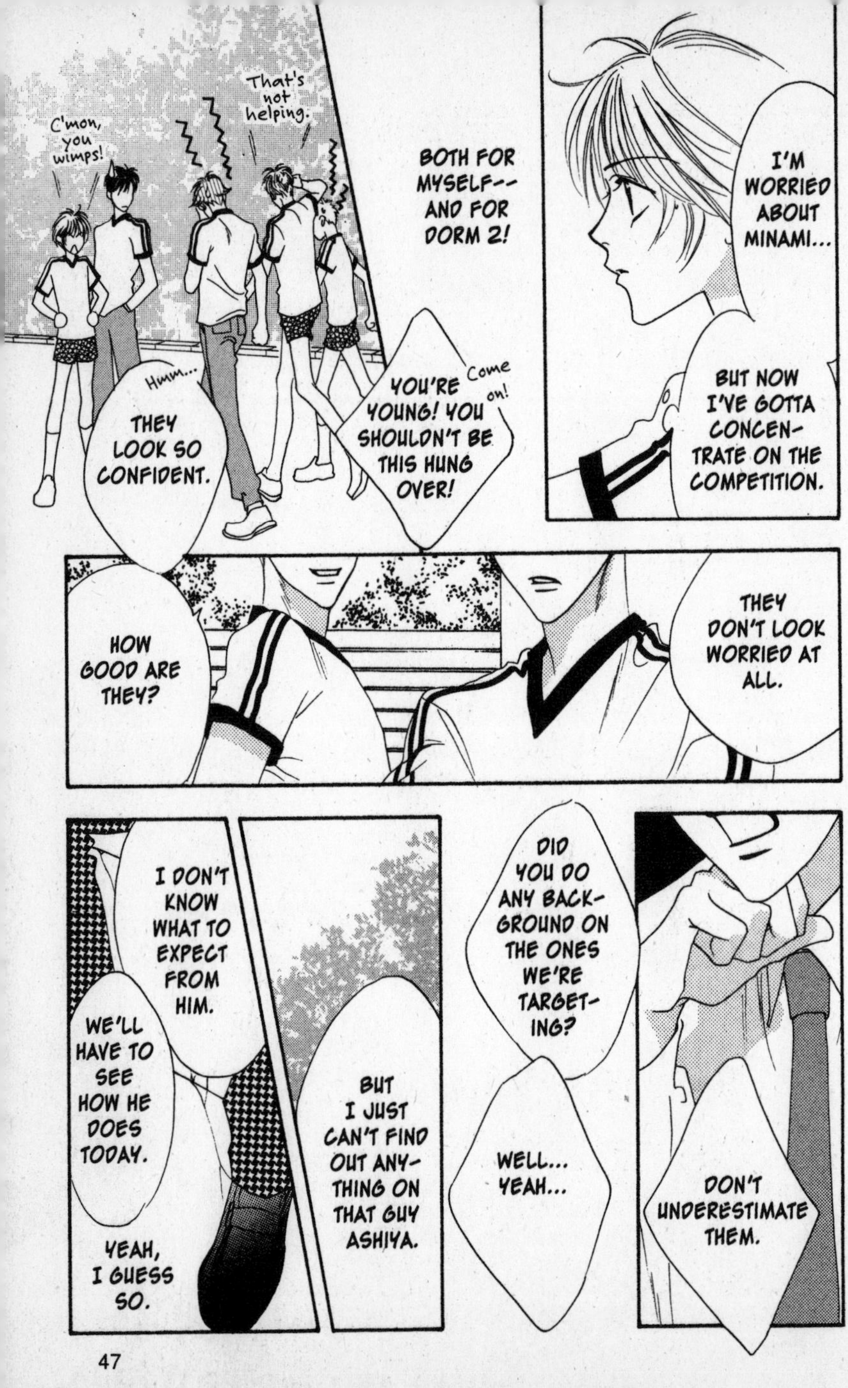
I'M WORRIED ABOUT MINAMI...
BUT NOW I'VE GOTTA CONCENTRATE ON THE COMPETITION.
BOTH FOR MYSELF-- AND FOR DORM 2!
That's not helping.
Come on!
YOU'RE YOUNG! YOU SHOULDN'T BE THIS HUNG OVER!
C'mon, you wimps!
Hmm...
THEY LOOK SO CONFIDENT.
THEY DON'T LOOK WORRIED AT ALL.
HOW GOOD ARE THEY?
DON'T UNDERESTIMATE THEM.
DID YOU DO ANY BACKGROUND ON THE ONES WE'RE TARGETING?
WELL... YEAH...
BUT I JUST CAN'T FIND OUT ANYTHING ON THAT GUY ASHIYA.
I DON'T KNOW WHAT TO EXPECT FROM HIM.
WE'LL HAVE TO SEE HOW HE DOES TODAY.
YEAH, I GUESS SO.

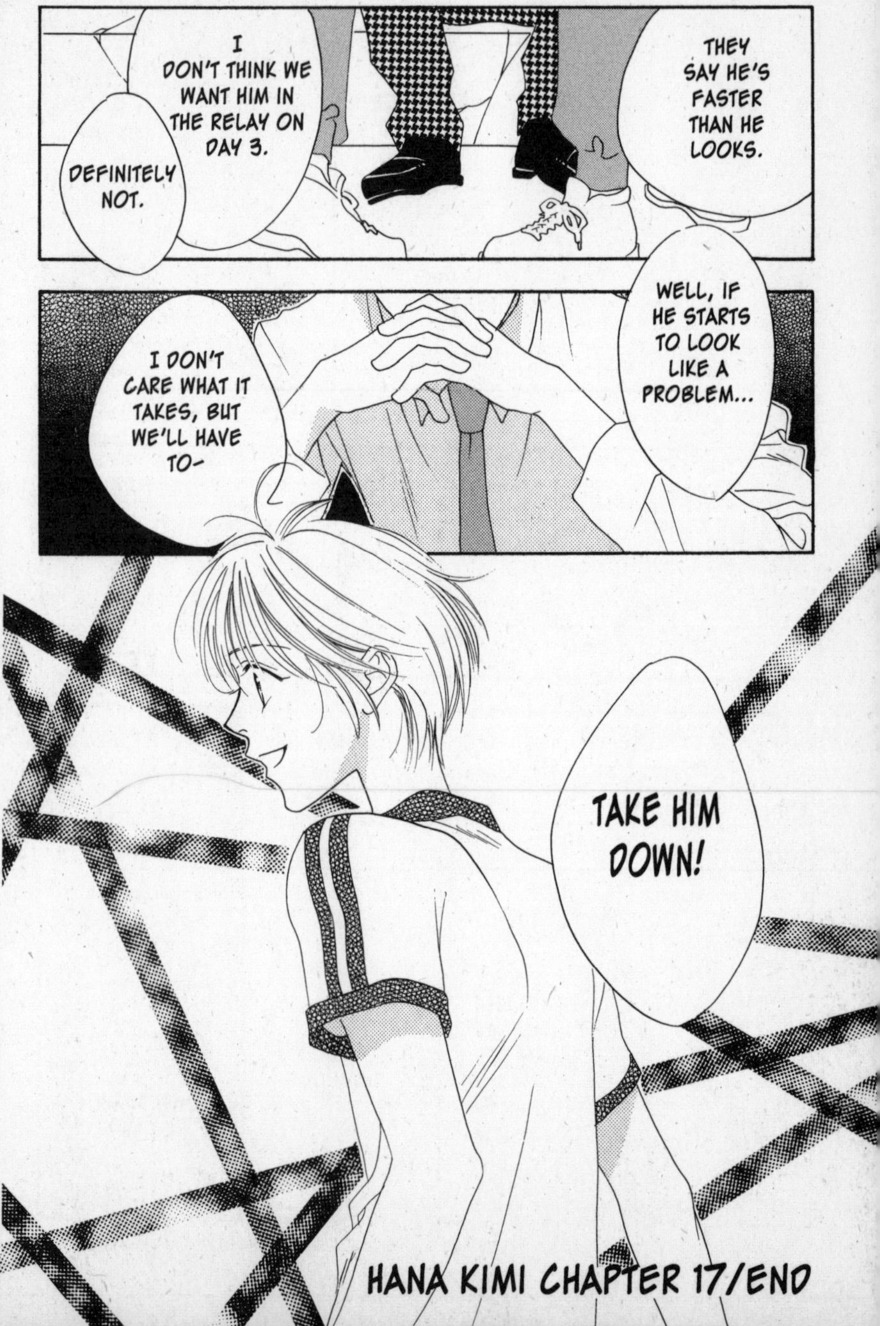
THEY SAY HE'S FASTER THAN HE LOOKS.
I DON'T THINK WE WANT HIM IN THE RELAY ON DAY 3.
DEFINITELY NOT.
WELL, IF HE STARTS TO LOOK LIKE A PROBLEM...
I DON'T CARE WHAT IT TAKES, BUT WE'LL HAVE TO-
TAKE HIM DOWN!
HANA KIMI CHAPTER 17/END

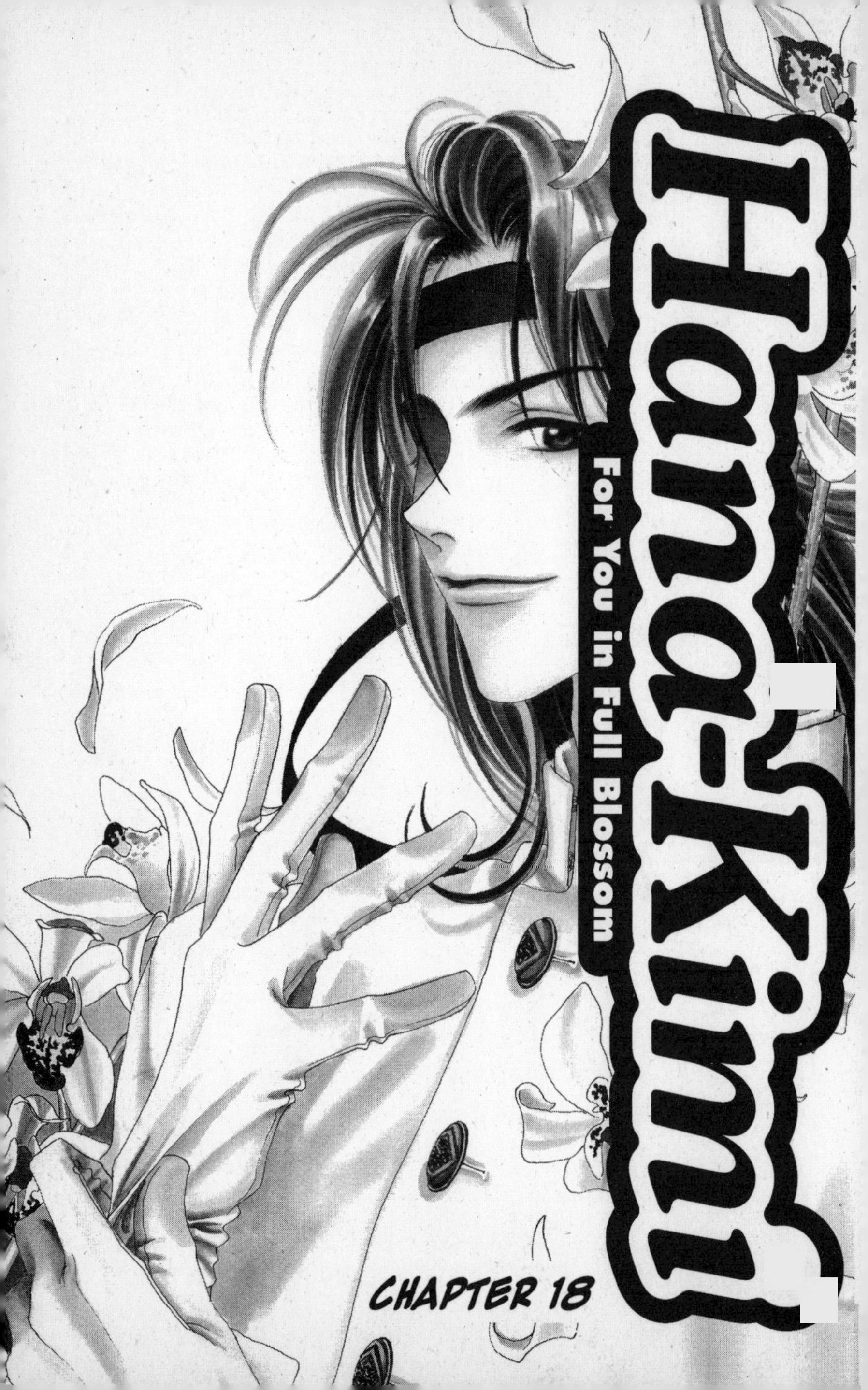
Hana-Kimi
For You in Full Blossom
CHAPTER 18

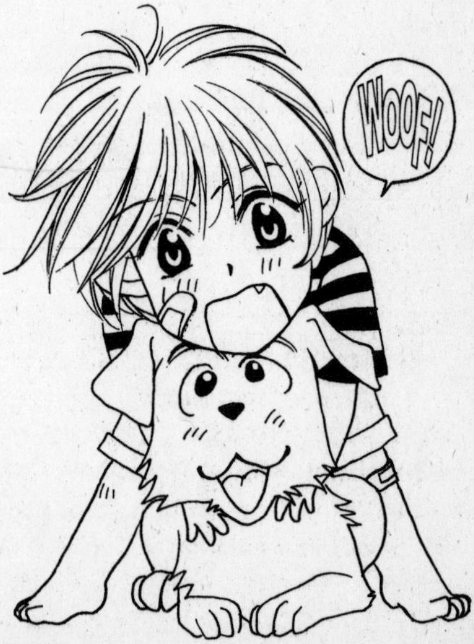
WOOF!

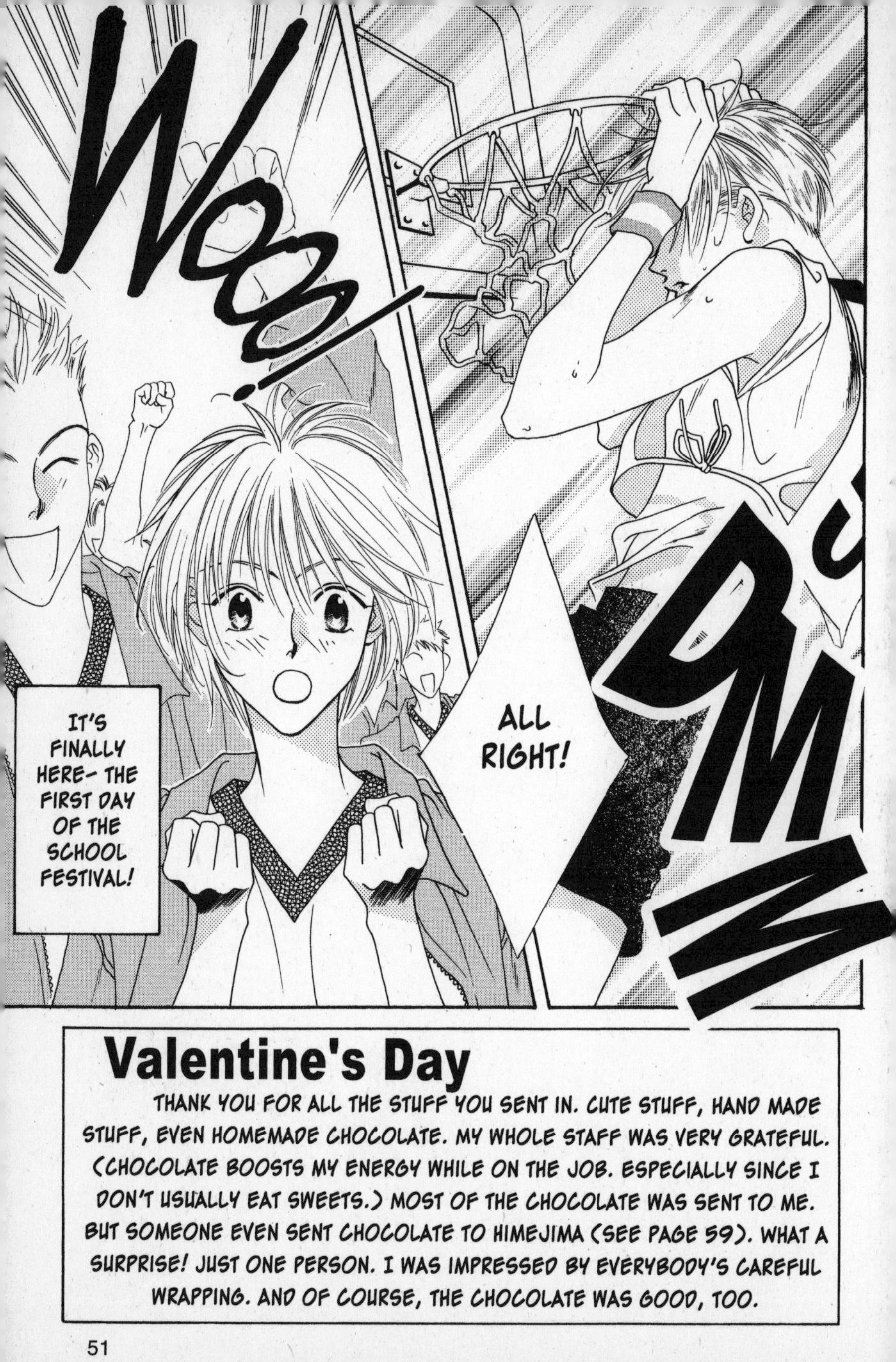
DMM
ALL RIGHT!
WOOO!
IT'S FINALLY HERE- THE FIRST DAY OF THE SCHOOL FESTIVAL!

Valentine's Day

THANK YOU FOR ALL THE STUFF YOU SENT IN. CUTE STUFF, HAND MADE STUFF, EVEN HOMEMADE CHOCOLATE. MY WHOLE STAFF WAS VERY GRATEFUL. (CHOCOLATE BOOSTS MY ENERGY WHILE ON THE JOB. ESPECIALLY SINCE I DON'T USUALLY EAT SWEETS.) MOST OF THE CHOCOLATE WAS SENT TO ME. BUT SOMEONE EVEN SENT CHOCOLATE TO HIMEJIMA (SEE PAGE 59). WHAT A SURPRISE! JUST ONE PERSON. I WAS IMPRESSED BY EVERYBODY'S CAREFUL WRAPPING. AND OF COURSE, THE CHOCOLATE WAS GOOD, TOO.

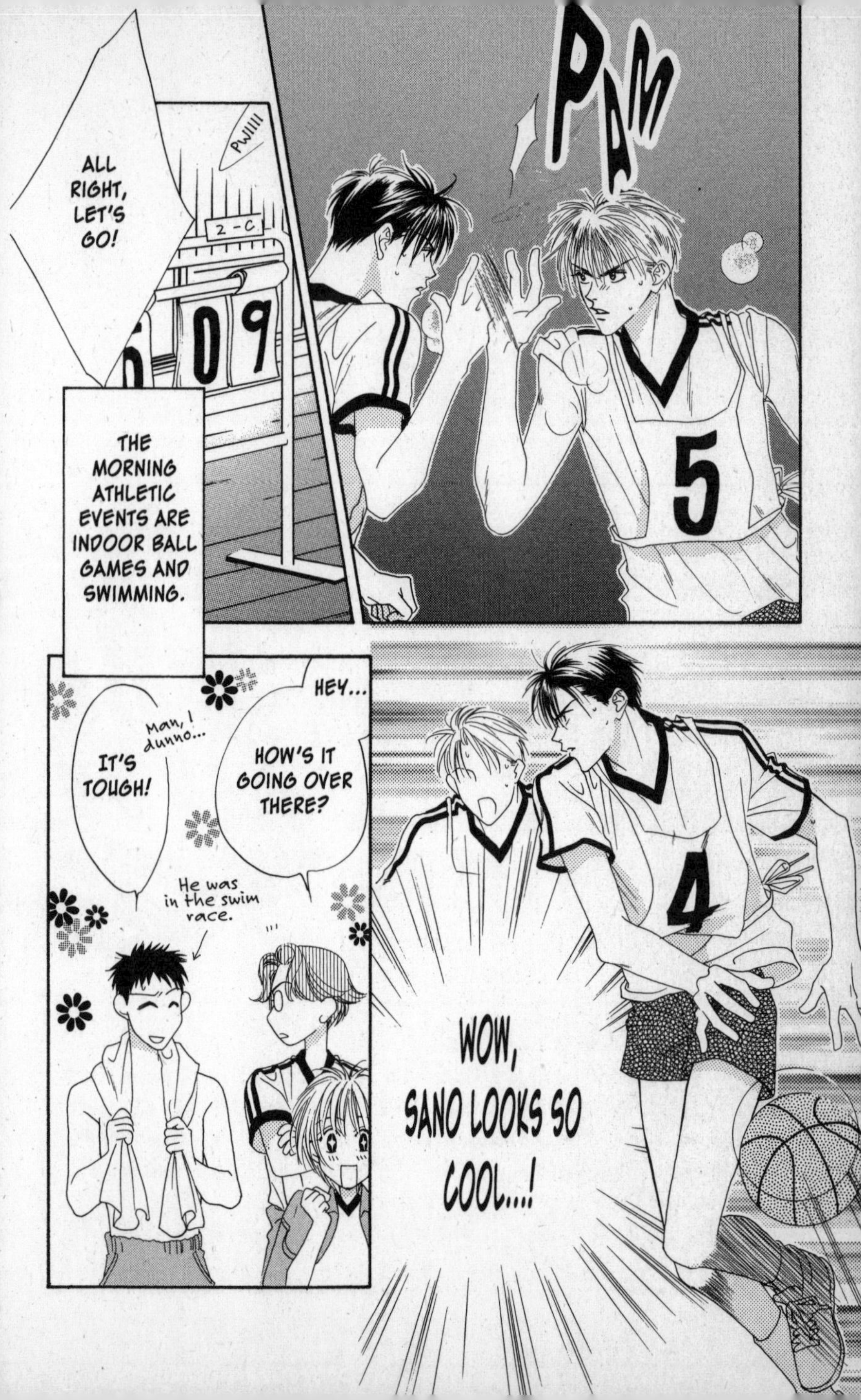
PAM
PWIIII
ALL RIGHT, LET'S GO!
2-C
THE MORNING ATHLETIC EVENTS ARE INDOOR BALL GAMES AND SWIMMING.
WOW, SANO LOOKS SO COOL...!
HEY... HOW'S IT GOING OVER THERE?
Man, I dunno...
IT'S TOUGH!
He was in the swim race.

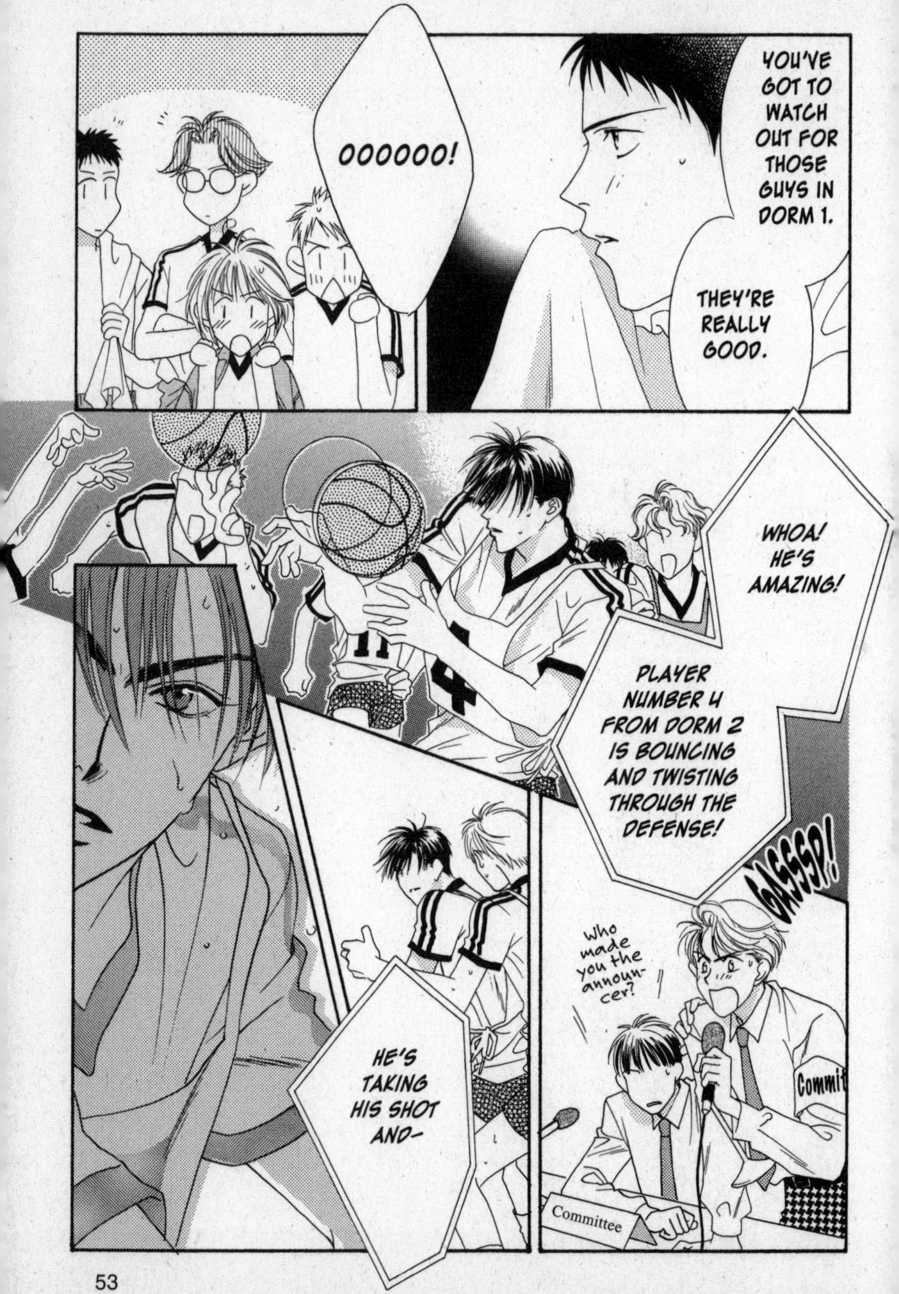
YOU'VE GOT TO WATCH OUT FOR THOSE GUYS IN DORM 1.
THEY'RE REALLY GOOD.
OOOOOO!
WHOA! HE'S AMAZING!
PLAYER NUMBER 4 FROM DORM 2 IS BOUNCING AND TWISTING THROUGH THE DEFENSE!
GASSSP!
Who made you the announcer?
Commit
Committee
HE'S TAKING HIS SHOT AND-

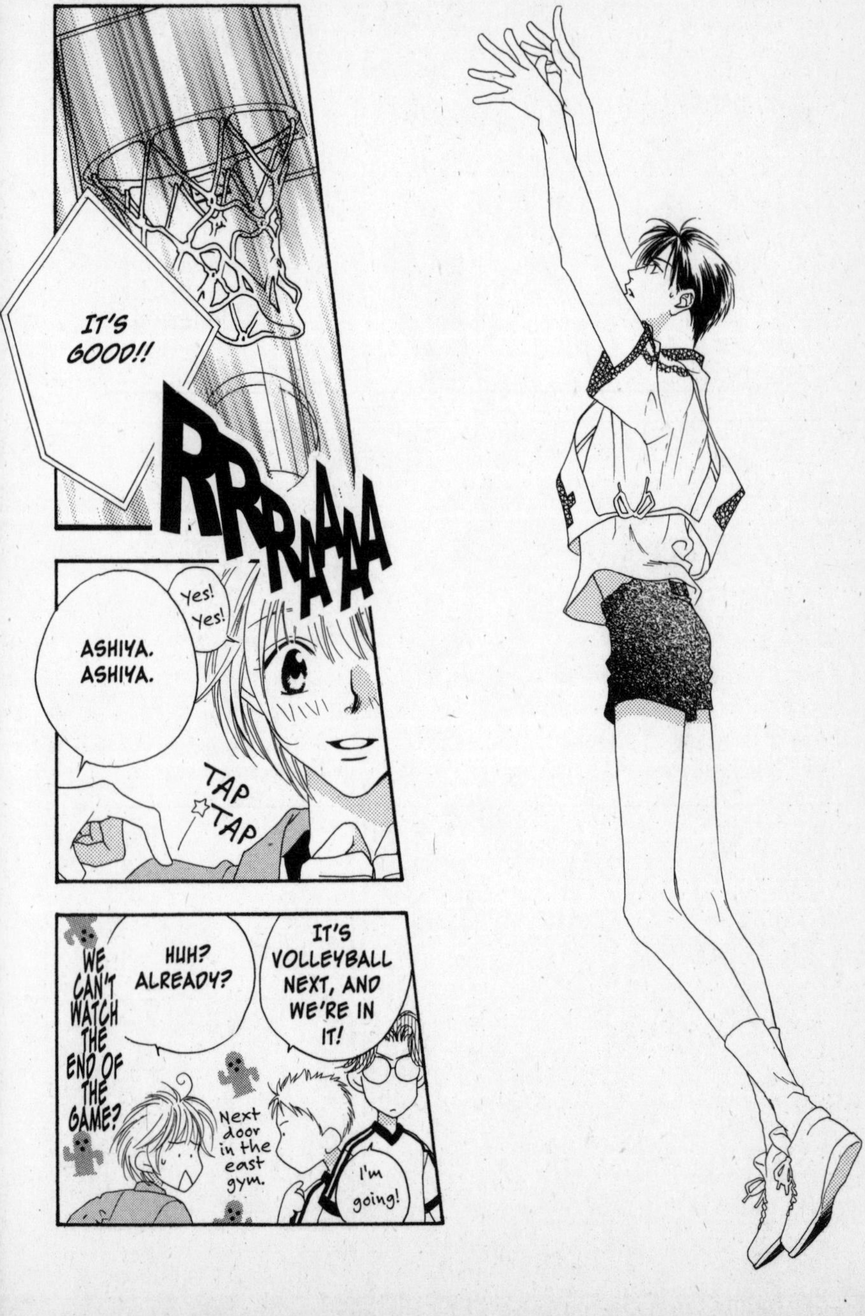
IT'S GOOD!!
RRRAAAA
ASHIYA. ASHIYA.
Yes! Yes!
TAP TAP
IT'S VOLLEYBALL NEXT, AND WE'RE IN IT!
I'm going!
HUH? ALREADY?
Next door in the east gym.
WE CAN'T WATCH THE END OF THE GAME?

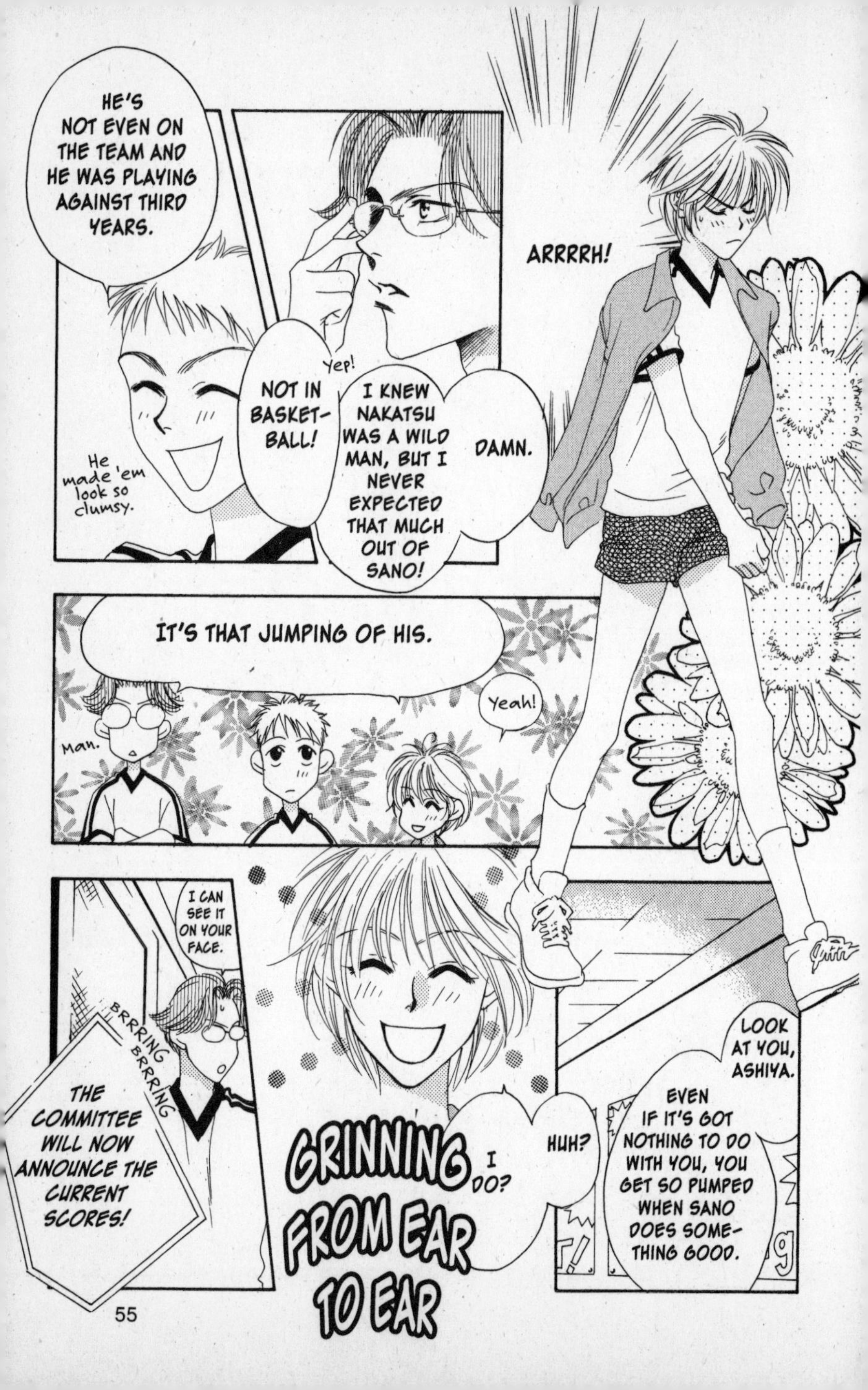
ARRRRH!
DAMN.
I KNEW NAKATSU WAS A WILD MAN, BUT I NEVER EXPECTED THAT MUCH OUT OF SANO!
Yep!
NOT IN BASKET-BALL!
HE'S NOT EVEN ON THE TEAM AND HE WAS PLAYING AGAINST THIRD YEARS.
He made 'em look so clumsy.
IT'S THAT JUMPING OF HIS.
Yeah!
Man.
LOOK AT YOU, ASHIYA.
EVEN IF IT'S GOT NOTHING TO DO WITH YOU, YOU GET SO PUMPED WHEN SANO DOES SOME-THING GOOD.
HUH?
I DO?
GRINNING FROM EAR TO EAR
I CAN SEE IT ON YOUR FACE.
BRRRING BRRRING
THE COMMITTEE WILL NOW ANNOUNCE THE CURRENT SCORES!

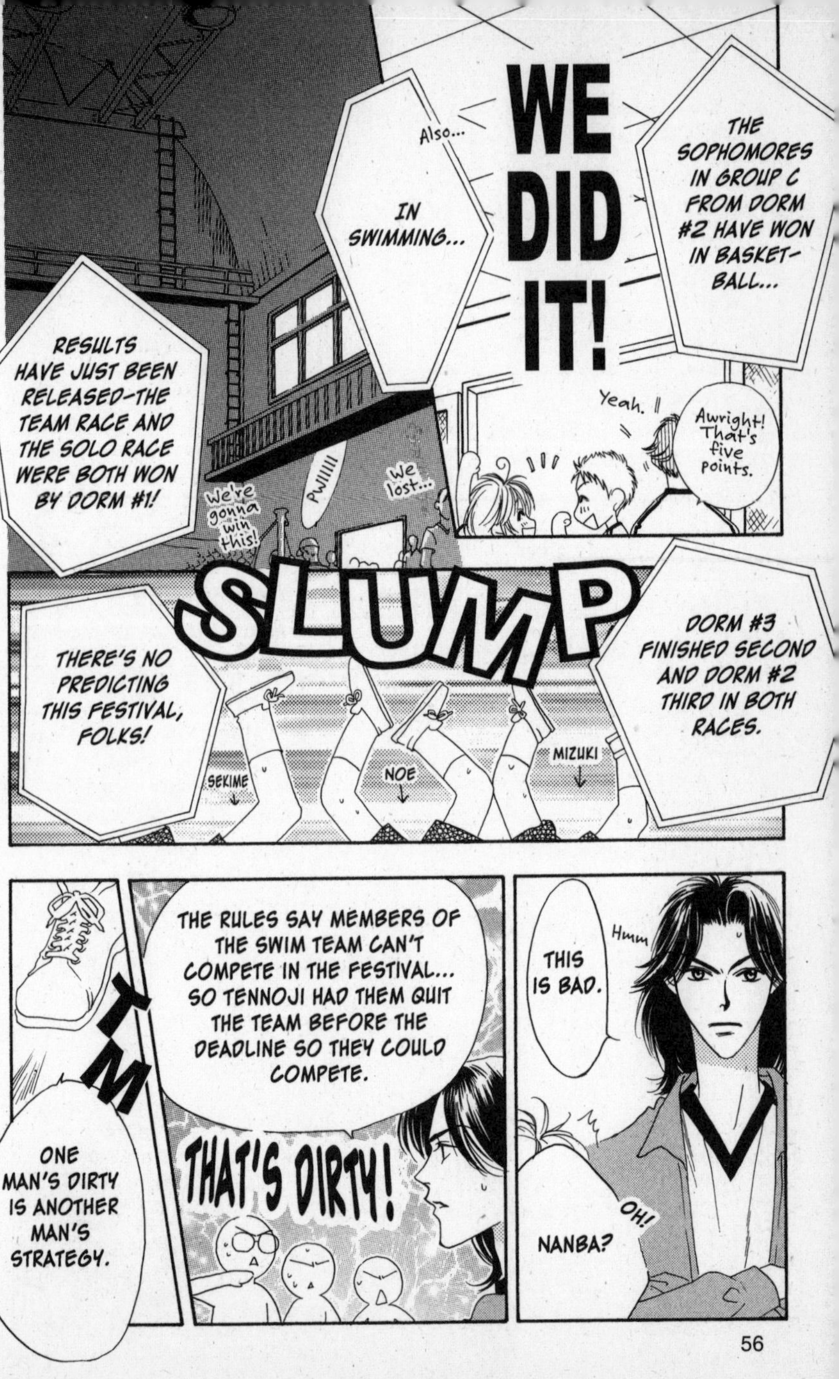
THE SOPHOMORES IN GROUP C FROM DORM #2 HAVE WON IN BASKET-BALL...
WE DID IT!
Also...
IN SWIMMING...
Awright! That's five points.
Yeah.
RESULTS HAVE JUST BEEN RELEASED—THE TEAM RACE AND THE SOLO RACE WERE BOTH WON BY DORM #1!
We lost...
PWIIIII
We're gonna win this!
DORM #3 FINISHED SECOND AND DORM #2 THIRD IN BOTH RACES.
SLUMP
MIZUKI
NOE
SEKIME
THERE'S NO PREDICTING THIS FESTIVAL, FOLKS!
Hmm
THIS IS BAD.
OH!
NANBA?
THE RULES SAY MEMBERS OF THE SWIM TEAM CAN'T COMPETE IN THE FESTIVAL... SO TENNOJI HAD THEM QUIT THE TEAM BEFORE THE DEADLINE SO THEY COULD COMPETE.
THAT'S DIRTY!
TM
ONE MAN'S DIRTY IS ANOTHER MAN'S STRATEGY.

Whispered Secrets

"MINAMI, THE LADIES MAN"

FOR SOME REASON, I WANTED TO DRAW NANBA WEARING A PEP SQUAD GOWN. THAT'S WHY I WROTE THIS STORY (HA HA). BOTH THE COVER ILLUSTRATION AND THE STORY WERE WELL RECEIVED, SO I WAS HAPPY.♡ A LOT OF GIRLS SAID THOSE IMAGES OF MINAMI REALLY KNOCKED THEM OUT. HE'S DEFINITELY A LADIES MAN. ON AN INTERNET MESSAGE BOARD THEY WERE TALKING ABOUT HANA-KIMI AND A GUY SAID, "I REALLY WANT TO SEE THE PICTURE OF MINAMI DRESSED LIKE A GIRL." (SEE PAGE 120.) SOMEONE ELSE SAID, "I LIKE THE PICTURES THAT NIHONBASHI SELLS MORE THAN THE ONE IO HAD."

By the way, my assistant Shibachi also liked Nihonbashi's photo of Minami. She said it looked like "Hyde."* She even took a copy home with her (heh heh).

* "HYDE" = JAPANESE MUSICIAN AND FORMER SINGER FOR THE BAND "L'ARC-EN-CIEL"

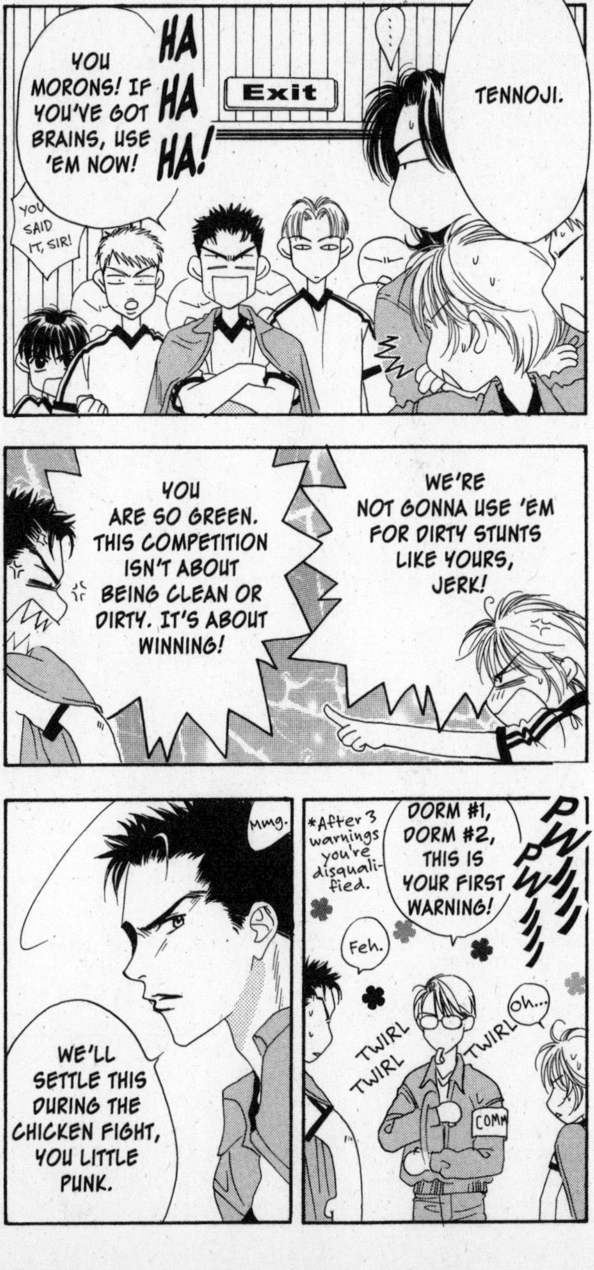
TENNOJI.
...
HA HA HA!
YOU MORONS! IF YOU'VE GOT BRAINS, USE 'EM NOW!
YOU SAID IT, SIR!
Exit
WE'RE NOT GONNA USE 'EM FOR DIRTY STUNTS LIKE YOURS, JERK!
YOU ARE SO GREEN. THIS COMPETITION ISN'T ABOUT BEING CLEAN OR DIRTY. IT'S ABOUT WINNING!
DORM #1, DORM #2, THIS IS YOUR FIRST WARNING!
*After 3 warnings you're disqualified.
Feh.
Oh...
TWIRL
TWIRL
TWIRL
COMM
Mmg.
WE'LL SETTLE THIS DURING THE CHICKEN FIGHT, YOU LITTLE PUNK.

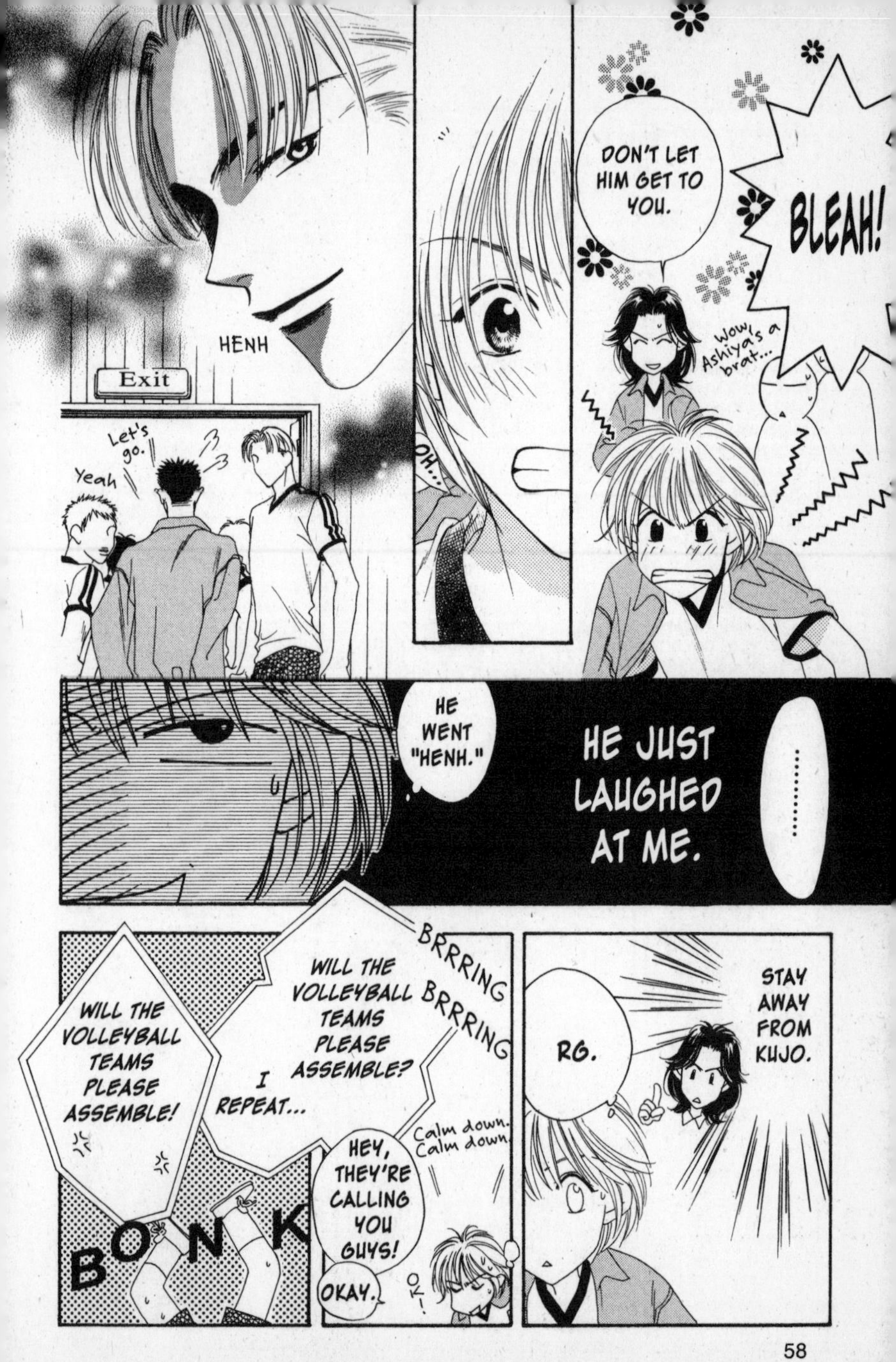
BLEAH!
DON'T LET HIM GET TO YOU.
Wow, Ashiya's a brat...
OH...
HENH
Exit
Let's go.
Yeah
......
HE JUST LAUGHED AT ME.
HE WENT "HENH."
STAY AWAY FROM KUJO.
RG.
BRRRING BRRRING
WILL THE VOLLEYBALL TEAMS PLEASE ASSEMBLE?
I REPEAT...
Calm down. Calm down.
HEY, THEY'RE CALLING YOU GUYS!
OK!
OKAY.
WILL THE VOLLEYBALL TEAMS PLEASE ASSEMBLE!
BONK

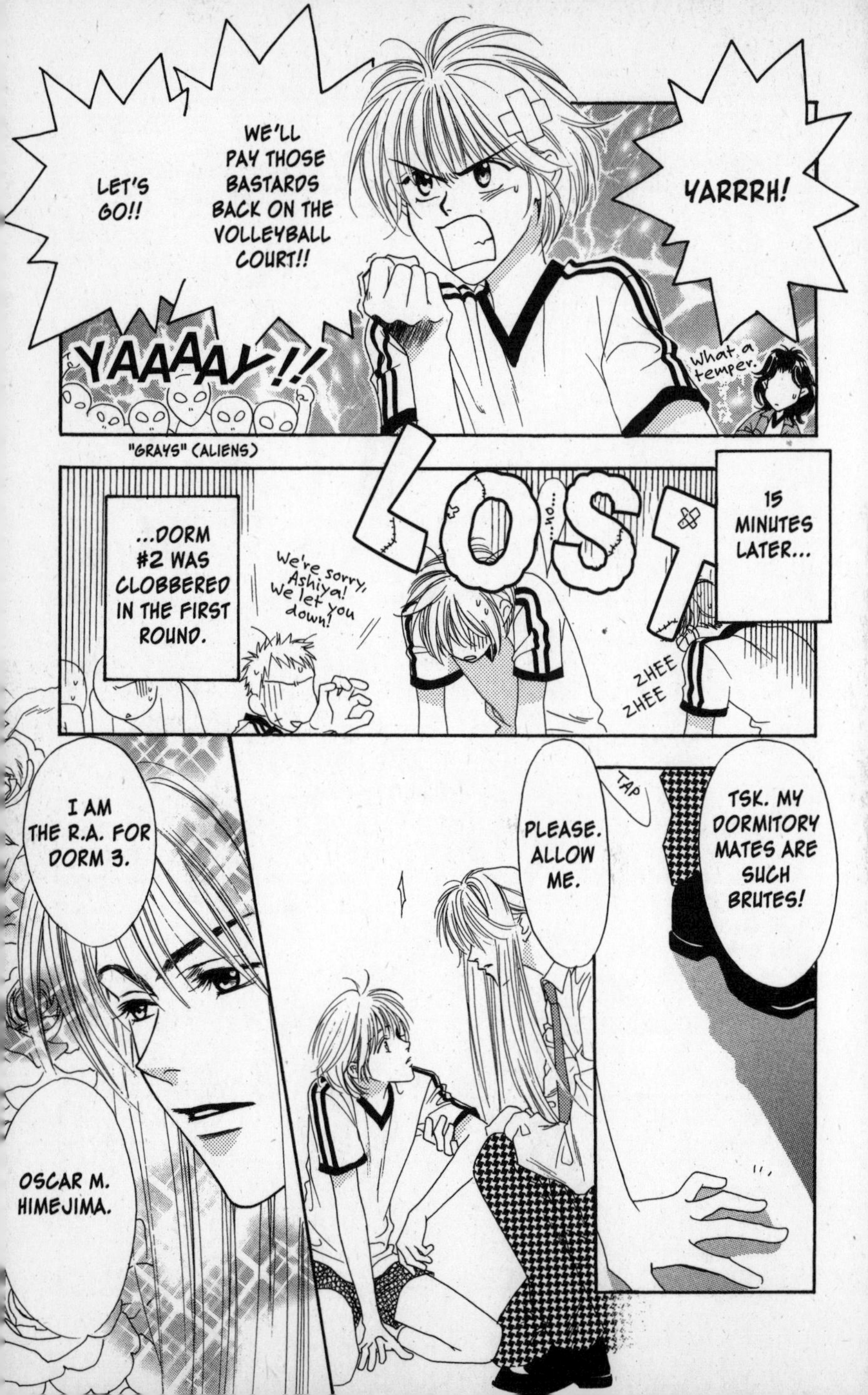
YARRRH!
WE'LL PAY THOSE BASTARDS BACK ON THE VOLLEYBALL COURT!!
LET'S GO!!
What a temper.
YAAAAY!!
"GRAYS" (ALIENS)
15 MINUTES LATER...
ZHEE ZHEE
LOST
...oh...
We're sorry, Ashiya! We let you down!
...DORM #2 WAS CLOBBERED IN THE FIRST ROUND.
TSK. MY DORMITORY MATES ARE SUCH BRUTES!
TAP
PLEASE. ALLOW ME.
I AM THE R.A. FOR DORM 3.
OSCAR M. HIMEJIMA.

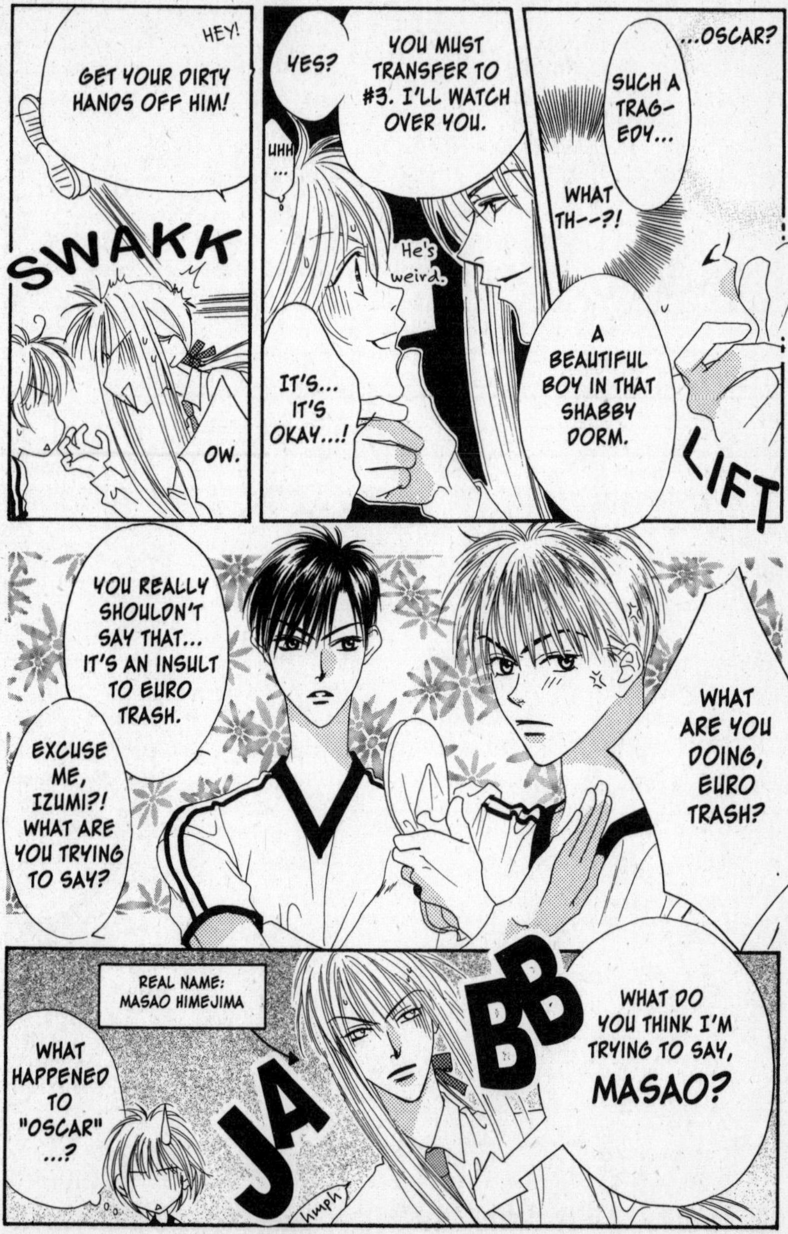
...OSCAR?
SUCH A TRAG-EDY...
WHAT TH--?!
A BEAUTIFUL BOY IN THAT SHABBY DORM.
LIFT
YES?
YOU MUST TRANSFER TO #3. I'LL WATCH OVER YOU.
UHH...
He's weird.
IT'S... IT'S OKAY...!
HEY!
GET YOUR DIRTY HANDS OFF HIM!
SWAKK
OW.
WHAT ARE YOU DOING, EURO TRASH?
YOU REALLY SHOULDN'T SAY THAT... IT'S AN INSULT TO EURO TRASH.
EXCUSE ME, IZUMI?! WHAT ARE YOU TRYING TO SAY?
WHAT DO YOU THINK I'M TRYING TO SAY, MASAO?
JABB
REAL NAME: MASAO HIMEJIMA
WHAT HAPPENED TO "OSCAR" ...?
hmph

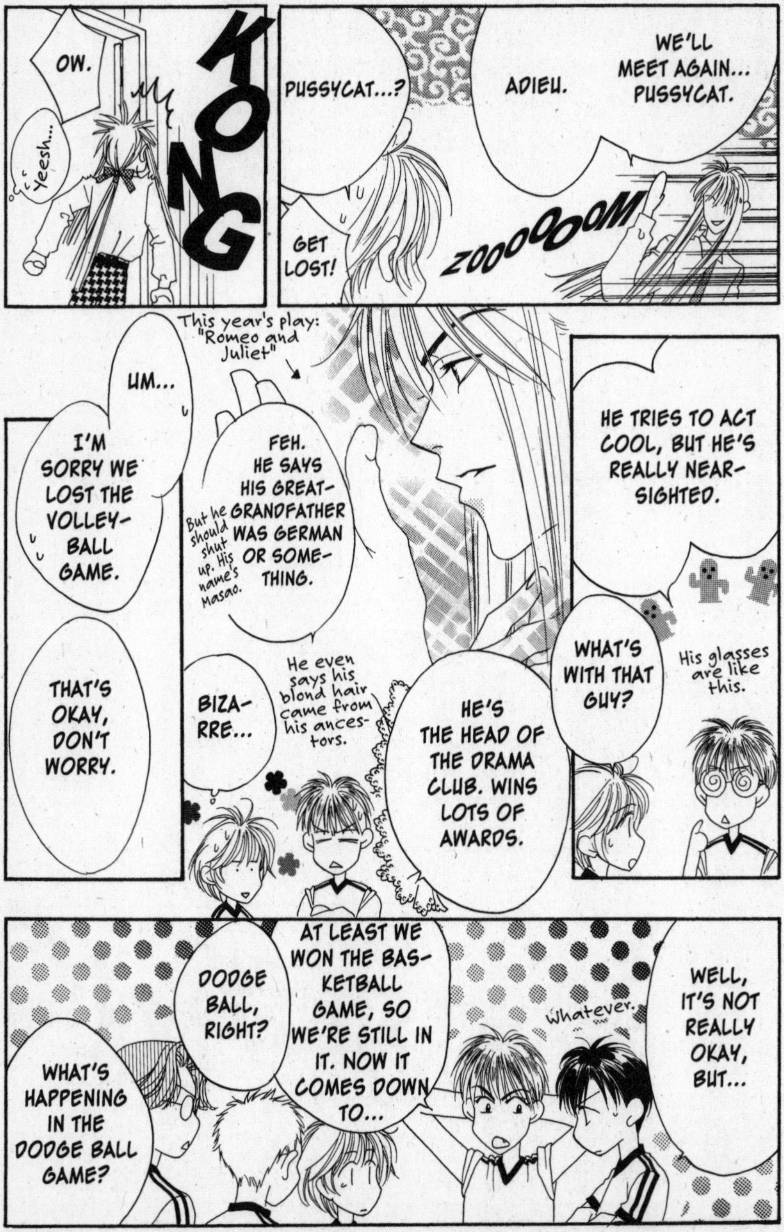
WE'LL MEET AGAIN... PUSSYCAT.
ADIEU.
PUSSYCAT...?
ZOOOOOOOM
GET LOST!
KONG
OW.
Yeesh...
HE TRIES TO ACT COOL, BUT HE'S REALLY NEAR-SIGHTED.
WHAT'S WITH THAT GUY?
His glasses are like this.
This year's play: "Romeo and Juliet"
FEH. HE SAYS HIS GREAT-GRANDFATHER WAS GERMAN OR SOMETHING.
But he should shut up. His name's Masao.
HE'S THE HEAD OF THE DRAMA CLUB. WINS LOTS OF AWARDS.
He even says his blond hair came from his ancestors.
BIZARRE...
UM...
I'M SORRY WE LOST THE VOLLEYBALL GAME.
THAT'S OKAY, DON'T WORRY.
WELL, IT'S NOT REALLY OKAY, BUT...
Whatever.
AT LEAST WE WON THE BASKETBALL GAME, SO WE'RE STILL IN IT. NOW IT COMES DOWN TO...
DODGE BALL, RIGHT?
WHAT'S HAPPENING IN THE DODGE BALL GAME?

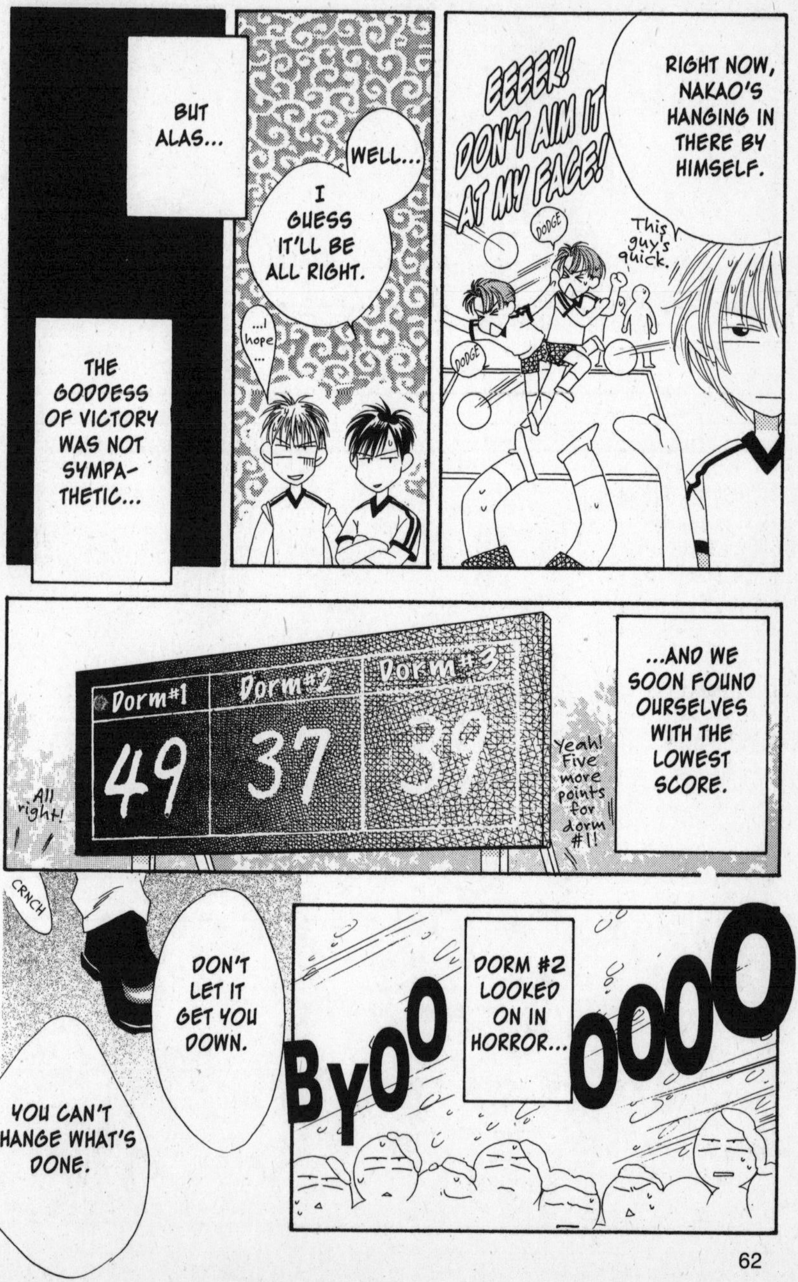
RIGHT NOW, NAKAO'S HANGING IN THERE BY HIMSELF.
EEEEK! DON'T AIM IT AT MY FACE!
This guy's quick.
DODGE
DODGE
WELL...
I GUESS IT'LL BE ALL RIGHT.
...I hope...
BUT ALAS...
THE GODDESS OF VICTORY WAS NOT SYMPATHETIC...
...AND WE SOON FOUND OURSELVES WITH THE LOWEST SCORE.
Yeah! Five more points for dorm #1!
Dorm#1 Dorm#2 Dorm#3
49 37 39
All right!
BYOOOOOOO
DORM #2 LOOKED ON IN HORROR...
CRNCH
DON'T LET IT GET YOU DOWN.
YOU CAN'T CHANGE WHAT'S DONE.

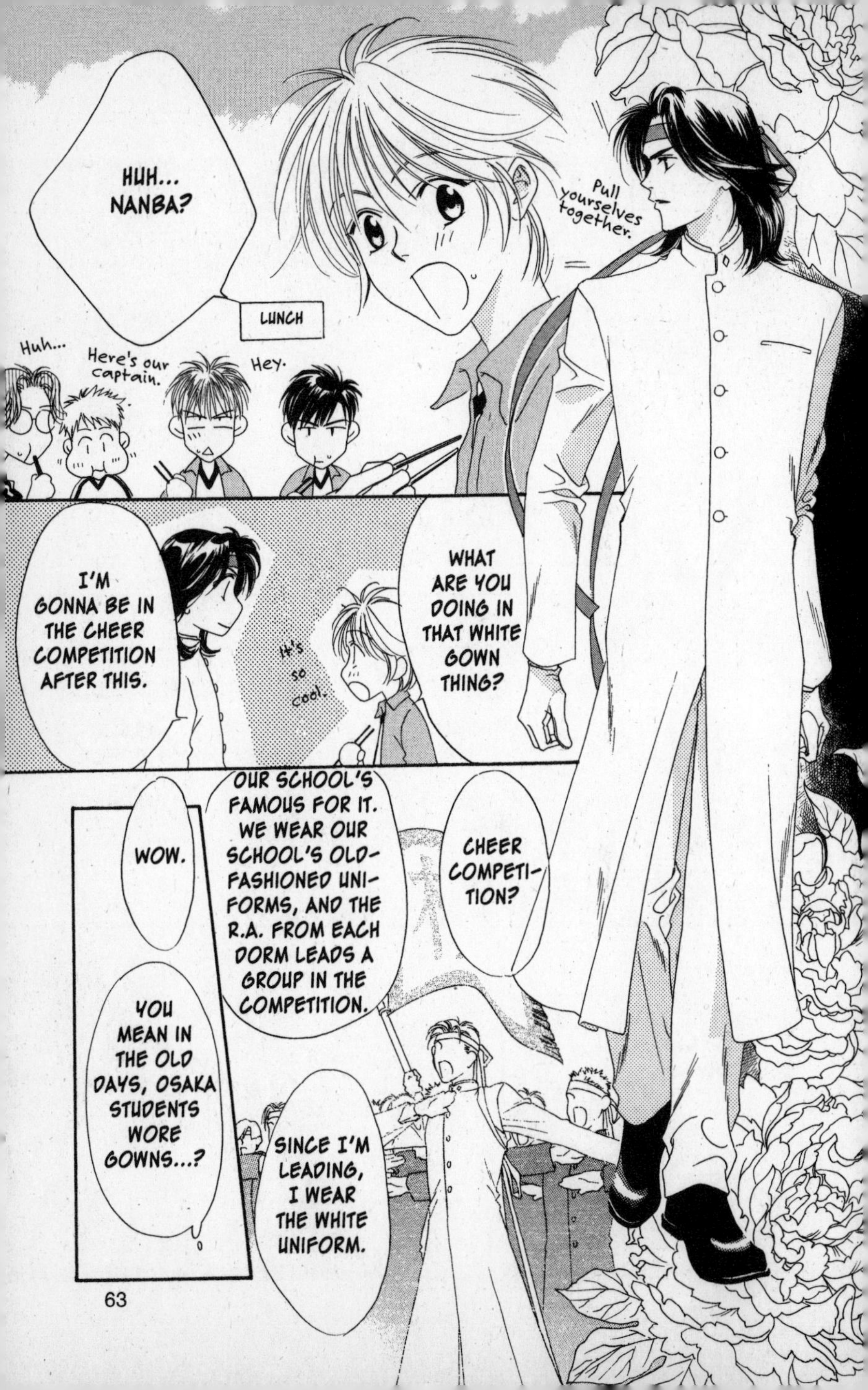
Pull yourselves together.
HUH... NANBA?
LUNCH
Hey.
Here's our captain.
Huh...
WHAT ARE YOU DOING IN THAT WHITE GOWN THING?
It's so cool.
I'M GONNA BE IN THE CHEER COMPETITION AFTER THIS.
CHEER COMPETITION?
OUR SCHOOL'S FAMOUS FOR IT. WE WEAR OUR SCHOOL'S OLD-FASHIONED UNIFORMS, AND THE R.A. FROM EACH DORM LEADS A GROUP IN THE COMPETITION.
SINCE I'M LEADING, I WEAR THE WHITE UNIFORM.
WOW.
YOU MEAN IN THE OLD DAYS, OSAKA STUDENTS WORE GOWNS...?

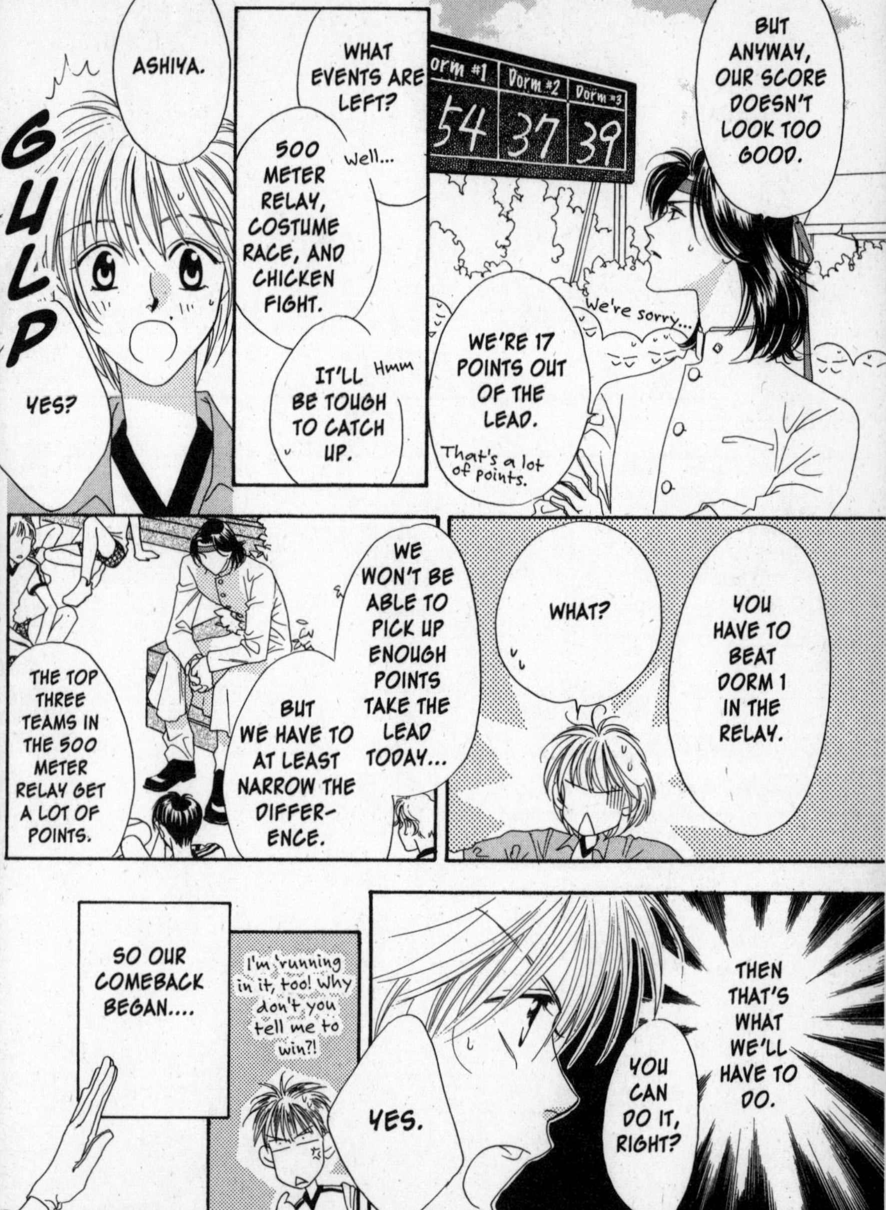
BUT ANYWAY, OUR SCORE DOESN'T LOOK TOO GOOD.
Dorm #1 Dorm #2 Dorm #3
54 37 39
We're sorry...
WE'RE 17 POINTS OUT OF THE LEAD.
That's a lot of points.
WHAT EVENTS ARE LEFT?
Well...
500 METER RELAY, COSTUME RACE, AND CHICKEN FIGHT.
Hmm
IT'LL BE TOUGH TO CATCH UP.
ASHIYA.
GULP
YES?
YOU HAVE TO BEAT DORM 1 IN THE RELAY.
WHAT?
WE WON'T BE ABLE TO PICK UP ENOUGH POINTS TAKE THE LEAD TODAY...
BUT WE HAVE TO AT LEAST NARROW THE DIFFER-ENCE.
THE TOP THREE TEAMS IN THE 500 METER RELAY GET A LOT OF POINTS.
THEN THAT'S WHAT WE'LL HAVE TO DO.
YOU CAN DO IT, RIGHT?
YES.
I'm running in it, too! Why don't you tell me to win?!
SO OUR COMEBACK BEGAN....

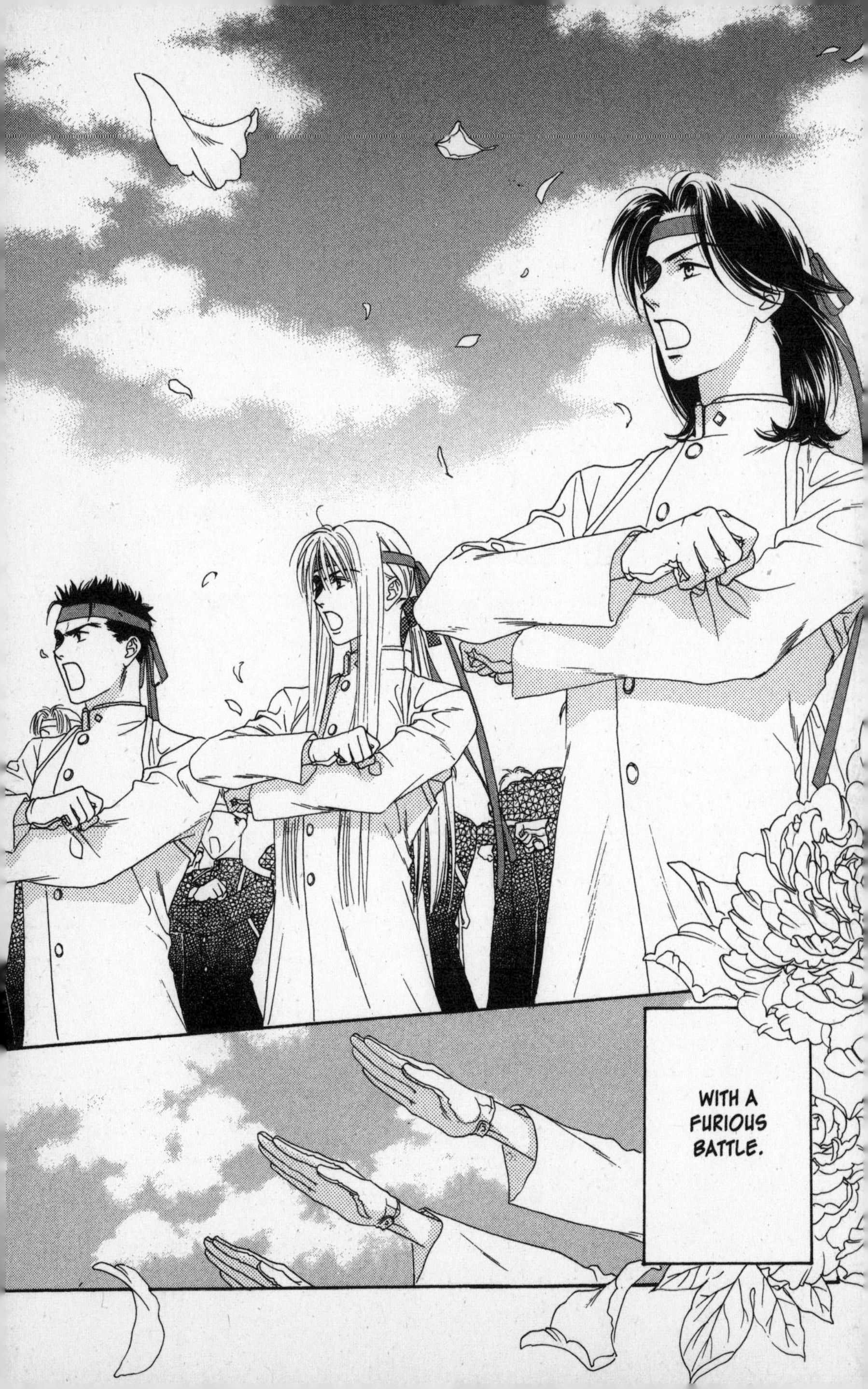
WITH A FURIOUS BATTLE.

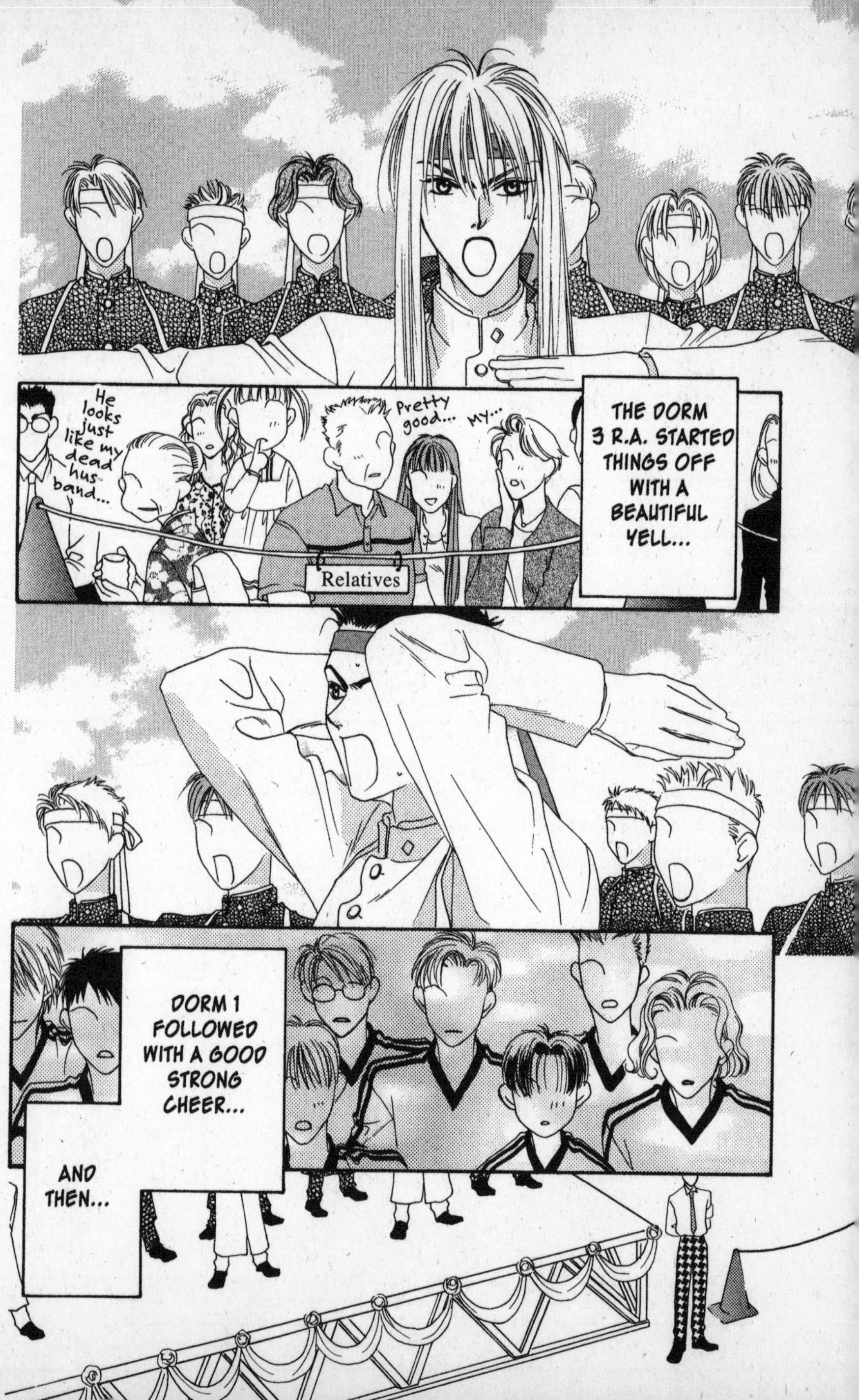
THE DORM 3 R.A. STARTED THINGS OFF WITH A BEAUTIFUL YELL...
My...
Pretty good...
Relatives
He looks just like my dead hus-band...
DORM 1 FOLLOWED WITH A GOOD STRONG CHEER...
AND THEN...

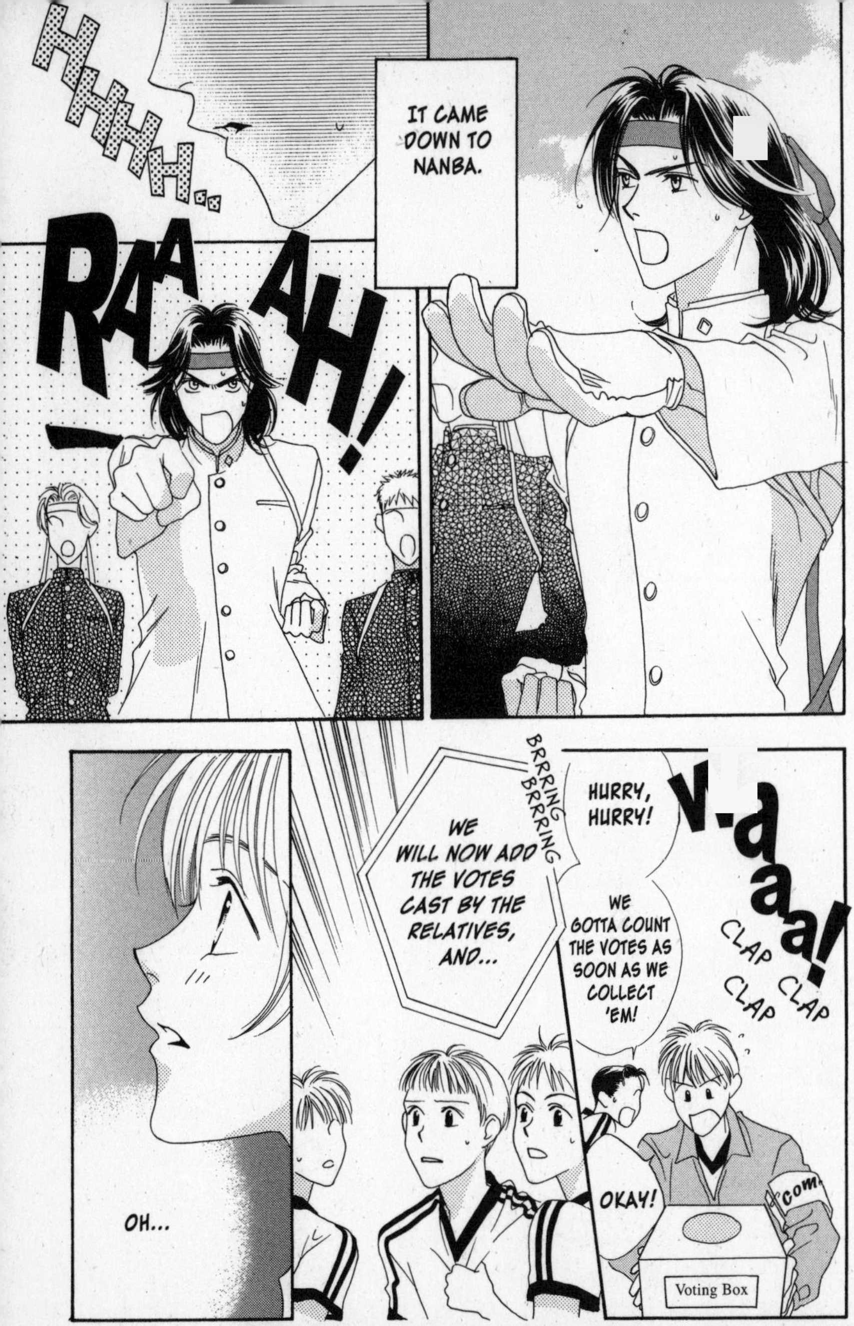
IT CAME DOWN TO NANBA.
HHHHH...
RAAAH!
BRRRING BRRRING
WE WILL NOW ADD THE VOTES CAST BY THE RELATIVES, AND...
HURRY, HURRY!
Waaa!
CLAP CLAP CLAP
WE GOTTA COUNT THE VOTES AS SOON AS WE COLLECT 'EM!
OKAY!
com.
Voting Box
OH...

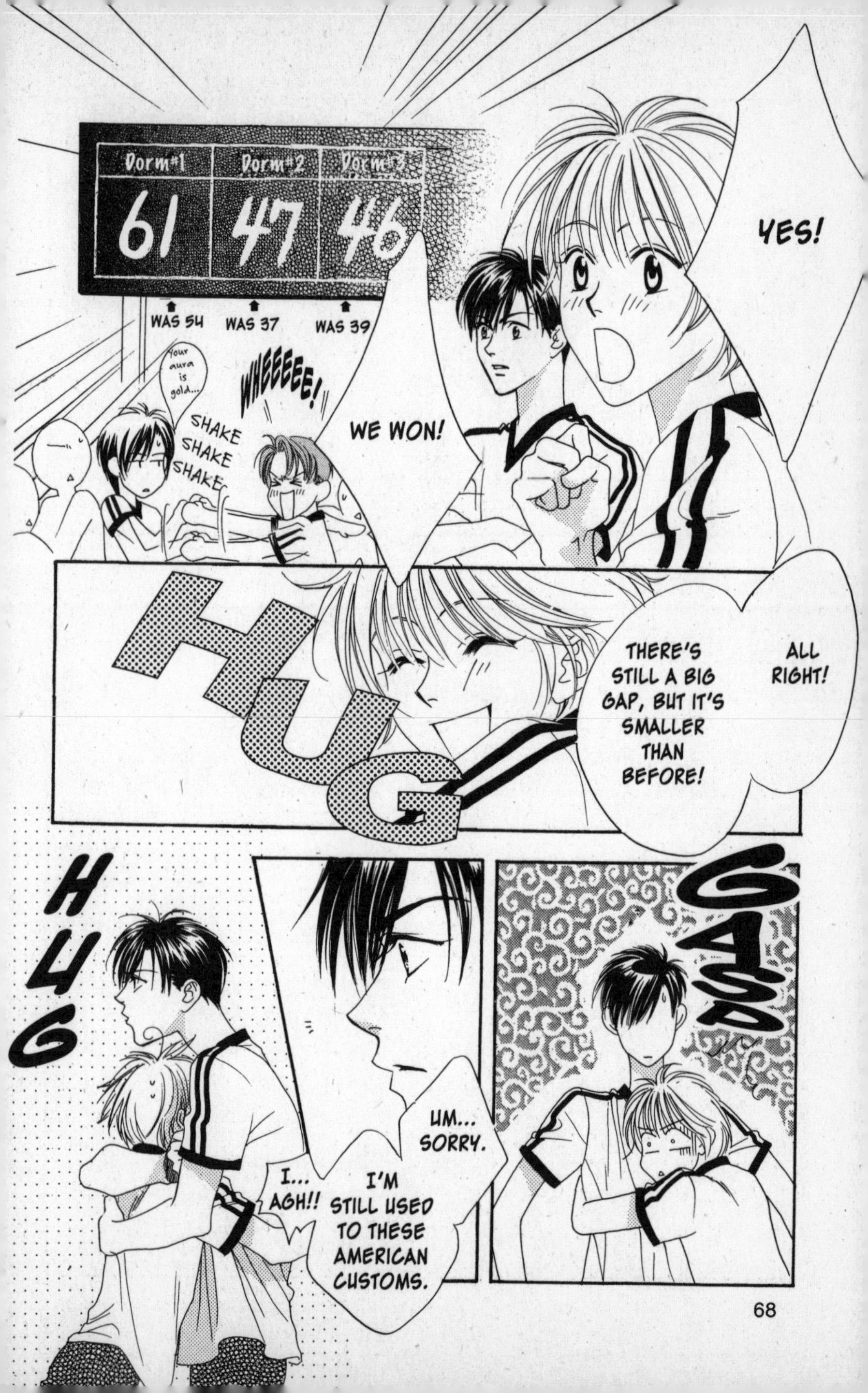
YES!
Dorm#1 Dorm#2 Dorm#3
61 47 46
WAS 54
WAS 37
WAS 39
WE WON!
WHEEEEE!
SHAKE SHAKE SHAKE
Your aura is gold...
ALL RIGHT!
THERE'S STILL A BIG GAP, BUT IT'S SMALLER THAN BEFORE!
HUG
GASP
UM... SORRY.
I'M STILL USED TO THESE AMERICAN CUSTOMS.
HUG
I... AGH!!

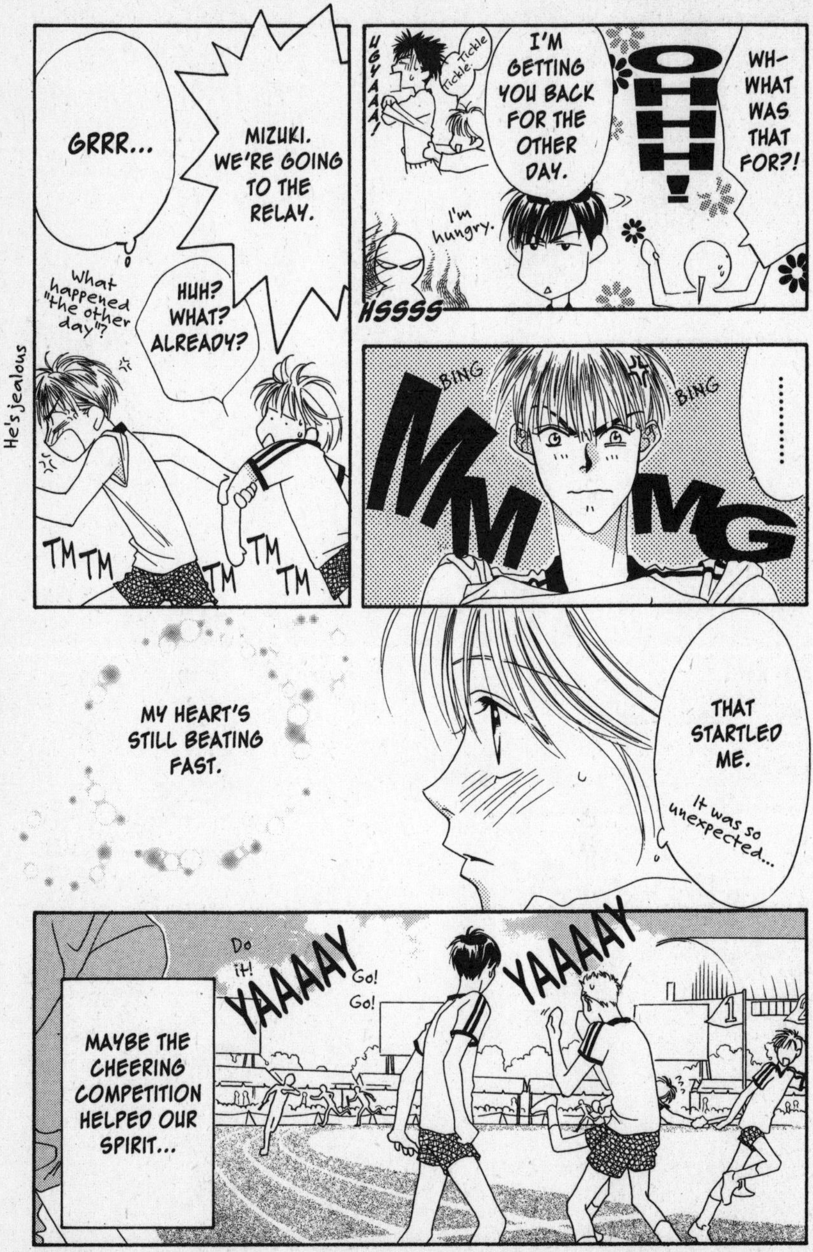
WH-WHAT WAS THAT FOR?!
OHH!
I'M GETTING YOU BACK FOR THE OTHER DAY.
Tickle Tickle
UGYAAAA!
I'm hungry.
HSSSS
BING
BING
......
MMMG
MIZUKI. WE'RE GOING TO THE RELAY.
GRRR...
HUH? WHAT? ALREADY?
What happened "the other day"?
He's jealous
TM TM TM TM TM
THAT STARTLED ME.
It was so unexpected...
MY HEART'S STILL BEATING FAST.
YAAAAY
Go! Go!
YAAAAY
Do it!
MAYBE THE CHEERING COMPETITION HELPED OUR SPIRIT...

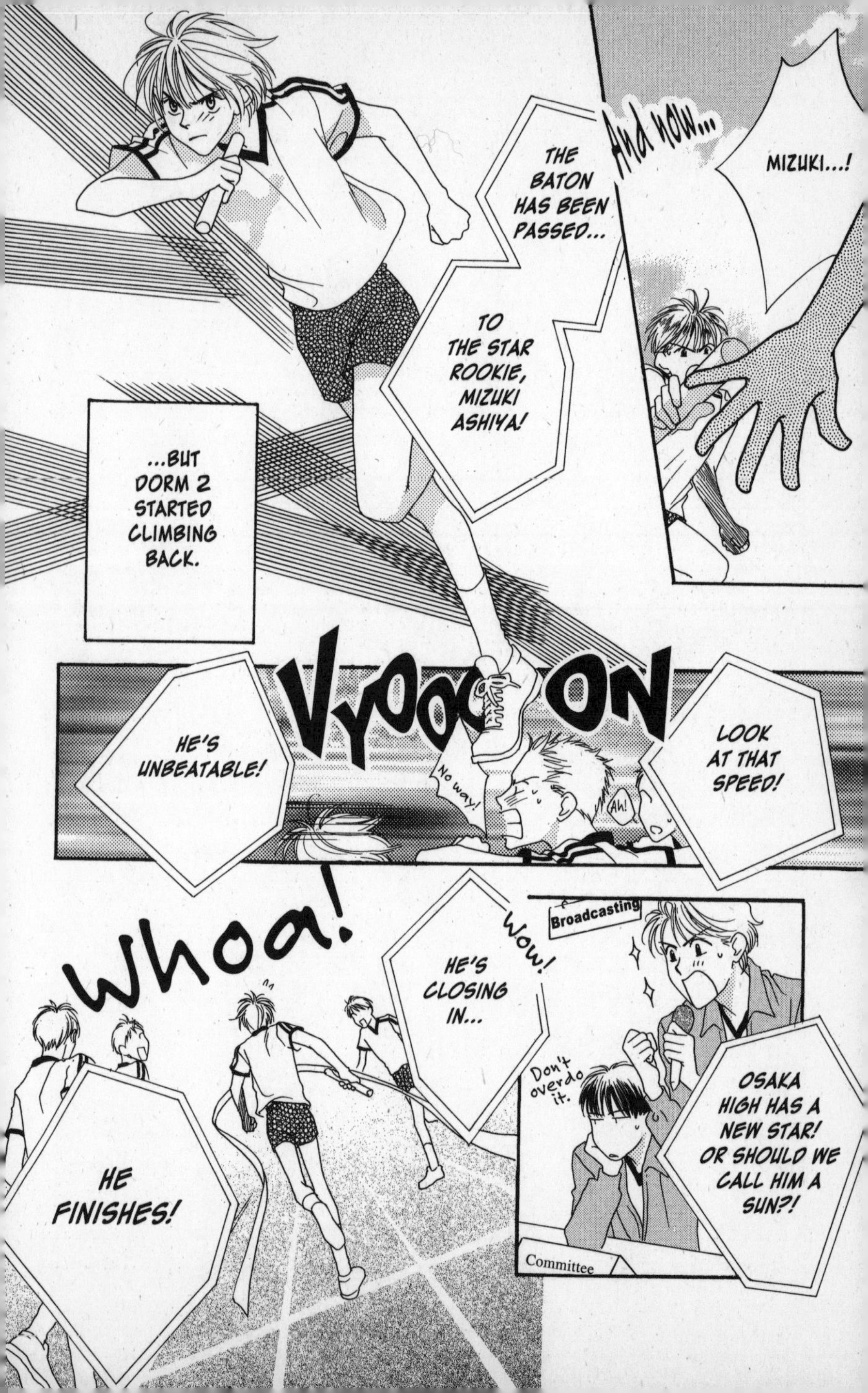

And now...
MIZUKI...!
THE BATON HAS BEEN PASSED...
TO THE STAR ROOKIE, MIZUKI ASHIYA!
...BUT DORM 2 STARTED CLIMBING BACK.
LOOK AT THAT SPEED!
Ah!
VROOOON
No way!
HE'S UNBEATABLE!
Broadcasting
Wow!
OSAKA HIGH HAS A NEW STAR! OR SHOULD WE CALL HIM A SUN?!
Don't overdo it.
Committee
HE'S CLOSING IN...
Whoa!
HE FINISHES!

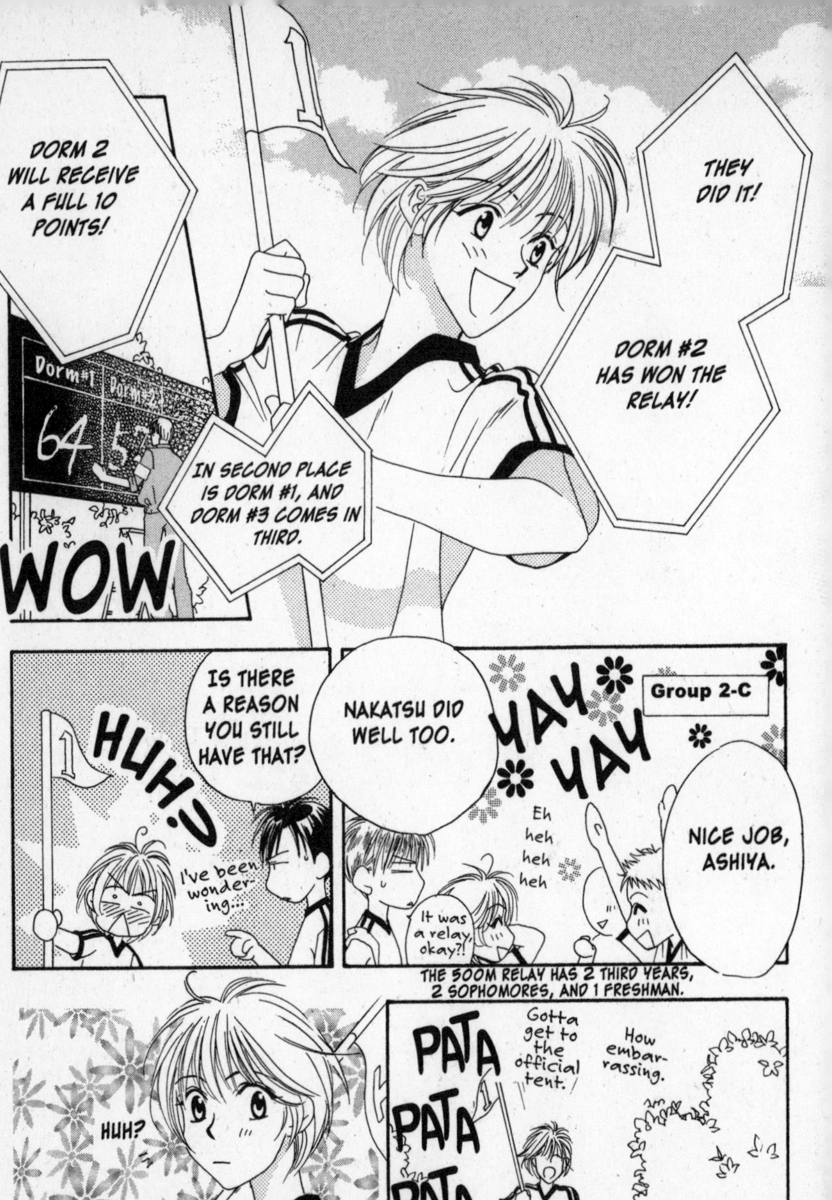

THEY DID IT!
DORM 2 WILL RECEIVE A FULL 10 POINTS!
DORM #2 HAS WON THE RELAY!
IN SECOND PLACE IS DORM #1, AND DORM #3 COMES IN THIRD.
Dorm#1 Dorm#2
64
WOW
Group 2-C
YAY YAY
NICE JOB, ASHIYA.
NAKATSU DID WELL TOO.
Eh heh heh heh
It was a relay, okay?!
IS THERE A REASON YOU STILL HAVE THAT?
HUH?
I've been wondering...
THE 500M RELAY HAS 2 THIRD YEARS, 2 SOPHOMORES, AND 1 FRESHMAN.
How embarrassing.
Gotta get to the official tent.
PATA PATA PATA
HUH?

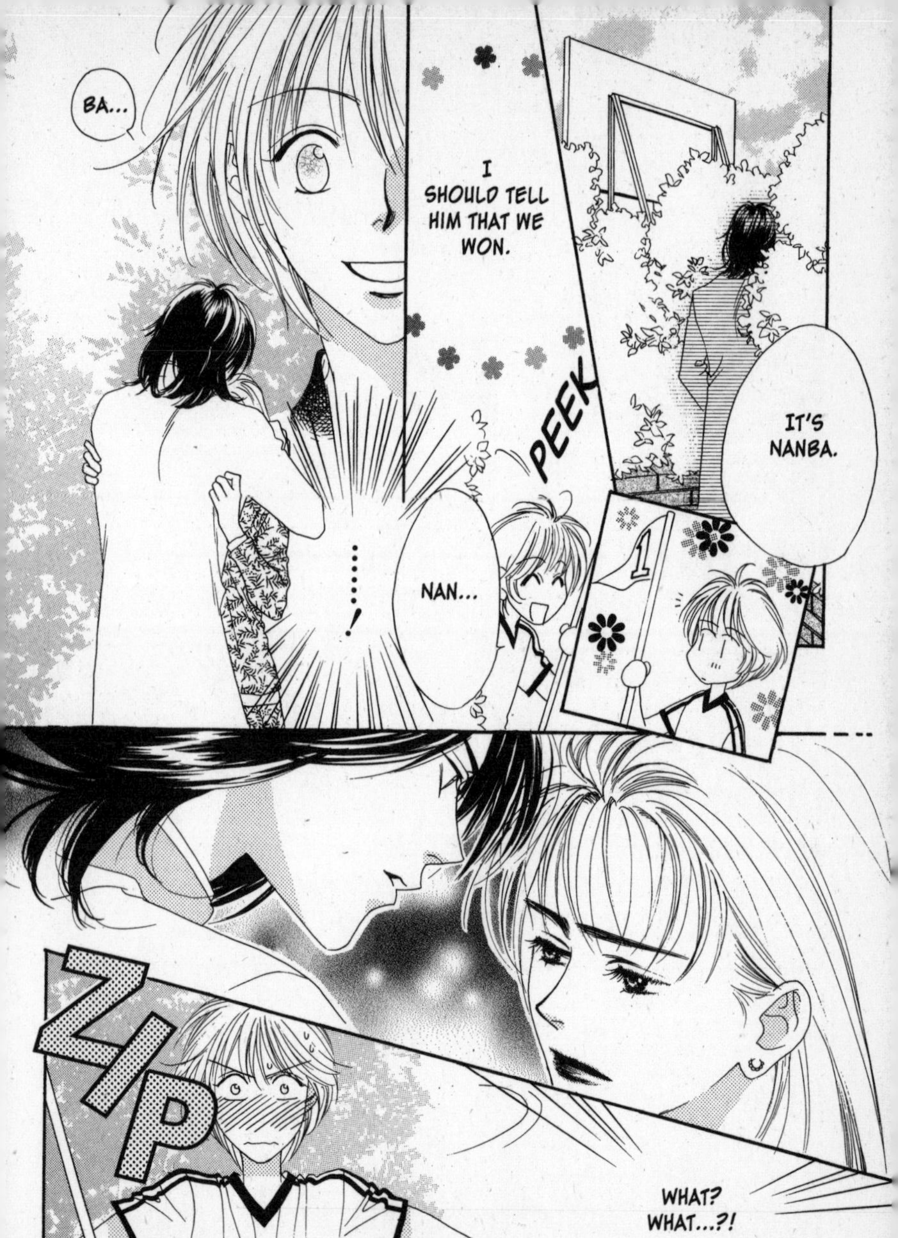
IT'S NANBA.
I SHOULD TELL HIM THAT WE WON.
PEEK
NAN...
BA...
.....!
ZIP
WHAT? WHAT...?!

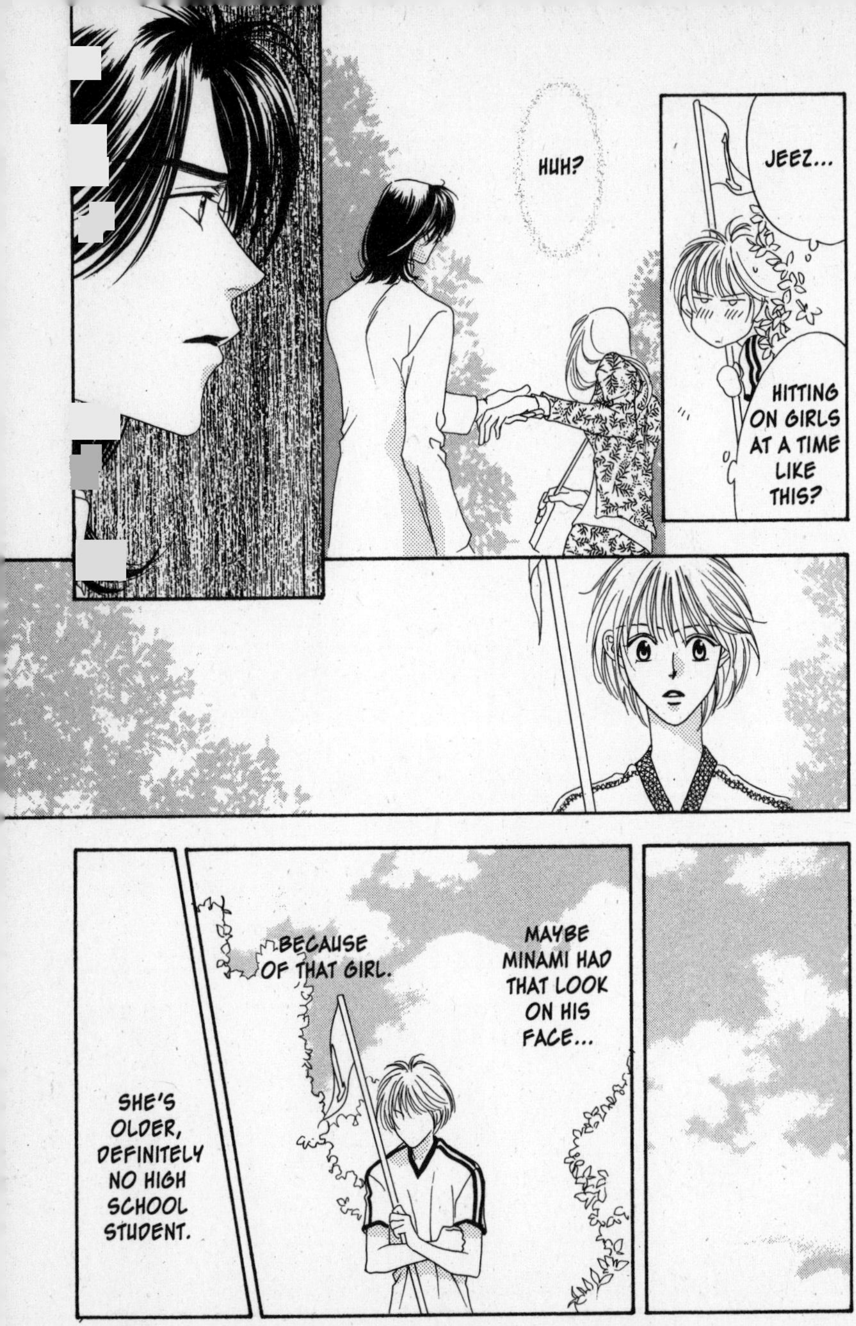
JEEZ...
HITTING ON GIRLS AT A TIME LIKE THIS?
HUH?
MAYBE MINAMI HAD THAT LOOK ON HIS FACE...
BECAUSE OF THAT GIRL.
SHE'S OLDER, DEFINITELY NO HIGH SCHOOL STUDENT.

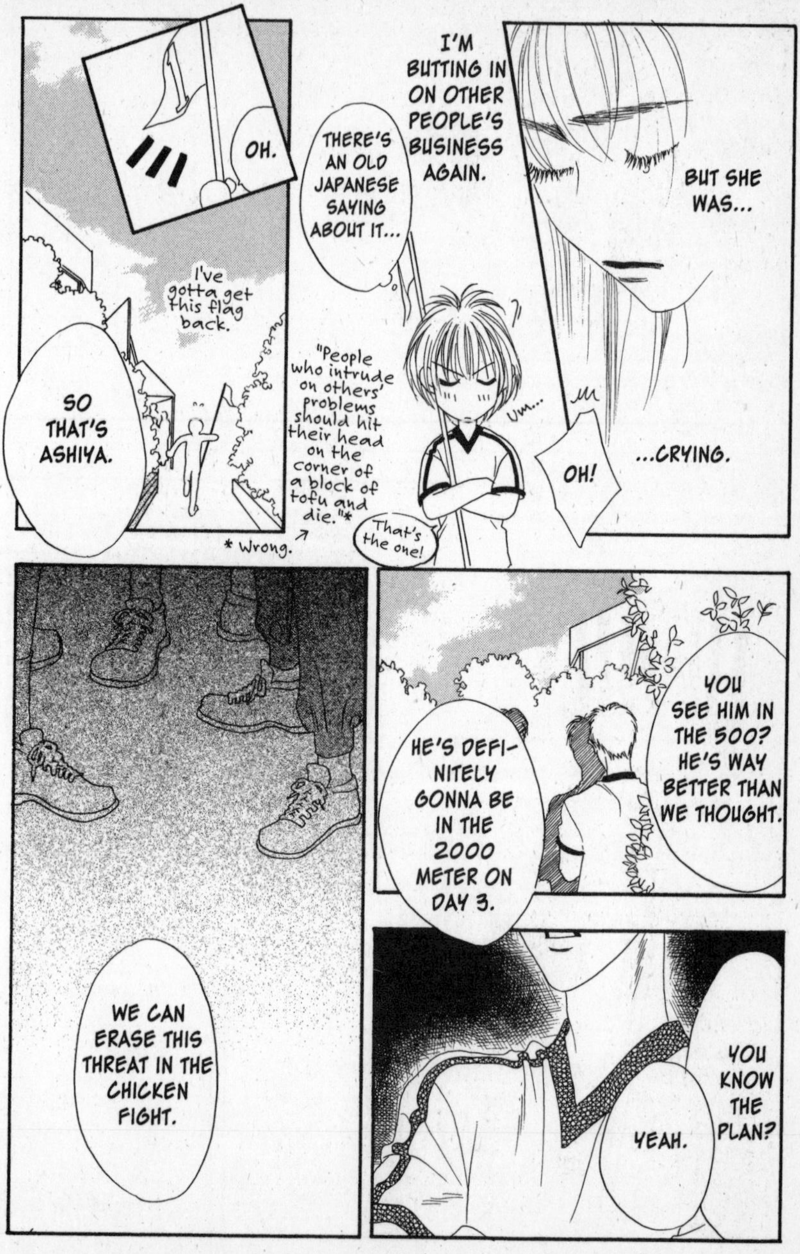
BUT SHE WAS...
...CRYING.
OH!
I'M BUTTING IN ON OTHER PEOPLE'S BUSINESS AGAIN.
THERE'S AN OLD JAPANESE SAYING ABOUT IT...
Um...
"People who intrude on others' problems should hit their head on the corner of a block of tofu and die."*
That's the one!
* Wrong.
OH.
I've gotta get this flag back.
SO THAT'S ASHIYA.
YOU SEE HIM IN THE 500? HE'S WAY BETTER THAN WE THOUGHT.
HE'S DEFINITELY GONNA BE IN THE 2000 METER ON DAY 3.
YOU KNOW THE PLAN?
YEAH.
WE CAN ERASE THIS THREAT IN THE CHICKEN FIGHT.

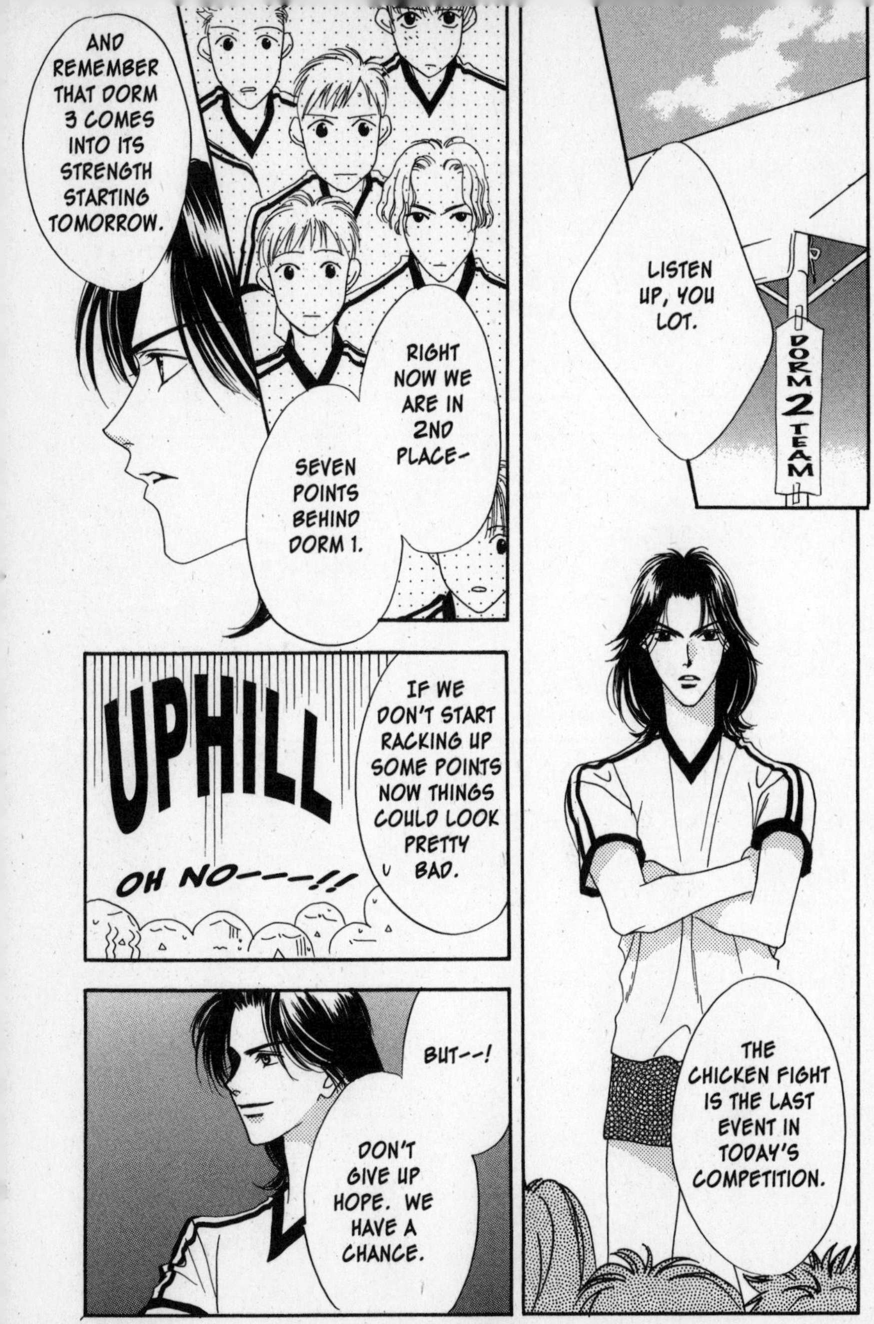
LISTEN UP, YOU LOT.
DORM 2 TEAM
THE CHICKEN FIGHT IS THE LAST EVENT IN TODAY'S COMPETITION.
RIGHT NOW WE ARE IN 2ND PLACE-
SEVEN POINTS BEHIND DORM 1.
AND REMEMBER THAT DORM 3 COMES INTO ITS STRENGTH STARTING TOMORROW.
IF WE DON'T START RACKING UP SOME POINTS NOW THINGS COULD LOOK PRETTY BAD.
UPHILL
OH NO---!!
BUT--!
DON'T GIVE UP HOPE. WE HAVE A CHANCE.

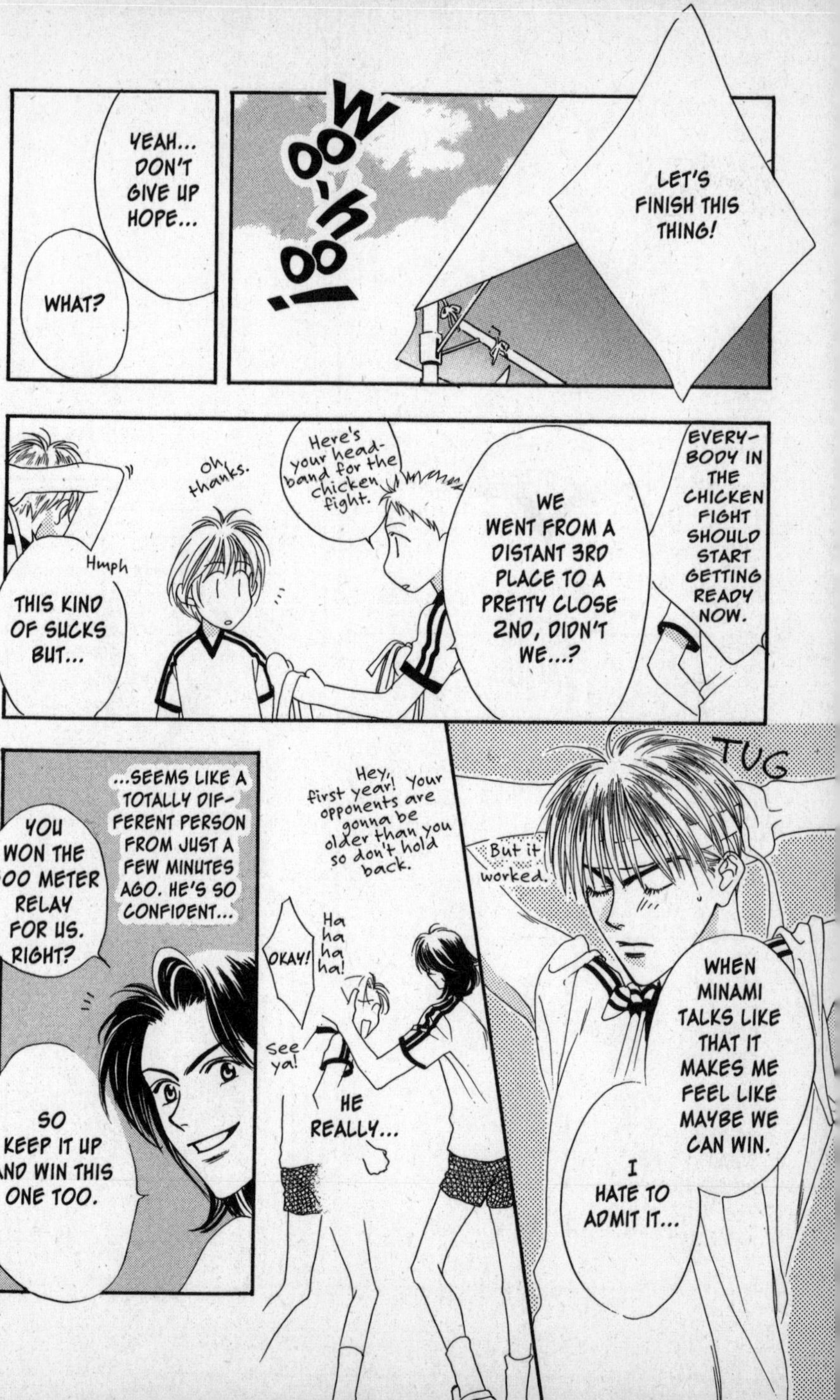
LET'S FINISH THIS THING!
WOO-HOO!
YEAH... DON'T GIVE UP HOPE...
WHAT?
EVERYBODY IN THE CHICKEN FIGHT SHOULD START GETTING READY NOW.
WE WENT FROM A DISTANT 3RD PLACE TO A PRETTY CLOSE 2ND, DIDN'T WE...?
Here's your headband for the chicken fight.
Oh thanks.
Hmph
THIS KIND OF SUCKS BUT...
TUG
But it worked.
WHEN MINAMI TALKS LIKE THAT IT MAKES ME FEEL LIKE MAYBE WE CAN WIN.
I HATE TO ADMIT IT...
Hey, first year! Your opponents are gonna be older than you so don't hold back.
OKAY!
Ha ha ha ha!
See ya!
HE REALLY...
...SEEMS LIKE A TOTALLY DIFFERENT PERSON FROM JUST A FEW MINUTES AGO. HE'S SO CONFIDENT...
YOU WON THE 500 METER RELAY FOR US. RIGHT?
SO KEEP IT UP AND WIN THIS ONE TOO.

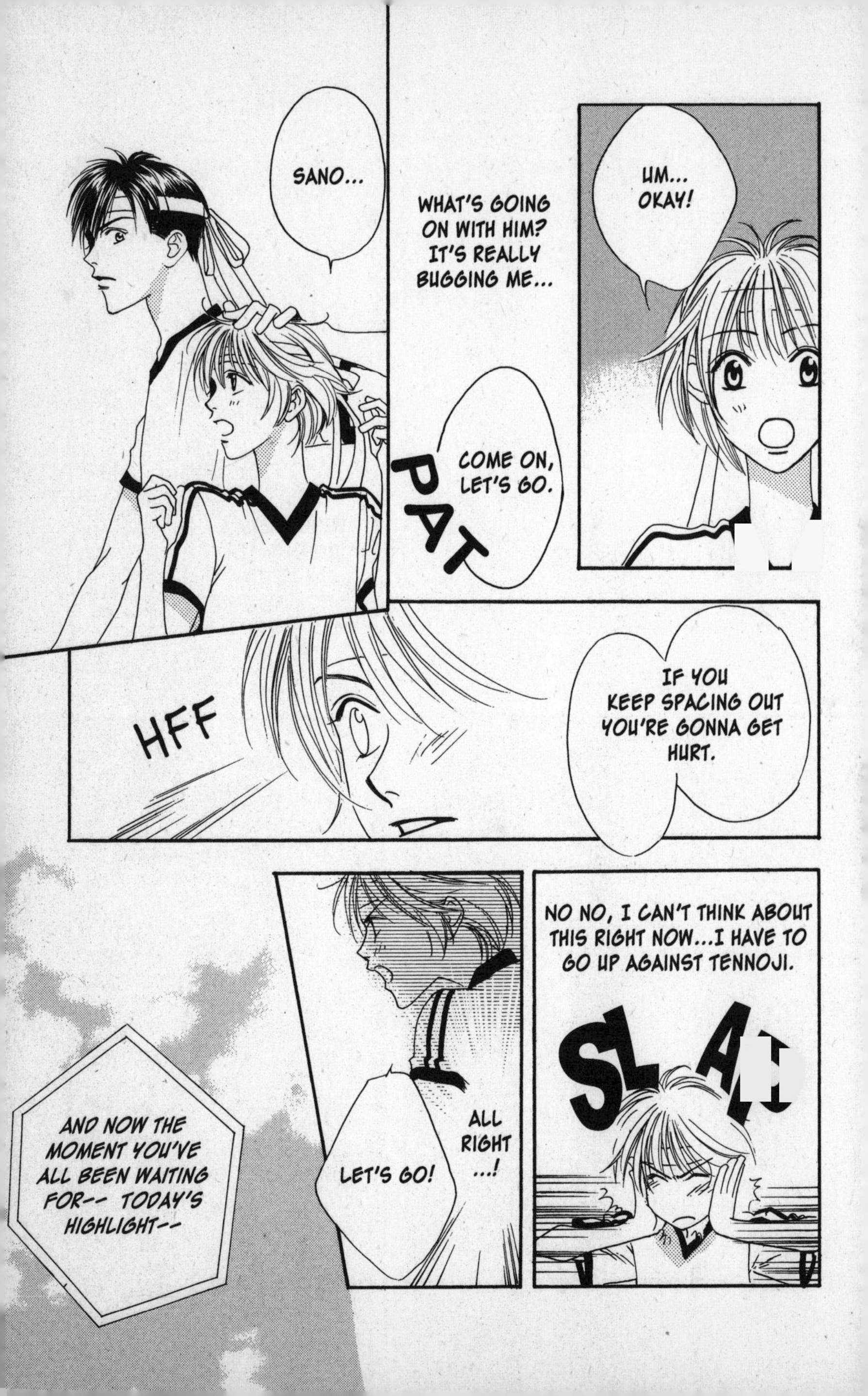

UM... OKAY!
WHAT'S GOING ON WITH HIM? IT'S REALLY BUGGING ME...
COME ON, LET'S GO.
PAT
SANO...
IF YOU KEEP SPACING OUT YOU'RE GONNA GET HURT.
HFF
NO NO, I CAN'T THINK ABOUT THIS RIGHT NOW...I HAVE TO GO UP AGAINST TENNOJI.
SLA
ALL RIGHT ...!
LET'S GO!
AND NOW THE MOMENT YOU'VE ALL BEEN WAITING FOR-- TODAY'S HIGHLIGHT--

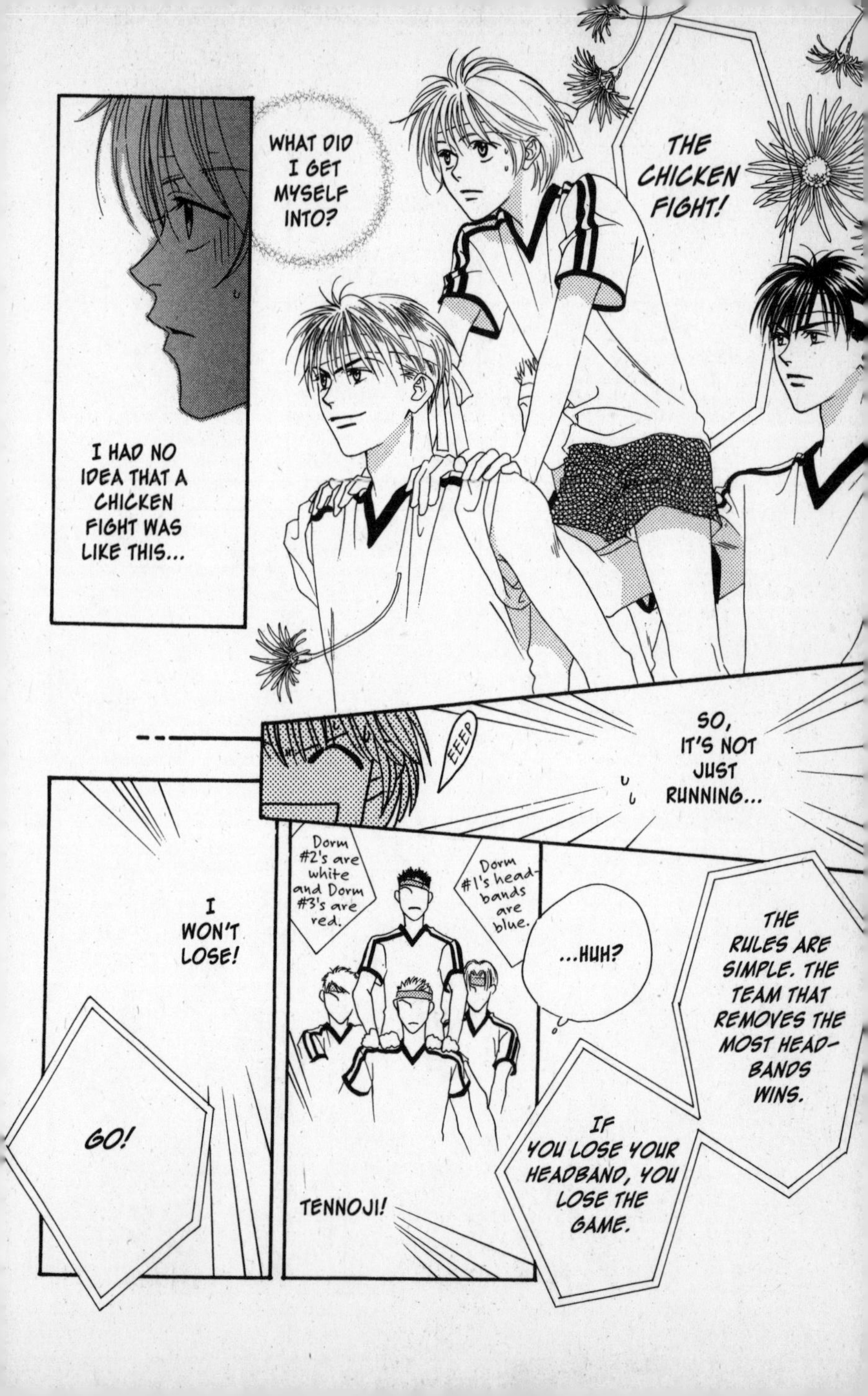
THE CHICKEN FIGHT!
WHAT DID I GET MYSELF INTO?
I HAD NO IDEA THAT A CHICKEN FIGHT WAS LIKE THIS...
SO, IT'S NOT JUST RUNNING...
EEEP
--
THE RULES ARE SIMPLE. THE TEAM THAT REMOVES THE MOST HEAD-BANDS WINS.
IF YOU LOSE YOUR HEADBAND, YOU LOSE THE GAME.
...HUH?
Dorm #1's head-bands are blue.
Dorm #2's are white and Dorm #3's are red.
TENNOJI!
I WON'T LOSE!
GO!

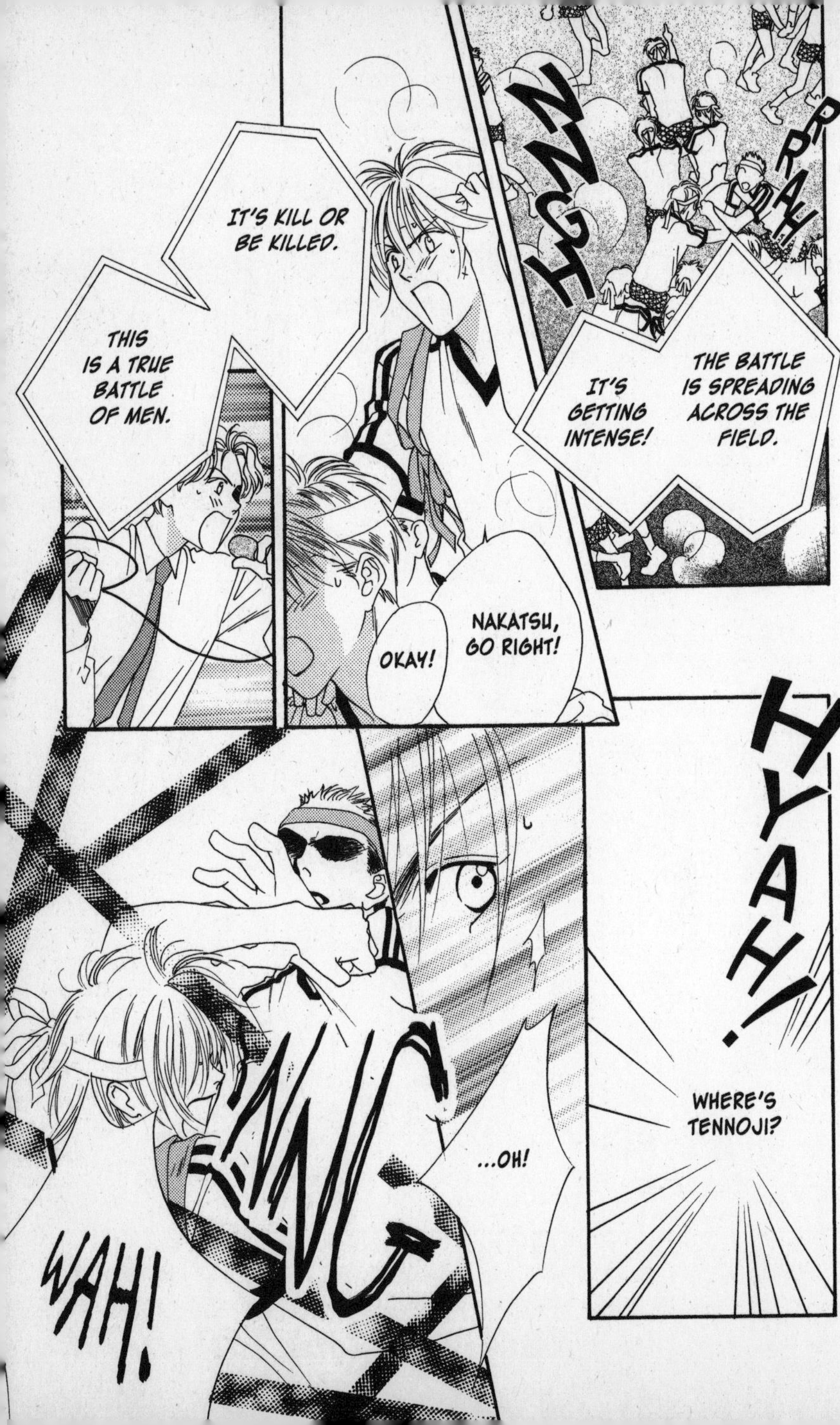
RRAH!
THE BATTLE IS SPREADING ACROSS THE FIELD.
IT'S GETTING INTENSE!
IT'S KILL OR BE KILLED.
THIS IS A TRUE BATTLE OF MEN.
NAKATSU, GO RIGHT!
OKAY!
HYAH!
WHERE'S TENNOJI?
...OH!
WAH!

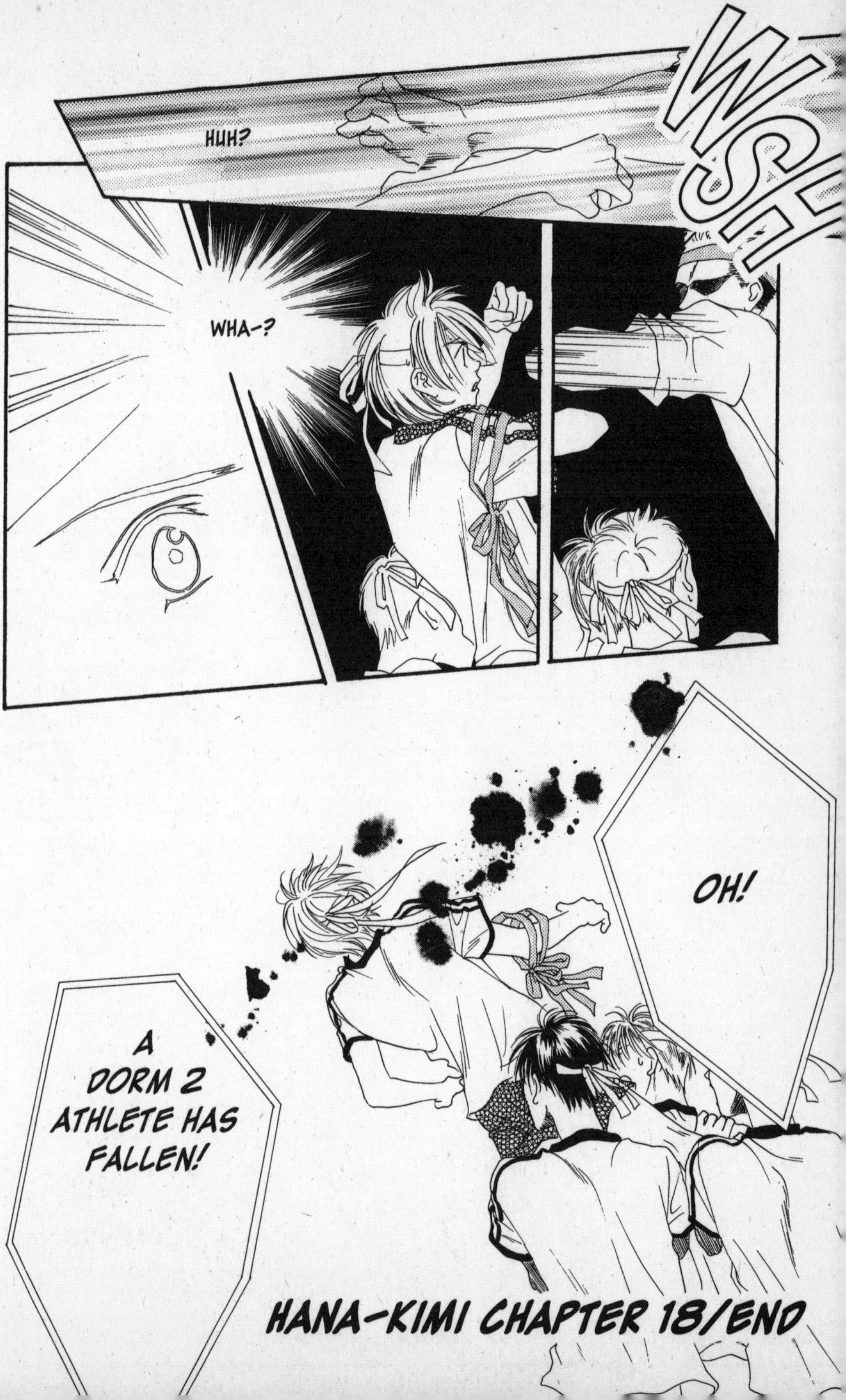
WSH
HUH?
WHA-?
OH!
A DORM 2 ATHLETE HAS FALLEN!
HANA-KIMI CHAPTER 18/END

CHAPTER 19

Hana-Kimi

For You in Full Blossom

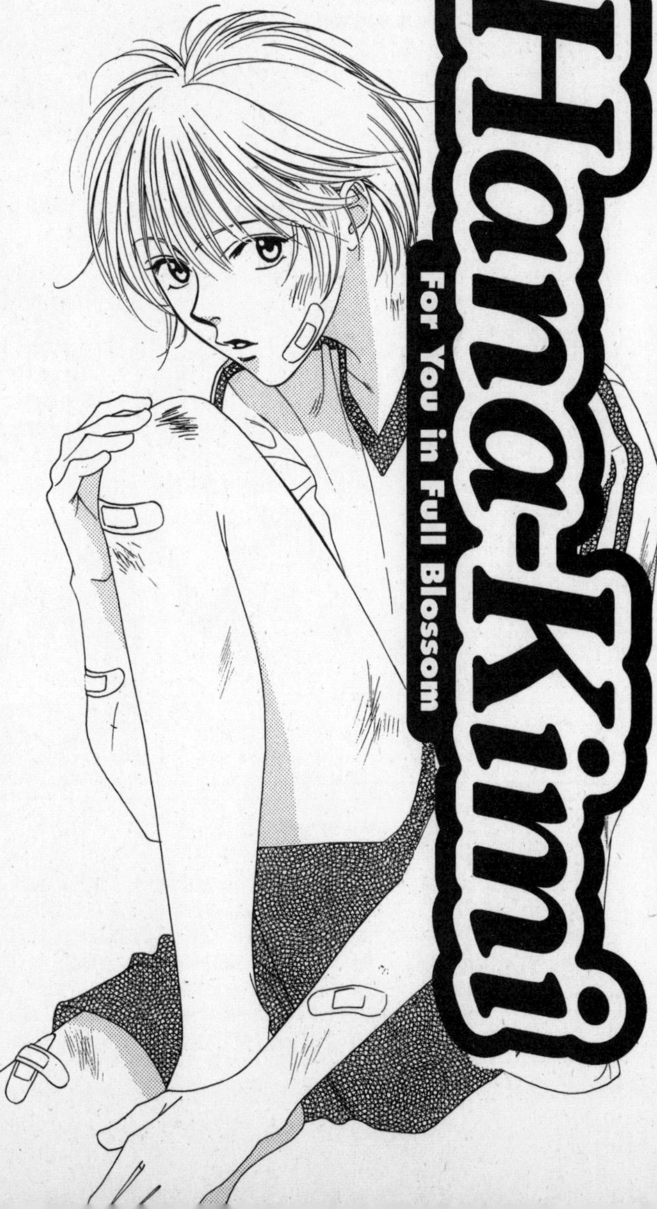

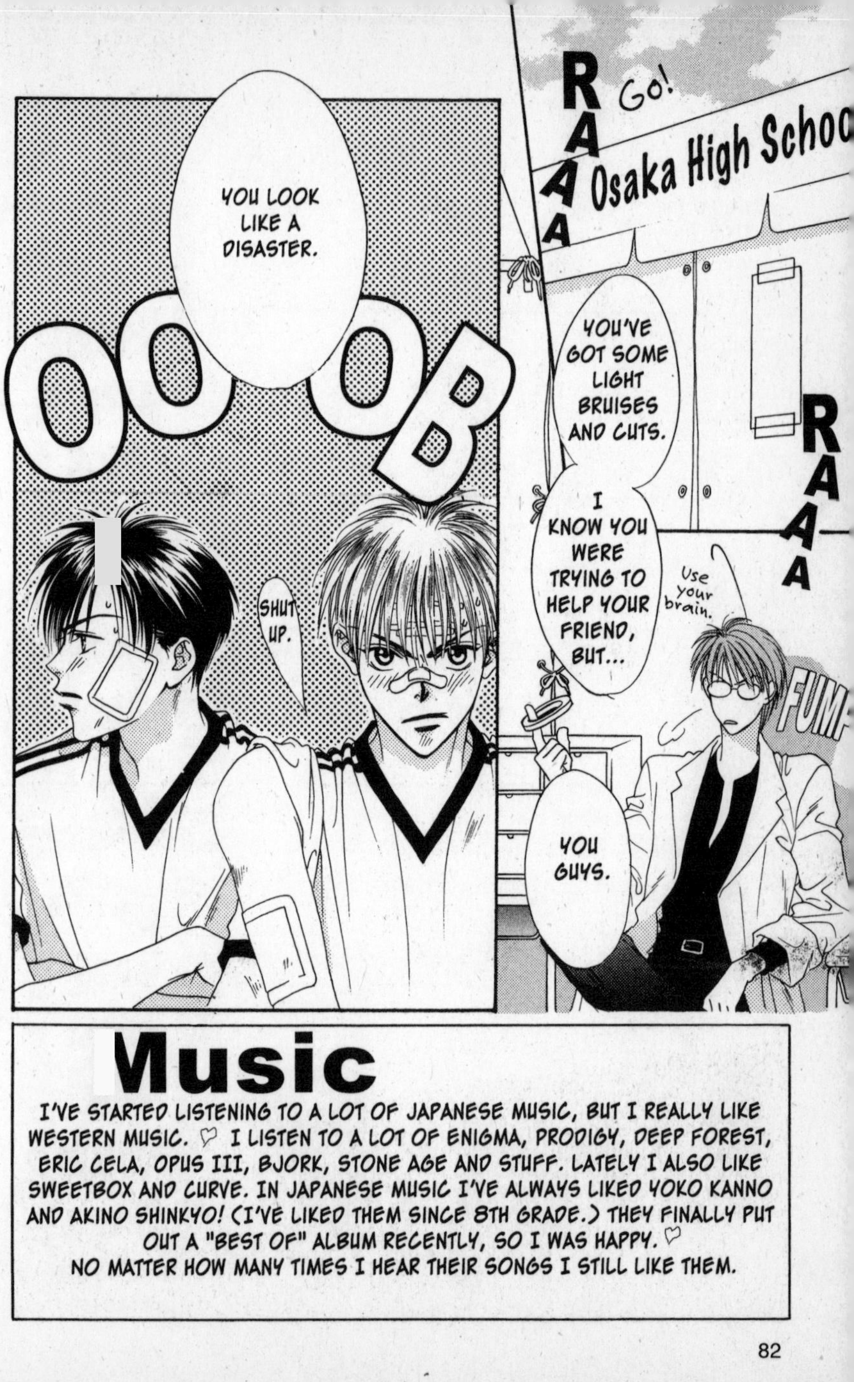
RAAAA
Go!
Osaka High Schoo
YOU'VE GOT SOME LIGHT BRUISES AND CUTS.
I KNOW YOU WERE TRYING TO HELP YOUR FRIEND, BUT...
Use your brain.
RAAAA
FUMI
YOU GUYS.
YOU LOOK LIKE A DISASTER.
OOOB
SHUT UP.

Music

I'VE STARTED LISTENING TO A LOT OF JAPANESE MUSIC, BUT I REALLY LIKE WESTERN MUSIC. ♡ I LISTEN TO A LOT OF ENIGMA, PRODIGY, DEEP FOREST, ERIC CELA, OPUS III, BJORK, STONE AGE AND STUFF. LATELY I ALSO LIKE SWEETBOX AND CURVE. IN JAPANESE MUSIC I'VE ALWAYS LIKED YOKO KANNO AND AKINO SHINKYO! (I'VE LIKED THEM SINCE 8TH GRADE.) THEY FINALLY PUT OUT A "BEST OF" ALBUM RECENTLY, SO I WAS HAPPY. ♡
NO MATTER HOW MANY TIMES I HEAR THEIR SONGS I STILL LIKE THEM.

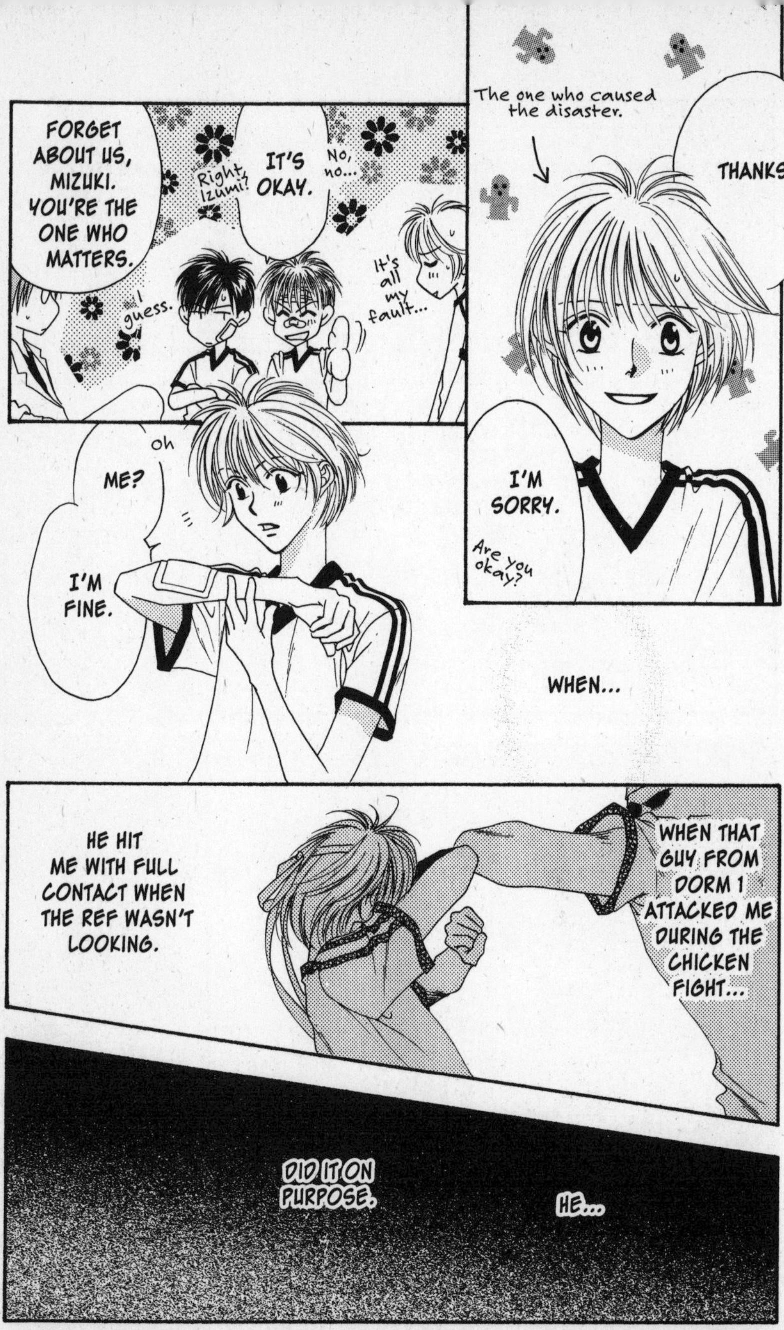
The one who caused the disaster.
THANKS.
I'M SORRY.
Are you okay?
It's all my fault...
No, no...
IT'S OKAY.
Right, Izumi?
FORGET ABOUT US, MIZUKI. YOU'RE THE ONE WHO MATTERS.
I guess.
oh
ME?
I'M FINE.
WHEN...
WHEN THAT GUY FROM DORM 1 ATTACKED ME DURING THE CHICKEN FIGHT...
HE HIT ME WITH FULL CONTACT WHEN THE REF WASN'T LOOKING.
HE...
DID IT ON PURPOSE.

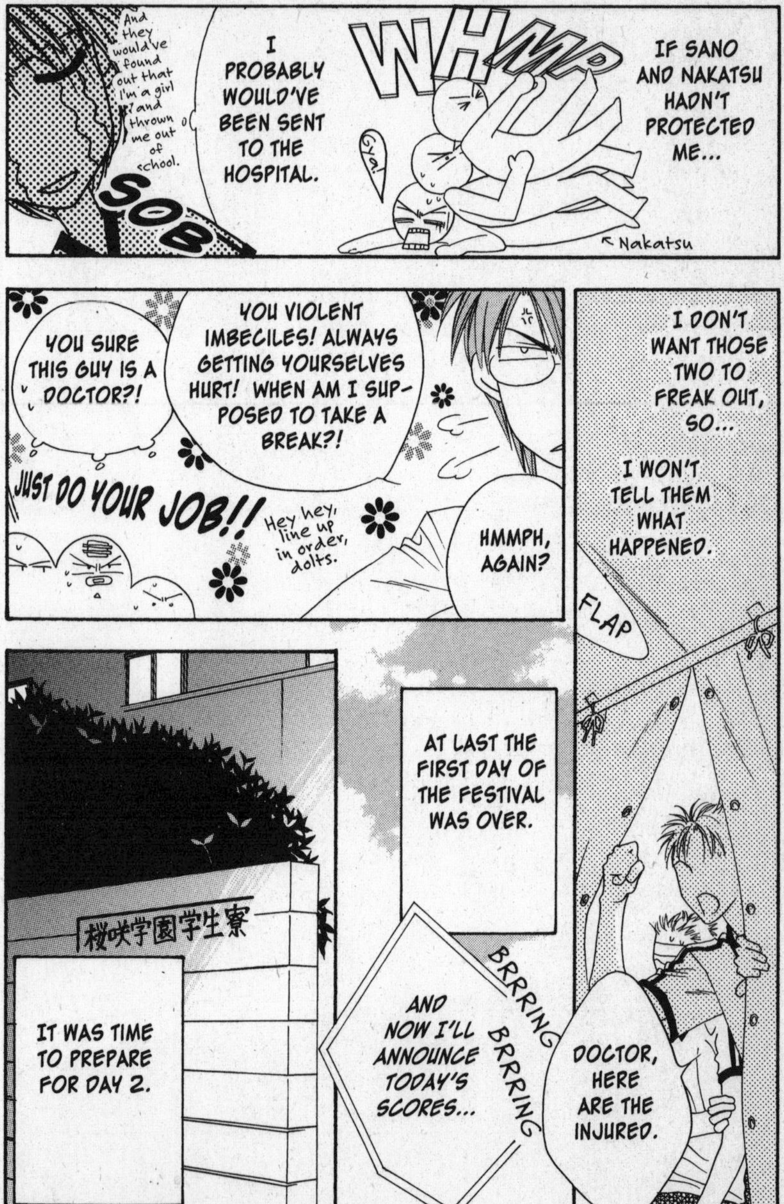
IF SANO AND NAKATSU HADN'T PROTECTED ME...
WHMP
Gya!
← Nakatsu
I PROBABLY WOULD'VE BEEN SENT TO THE HOSPITAL.
And they would've found out that I'm a girl and thrown me out of school.
SOB
I DON'T WANT THOSE TWO TO FREAK OUT, SO...
I WON'T TELL THEM WHAT HAPPENED.
FLAP
DOCTOR, HERE ARE THE INJURED.
HMMPH, AGAIN?
YOU VIOLENT IMBECILES! ALWAYS GETTING YOURSELVES HURT! WHEN AM I SUP-POSED TO TAKE A BREAK?!
YOU SURE THIS GUY IS A DOCTOR?!
Hey hey, line up in order, dolts.
JUST DO YOUR JOB!!
AT LAST THE FIRST DAY OF THE FESTIVAL WAS OVER.
BRRRING BRRRING
AND NOW I'LL ANNOUNCE TODAY'S SCORES...
桜咲学園学生寮
IT WAS TIME TO PREPARE FOR DAY 2.

Osaka High School Dormitory

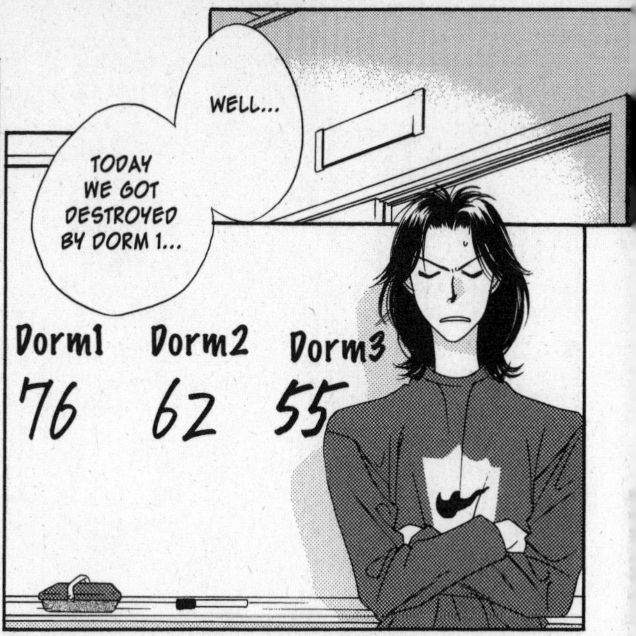
WELL...
TODAY WE GOT DESTROYED BY DORM 1...
Dorm1 76
Dorm2 62
Dorm3 55

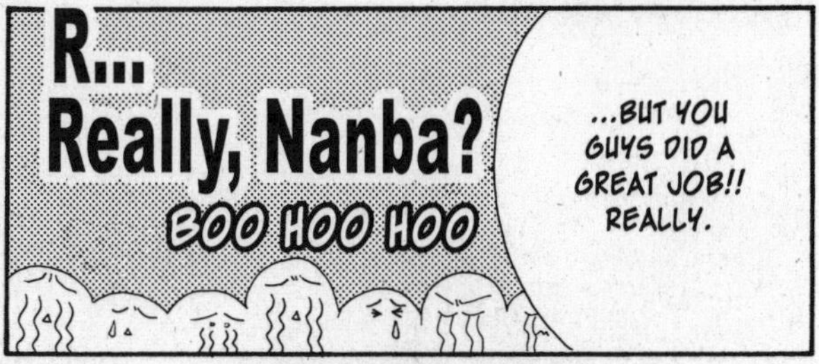
...BUT YOU GUYS DID A GREAT JOB!! REALLY.
R... Really, Nanba?
BOO HOO HOO

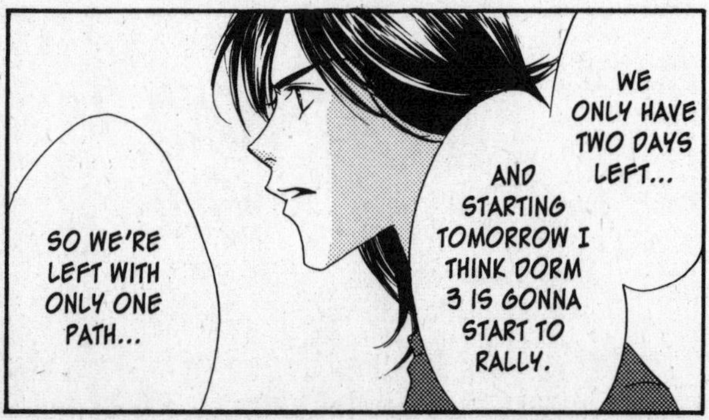
WE ONLY HAVE TWO DAYS LEFT...
AND STARTING TOMORROW I THINK DORM 3 IS GONNA START TO RALLY.
SO WE'RE LEFT WITH ONLY ONE PATH...

Whispered secrets

Costumes

THIS TIME I GOT TO DRAW SOME COOL STUFF, SO IT WAS REALLY FUN! ♡ I LOVED DRAWING MIZUKI AS ALICE IN WONDERLAND AND NAKAO AS SNOW WHITE, BUT THE BEST WAS THE THREE IDIOTS DRESSED AS CHARACTERS FROM "HEIDI" ("ALPS NO SHOJO HEIDI" IN JAPANESE). I KNEW THEY WERE GONNA LOOK LIKE THAT! ♡ BUT SANO WAS DEFINITELY THE FAVORITE. APPARENTLY HE'S BEEN GETTING SEXIER AND SEXIER. WHAT DID YOU THINK? (HA-HA) I KNEW I WOULDN'T GET THE CHANCE TO DRAW THEM IN GIRLS' CLOTHES AGAIN SO I HAD FUN.

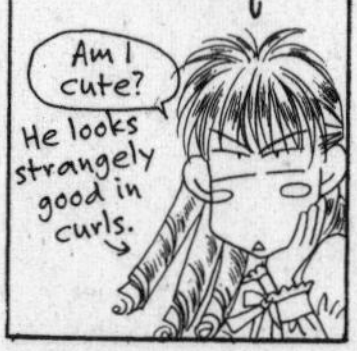
Am I cute?
He looks strangely good in curls.

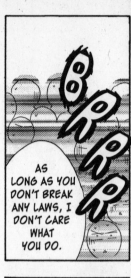

AND THAT IS...
BOOM!!
A BATTLE OF BRAINS!
ACCORDING TO THE COMMITTEE, OUR FRESHMEN WILL BE DOING AN ARCADE, THE SOPHOMORES WILL DO A CAFE,
AND US THIRD YEARS WILL PUT ON A MYSTERY THEATER.
UM...
THE COSTUMES ARE LATE COMING TOGETHER. THEY'LL BE DONE TOMORROW.
HUH? ON THE DAY OF THE EVENT?
THIS IS A BIG DEAL.
WHATEVER YOU DO...
DON'T HOLD BACK.
BRRRR
AS LONG AS YOU DON'T BREAK ANY LAWS, I DON'T CARE WHAT YOU DO.
BUT DON'T STRESS OUT! IT'S GONNA BE FINE.
HA HA HA
WE'VE ALREADY DECIDED WHAT WE ARE GONNA DO. NOW WE JUST NEED TO GET THE STUDENTS' AND THE AUDIENCE'S VOTES.
UH-OH...
SSHHH
GULP...
I'VE GOT A BAD FEELING.

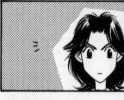

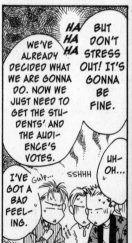

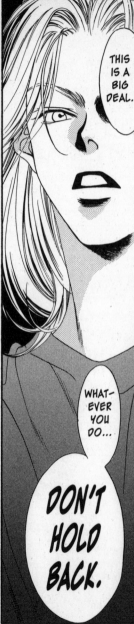

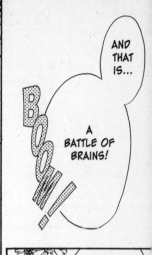

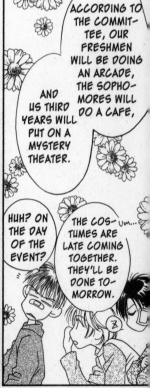

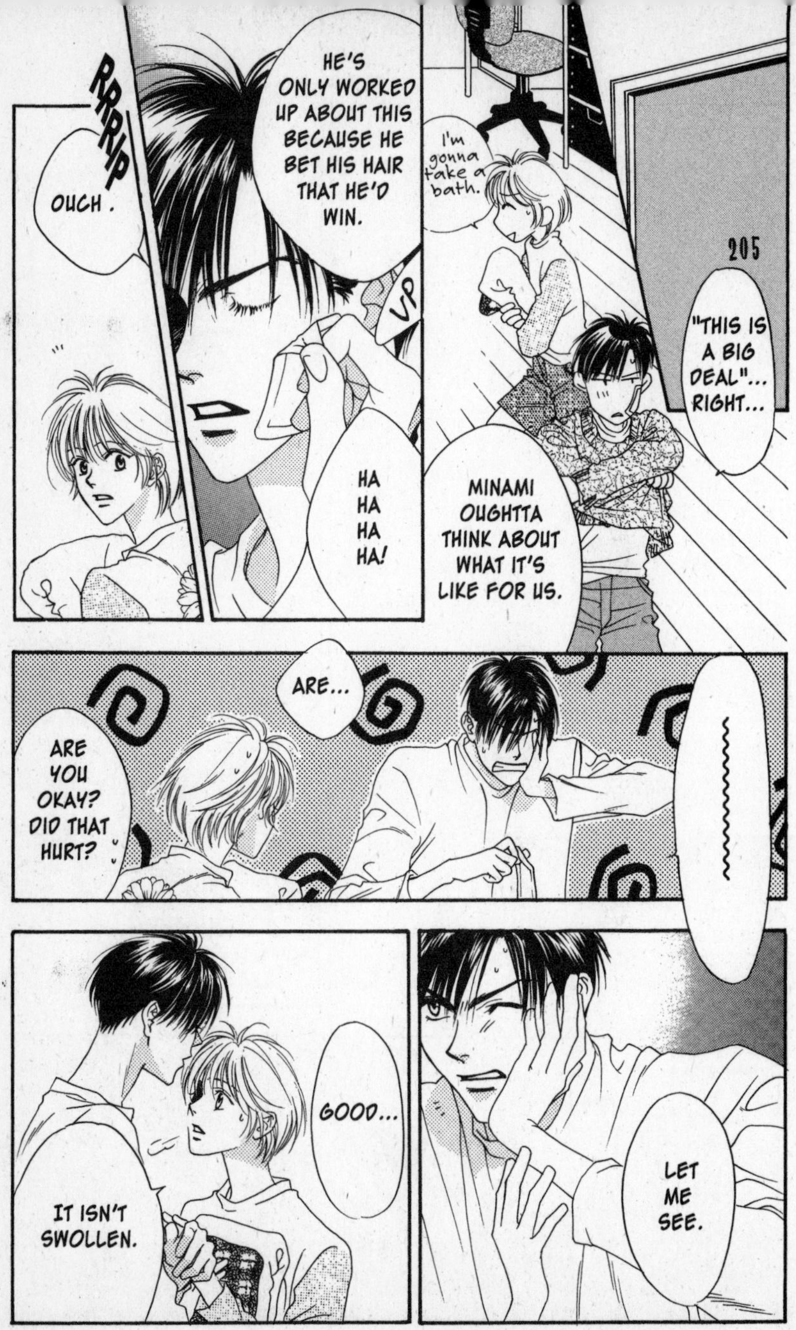
I'm gonna take a bath.
205
"THIS IS A BIG DEAL"... RIGHT...
MINAMI OUGHTTA THINK ABOUT WHAT IT'S LIKE FOR US.
HE'S ONLY WORKED UP ABOUT THIS BECAUSE HE BET HIS HAIR THAT HE'D WIN.
HA HA HA HA!
RRRRIP
OUCH.
ARE...
ARE YOU OKAY? DID THAT HURT?
LET ME SEE.
GOOD...
IT ISN'T SWOLLEN.

DOES IT STILL HURT?

I'M SORRY.

FLOWER

SHIVER

IT'S NOTHING.

GWMP—

PUSH

IT'S MY FAULT THAT YOU...

GRAB

R

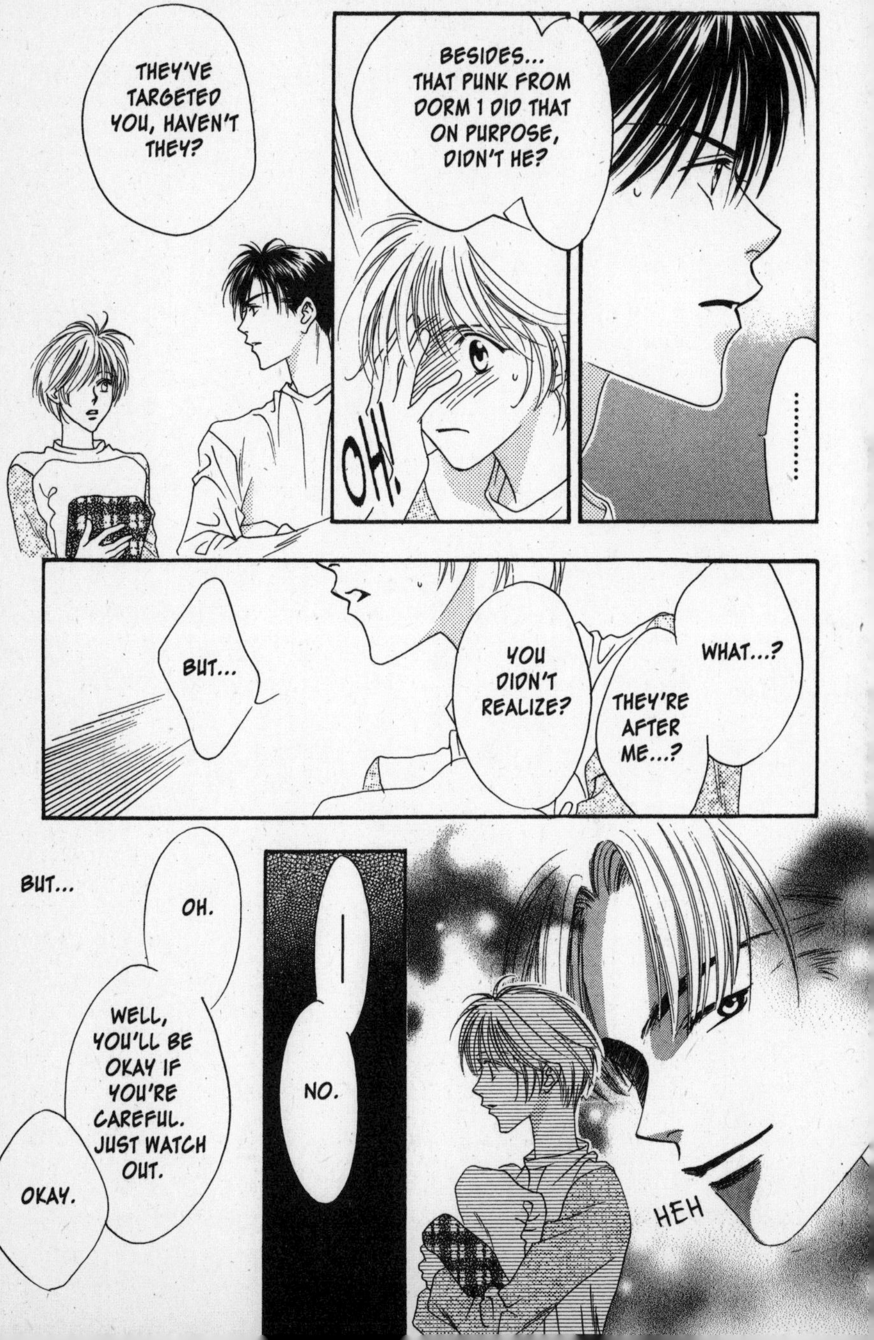

......
BESIDES... THAT PUNK FROM DORM 1 DID THAT ON PURPOSE, DIDN'T HE?
OH!
THEY'VE TARGETED YOU, HAVEN'T THEY?
WHAT...?
THEY'RE AFTER ME...?
YOU DIDN'T REALIZE?
BUT...
HEH
NO.
OH.
BUT...
WELL, YOU'LL BE OKAY IF YOU'RE CAREFUL. JUST WATCH OUT.
OKAY.

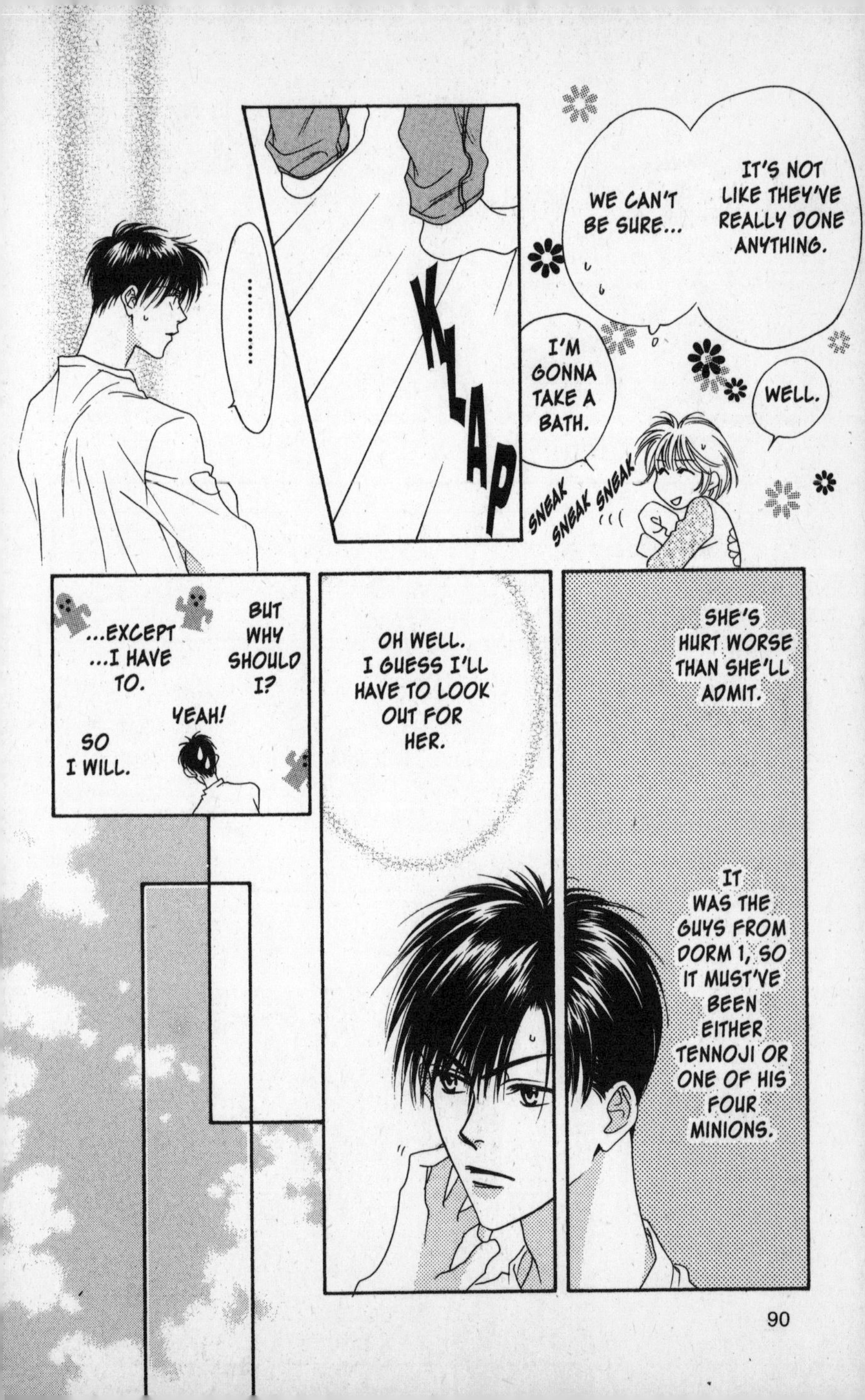

IT'S NOT LIKE THEY'VE REALLY DONE ANYTHING.
WE CAN'T BE SURE...
WELL.
I'M GONNA TAKE A BATH.
SNEAK SNEAK SNEAK
KLAP
......
SHE'S HURT WORSE THAN SHE'LL ADMIT.
IT WAS THE GUYS FROM DORM 1, SO IT MUST'VE BEEN EITHER TENNOJI OR ONE OF HIS FOUR MINIONS.
OH WELL. I GUESS I'LL HAVE TO LOOK OUT FOR HER.
BUT WHY SHOULD I?
...EXCEPT ...I HAVE TO.
YEAH!
SO I WILL.

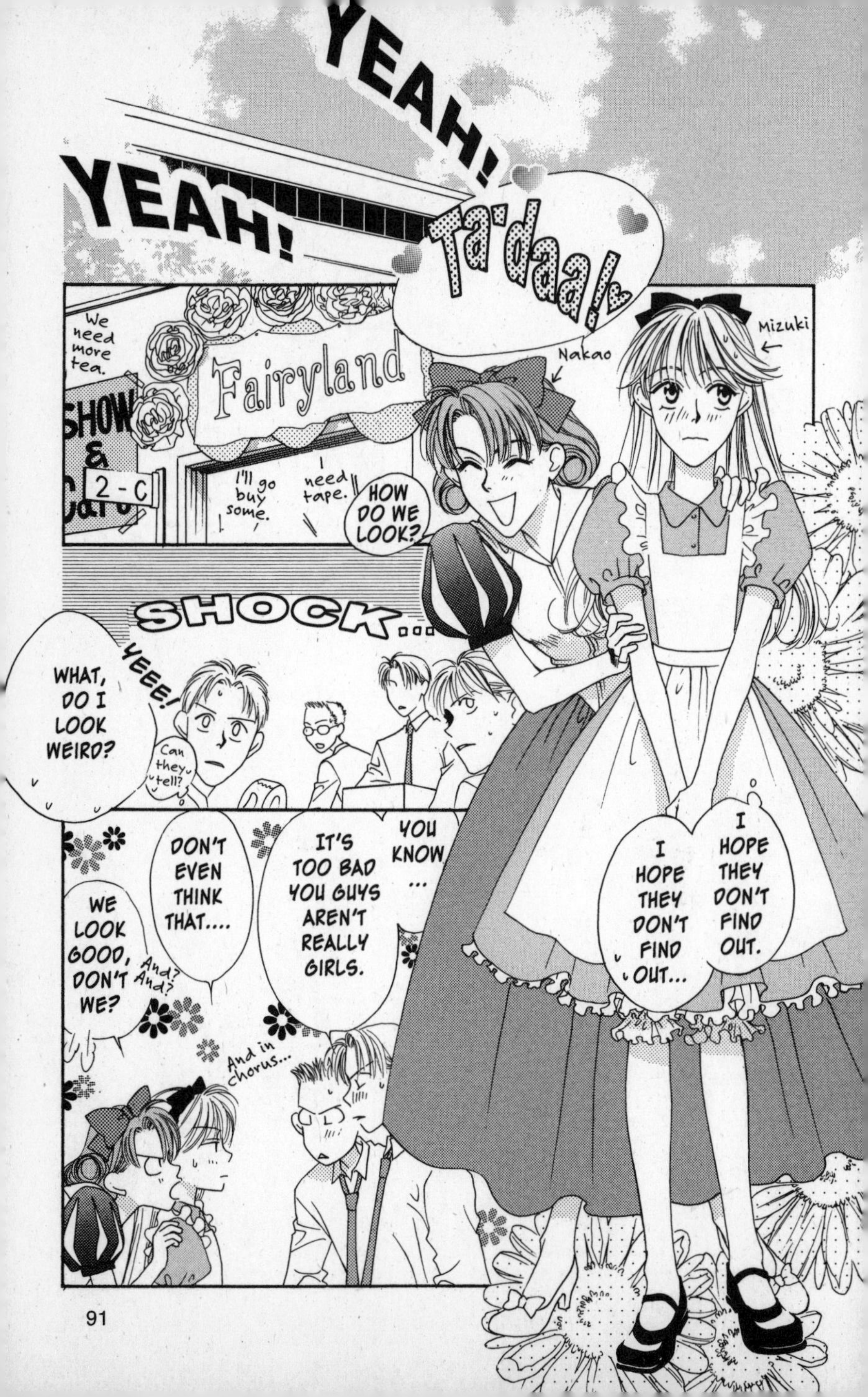
YEAH!
YEAH!
Ta'daa!
Mizuki
Nakao
HOW DO WE LOOK?
I need tape.
I'll go buy some.
We need more tea.
Fairyland
SHOW & Cafe
2-C
SHOCK...
YEEEE!
Can they tell?
WHAT, DO I LOOK WEIRD?
I HOPE THEY DON'T FIND OUT.
I HOPE THEY DON'T FIND OUT...
YOU KNOW...
IT'S TOO BAD YOU GUYS AREN'T REALLY GIRLS.
DON'T EVEN THINK THAT....
WE LOOK GOOD, DON'T WE?
And? And?
And in chorus...

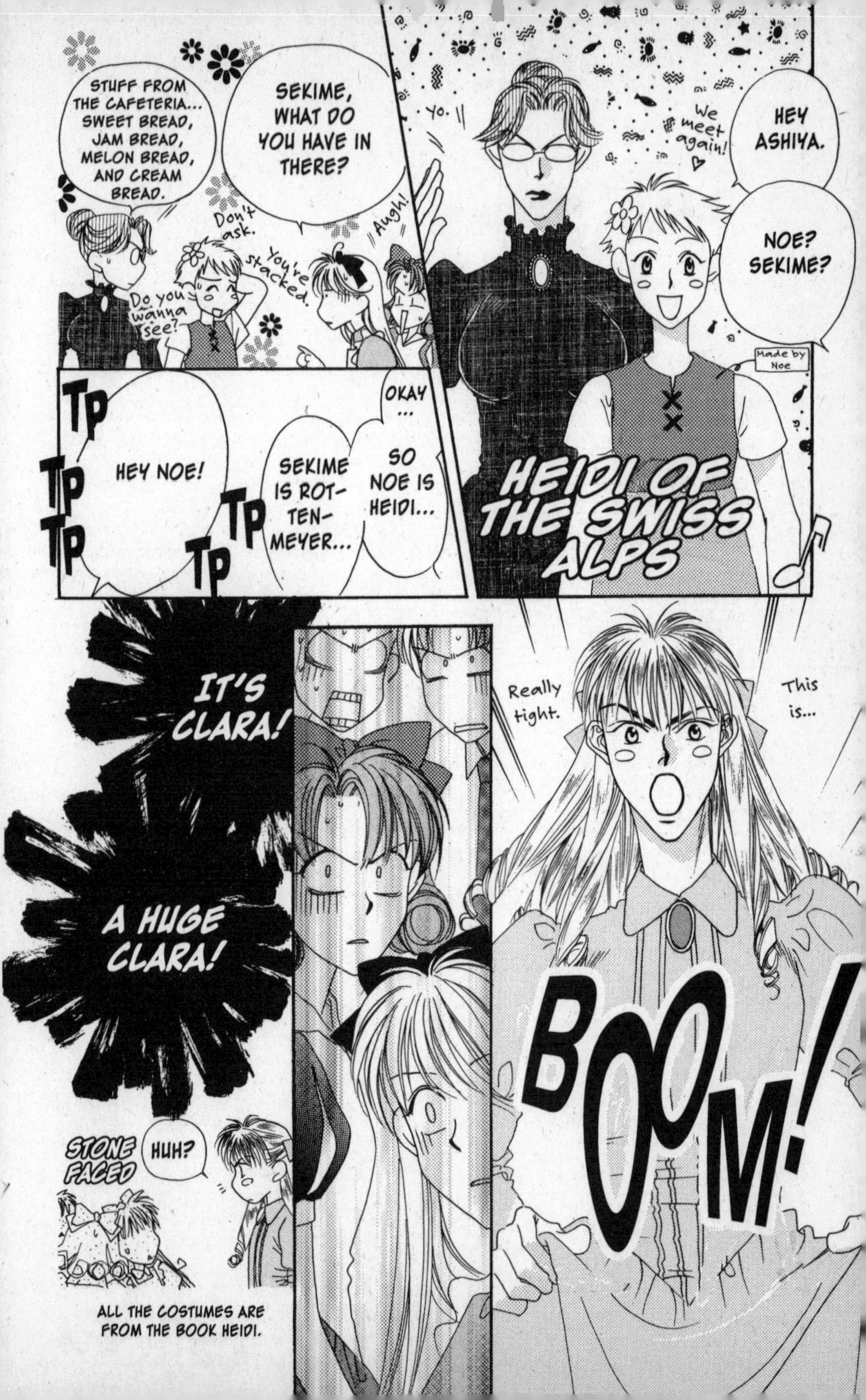
HEY ASHIYA.
NOE? SEKIME?
Yo.
We meet again!
Made by Noe
HEIDI OF THE SWISS ALPS
SEKIME, WHAT DO YOU HAVE IN THERE?
STUFF FROM THE CAFETERIA... SWEET BREAD, JAM BREAD, MELON BREAD, AND CREAM BREAD.
Augh!
You're stacked.
Don't ask.
Do you wanna see?
OKAY ...
SO NOE IS HEIDI...
SEKIME IS ROT-TEN-MEYER...
TP TP
HEY NOE!
TP TP TP
This is...
Really tight.
BOOM!
IT'S CLARA!
A HUGE CLARA!
HUH?
STONE FACED
ALL THE COSTUMES ARE FROM THE BOOK HEIDI.

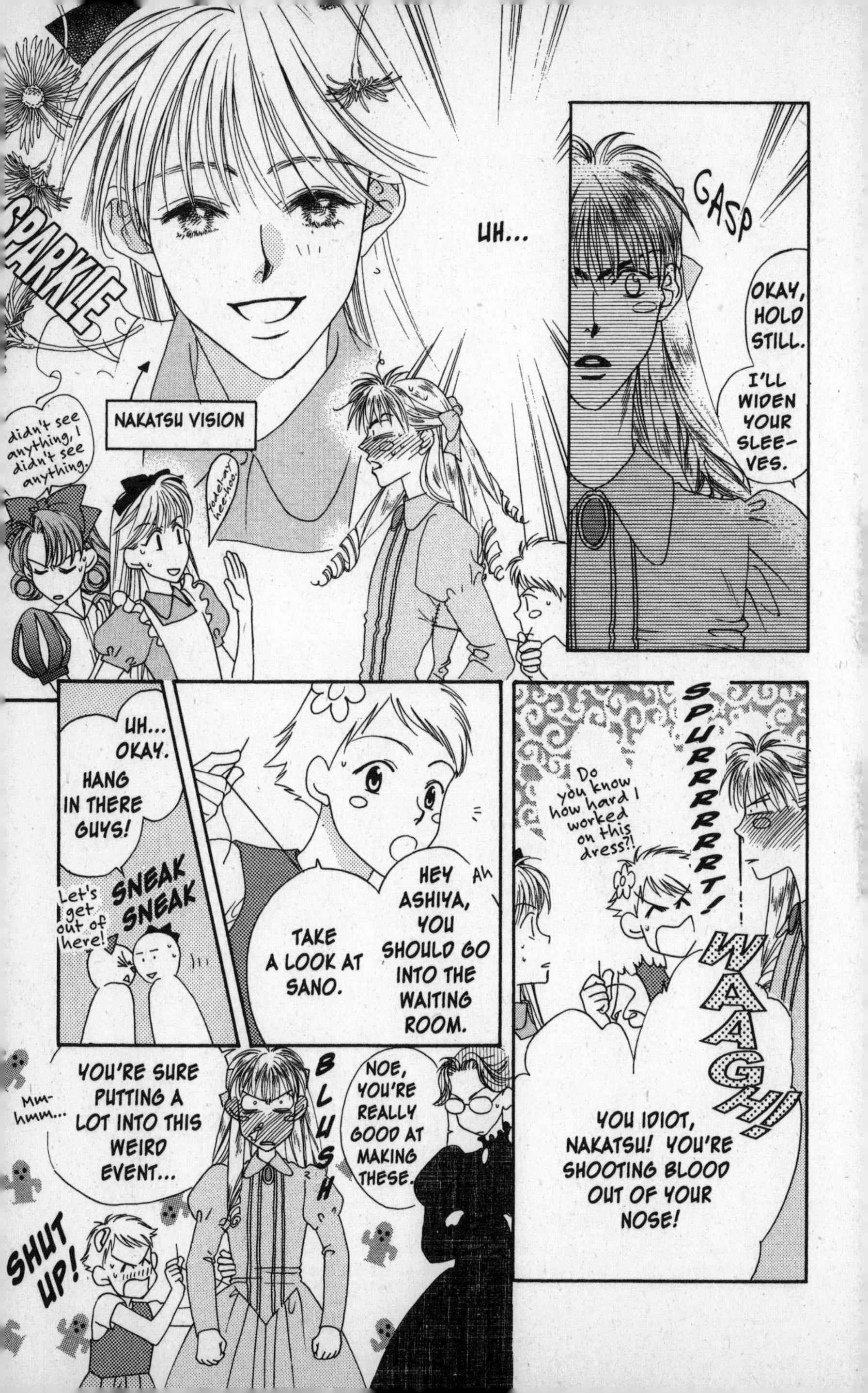
GASP
OKAY, HOLD STILL.
I'LL WIDEN YOUR SLEE-VES.
UH...
SPARKLE
NAKATSU VISION
didn't see anything, I didn't see anything.
Yodel-ay hee-hoo.
SPURRRRRRT!
Do you know how hard I worked on this dress?!
WAAGH!
YOU IDIOT, NAKATSU! YOU'RE SHOOTING BLOOD OUT OF YOUR NOSE!
HEY ASHIYA, YOU SHOULD GO INTO THE WAITING ROOM.
Ah
TAKE A LOOK AT SANO.
UH... OKAY.
HANG IN THERE GUYS!
SNEAK SNEAK
Let's get out of here!
NOE, YOU'RE REALLY GOOD AT MAKING THESE.
BLUSH
YOU'RE SURE PUTTING A LOT INTO THIS WEIRD EVENT...
Mm-hmm...
SHUT UP!

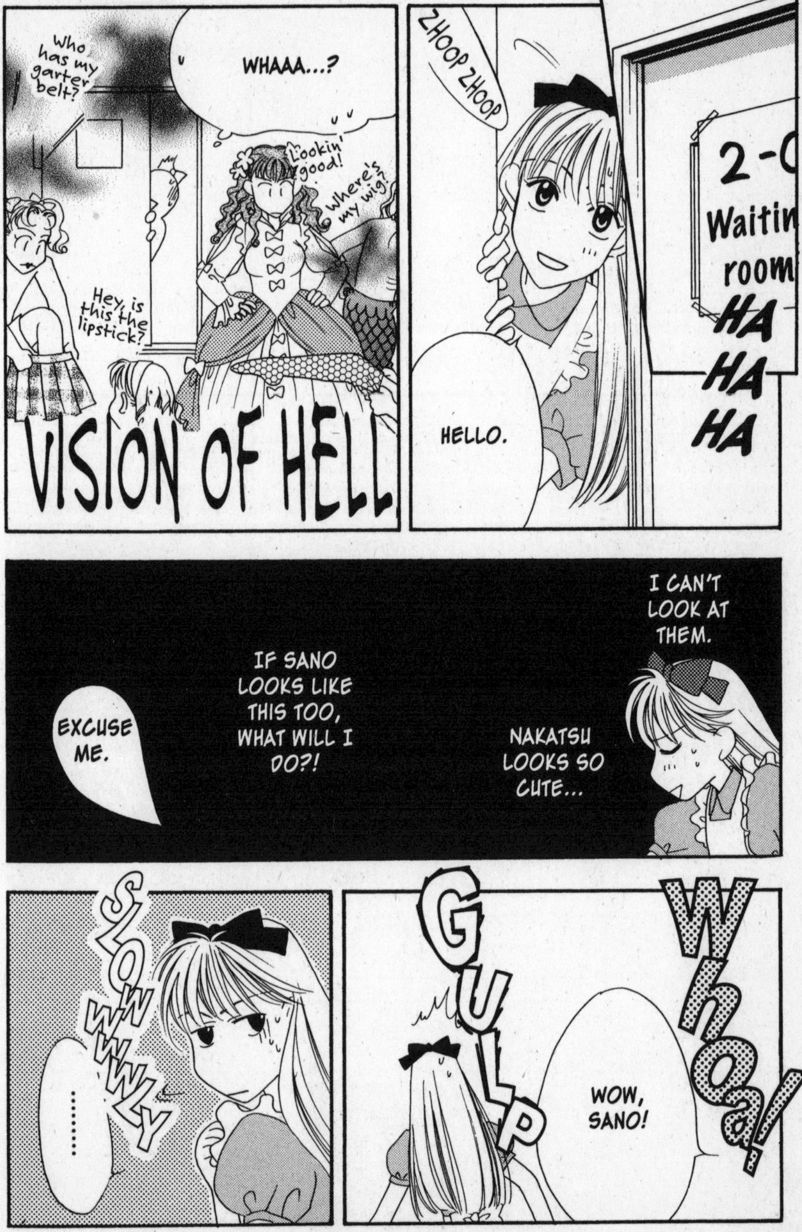
ZHOOP ZHOOP
2-C
Waitin
room
HA HA HA
HELLO.
WHAAA...?
Who has my garter belt?
Lookin' good!
Where's my wig?
Hey, is this the lipstick?
VISION OF HELL
I CAN'T LOOK AT THEM.
NAKATSU LOOKS SO CUTE...
IF SANO LOOKS LIKE THIS TOO, WHAT WILL I DO?!
EXCUSE ME.
Whoa!
WOW, SANO!
GULP
SLOWWWWLY
......

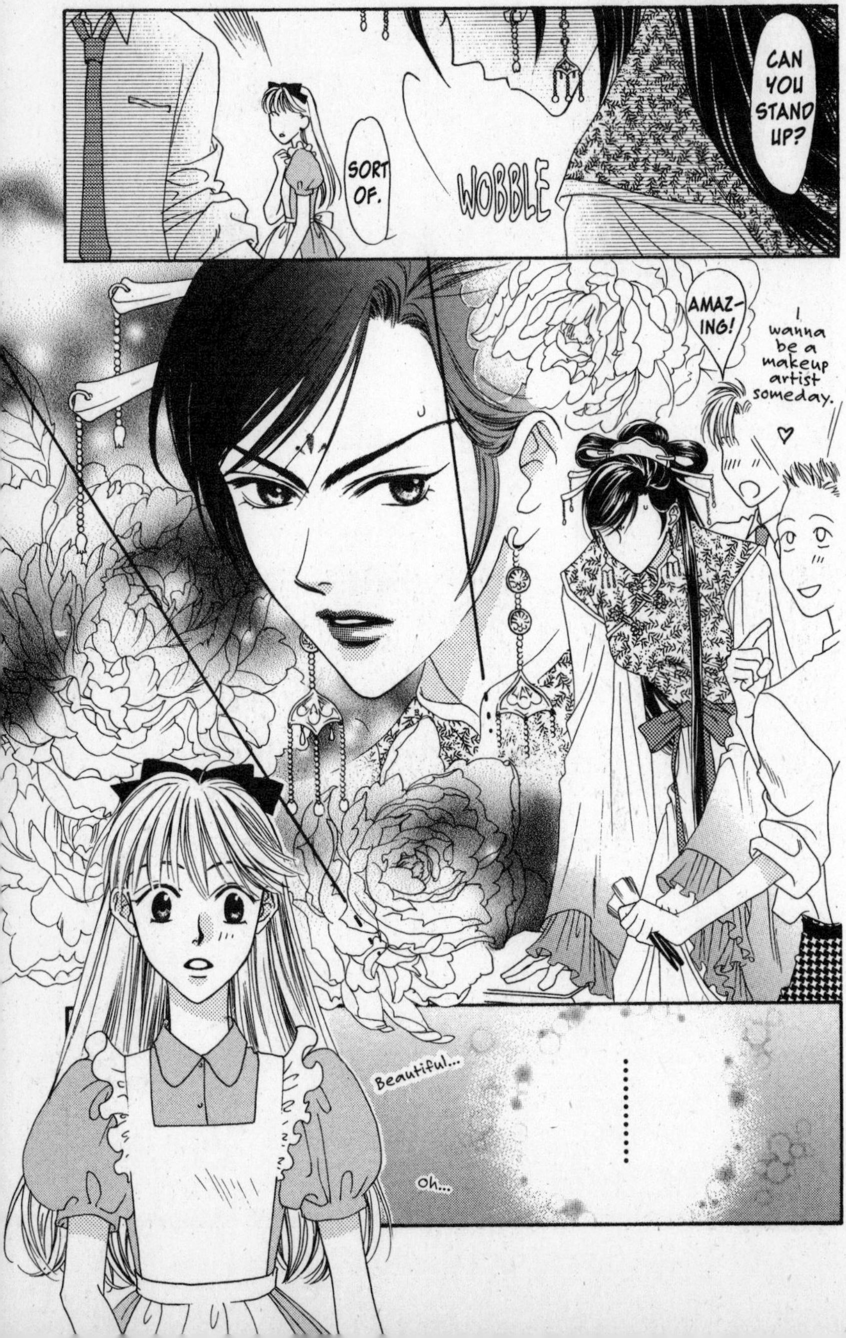
CAN YOU STAND UP?
WOBBLE
SORT OF.
I wanna be a makeup artist someday.
AMAZ-ING!
......
Beautiful...
Oh...

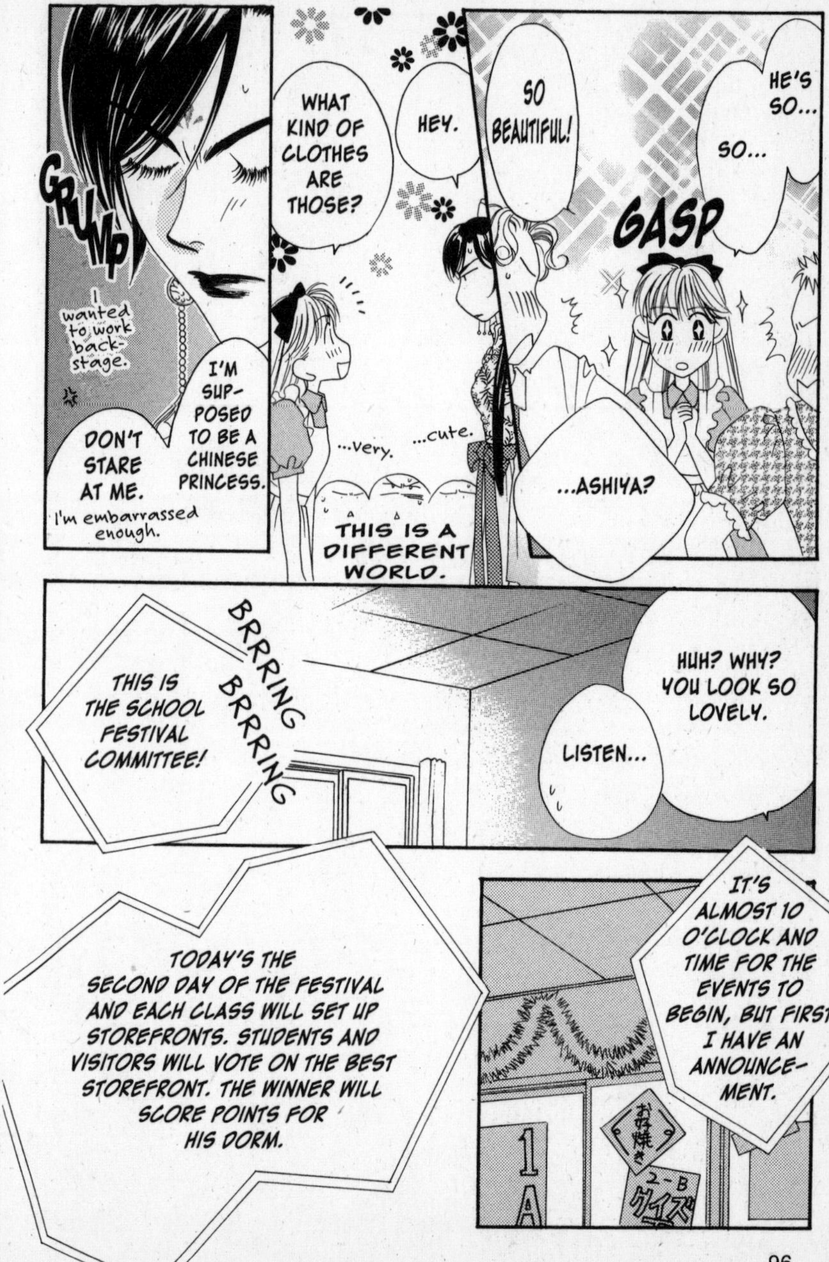
HE'S SO...
SO...
SO BEAUTIFUL!
GASP
...ASHIYA?
HEY.
WHAT KIND OF CLOTHES ARE THOSE?
...very.
...cute.
THIS IS A DIFFERENT WORLD.
GRUMP
I wanted to work back-stage.
I'M SUP-POSED TO BE A CHINESE PRINCESS.
DON'T STARE AT ME.
I'm embarrassed enough.
HUH? WHY? YOU LOOK SO LOVELY.
LISTEN...
BRRRING BRRRING
THIS IS THE SCHOOL FESTIVAL COMMITTEE!
IT'S ALMOST 10 O'CLOCK AND TIME FOR THE EVENTS TO BEGIN, BUT FIRST I HAVE AN ANNOUNCE-MENT.
1 A
お好焼き
2-B
クイズ
TODAY'S THE SECOND DAY OF THE FESTIVAL AND EACH CLASS WILL SET UP STOREFRONTS. STUDENTS AND VISITORS WILL VOTE ON THE BEST STOREFRONT. THE WINNER WILL SCORE POINTS FOR HIS DORM.

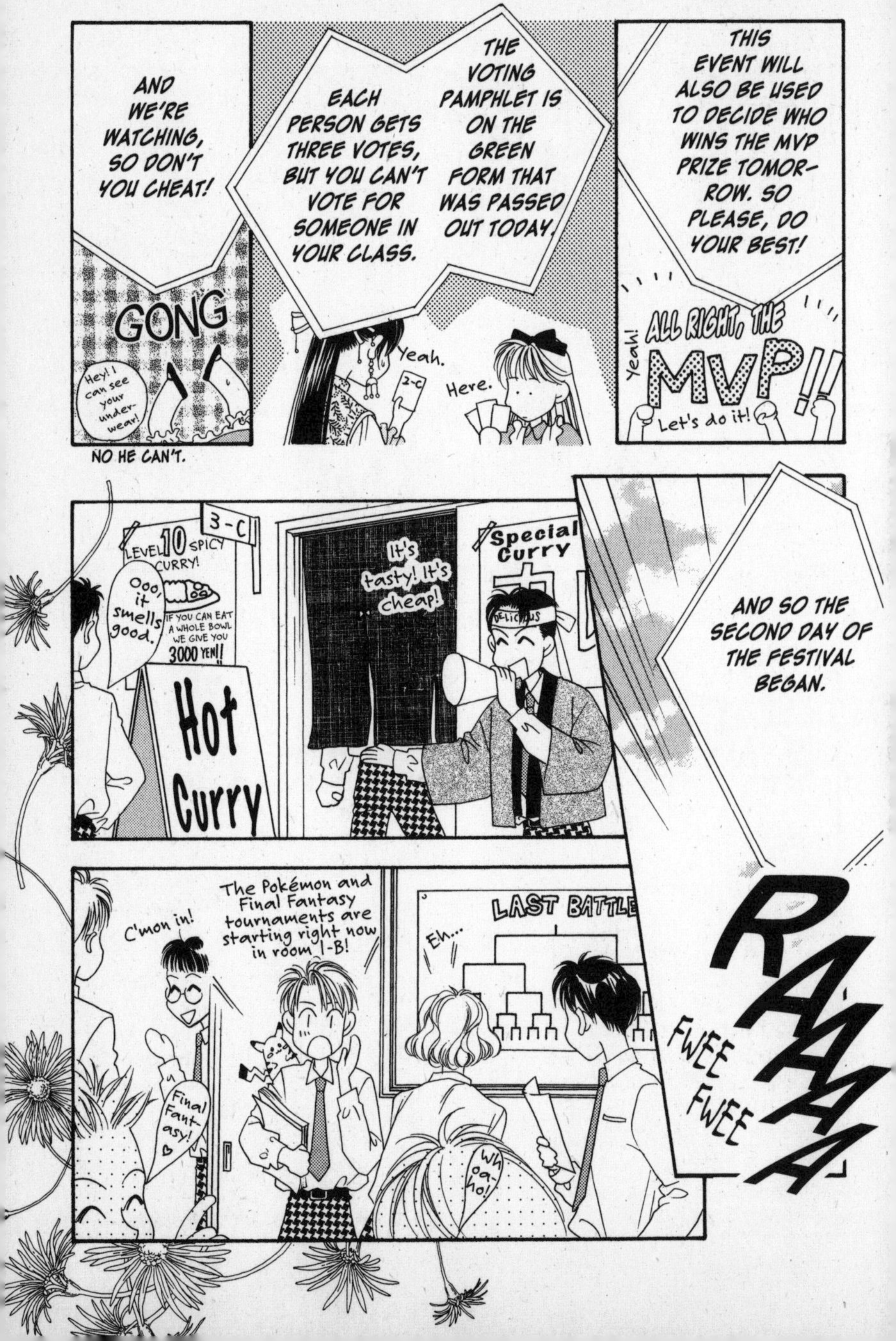
THIS EVENT WILL ALSO BE USED TO DECIDE WHO WINS THE MVP PRIZE TOMORROW. SO PLEASE, DO YOUR BEST!
ALL RIGHT, THE MVP!!
Yeah!
Let's do it!
THE VOTING PAMPHLET IS ON THE GREEN FORM THAT WAS PASSED OUT TODAY.
EACH PERSON GETS THREE VOTES, BUT YOU CAN'T VOTE FOR SOMEONE IN YOUR CLASS.
Here.
Yeah.
2-C
AND WE'RE WATCHING, SO DON'T YOU CHEAT!
GONG
Hey! I can see your underwear!
NO HE CAN'T.
AND SO THE SECOND DAY OF THE FESTIVAL BEGAN.
RAAAA
FWEE FWEE
Special Curry
DELICIOUS
It's tasty! It's cheap!
3-C
LEVEL 10 SPICY CURRY!
IF YOU CAN EAT A WHOLE BOWL WE GIVE YOU 3000 YEN!
Ooo, it smells good.
Hot Curry
LAST BATTLE
Eh...
Whoa-ho!
The Pokémon and Final Fantasy tournaments are starting right now in room 1-B!
C'mon in!
Final Fantasy!

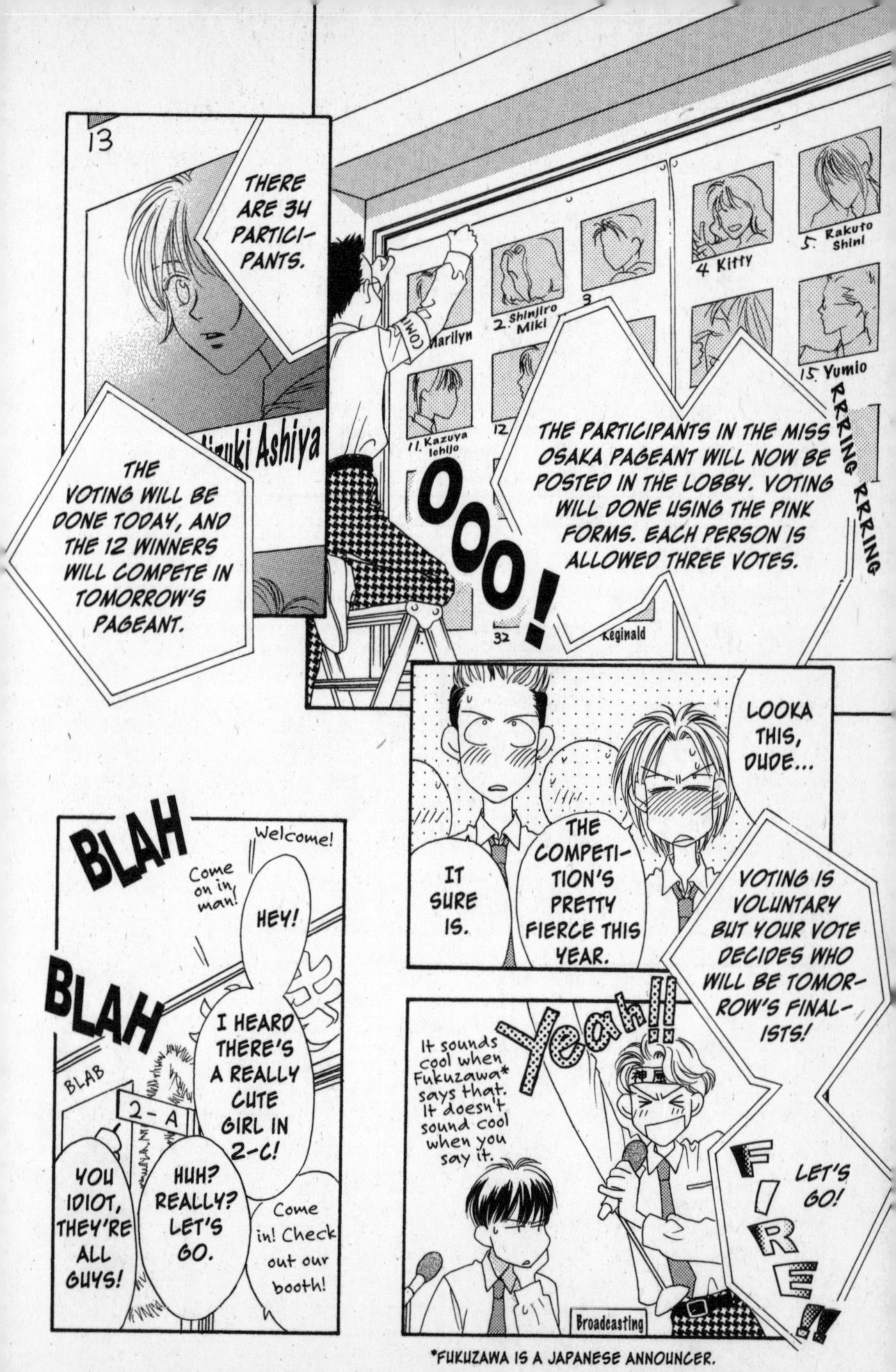
THE PARTICIPANTS IN THE MISS OSAKA PAGEANT WILL NOW BE POSTED IN THE LOBBY. VOTING WILL DONE USING THE PINK FORMS. EACH PERSON IS ALLOWED THREE VOTES.
RRRING RRRING
OOO!
4 Kitty
5. Rakuto Shini
15. Yumio
2. Shinjiro Miki
3
Marilyn
11. Kazuya Ichijo
12
32
Reginald
13
THERE ARE 34 PARTICIPANTS.
THE VOTING WILL BE DONE TODAY, AND THE 12 WINNERS WILL COMPETE IN TOMORROW'S PAGEANT.
LOOKA THIS, DUDE...
THE COMPETITION'S PRETTY FIERCE THIS YEAR.
IT SURE IS.
VOTING IS VOLUNTARY BUT YOUR VOTE DECIDES WHO WILL BE TOMORROW'S FINALISTS!
Yeah!!
LET'S GO!
FIRE!!
It sounds cool when Fukuzawa* says that. It doesn't sound cool when you say it.
Broadcasting
Welcome!
Come on in man!
HEY!
BLAH
BLAH
BLAB
2-A
I HEARD THERE'S A REALLY CUTE GIRL IN 2-C!
HUH? REALLY? LET'S GO.
YOU IDIOT, THEY'RE ALL GUYS!
Come in! Check out our booth!

*FUKUZAWA IS A JAPANESE ANNOUNCER.

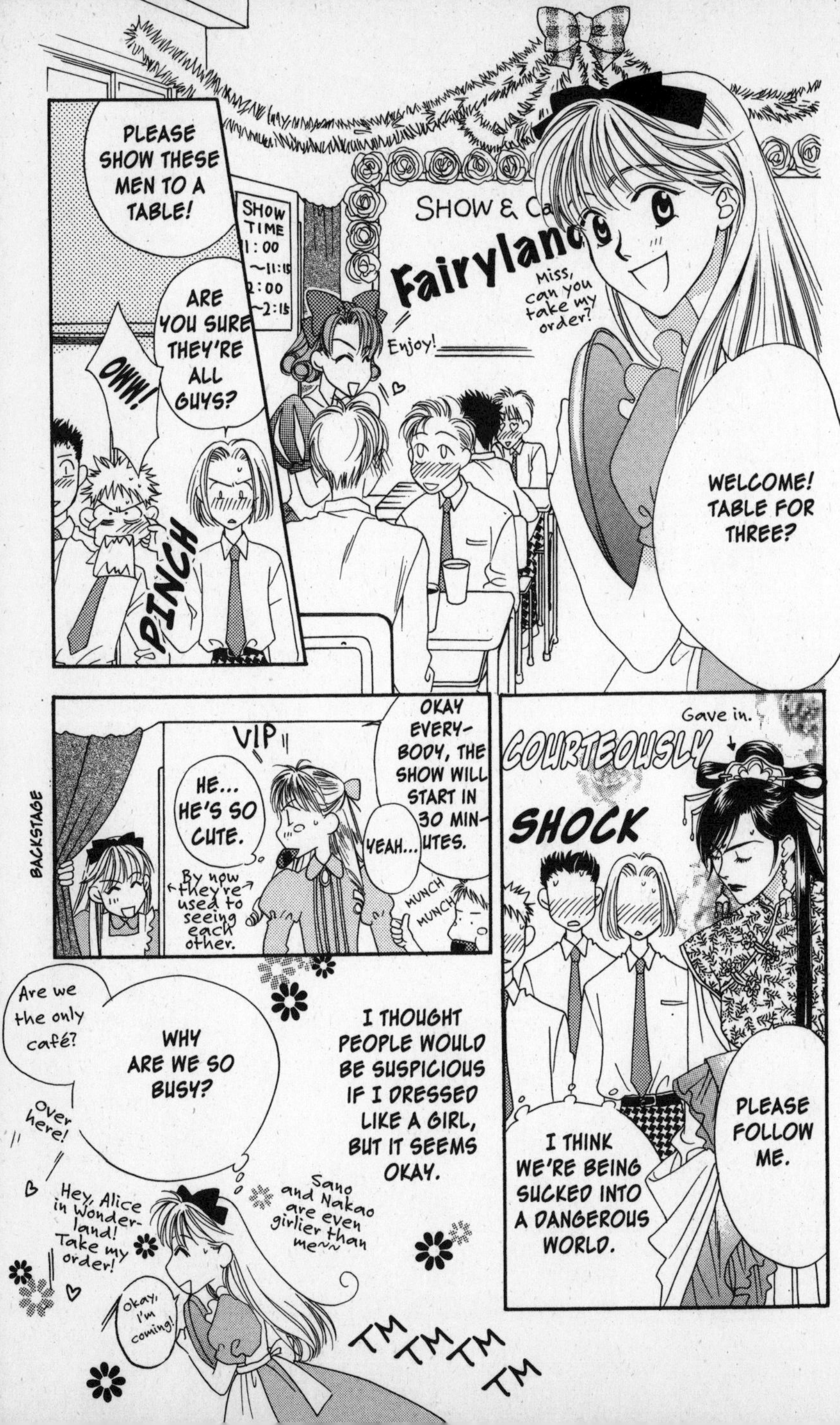
SHOW & Ca
Fairyland
Miss, can you take my order?
Enjoy!
WELCOME! TABLE FOR THREE?
PLEASE SHOW THESE MEN TO A TABLE!
SHOW TIME 1:00 ~11:15 2:00 ~2:15
ARE YOU SURE THEY'RE ALL GUYS?
OWW!
PINCH
Gave in.
COURTEOUSLY
SHOCK
PLEASE FOLLOW ME.
I THINK WE'RE BEING SUCKED INTO A DANGEROUS WORLD.
OKAY EVERYBODY, THE SHOW WILL START IN 30 MINUTES.
VIP
YEAH...
HE... HE'S SO CUTE.
MUNCH MUNCH
By now they're used to seeing each other.
BACKSTAGE
I THOUGHT PEOPLE WOULD BE SUSPICIOUS IF I DRESSED LIKE A GIRL, BUT IT SEEMS OKAY.
Sano and Nakao are even girlier than me~~
WHY ARE WE SO BUSY?
Are we the only café?
Over here!
Hey, Alice in Wonderland! Take my order!
Okay, I'm coming!
TM TM TM TM

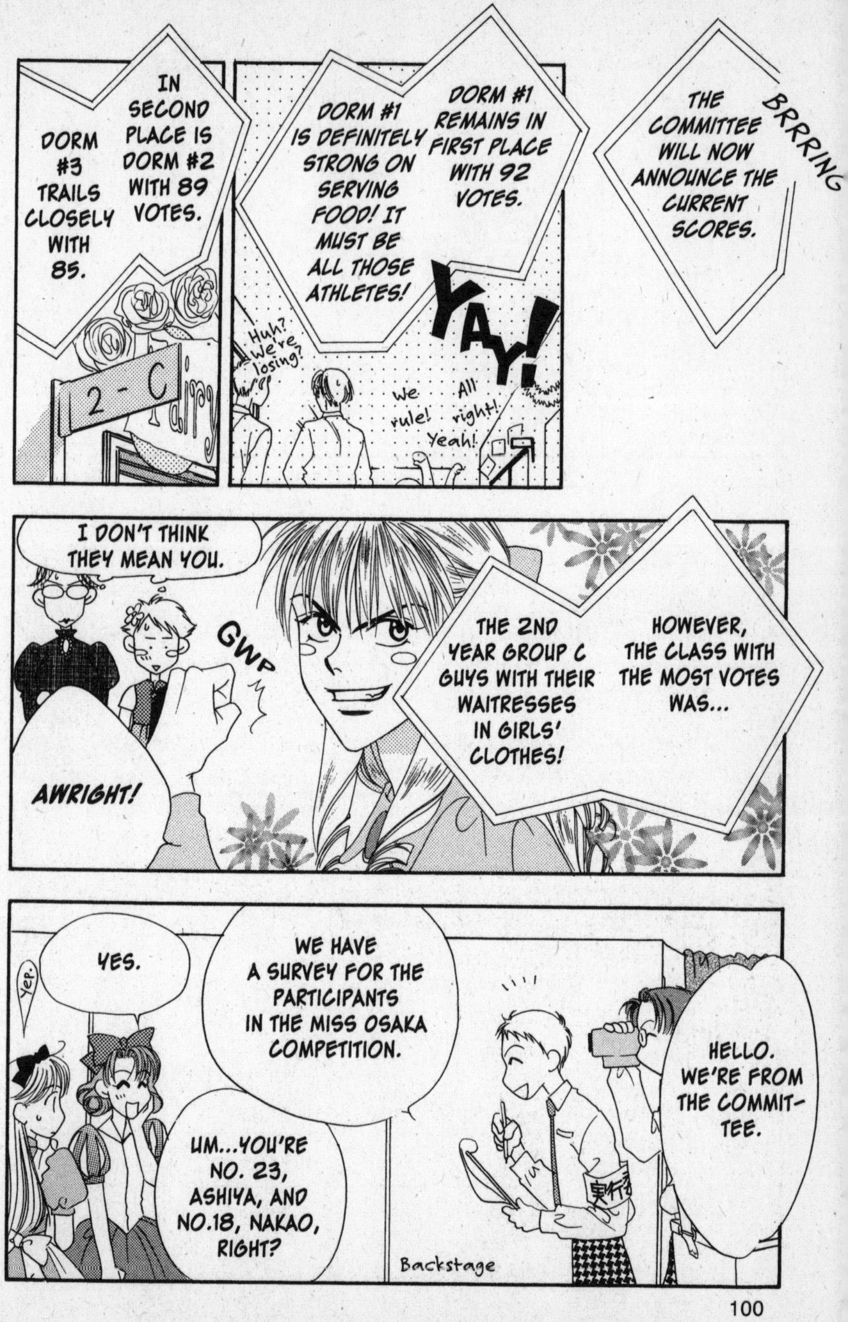
BRRRING
THE COMMITTEE WILL NOW ANNOUNCE THE CURRENT SCORES.
DORM #1 REMAINS IN FIRST PLACE WITH 92 VOTES.
DORM #1 IS DEFINITELY STRONG ON SERVING FOOD! IT MUST BE ALL THOSE ATHLETES!
YAY!
All right!
We rule!
Yeah!
Huh? We're losing?
IN SECOND PLACE IS DORM #2 WITH 89 VOTES.
DORM #3 TRAILS CLOSELY WITH 85.
2-C
Fairy
HOWEVER, THE CLASS WITH THE MOST VOTES WAS...
THE 2ND YEAR GROUP C GUYS WITH THEIR WAITRESSES IN GIRLS' CLOTHES!
GWP
AWRIGHT!
I DON'T THINK THEY MEAN YOU.
HELLO. WE'RE FROM THE COMMIT-TEE.
Backstage
WE HAVE A SURVEY FOR THE PARTICIPANTS IN THE MISS OSAKA COMPETITION.
UM...YOU'RE NO. 23, ASHIYA, AND NO.18, NAKAO, RIGHT?
YES.
Yep.

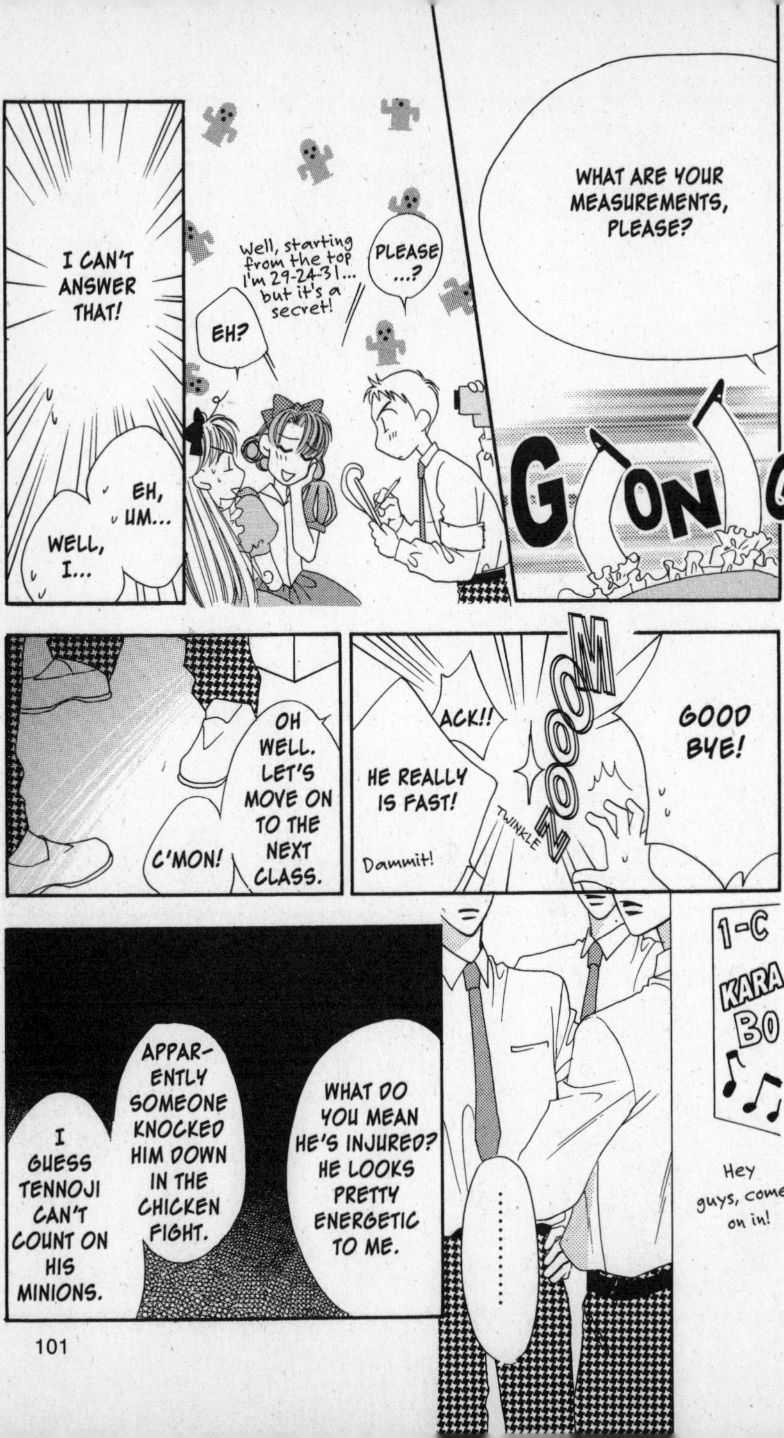
WHAT ARE YOUR MEASUREMENTS, PLEASE?
GONG
PLEASE ...?
Well, starting from the top I'm 29-24-31... but it's a secret!
EH?
I CAN'T ANSWER THAT!
EH, UM...
WELL, I...
GOOD BYE!
ZOOOOM
ACK!!
HE REALLY IS FAST!
TWINKLE
Dammit!
OH WELL. LET'S MOVE ON TO THE NEXT CLASS.
C'MON!
1-C KARA BO
Hey guys, come on in!
......
WHAT DO YOU MEAN HE'S INJURED? HE LOOKS PRETTY ENERGETIC TO ME.
APPARENTLY SOMEONE KNOCKED HIM DOWN IN THE CHICKEN FIGHT.
I GUESS TENNOJI CAN'T COUNT ON HIS MINIONS.

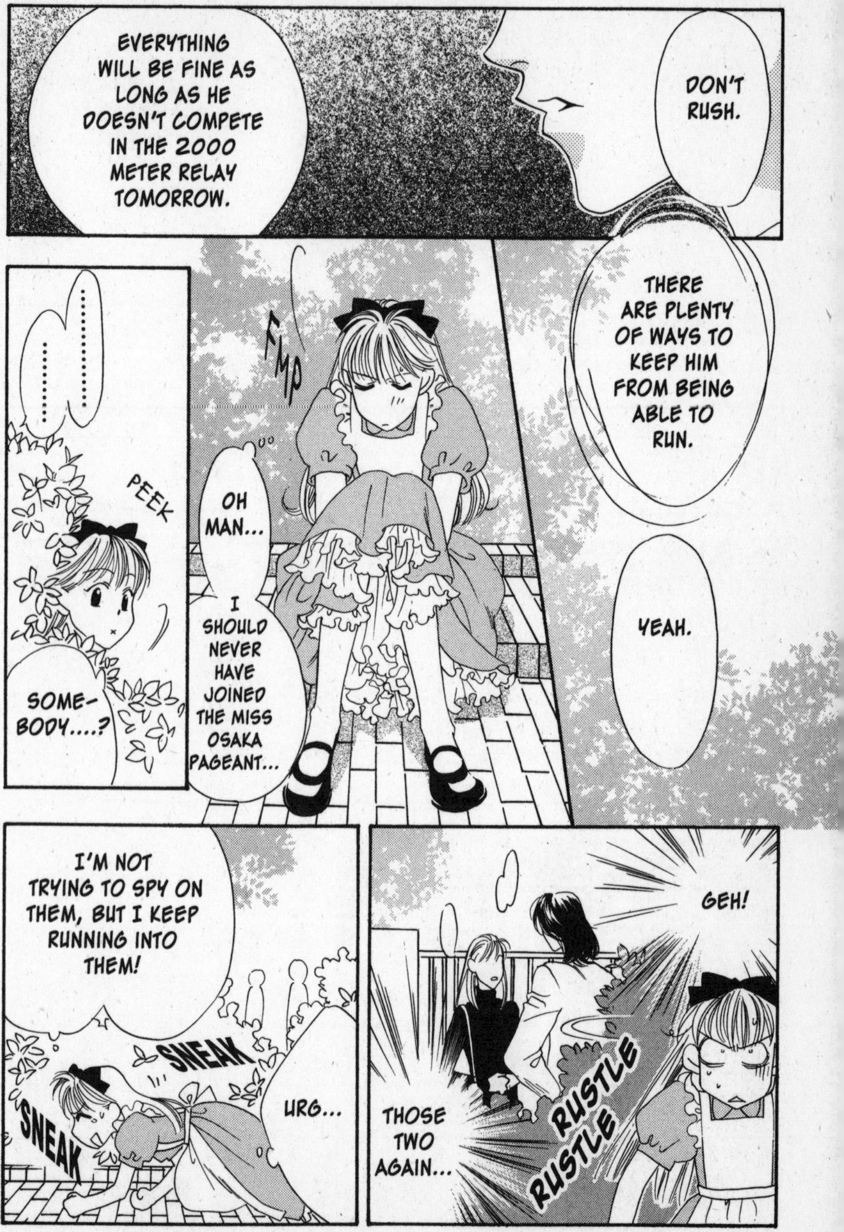
DON'T RUSH.
EVERYTHING WILL BE FINE AS LONG AS HE DOESN'T COMPETE IN THE 2000 METER RELAY TOMORROW.
THERE ARE PLENTY OF WAYS TO KEEP HIM FROM BEING ABLE TO RUN.
YEAH.
FMP
OH MAN...
I SHOULD NEVER HAVE JOINED THE MISS OSAKA PAGEANT...
......
......
PEEK
SOME-BODY....?
GEH!
RUSTLE RUSTLE
THOSE TWO AGAIN...
I'M NOT TRYING TO SPY ON THEM, BUT I KEEP RUNNING INTO THEM!
SNEAK
SNEAK
URG...

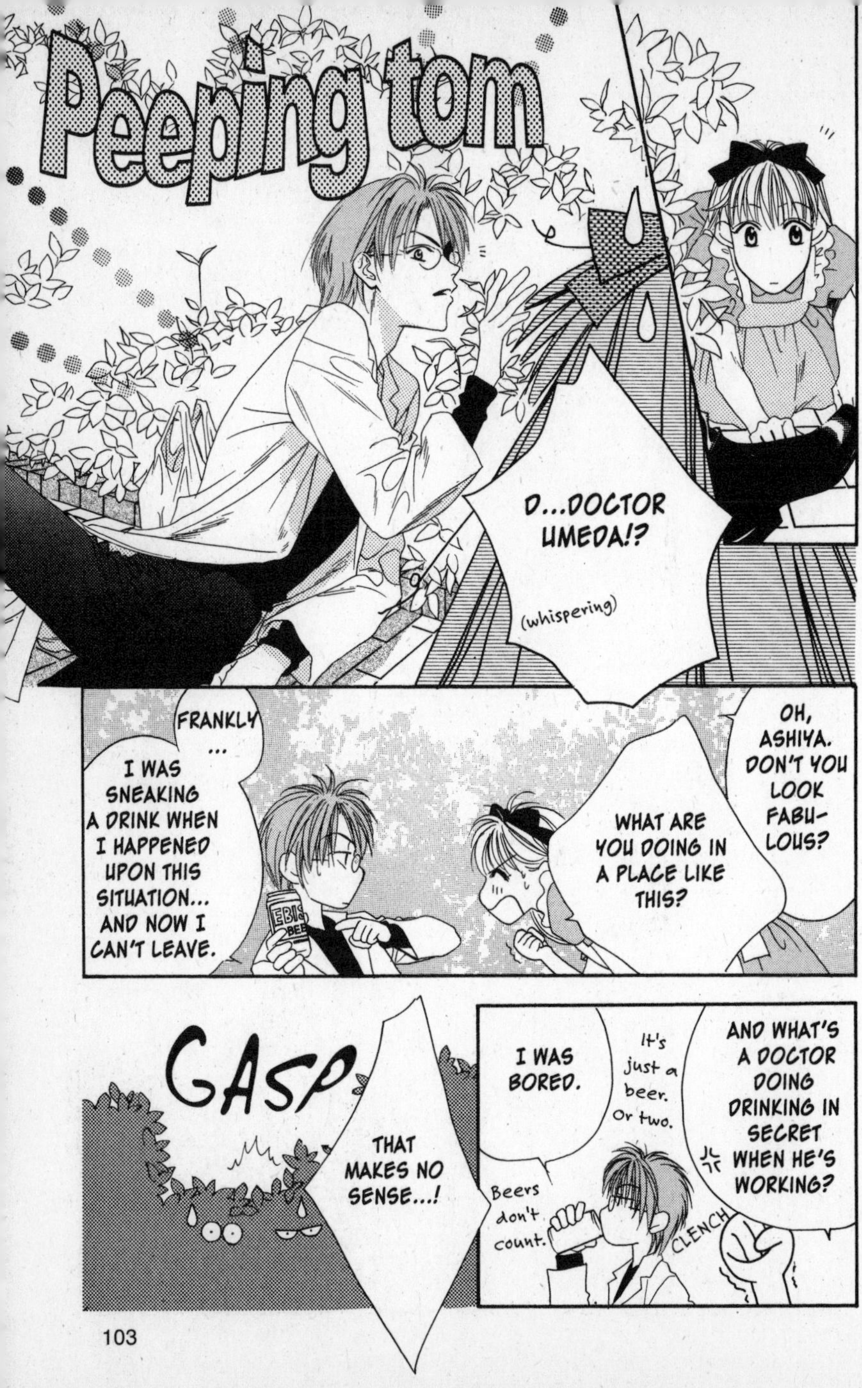
Peeping tom
D...DOCTOR UMEDA!?
(whispering)
OH, ASHIYA. DON'T YOU LOOK FABULOUS?
WHAT ARE YOU DOING IN A PLACE LIKE THIS?
FRANKLY... I WAS SNEAKING A DRINK WHEN I HAPPENED UPON THIS SITUATION... AND NOW I CAN'T LEAVE.
AND WHAT'S A DOCTOR DOING DRINKING IN SECRET WHEN HE'S WORKING?
It's just a beer. Or two.
I WAS BORED.
Beers don't count.
CLENCH
THAT MAKES NO SENSE...!
GASP

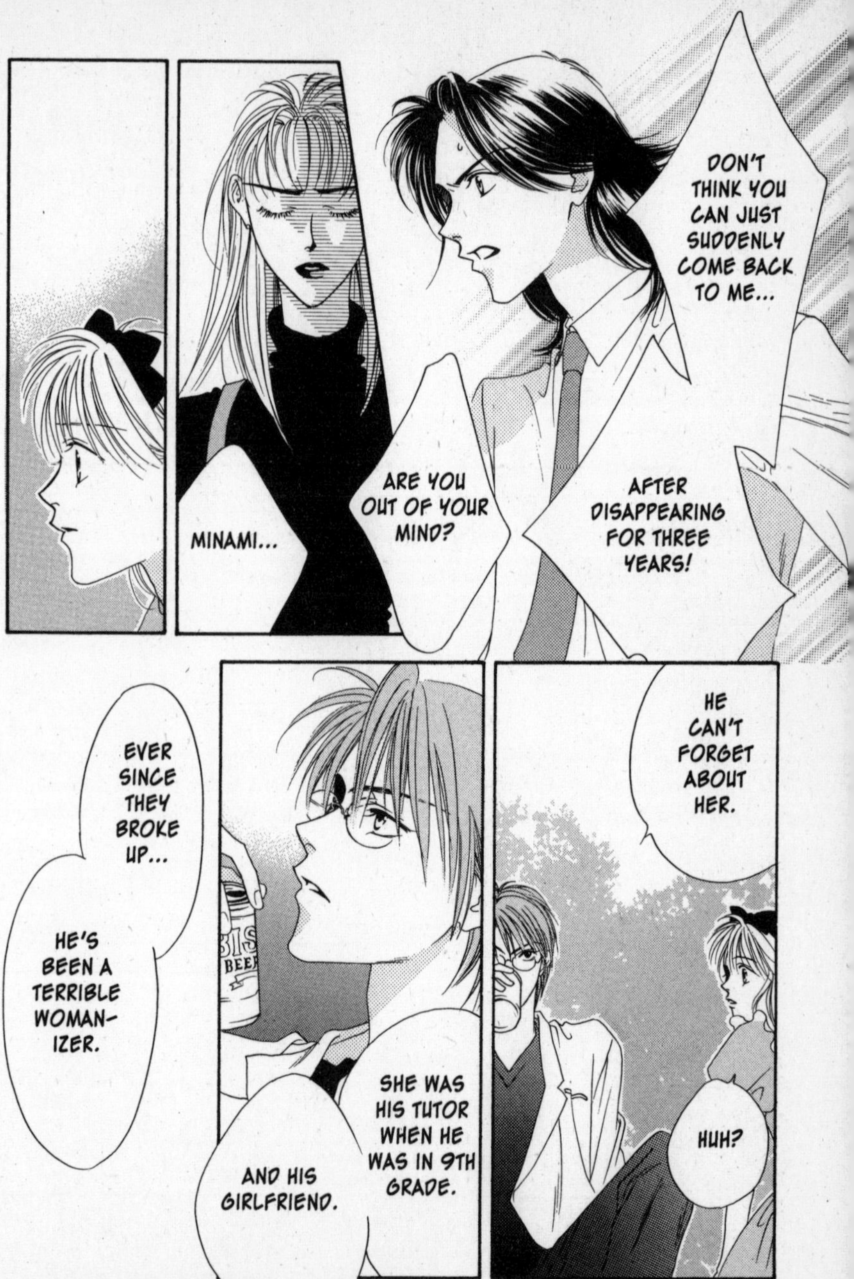
DON'T THINK YOU CAN JUST SUDDENLY COME BACK TO ME...
AFTER DISAPPEARING FOR THREE YEARS!
ARE YOU OUT OF YOUR MIND?
MINAMI...
HE CAN'T FORGET ABOUT HER.
HUH?
SHE WAS HIS TUTOR WHEN HE WAS IN 9TH GRADE.
AND HIS GIRLFRIEND.
EVER SINCE THEY BROKE UP...
HE'S BEEN A TERRIBLE WOMAN-IZER.

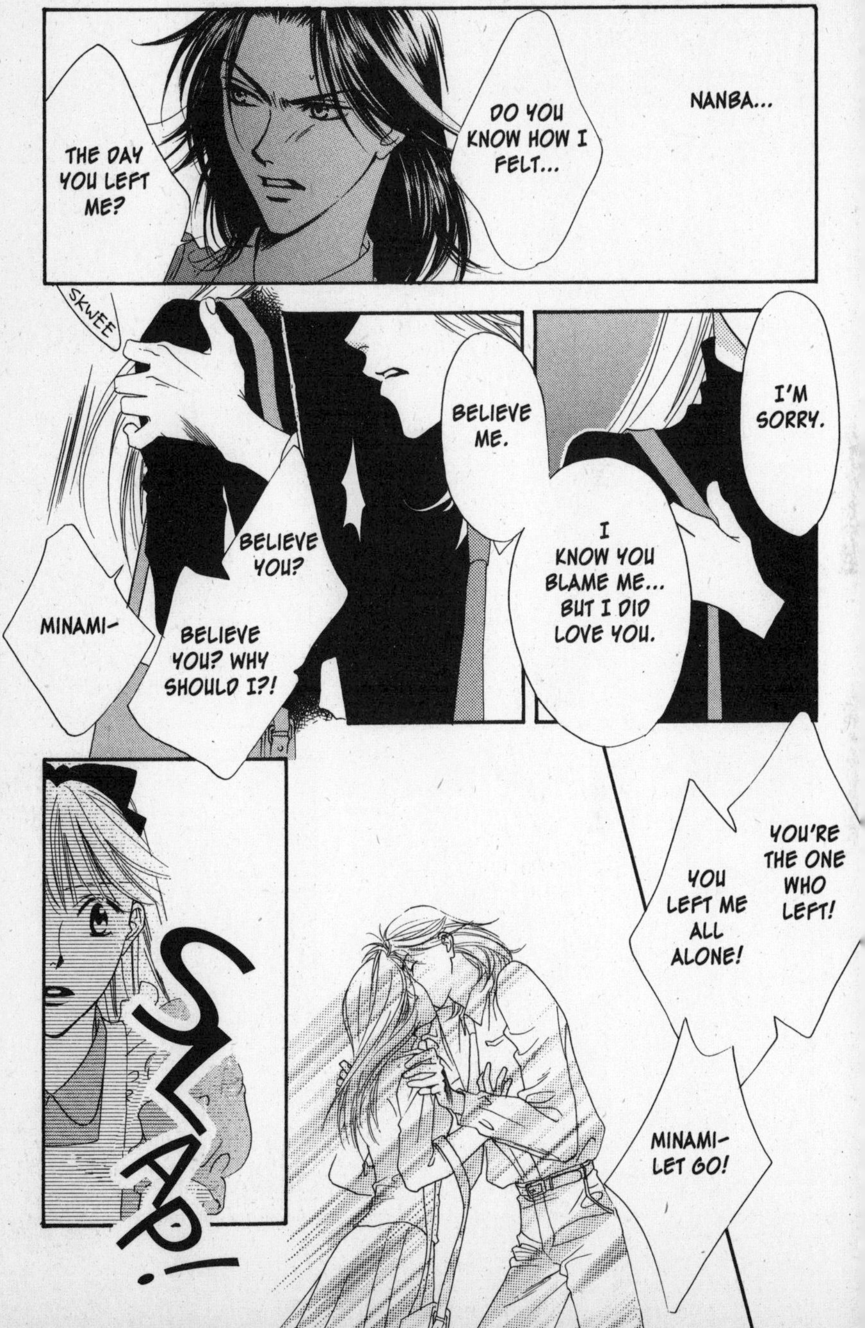
NANBA...
DO YOU KNOW HOW I FELT...
THE DAY YOU LEFT ME?
I'M SORRY.
I KNOW YOU BLAME ME... BUT I DID LOVE YOU.
BELIEVE ME.
SKWEE
BELIEVE YOU?
BELIEVE YOU? WHY SHOULD I?!
MINAMI-
YOU'RE THE ONE WHO LEFT!
YOU LEFT ME ALL ALONE!
MINAMI- LET GO!
SLAP!

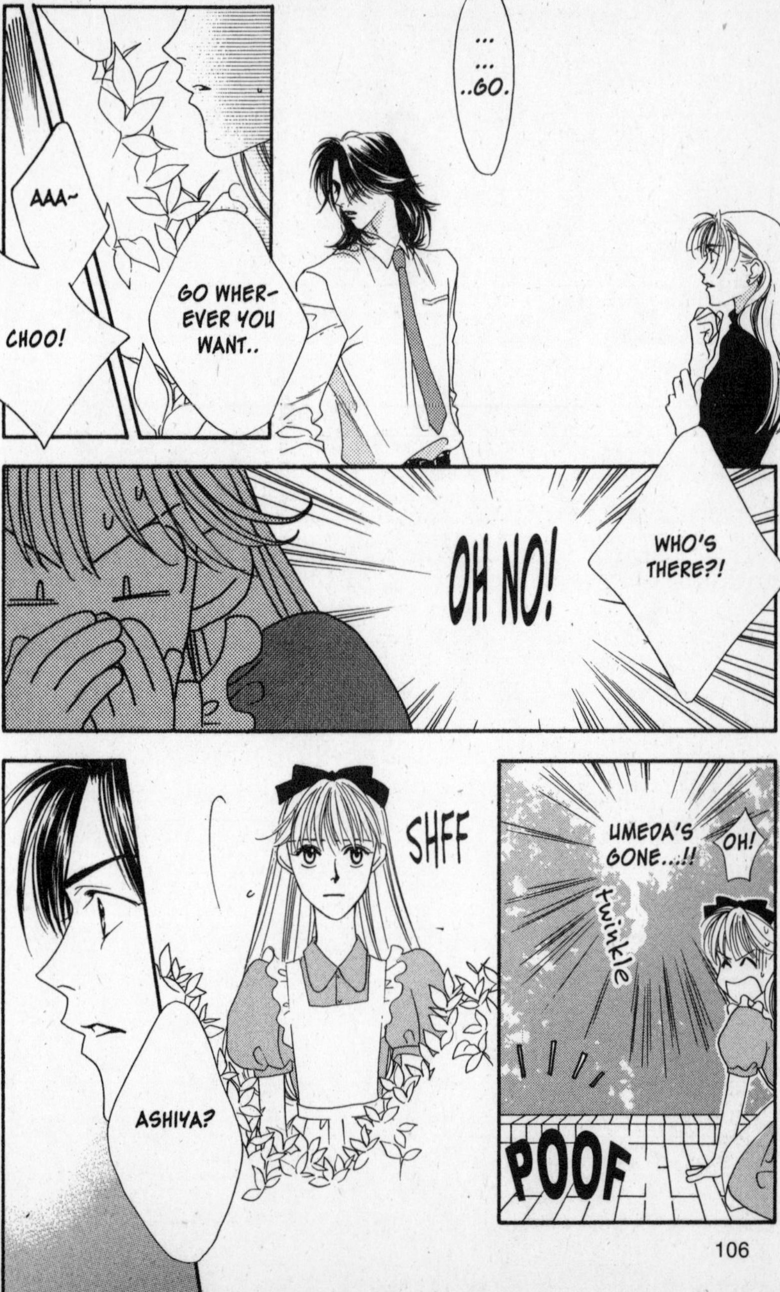
... .GO.
GO WHER-EVER YOU WANT..
AAA~
CHOO!
WHO'S THERE?!
OH NO!
OH!
UMEDA'S GONE...!!
twinkle
POOF
SHFF
ASHIYA?

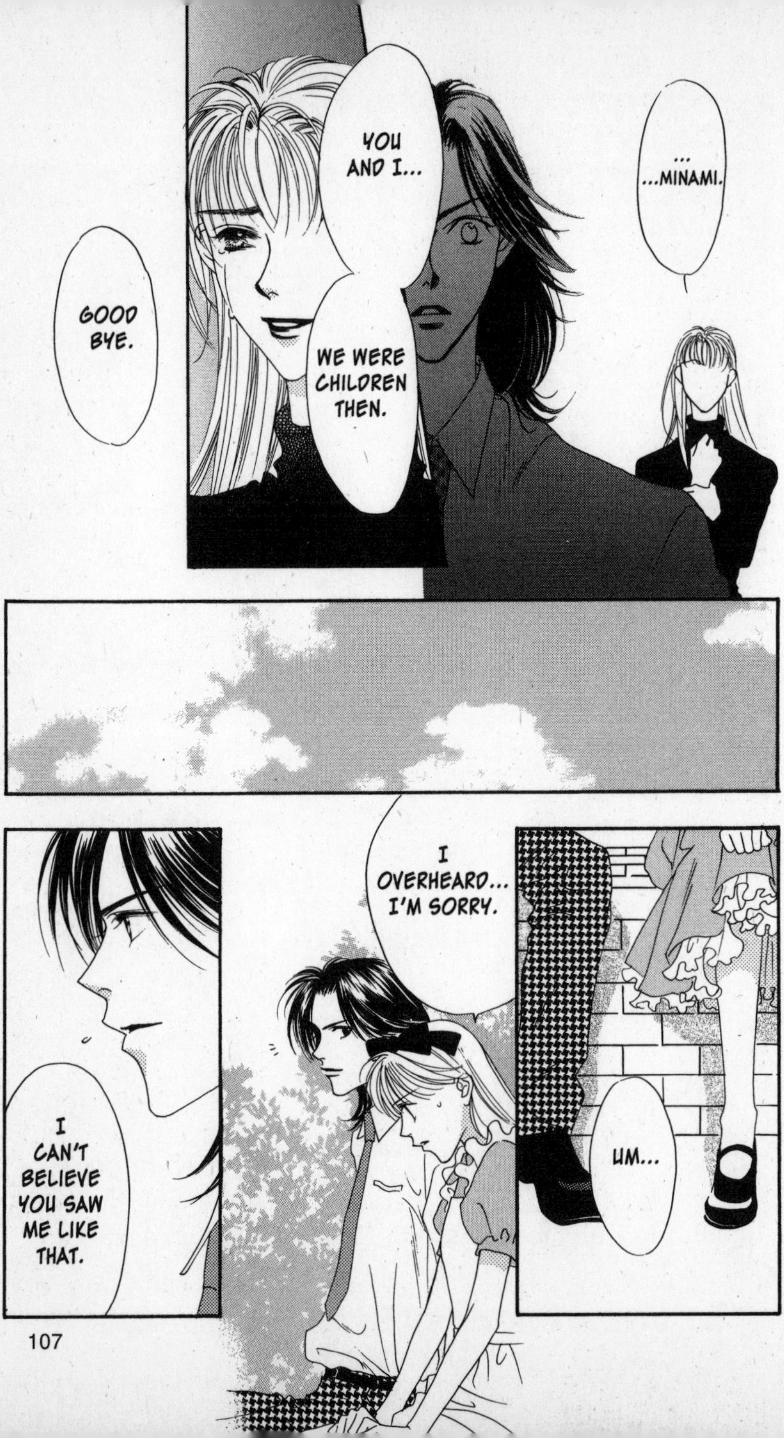
...
...MINAMI.
YOU AND I...
WE WERE CHILDREN THEN.
GOOD BYE.
UM...
I OVERHEARD... I'M SORRY.
I CAN'T BELIEVE YOU SAW ME LIKE THAT.

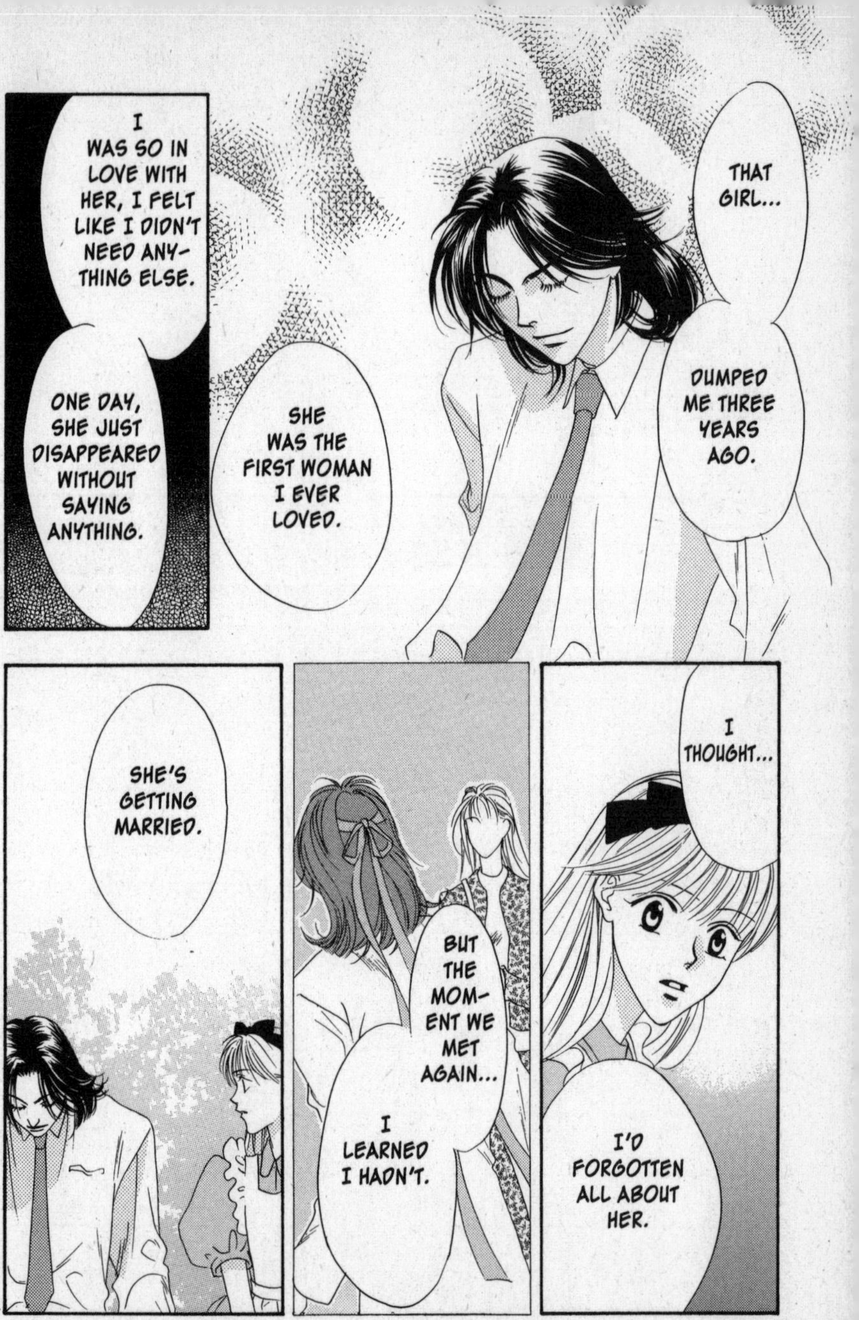
THAT GIRL...
DUMPED ME THREE YEARS AGO.
SHE WAS THE FIRST WOMAN I EVER LOVED.
I WAS SO IN LOVE WITH HER, I FELT LIKE I DIDN'T NEED ANY-THING ELSE.
ONE DAY, SHE JUST DISAPPEARED WITHOUT SAYING ANYTHING.
I THOUGHT...
I'D FORGOTTEN ALL ABOUT HER.
BUT THE MOM-ENT WE MET AGAIN...
I LEARNED I HADN'T.
SHE'S GETTING MARRIED.

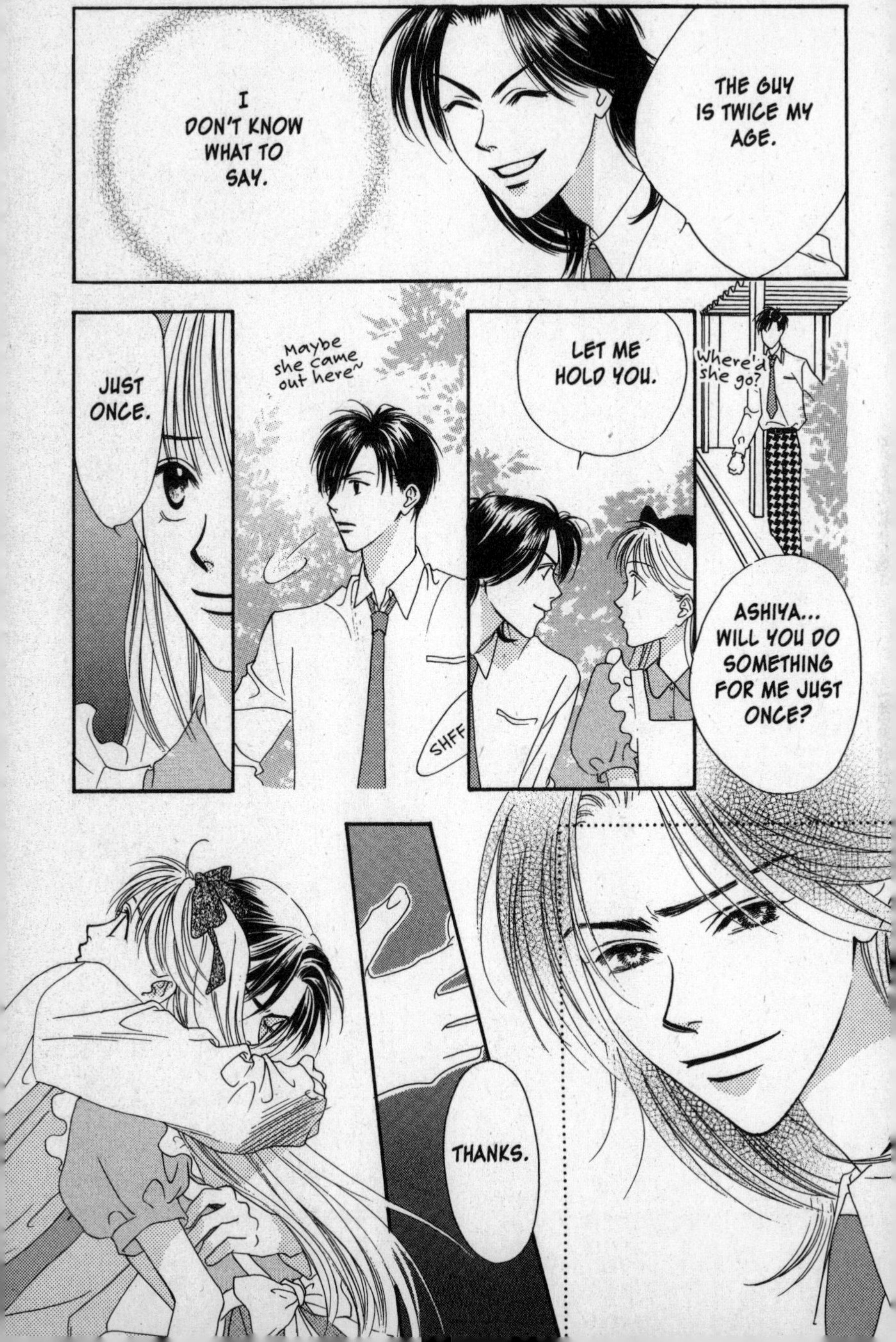
THE GUY IS TWICE MY AGE.
I DON'T KNOW WHAT TO SAY.
Where'd she go?
ASHIYA... WILL YOU DO SOMETHING FOR ME JUST ONCE?
LET ME HOLD YOU.
SHFF
Maybe she came out here~
JUST ONCE.
THANKS.

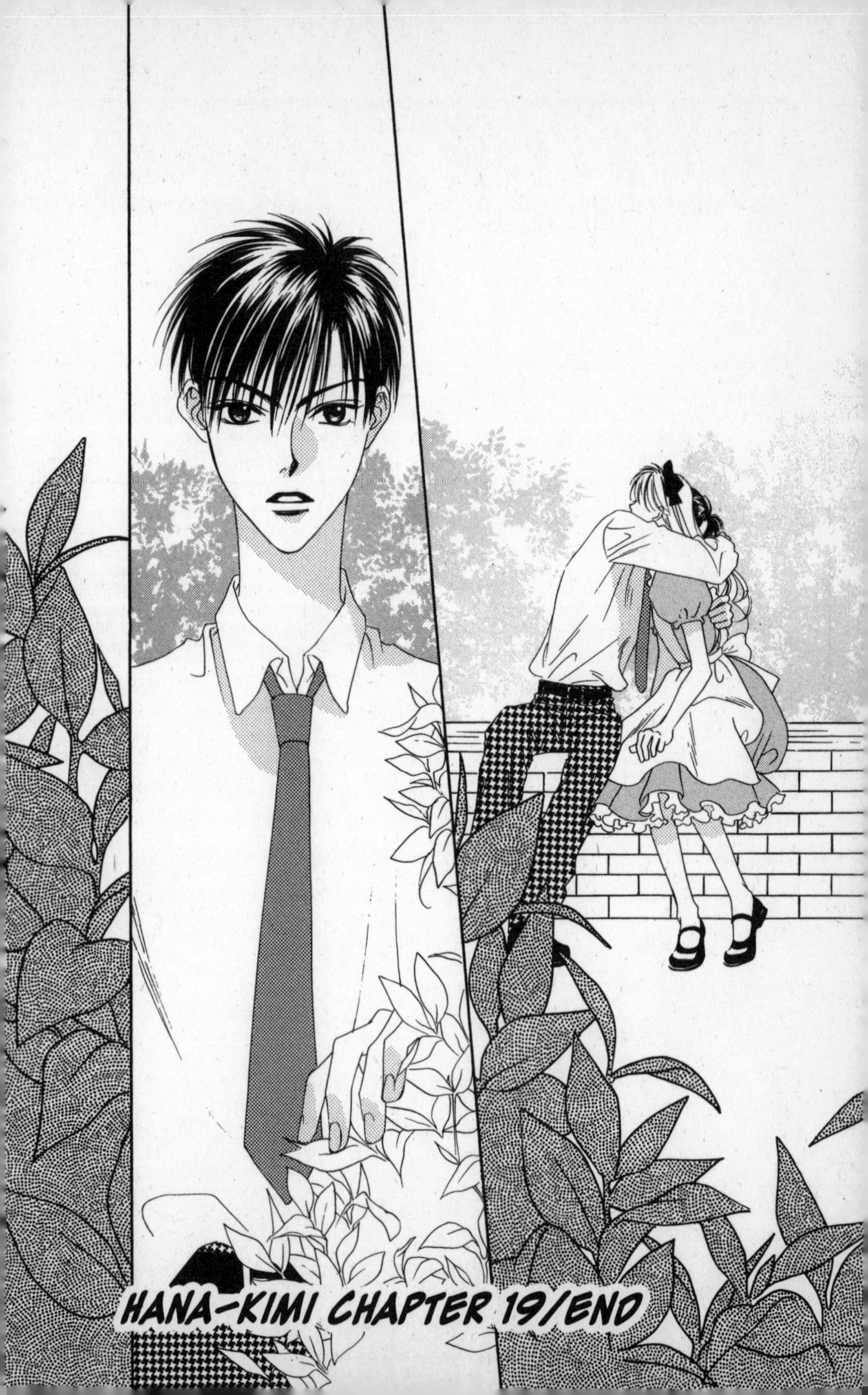
HANA-KIMI CHAPTER 19/END

Hana-Kimi

For You in Full Blossom

CHAPTER 20

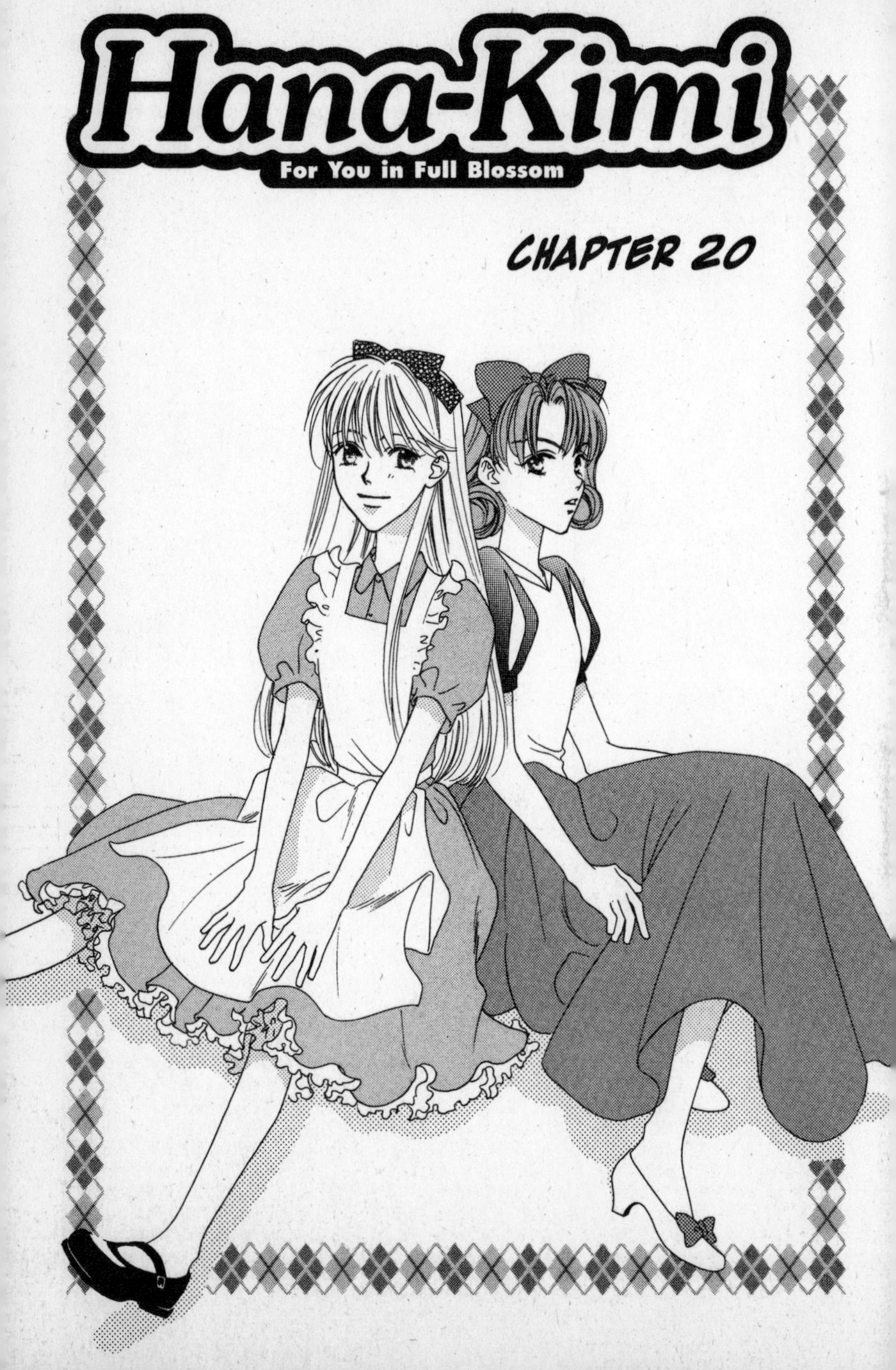

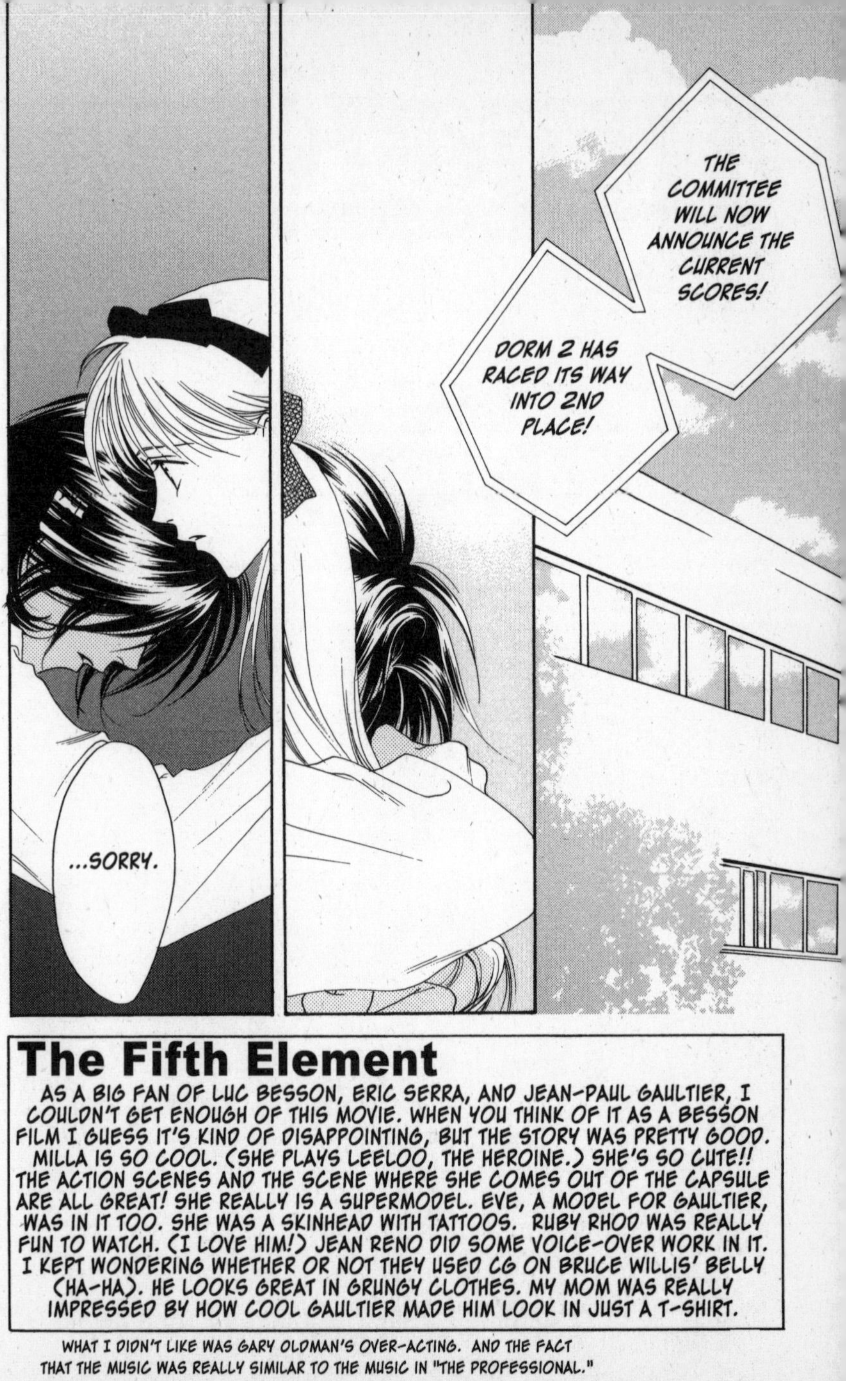
THE COMMITTEE WILL NOW ANNOUNCE THE CURRENT SCORES!
DORM 2 HAS RACED ITS WAY INTO 2ND PLACE!
...SORRY.

The Fifth Element

AS A BIG FAN OF LUC BESSON, ERIC SERRA, AND JEAN-PAUL GAULTIER, I COULDN'T GET ENOUGH OF THIS MOVIE. WHEN YOU THINK OF IT AS A BESSON FILM I GUESS IT'S KIND OF DISAPPOINTING, BUT THE STORY WAS PRETTY GOOD. MILLA IS SO COOL. (SHE PLAYS LEELOO, THE HEROINE.) SHE'S SO CUTE!! THE ACTION SCENES AND THE SCENE WHERE SHE COMES OUT OF THE CAPSULE ARE ALL GREAT! SHE REALLY IS A SUPERMODEL. EVE, A MODEL FOR GAULTIER, WAS IN IT TOO. SHE WAS A SKINHEAD WITH TATTOOS. RUBY RHOD WAS REALLY FUN TO WATCH. (I LOVE HIM!) JEAN RENO DID SOME VOICE-OVER WORK IN IT. I KEPT WONDERING WHETHER OR NOT THEY USED CG ON BRUCE WILLIS' BELLY (HA-HA). HE LOOKS GREAT IN GRUNGY CLOTHES. MY MOM WAS REALLY IMPRESSED BY HOW COOL GAULTIER MADE HIM LOOK IN JUST A T-SHIRT.

WHAT I DIDN'T LIKE WAS GARY OLDMAN'S OVER-ACTING. AND THE FACT THAT THE MUSIC WAS REALLY SIMILAR TO THE MUSIC IN "THE PROFESSIONAL."

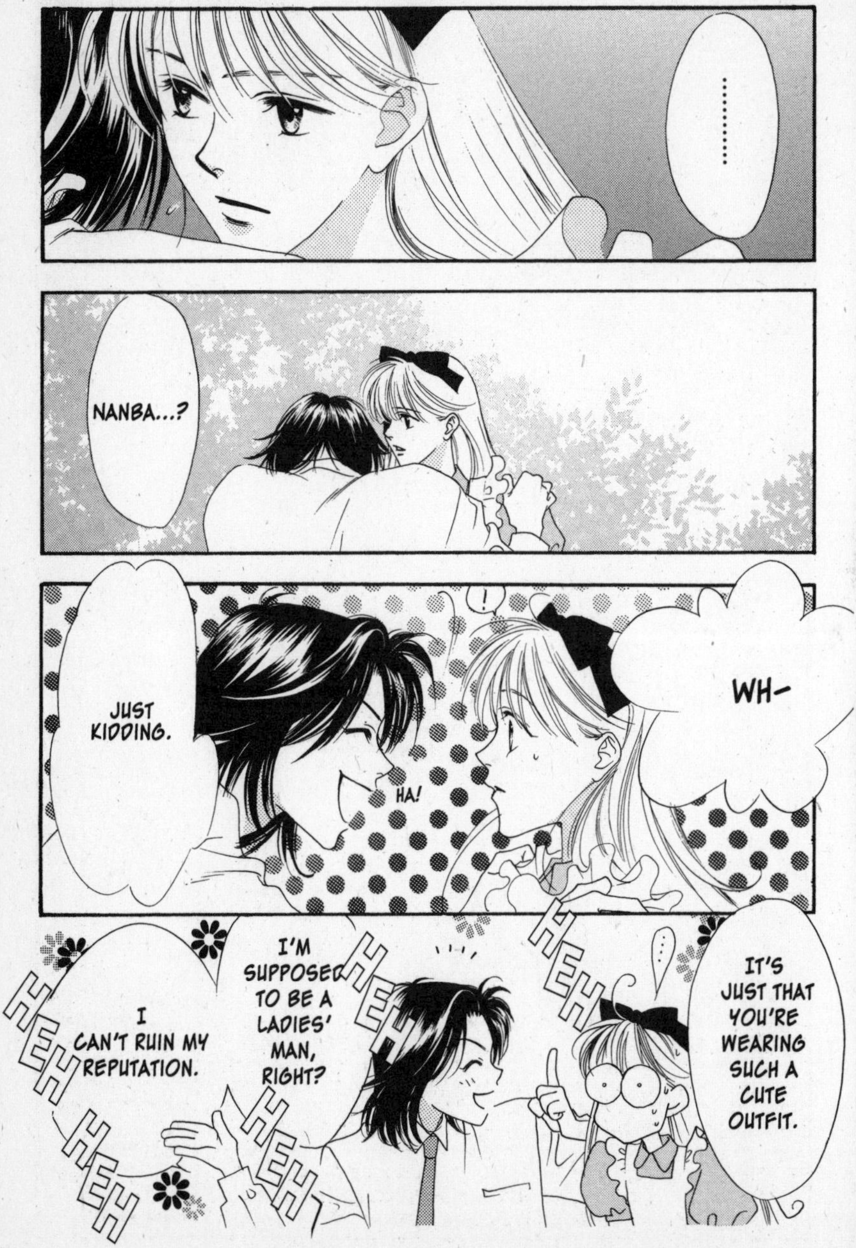
......
NANBA...?
WH-
!
JUST KIDDING.
HA!
IT'S JUST THAT YOU'RE WEARING SUCH A CUTE OUTFIT.
...
HEH HEH
I'M SUPPOSED TO BE A LADIES' MAN, RIGHT?
HEH HEH
I CAN'T RUIN MY REPUTATION.
HEH HEH

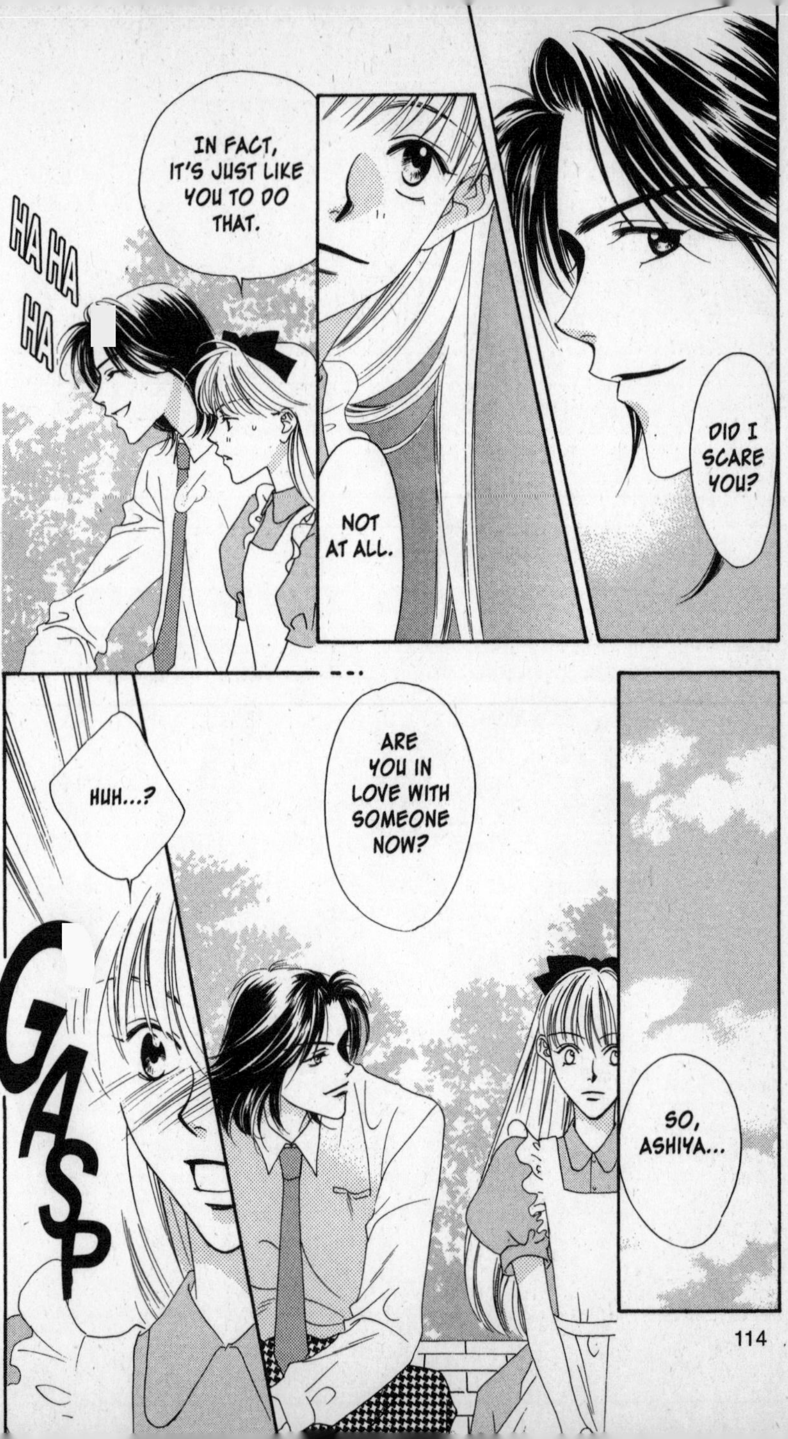
DID I SCARE YOU?
NOT AT ALL.
IN FACT, IT'S JUST LIKE YOU TO DO THAT.
HA HA HA
SO, ASHIYA...
ARE YOU IN LOVE WITH SOMEONE NOW?
HUH...?
GASP

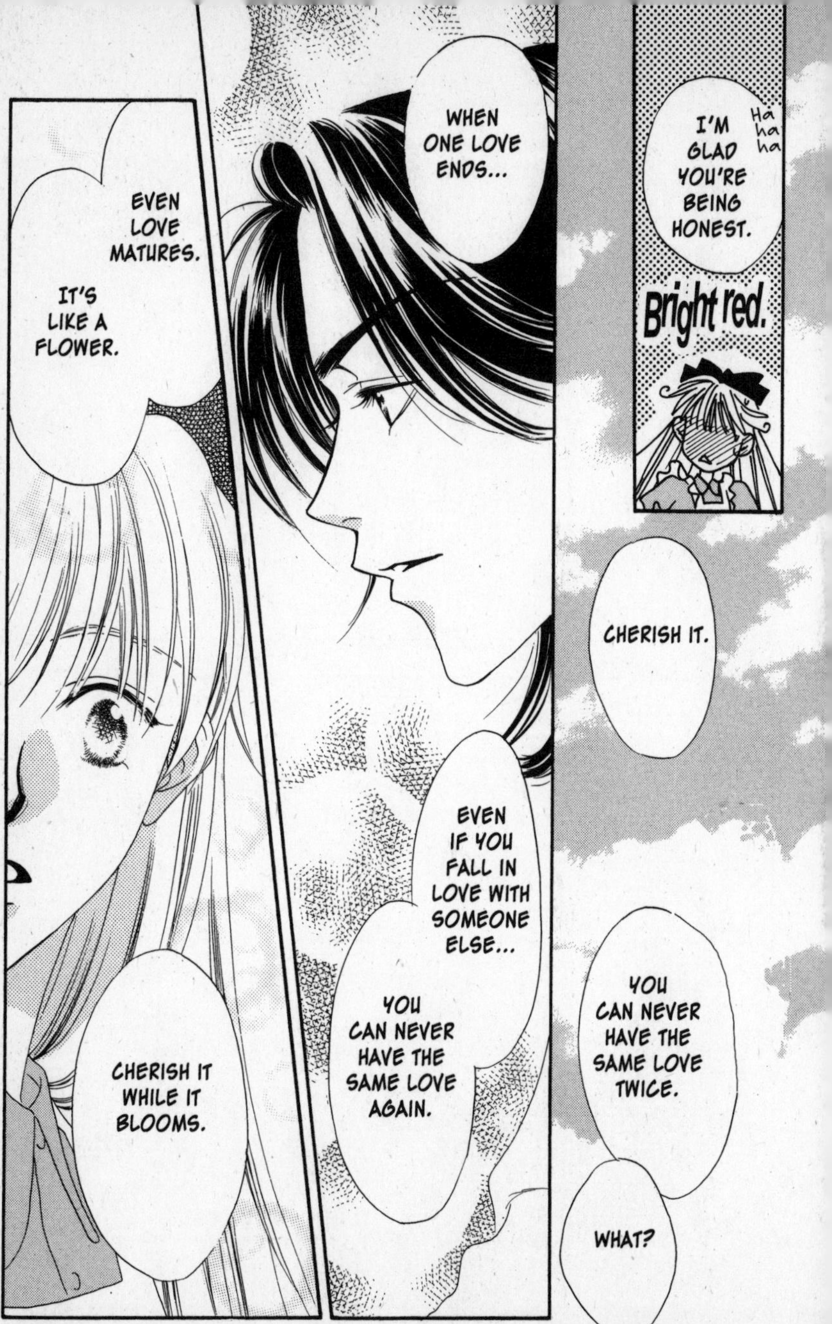

I'M GLAD YOU'RE BEING HONEST.
Ha ha ha
Bright red.
CHERISH IT.
YOU CAN NEVER HAVE THE SAME LOVE TWICE.
WHAT?
WHEN ONE LOVE ENDS...
EVEN IF YOU FALL IN LOVE WITH SOMEONE ELSE...
YOU CAN NEVER HAVE THE SAME LOVE AGAIN.
EVEN LOVE MATURES.
IT'S LIKE A FLOWER.
CHERISH IT WHILE IT BLOOMS.

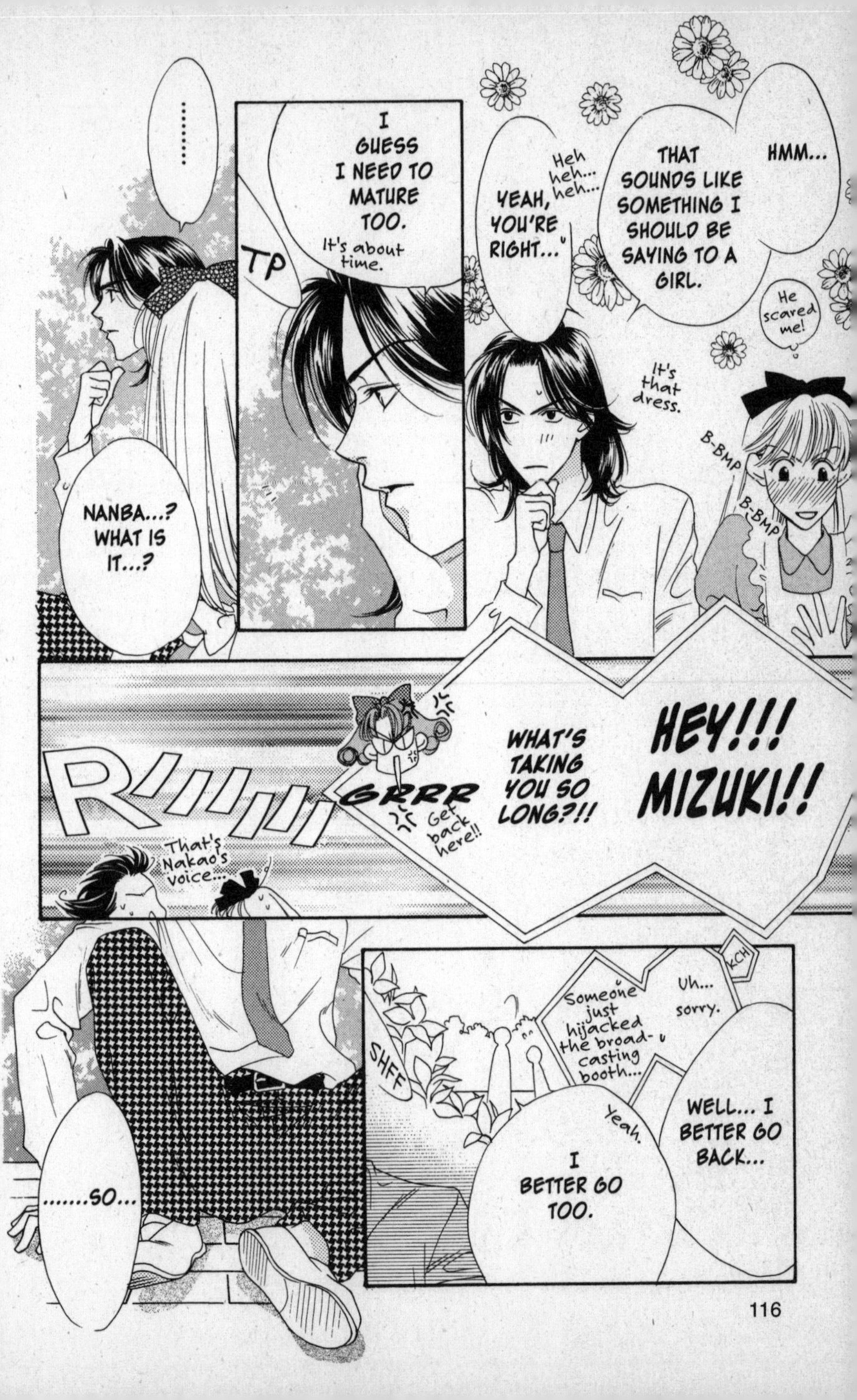
HMM...
THAT SOUNDS LIKE SOMETHING I SHOULD BE SAYING TO A GIRL.
He scared me!
YEAH, YOU'RE RIGHT...
Heh heh... heh...
It's that dress.
B-BMP
B-BMP
I GUESS I NEED TO MATURE TOO.
It's about time.
TP
......
NANBA...? WHAT IS IT...?
HEY!!! MIZUKI!!
WHAT'S TAKING YOU SO LONG?!!
GRRR
Get back here!!
RIIIIII
That's Nakao's voice...
KCH
Uh... sorry.
Someone just hijacked the broad-casting booth...
WELL... I BETTER GO BACK...
Yeah.
I BETTER GO TOO.
SHFF
.......SO...

Whispered Secrets
Karate vs. Music

THE CHARACTERS TENNOJI AND KUJO COME FROM MY LOVE FOR KARATE. IN K1, I LIKE ANDY HUG. IN KYOKUSHIN KARATE I LIKE GLAUBE FEITOSA. HIS ANKLE CHOP AND UPPER FLIP KICKS ARE REALLY COOL. I THINK THIN "REPLICANT" TYPE BODIES ARE BEAUTIFUL, BUT WELL-DEFINED MUSCULAR BODIES ARE NICE TOO. AND OSCAR M. HIMEJIMA IS BASED ON A SINGER FROM MALICE MIZER, NAMED GACKT. WHEN THEY FIRST CAME OUT SOME PEOPLE LIKED THEM AND SOME PEOPLE DIDN'T, BUT NOW THEY'RE GETTING VERY POPULAR!! (HE HAS A NICE VOICE...AND I'VE GOT A VOICE FETISH.)

But Himejima's voice is probably more like Koyasu Takehi-to's.

WHY SHOULD I HAVE TO HIDE...?

YOU'RE LATE!

eh heh heh...

SORRY!

Fairyla

BLAH BLAH

Look, it's Alice in Wonderland!

Hey Alice!

MOB!!

Oo! Cute!

117

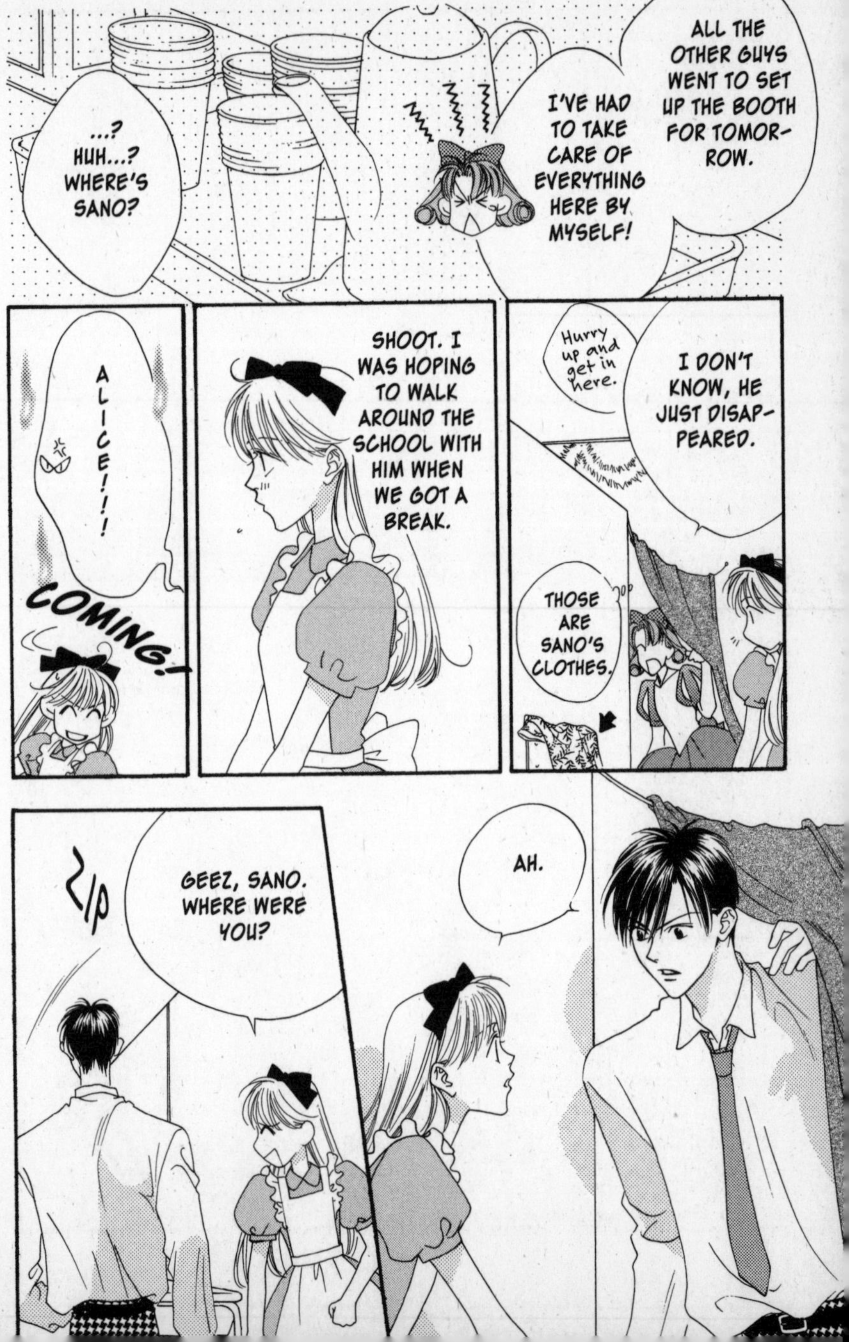

ALL THE OTHER GUYS WENT TO SET UP THE BOOTH FOR TOMOR-ROW.
I'VE HAD TO TAKE CARE OF EVERYTHING HERE BY MYSELF!
...? HUH...? WHERE'S SANO?
I DON'T KNOW, HE JUST DISAP-PEARED.
Hurry up and get in here.
THOSE ARE SANO'S CLOTHES.
SHOOT. I WAS HOPING TO WALK AROUND THE SCHOOL WITH HIM WHEN WE GOT A BREAK.
ALICE!!!
COMING!
AH.
ZIP
GEEZ, SANO. WHERE WERE YOU?

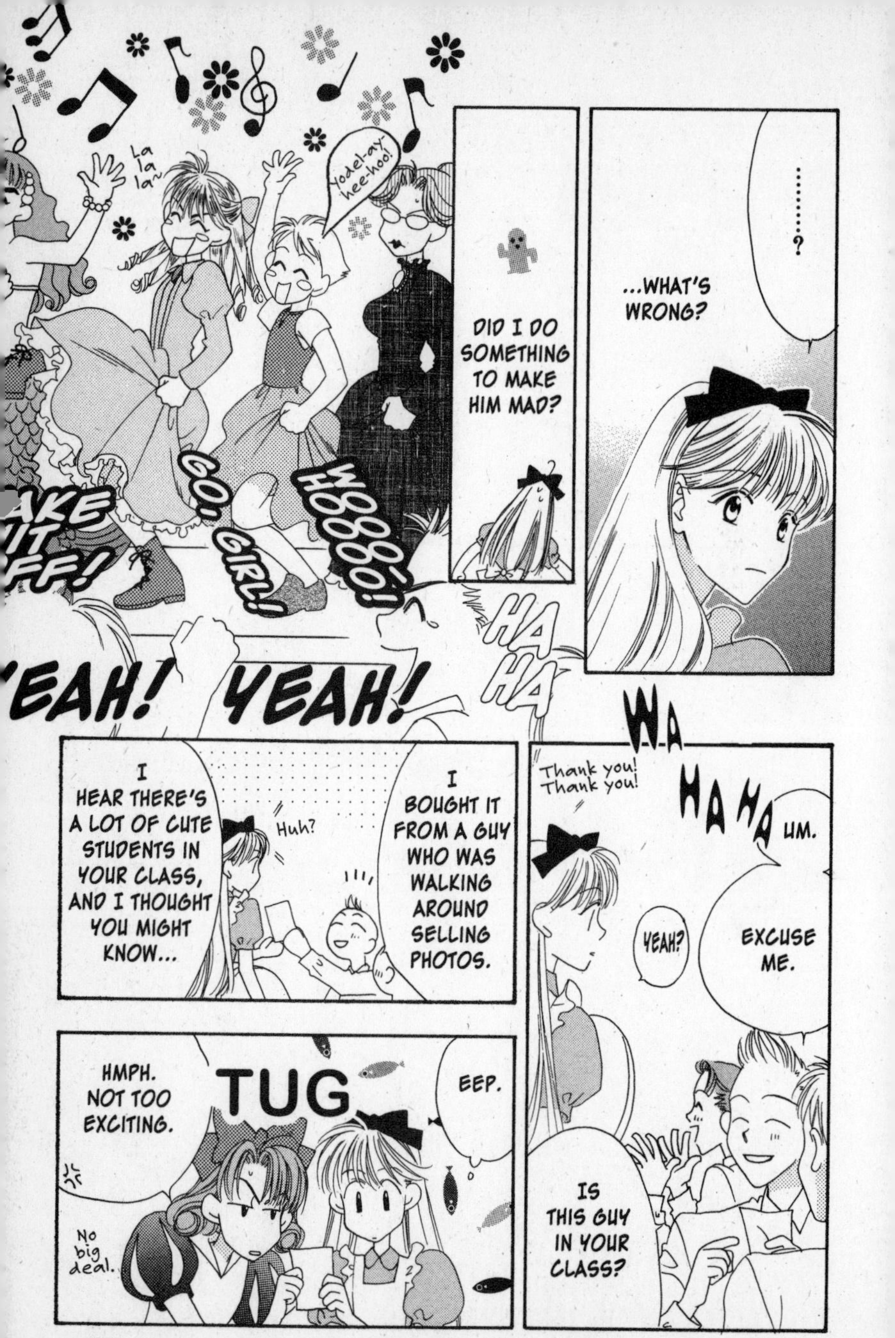
.......?
...WHAT'S WRONG?
DID I DO SOMETHING TO MAKE HIM MAD?
Yodel-ay-hee-hoo!
La la la~
WOOOO!
GO, GIRL!
AKE IT FF!
HA HA
YEAH! YEAH!
WA HA HA HA
UM.
Thank you! Thank you!
EXCUSE ME.
YEAH?
IS THIS GUY IN YOUR CLASS?
I BOUGHT IT FROM A GUY WHO WAS WALKING AROUND SELLING PHOTOS.
Huh?
I HEAR THERE'S A LOT OF CUTE STUDENTS IN YOUR CLASS, AND I THOUGHT YOU MIGHT KNOW...
EEP.
TUG
HMPH. NOT TOO EXCITING.
No big deal.

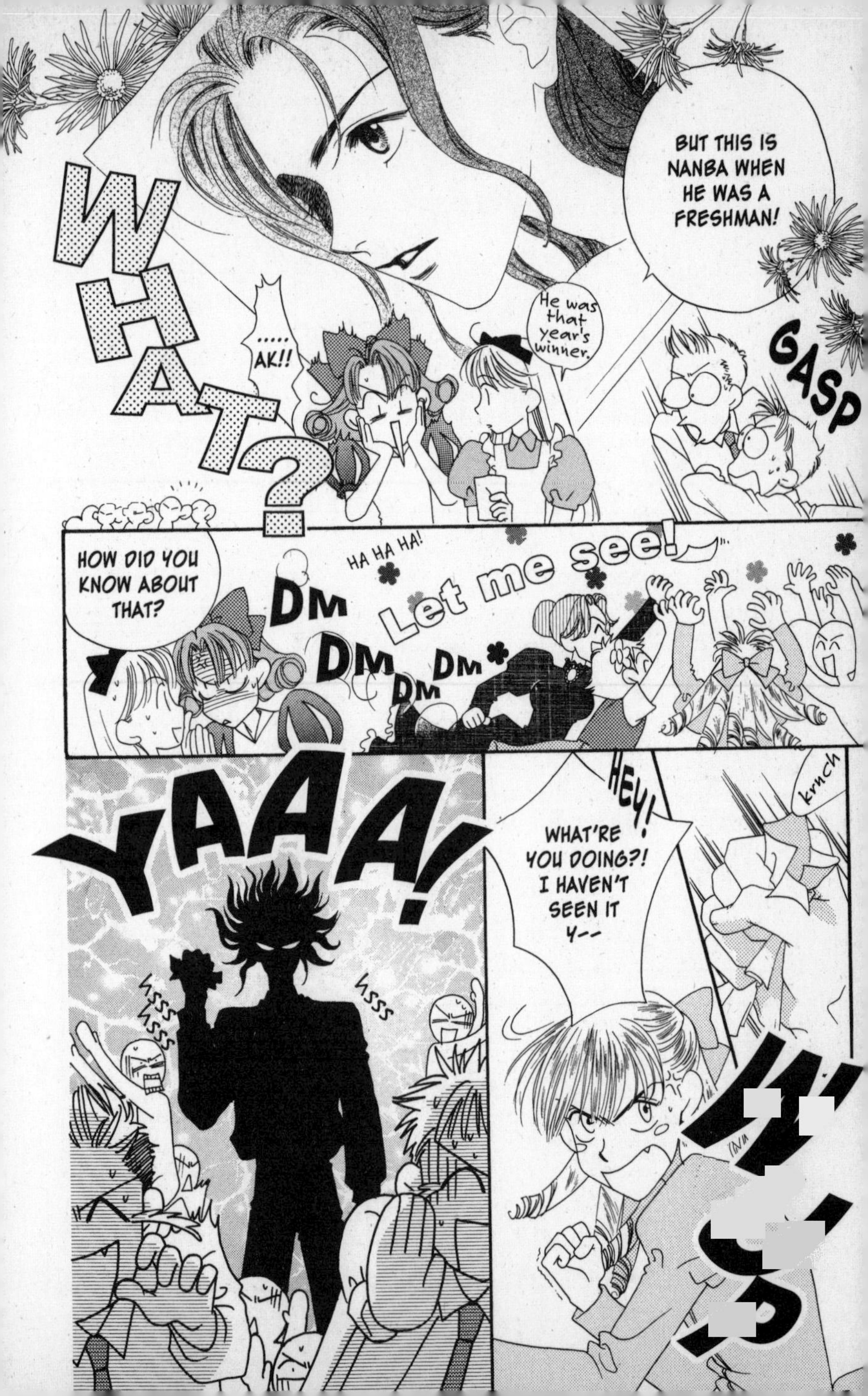
BUT THIS IS NANBA WHEN HE WAS A FRESHMAN!
GASP
He was that year's winner.
.....AK!!
WHAT?
Let me see!
HA HA HA!
DM DM DM DM
HOW DID YOU KNOW ABOUT THAT?
krunch
HEY!
WHAT'RE YOU DOING?! I HAVEN'T SEEN IT Y--
YAAAA!
hsss hsss
hsss

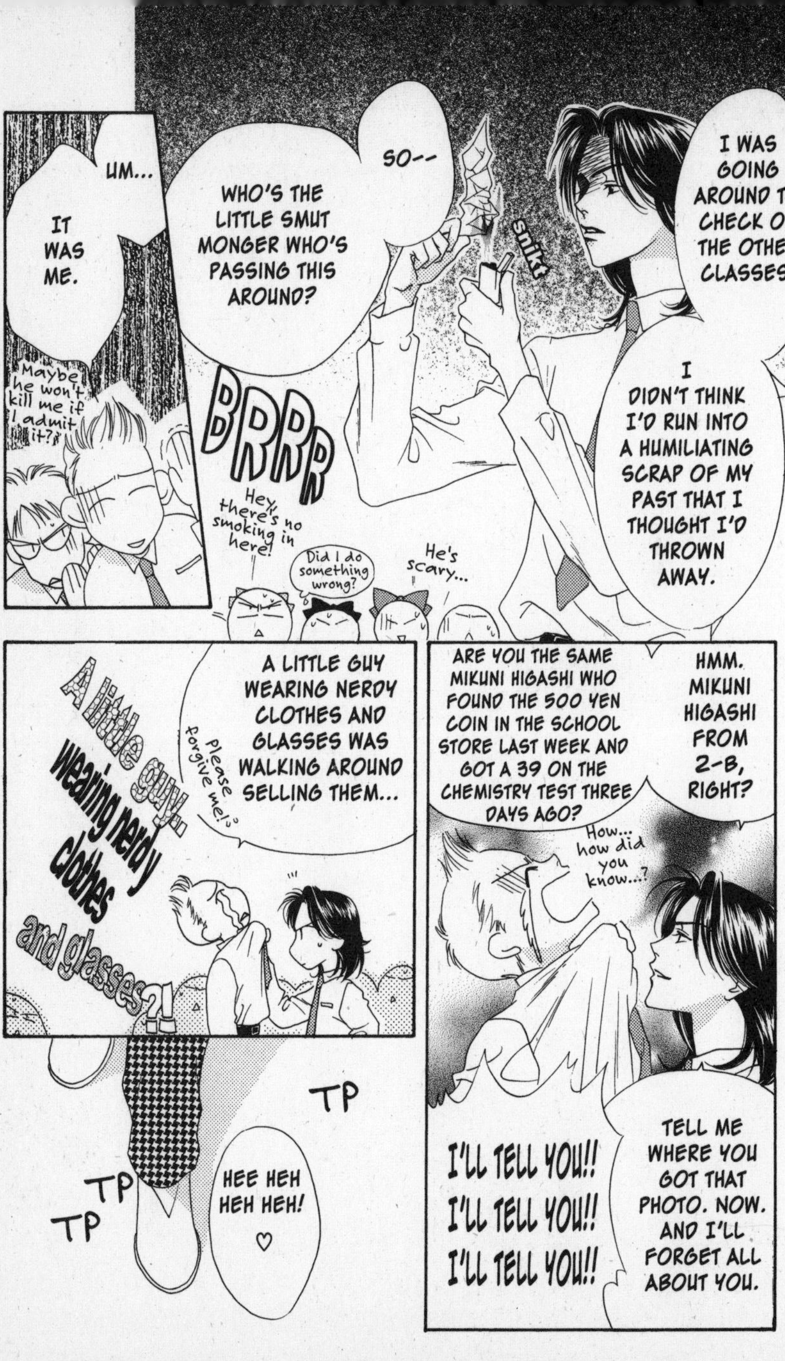
I WAS GOING AROUND TO CHECK ON THE OTHER CLASSES.
snikt
I DIDN'T THINK I'D RUN INTO A HUMILIATING SCRAP OF MY PAST THAT I THOUGHT I'D THROWN AWAY.
SO--
WHO'S THE LITTLE SMUT MONGER WHO'S PASSING THIS AROUND?
BRRRR
Hey, there's no smoking in here!
Did I do something wrong?
He's scary...
UM...
IT WAS ME.
Maybe he won't kill me if I admit it?
HMM. MIKUNI HIGASHI FROM 2-B, RIGHT?
ARE YOU THE SAME MIKUNI HIGASHI WHO FOUND THE 500 YEN COIN IN THE SCHOOL STORE LAST WEEK AND GOT A 39 ON THE CHEMISTRY TEST THREE DAYS AGO?
How... how did you know...?
TELL ME WHERE YOU GOT THAT PHOTO. NOW. AND I'LL FORGET ALL ABOUT YOU.
I'LL TELL YOU!! I'LL TELL YOU!! I'LL TELL YOU!!
A LITTLE GUY WEARING NERDY CLOTHES AND GLASSES WAS WALKING AROUND SELLING THEM...
Please forgive me!
A little guy, wearing nerdy clothes and glasses?!
TP
HEE HEH HEH HEH! ♡
TP TP

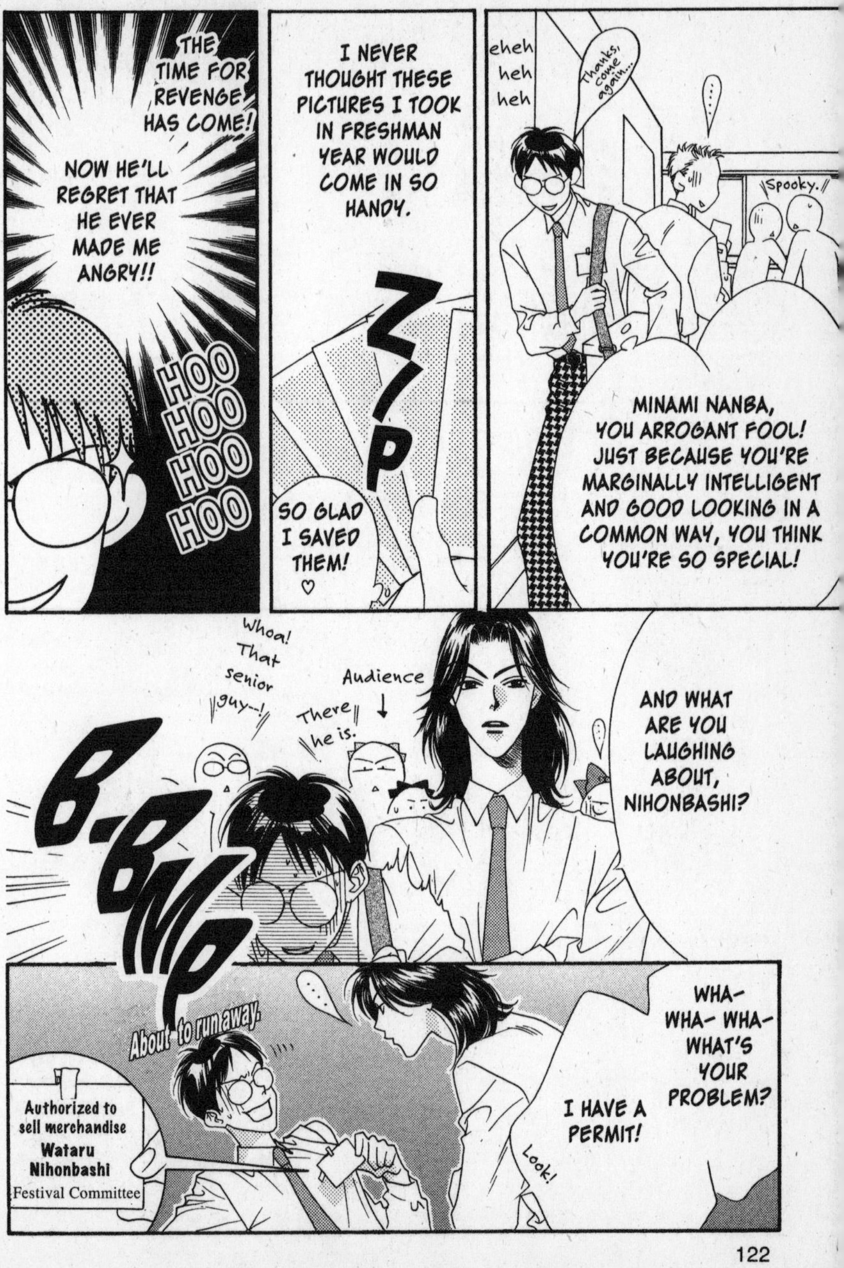
eheh heh heh
Thanks, come again...
!
Spooky.
MINAMI NANBA, YOU ARROGANT FOOL! JUST BECAUSE YOU'RE MARGINALLY INTELLIGENT AND GOOD LOOKING IN A COMMON WAY, YOU THINK YOU'RE SO SPECIAL!
I NEVER THOUGHT THESE PICTURES I TOOK IN FRESHMAN YEAR WOULD COME IN SO HANDY.
ZIP
SO GLAD I SAVED THEM! ♡
THE TIME FOR REVENGE HAS COME!
NOW HE'LL REGRET THAT HE EVER MADE ME ANGRY!!
HOO HOO HOO HOO
AND WHAT ARE YOU LAUGHING ABOUT, NIHONBASHI?
Audience
There he is.
Whoa! That senior guy--!
B-BMP
WHA- WHA- WHA- WHAT'S YOUR PROBLEM?
I HAVE A PERMIT!
Look!
About to run away.
Authorized to sell merchandise
Wataru Nihonbashi
Festival Committee

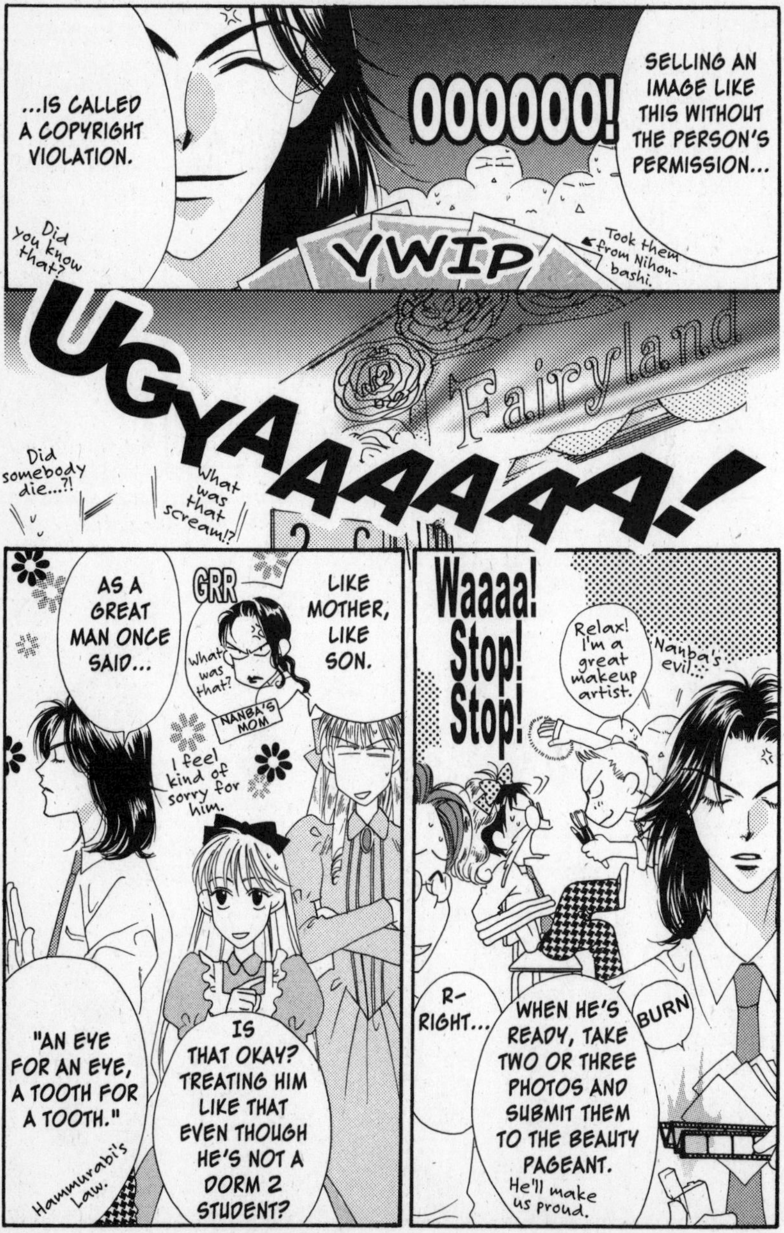

SELLING AN IMAGE LIKE THIS WITHOUT THE PERSON'S PERMISSION...
OOOOOO!
Took them from Nihon-bashi.
YWIP
...IS CALLED A COPYRIGHT VIOLATION.
Did you know that?
UGYAAAAAA!
Fairyland
What was that scream!?
Did somebody die...?!
Waaaa! Stop! Stop!
Nanba's evil...
Relax! I'm a great makeup artist.
BURN
WHEN HE'S READY, TAKE TWO OR THREE PHOTOS AND SUBMIT THEM TO THE BEAUTY PAGEANT.
He'll make us proud.
R-RIGHT...
LIKE MOTHER, LIKE SON.
GRR
What was that?
NANBA'S MOM
AS A GREAT MAN ONCE SAID...
I feel kind of sorry for him.
IS THAT OKAY? TREATING HIM LIKE THAT EVEN THOUGH HE'S NOT A DORM 2 STUDENT?
"AN EYE FOR AN EYE, A TOOTH FOR A TOOTH."
Hammurabi's Law.

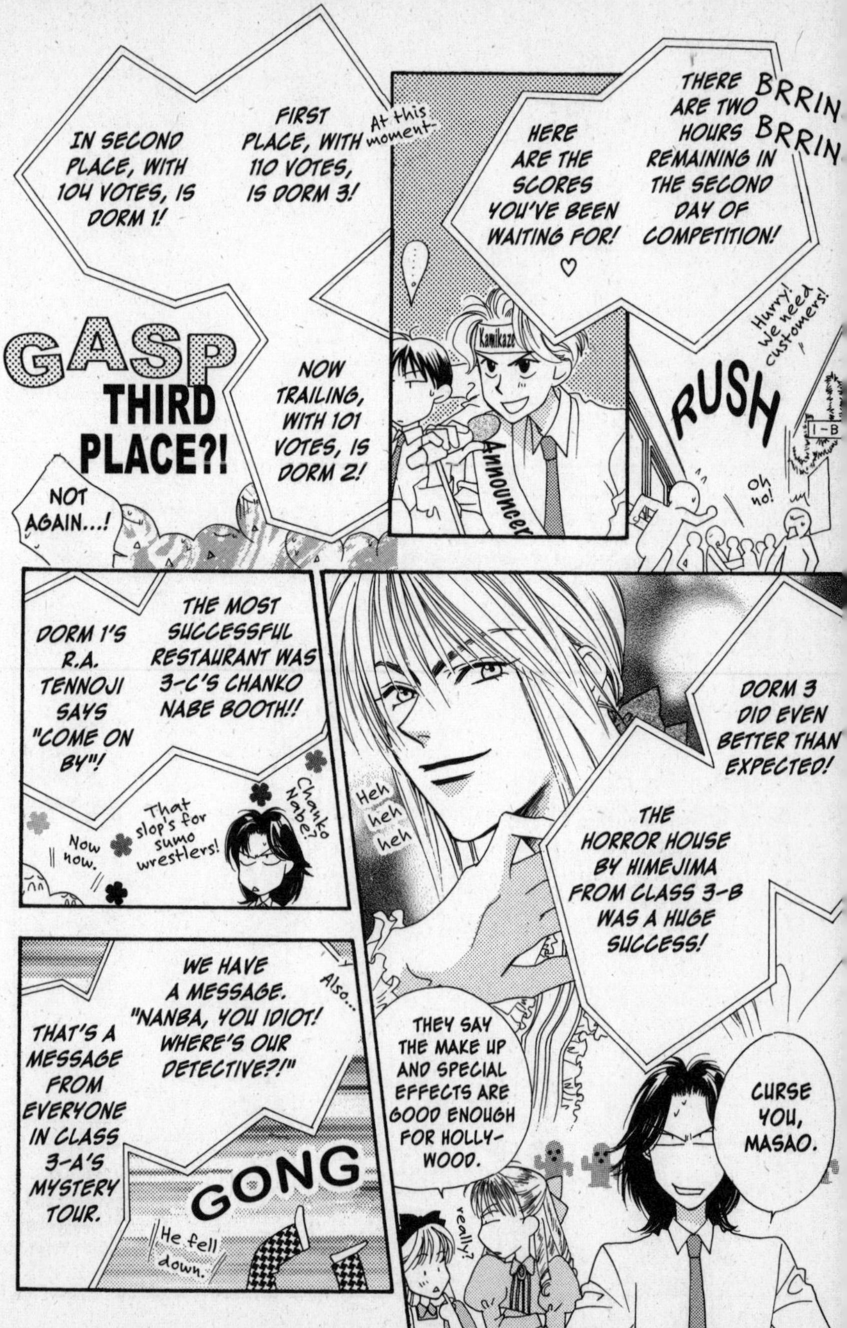
THERE ARE TWO HOURS REMAINING IN THE SECOND DAY OF COMPETITION!
BRRIN BRRIN
HERE ARE THE SCORES YOU'VE BEEN WAITING FOR! ♡
Hurry! We need customers!
RUSH
1-B
Oh no!
Kamikaze
Announcer
At this moment-
FIRST PLACE, WITH 110 VOTES, IS DORM 3!
IN SECOND PLACE, WITH 104 VOTES, IS DORM 1!
NOW TRAILING, WITH 101 VOTES, IS DORM 2!
GASP
THIRD PLACE?!
NOT AGAIN...!
DORM 3 DID EVEN BETTER THAN EXPECTED!
THE HORROR HOUSE BY HIMEJIMA FROM CLASS 3-B WAS A HUGE SUCCESS!
Heh heh heh
CURSE YOU, MASAO.
THEY SAY THE MAKE UP AND SPECIAL EFFECTS ARE GOOD ENOUGH FOR HOLLY-WOOD.
really?
THE MOST SUCCESSFUL RESTAURANT WAS 3-C'S CHANKO NABE BOOTH!!
DORM 1'S R.A. TENNOJI SAYS "COME ON BY"!
Chanko Nabe?
That slop's for sumo wrestlers!
Now now.
Also...
WE HAVE A MESSAGE. "NANBA, YOU IDIOT! WHERE'S OUR DETECTIVE?!"
THAT'S A MESSAGE FROM EVERYONE IN CLASS 3-A'S MYSTERY TOUR.
GONG
He fell down.

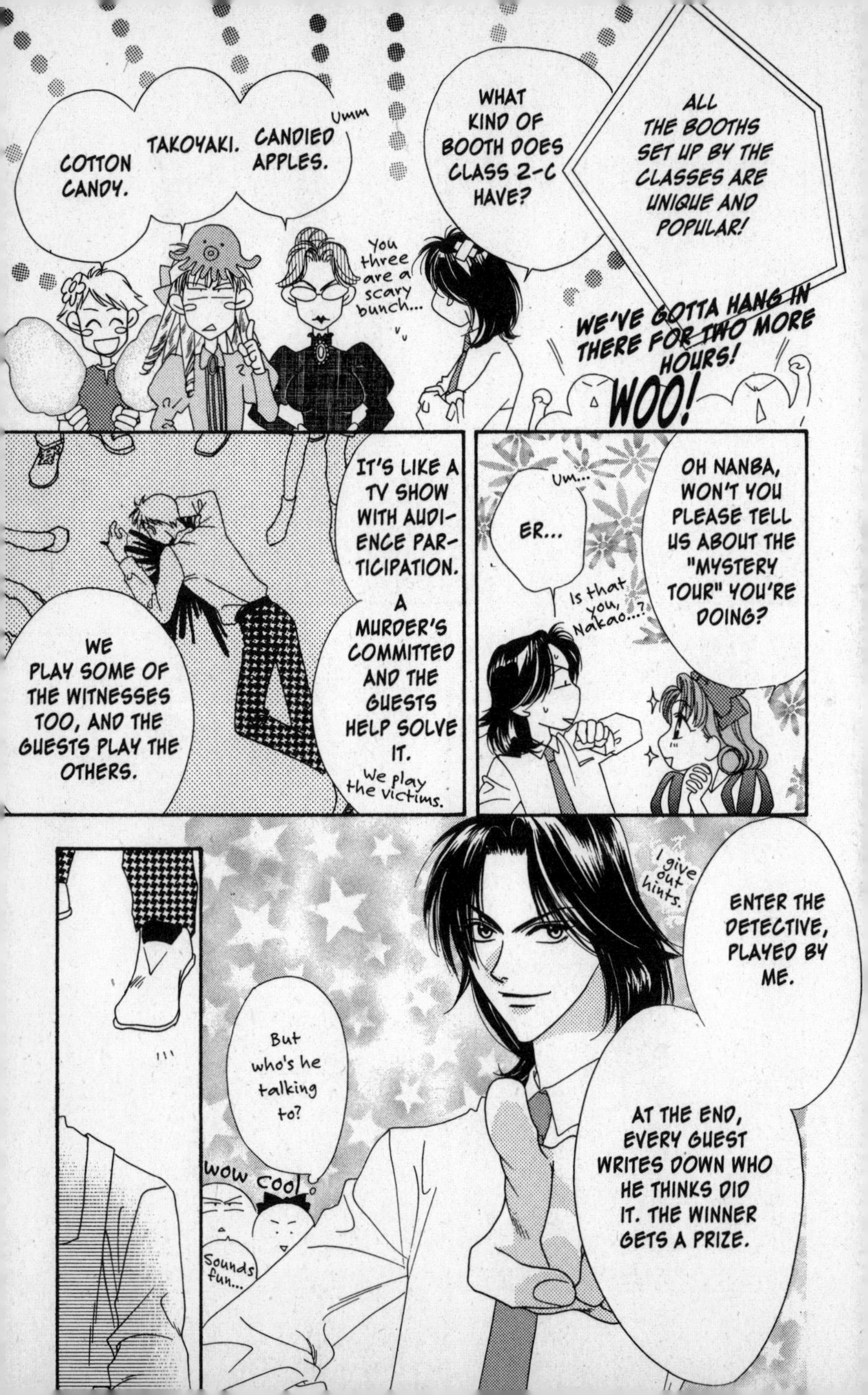
ALL THE BOOTHS SET UP BY THE CLASSES ARE UNIQUE AND POPULAR!
WE'VE GOTTA HANG IN THERE FOR TWO MORE HOURS!
WOO!
WHAT KIND OF BOOTH DOES CLASS 2-C HAVE?
Umm
CANDIED APPLES.
TAKOYAKI.
COTTON CANDY.
You three are a scary bunch...
OH NANBA, WON'T YOU PLEASE TELL US ABOUT THE "MYSTERY TOUR" YOU'RE DOING?
Um...
ER...
Is that you, Nakao...?
IT'S LIKE A TV SHOW WITH AUDI-ENCE PAR-TICIPATION.
A MURDER'S COMMITTED AND THE GUESTS HELP SOLVE IT.
We play the victims.
WE PLAY SOME OF THE WITNESSES TOO, AND THE GUESTS PLAY THE OTHERS.
I give out hints.
ENTER THE DETECTIVE, PLAYED BY ME.
AT THE END, EVERY GUEST WRITES DOWN WHO HE THINKS DID IT. THE WINNER GETS A PRIZE.
But who's he talking to?
WOW COOL
Sounds fun...

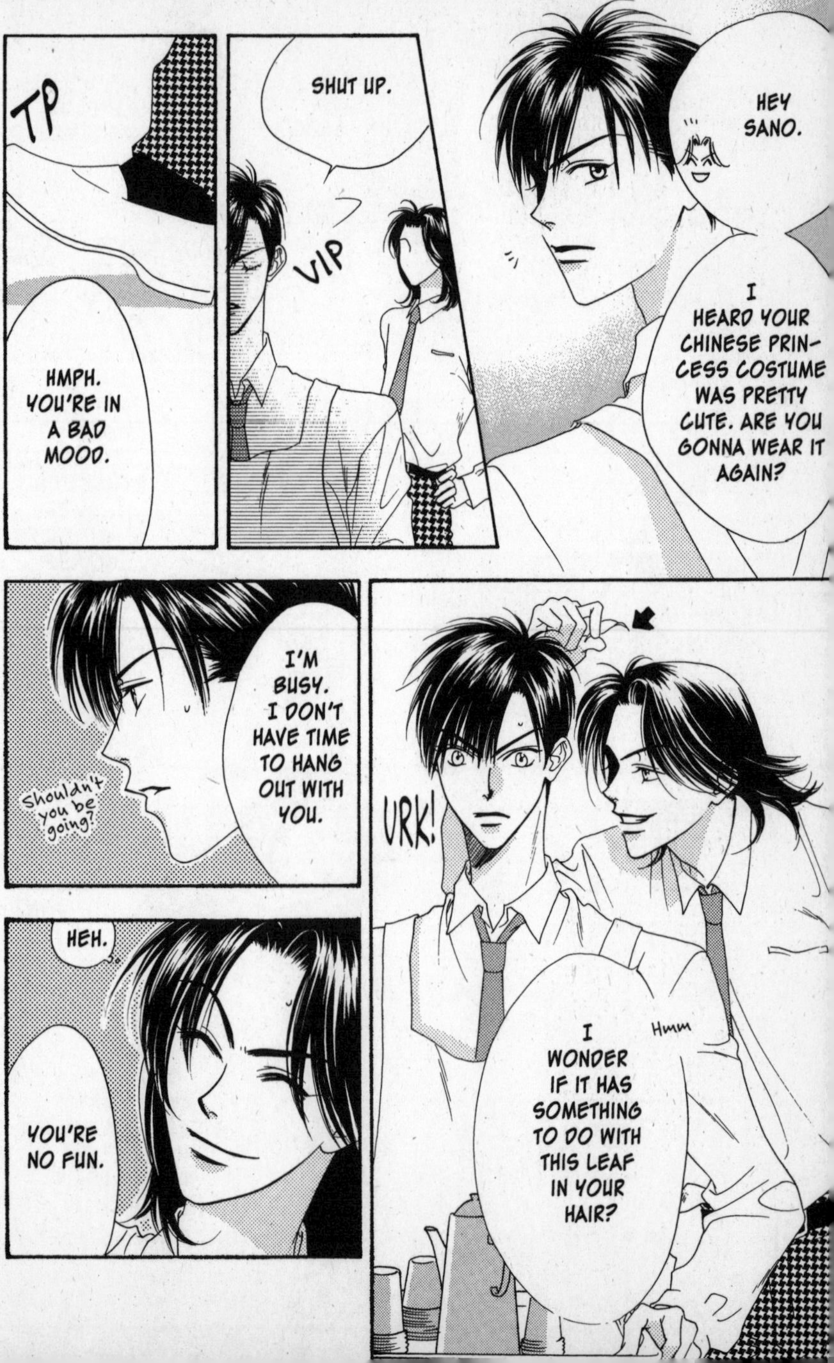
HEY SANO.
I HEARD YOUR CHINESE PRINCESS COSTUME WAS PRETTY CUTE. ARE YOU GONNA WEAR IT AGAIN?
SHUT UP.
VIP
TP
HMPH. YOU'RE IN A BAD MOOD.
URK!
Hmm
I WONDER IF IT HAS SOMETHING TO DO WITH THIS LEAF IN YOUR HAIR?
I'M BUSY. I DON'T HAVE TIME TO HANG OUT WITH YOU.
Shouldn't you be going?
HEH.
YOU'RE NO FUN.

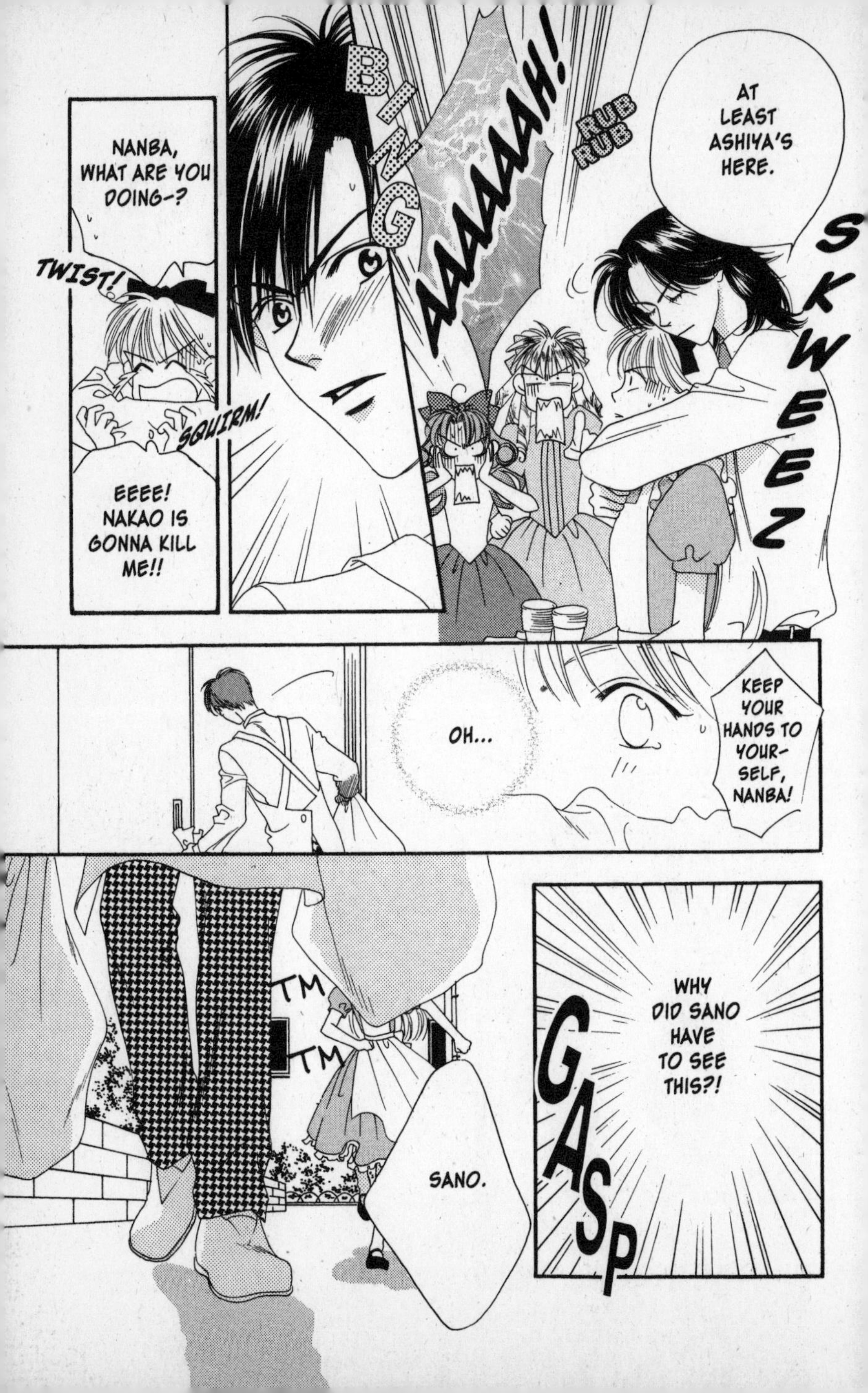
AT LEAST ASHIYA'S HERE.
SKWEEZ
RUB RUB
AAAAAH!
BING
NANBA, WHAT ARE YOU DOING-?
TWIST!
SQUIRM!
EEEE! NAKAO IS GONNA KILL ME!!
KEEP YOUR HANDS TO YOUR-SELF, NANBA!
OH...
WHY DID SANO HAVE TO SEE THIS?!
GASP
SANO.
TM
TM

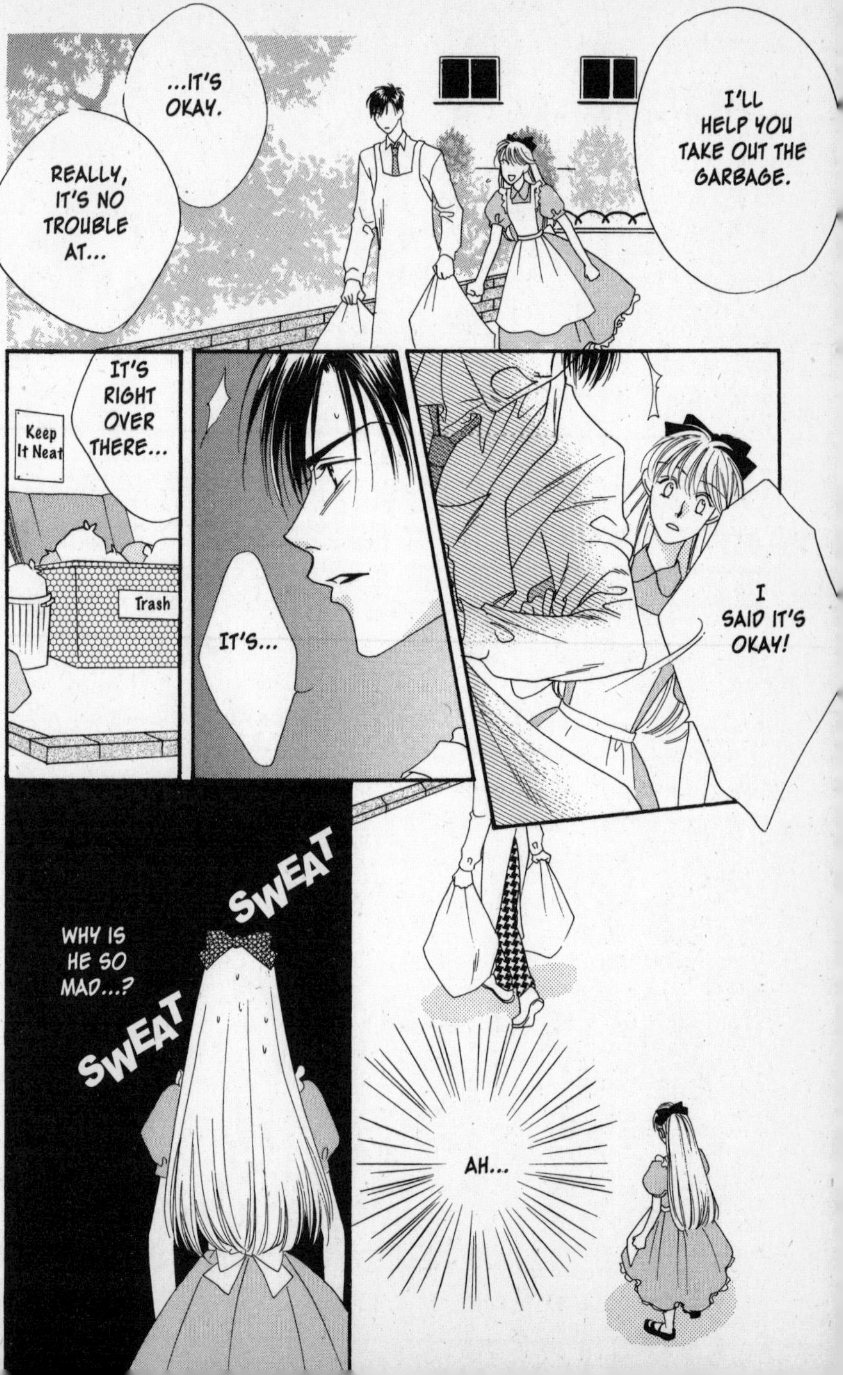
I'LL HELP YOU TAKE OUT THE GARBAGE.
...IT'S OKAY.
REALLY, IT'S NO TROUBLE AT...
I SAID IT'S OKAY!
IT'S...
IT'S RIGHT OVER THERE...
Keep It Neat
Trash
AH...
SWEAT
SWEAT
WHY IS HE SO MAD...?

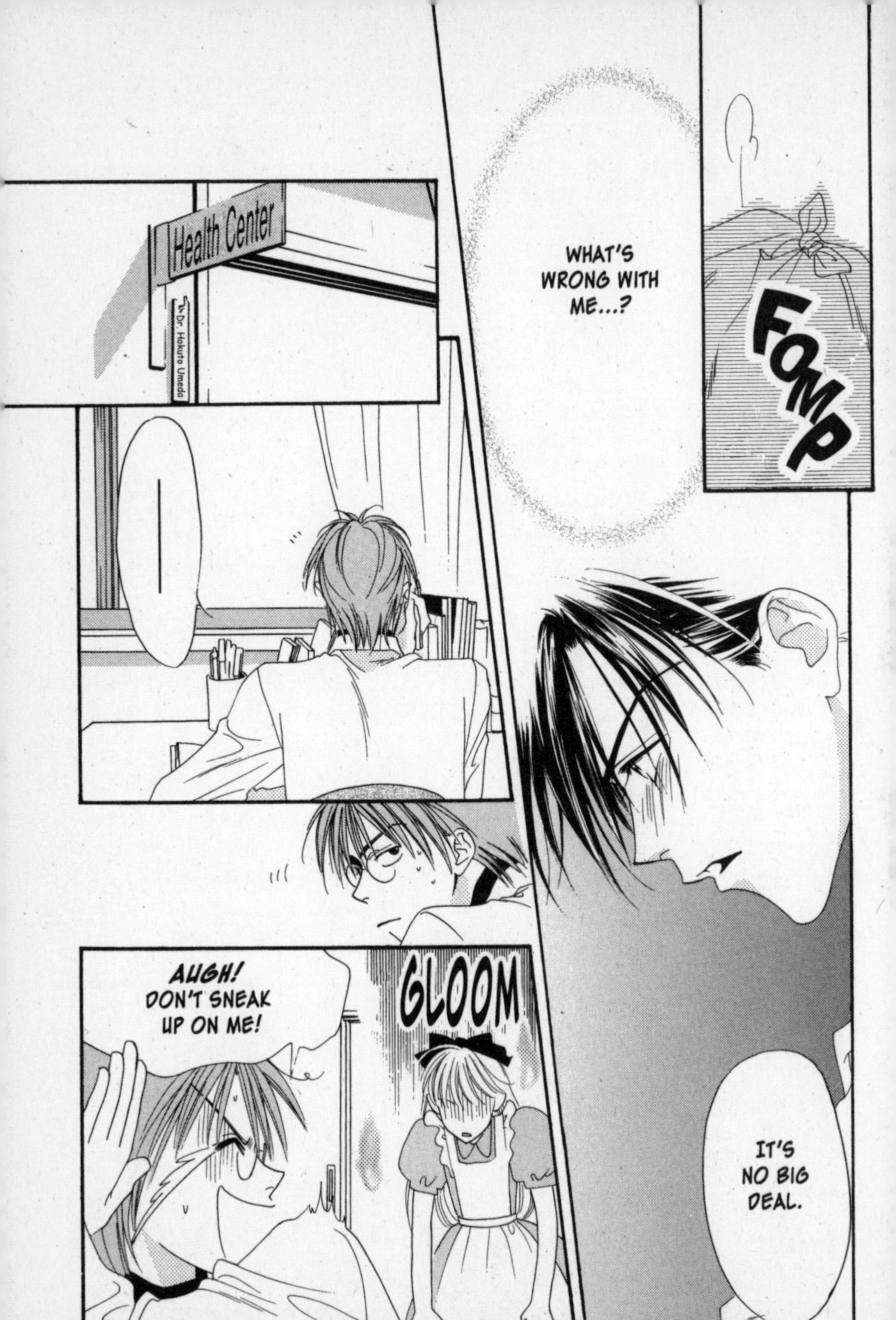
FOMP
WHAT'S WRONG WITH ME...?
IT'S NO BIG DEAL.
Health Center
Dr. Hokuto Umeda
AUGH! DON'T SNEAK UP ON ME!
GLOOM

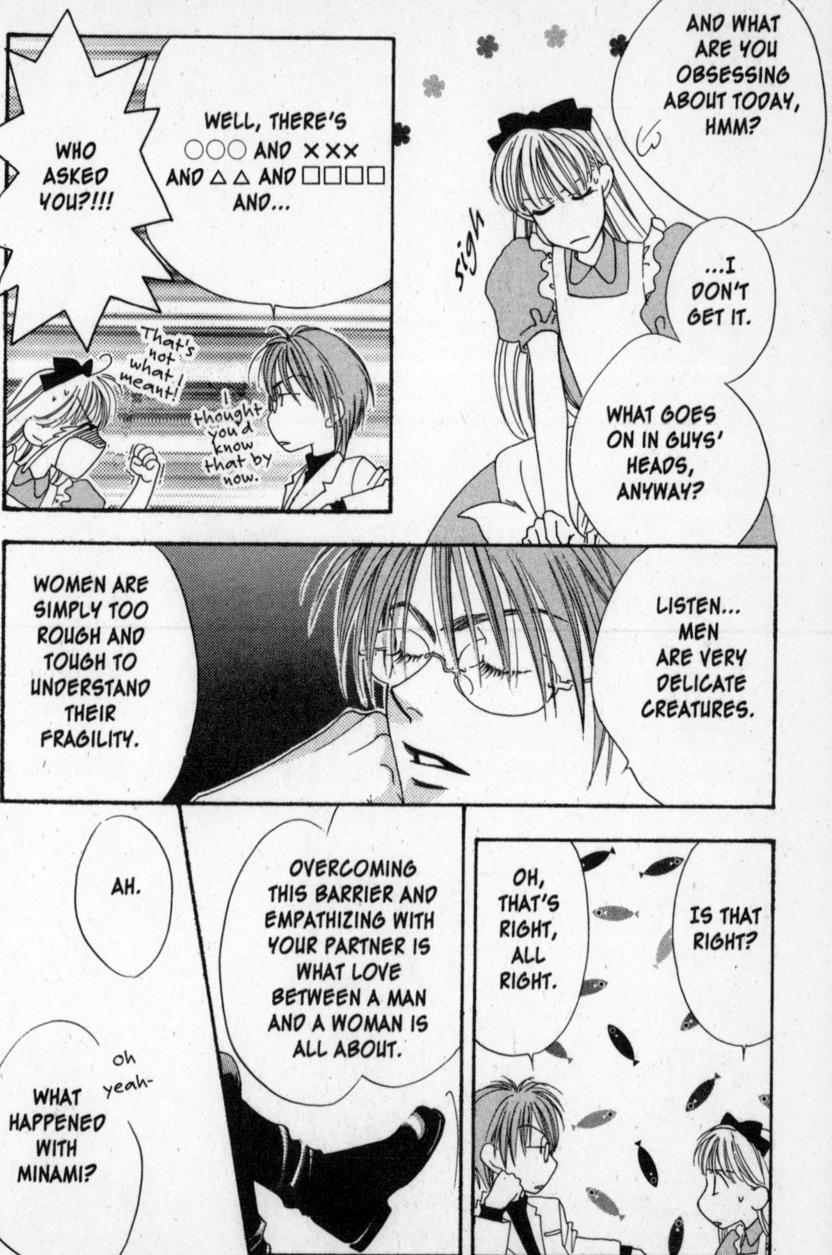
AND WHAT ARE YOU OBSESSING ABOUT TODAY, HMM?
sigh
...I DON'T GET IT.
WHAT GOES ON IN GUYS' HEADS, ANYWAY?
WELL, THERE'S ○○○ AND ××× AND △△ AND □□□□ AND...
WHO ASKED YOU?!!!
That's not what I meant!
I thought you'd know that by now.
LISTEN... MEN ARE VERY DELICATE CREATURES.
WOMEN ARE SIMPLY TOO ROUGH AND TOUGH TO UNDERSTAND THEIR FRAGILITY.
IS THAT RIGHT?
OH, THAT'S RIGHT, ALL RIGHT.
OVERCOMING THIS BARRIER AND EMPATHIZING WITH YOUR PARTNER IS WHAT LOVE BETWEEN A MAN AND A WOMAN IS ALL ABOUT.
AH.
oh yeah-
WHAT HAPPENED WITH MINAMI?

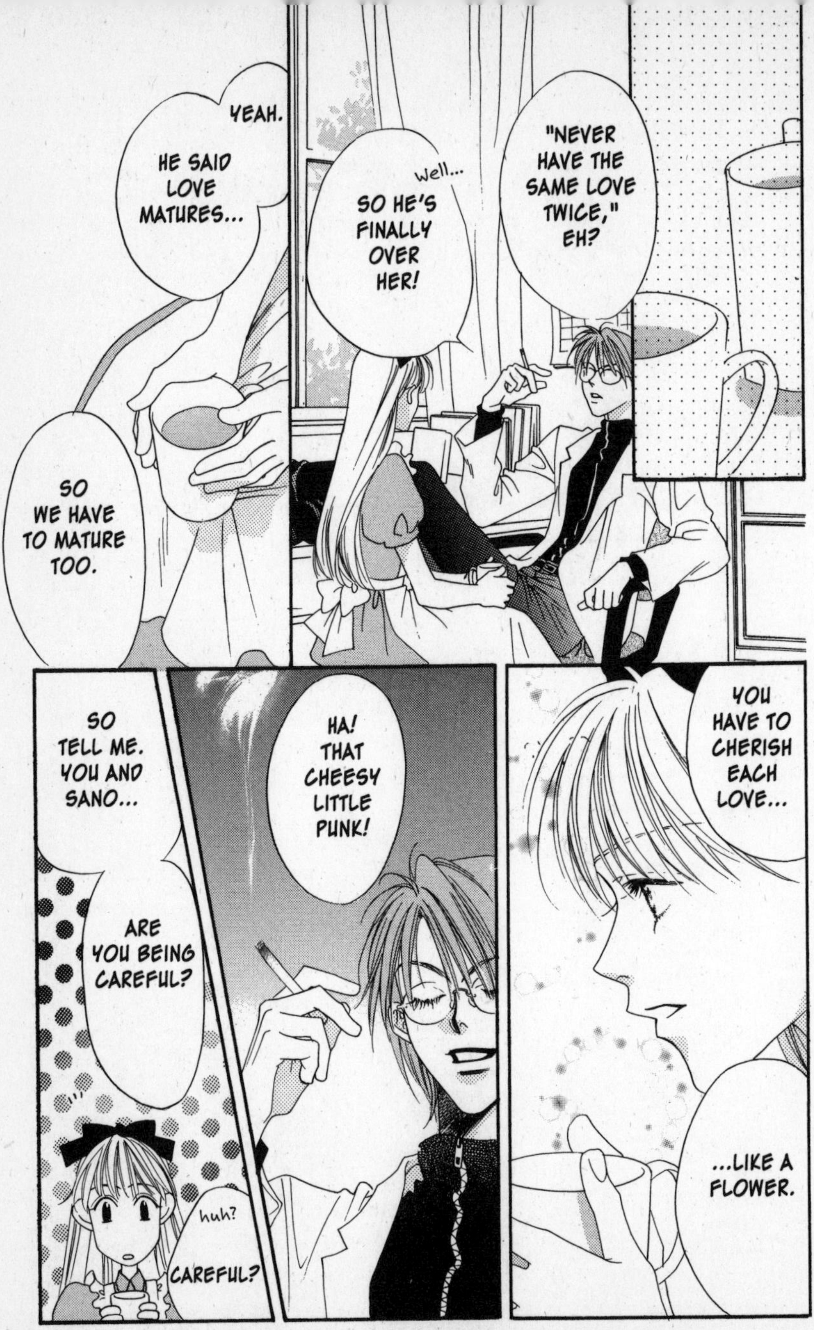
"NEVER HAVE THE SAME LOVE TWICE," EH?
Well...
SO HE'S FINALLY OVER HER!
YEAH.
HE SAID LOVE MATURES...
SO WE HAVE TO MATURE TOO.
YOU HAVE TO CHERISH EACH LOVE...
...LIKE A FLOWER.
HA! THAT CHEESY LITTLE PUNK!
SO TELL ME. YOU AND SANO...
ARE YOU BEING CAREFUL?
huh?
CAREFUL?

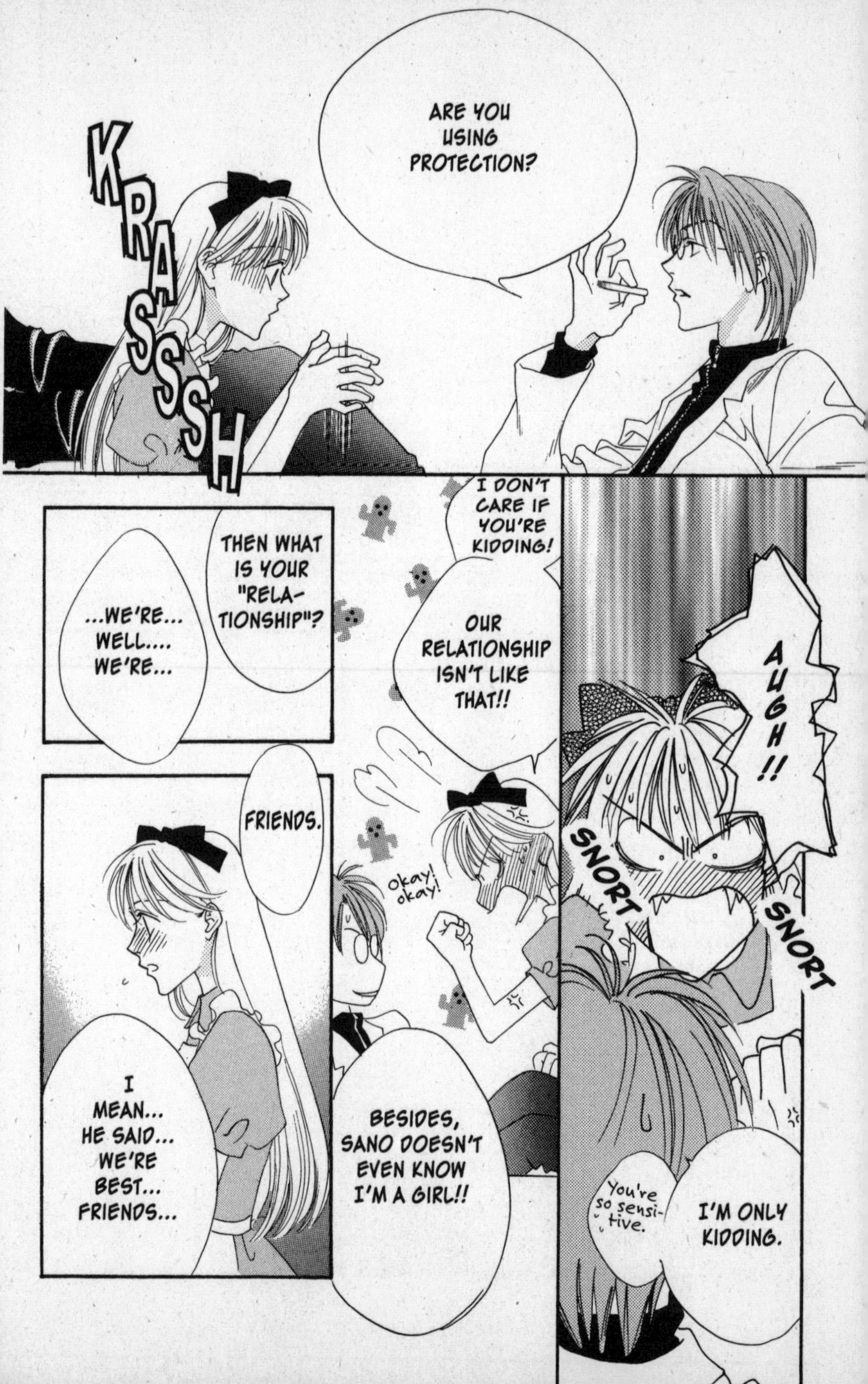
ARE YOU USING PROTECTION?
KRASSSH
AUGH!!
SNORT SNORT
I'M ONLY KIDDING.
You're so sensitive.
I DON'T CARE IF YOU'RE KIDDING!
OUR RELATIONSHIP ISN'T LIKE THAT!!
okay! okay!
BESIDES, SANO DOESN'T EVEN KNOW I'M A GIRL!!
THEN WHAT IS YOUR "RELATIONSHIP"?
...WE'RE... WELL.... WE'RE...
FRIENDS.
I MEAN... HE SAID... WE'RE BEST... FRIENDS...

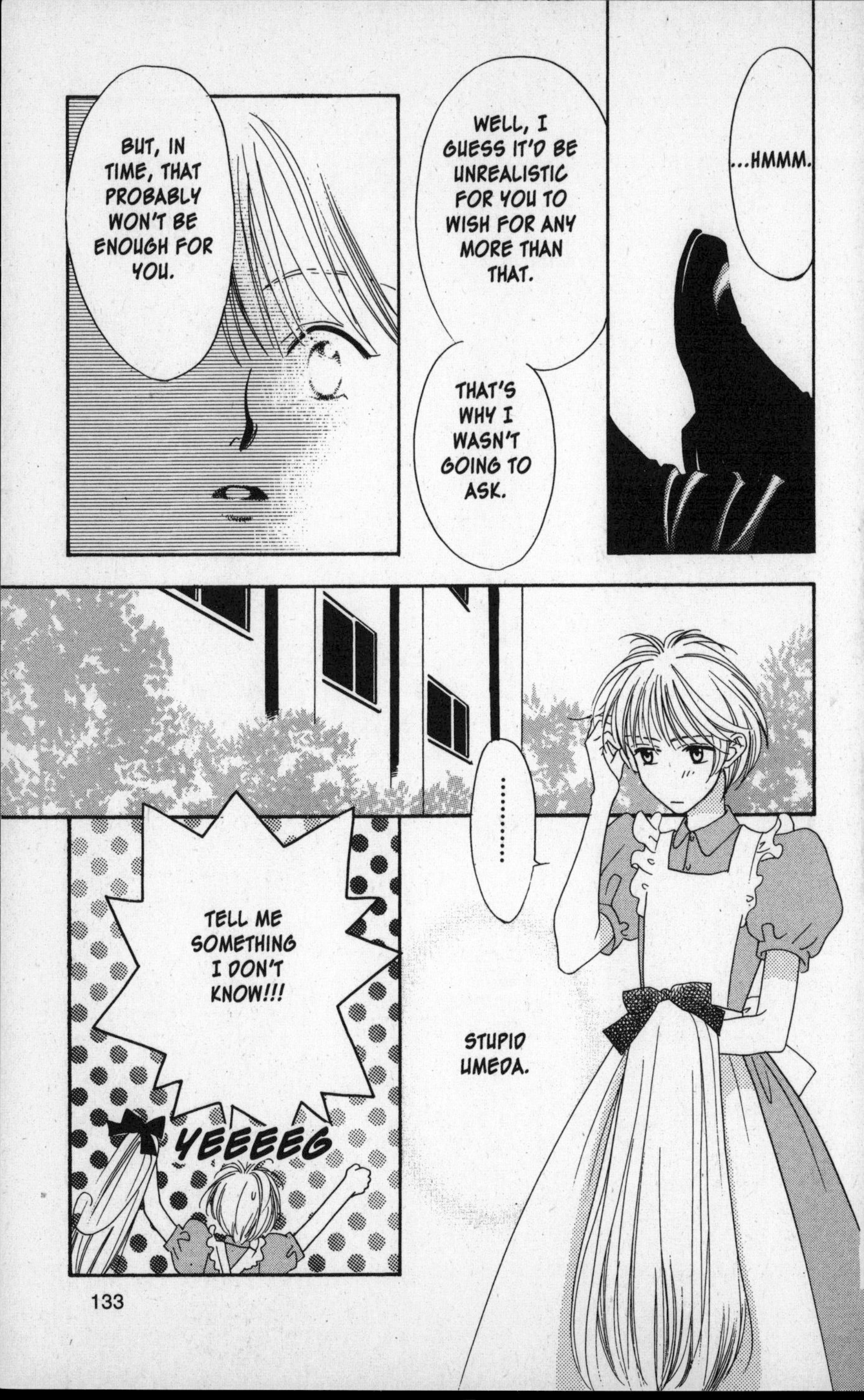
...HMMM.
WELL, I GUESS IT'D BE UNREALISTIC FOR YOU TO WISH FOR ANY MORE THAN THAT.
THAT'S WHY I WASN'T GOING TO ASK.
BUT, IN TIME, THAT PROBABLY WON'T BE ENOUGH FOR YOU.
....
STUPID UMEDA.
TELL ME SOMETHING I DON'T KNOW!!!
YEEEEG

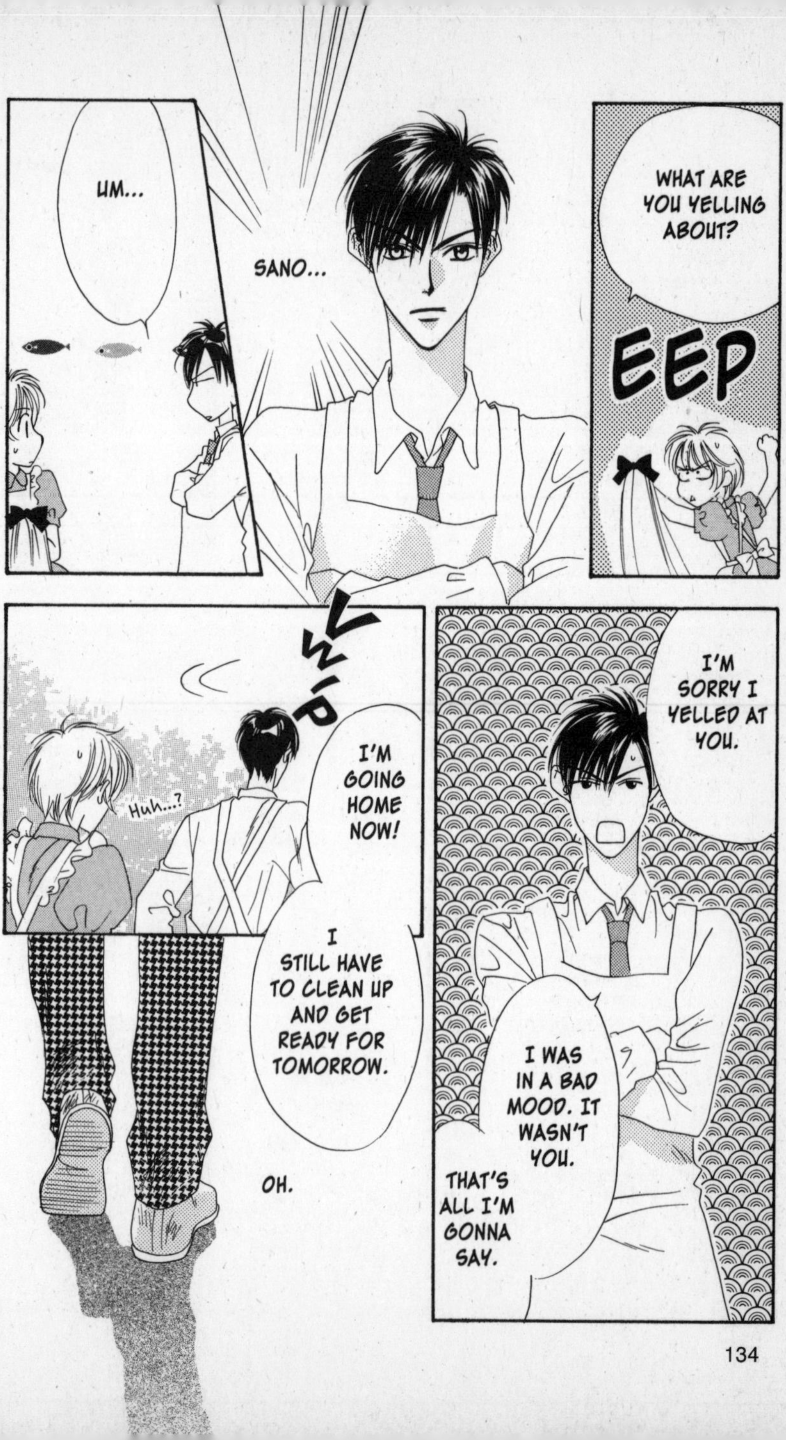
WHAT ARE YOU YELLING ABOUT?
EEP
SANO...
UM...
I'M SORRY I YELLED AT YOU.
I WAS IN A BAD MOOD. IT WASN'T YOU.
THAT'S ALL I'M GONNA SAY.
OH.
VWIP
I'M GOING HOME NOW!
Huh...?
I STILL HAVE TO CLEAN UP AND GET READY FOR TOMORROW.

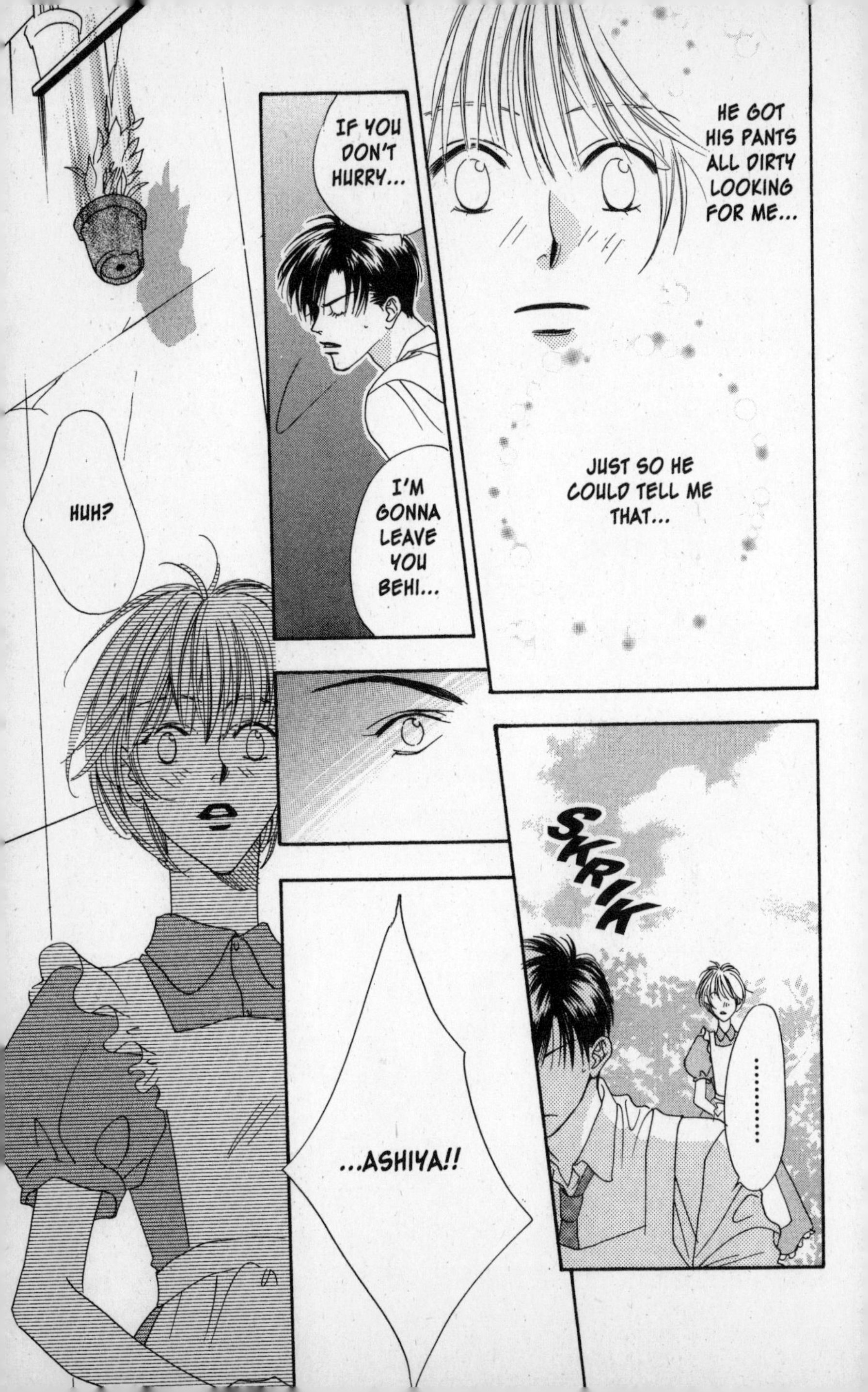
HE GOT HIS PANTS ALL DIRTY LOOKING FOR ME...
JUST SO HE COULD TELL ME THAT...
IF YOU DON'T HURRY...
I'M GONNA LEAVE YOU BEHI...
SKRIK
....
...ASHIYA!!
HUH?

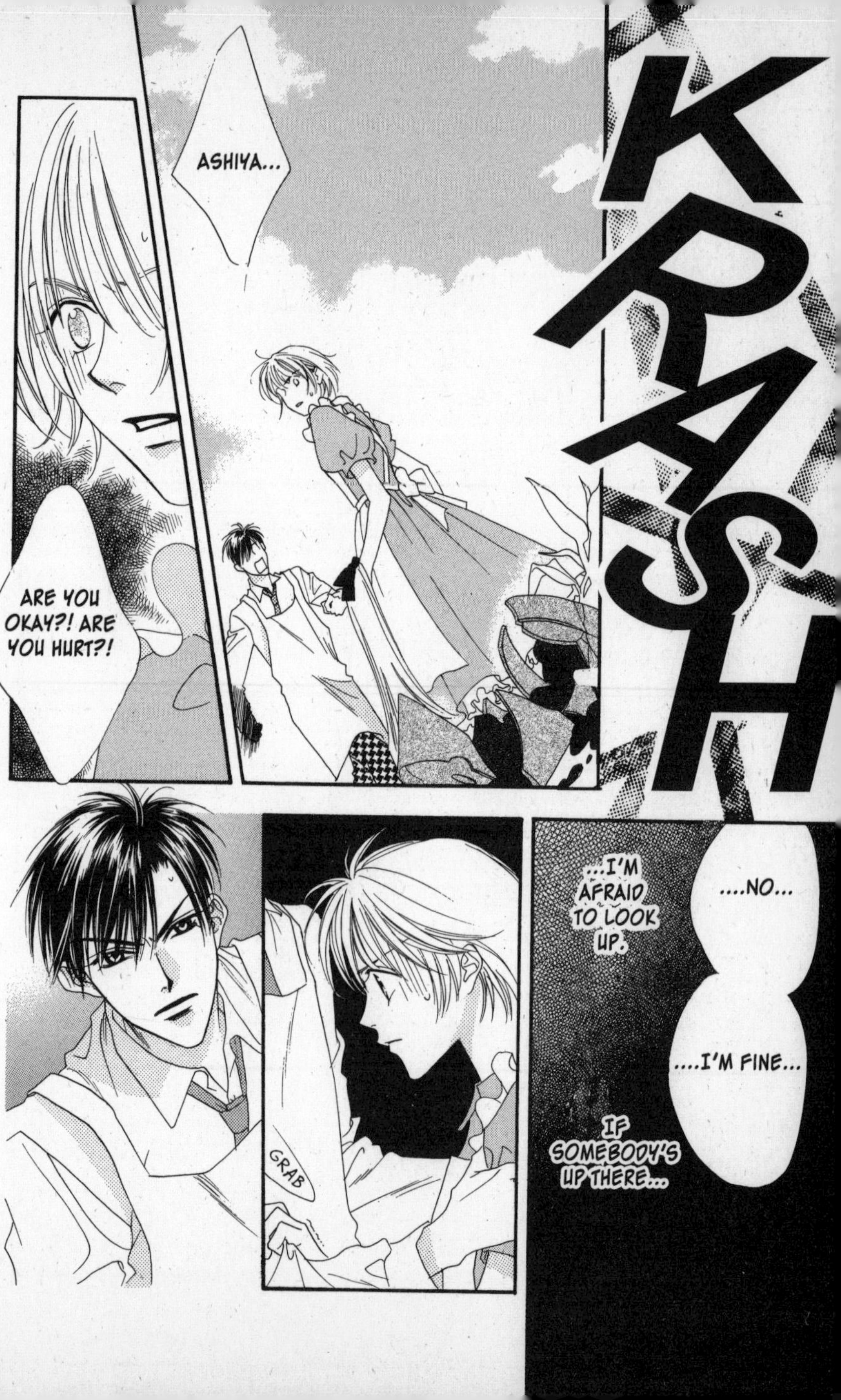
KRASH
ASHIYA...
ARE YOU OKAY?! ARE YOU HURT?!
....NO...
...I'M AFRAID TO LOOK UP.
....I'M FINE...
IF SOMEBODY'S UP THERE...
GRAB

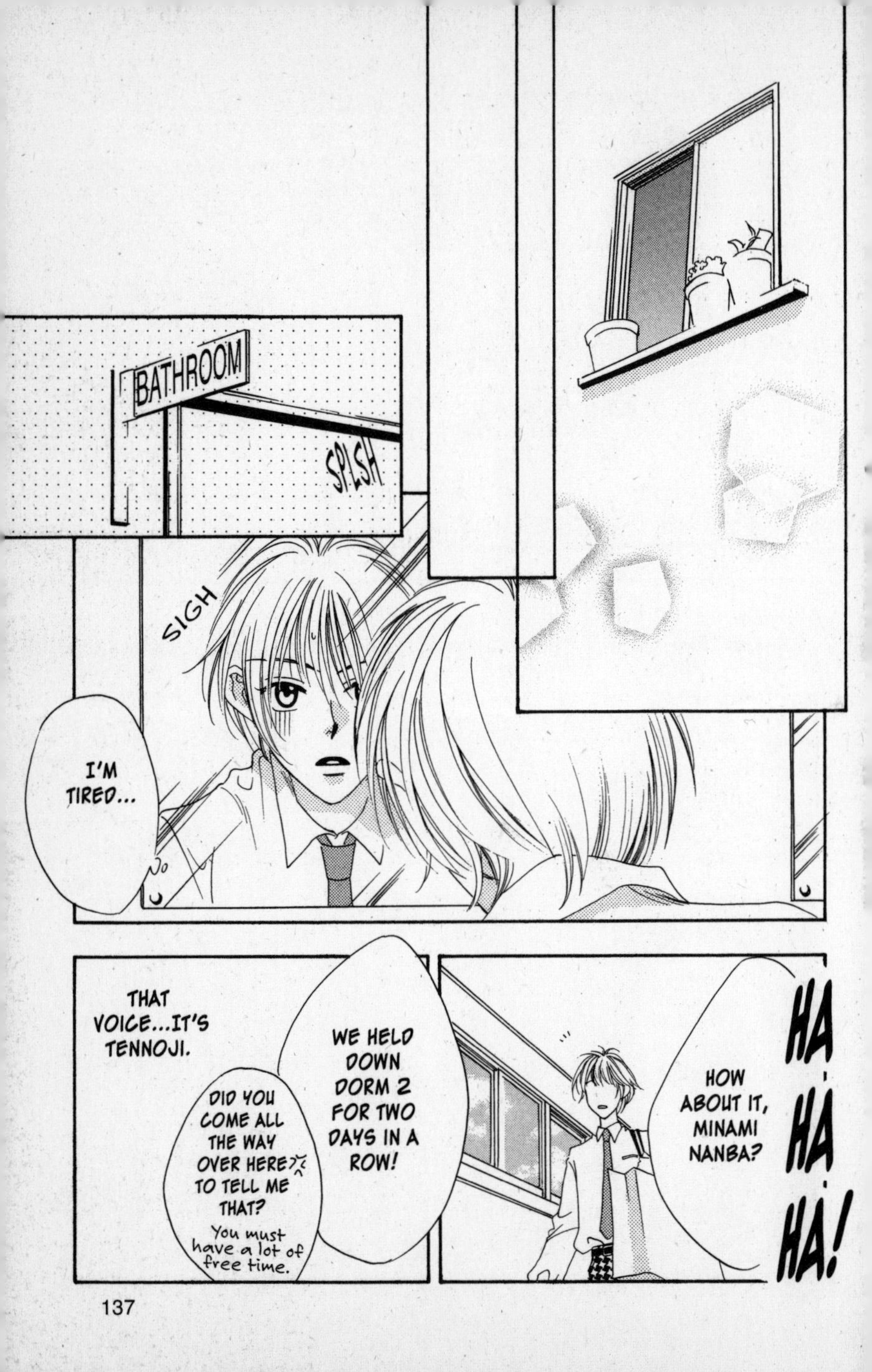
BATHROOM
SPLSH
SIGH
I'M TIRED...
HA HA HA!
HOW ABOUT IT, MINAMI NANBA?
WE HELD DOWN DORM 2 FOR TWO DAYS IN A ROW!
THAT VOICE...IT'S TENNOJI.
DID YOU COME ALL THE WAY OVER HERE TO TELL ME THAT?
You must have a lot of free time.

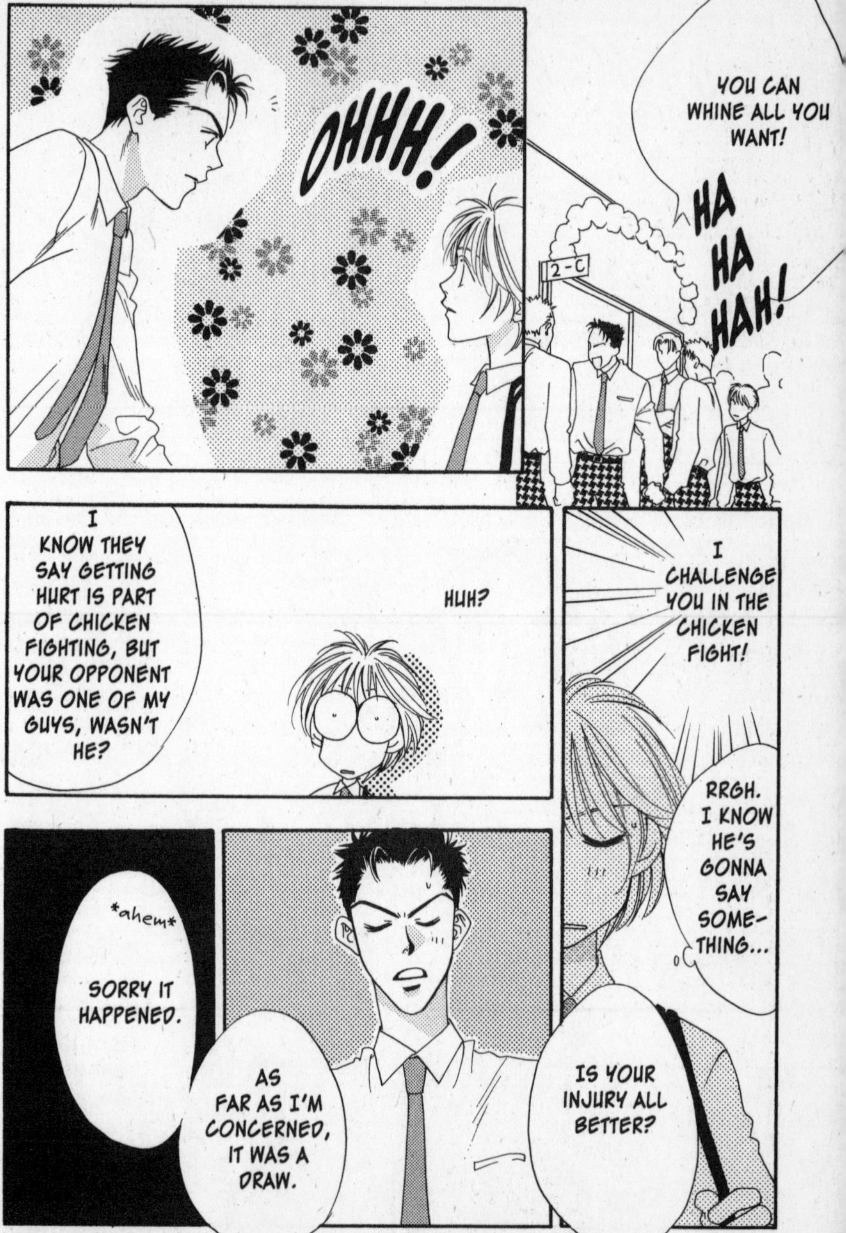
YOU CAN WHINE ALL YOU WANT!
HA HA HAH!
2-C
OHHH!
I CHALLENGE YOU IN THE CHICKEN FIGHT!
RRGH. I KNOW HE'S GONNA SAY SOME-THING...
IS YOUR INJURY ALL BETTER?
HUH?
I KNOW THEY SAY GETTING HURT IS PART OF CHICKEN FIGHTING, BUT YOUR OPPONENT WAS ONE OF MY GUYS, WASN'T HE?
AS FAR AS I'M CONCERNED, IT WAS A DRAW.
ahem
SORRY IT HAPPENED.

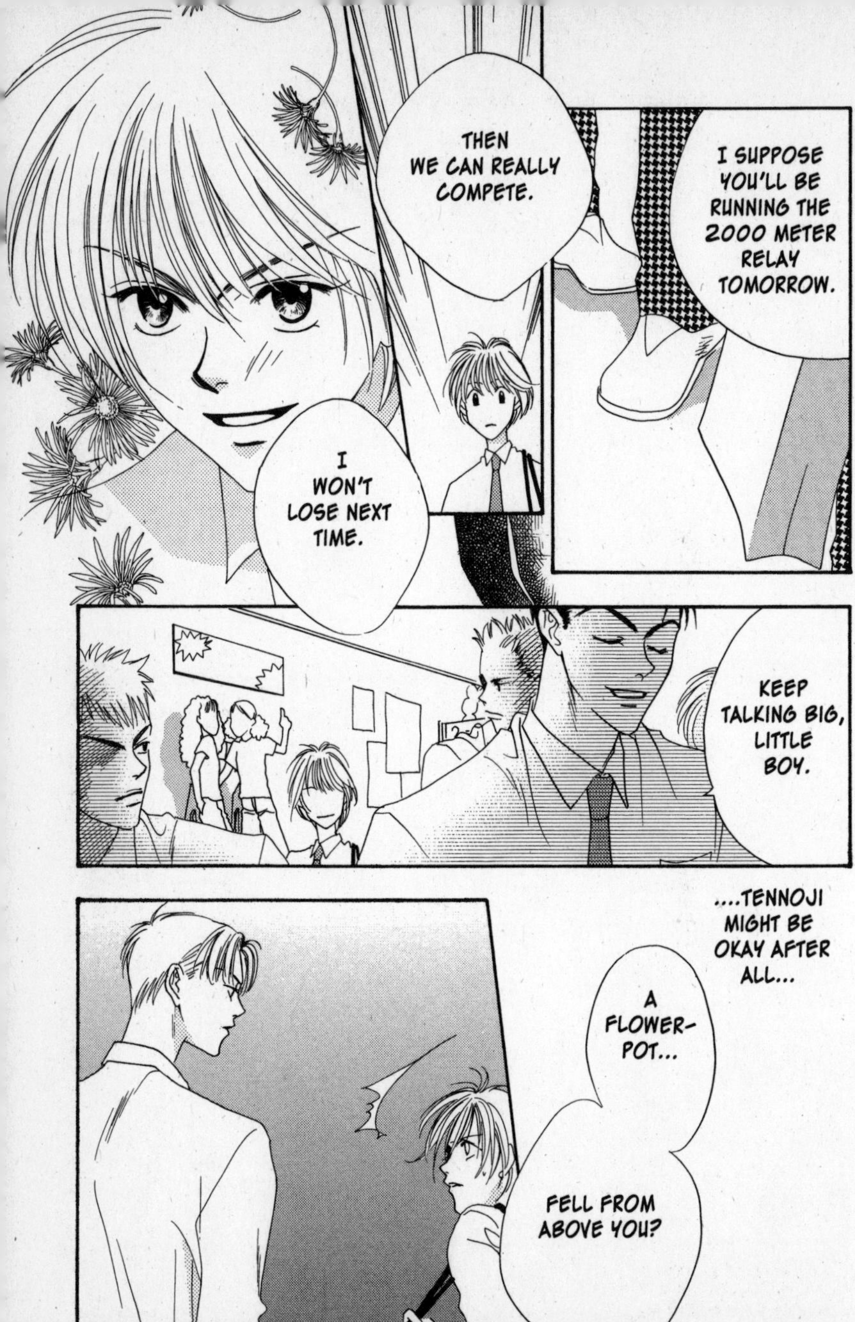
I SUPPOSE YOU'LL BE RUNNING THE 2000 METER RELAY TOMORROW.
THEN WE CAN REALLY COMPETE.
I WON'T LOSE NEXT TIME.
KEEP TALKING BIG, LITTLE BOY.
....TENNOJI MIGHT BE OKAY AFTER ALL...
A FLOWER-POT...
FELL FROM ABOVE YOU?

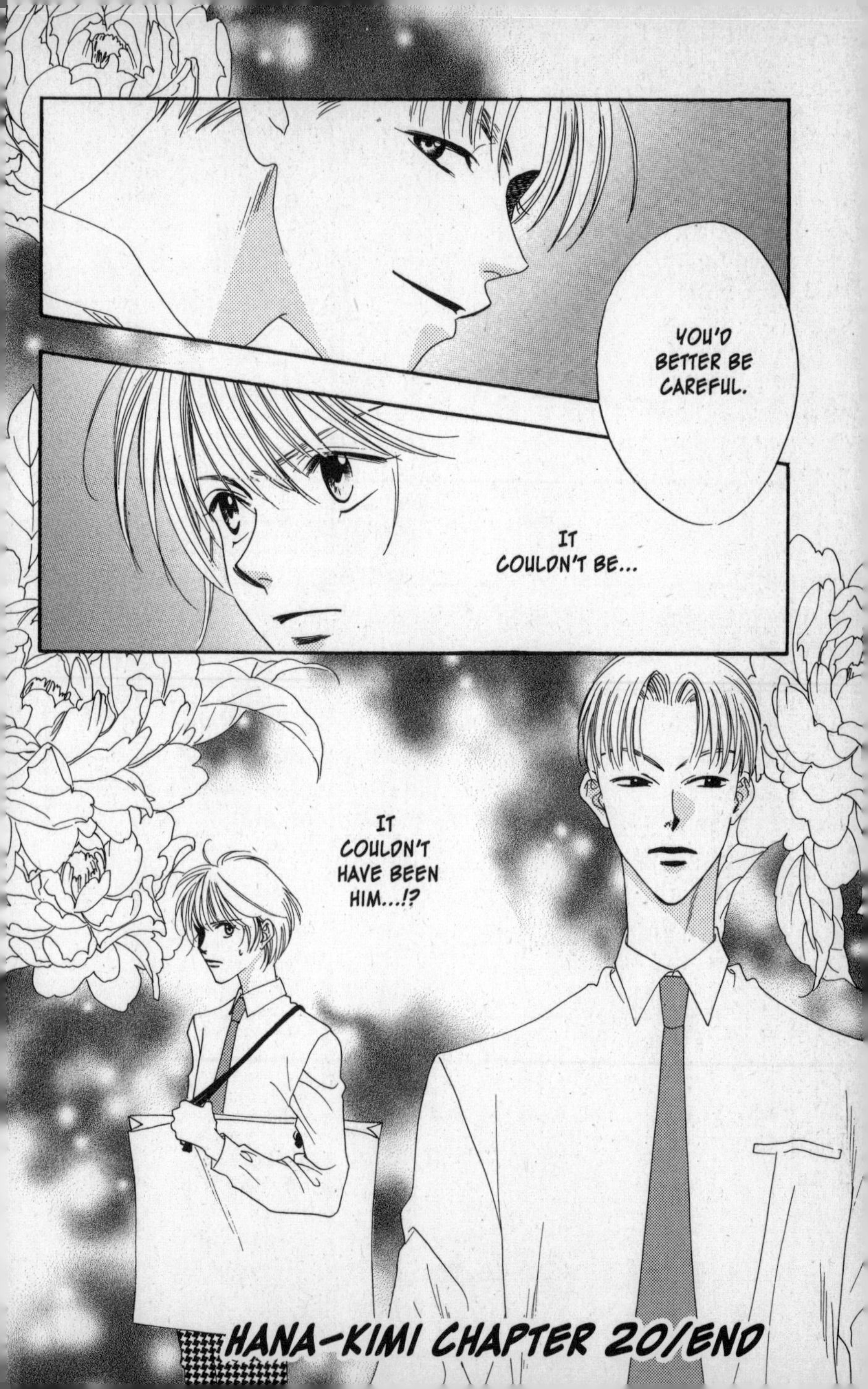
YOU'D BETTER BE CAREFUL.
IT COULDN'T BE...
IT COULDN'T HAVE BEEN HIM...!?
HANA-KIMI CHAPTER 20/END

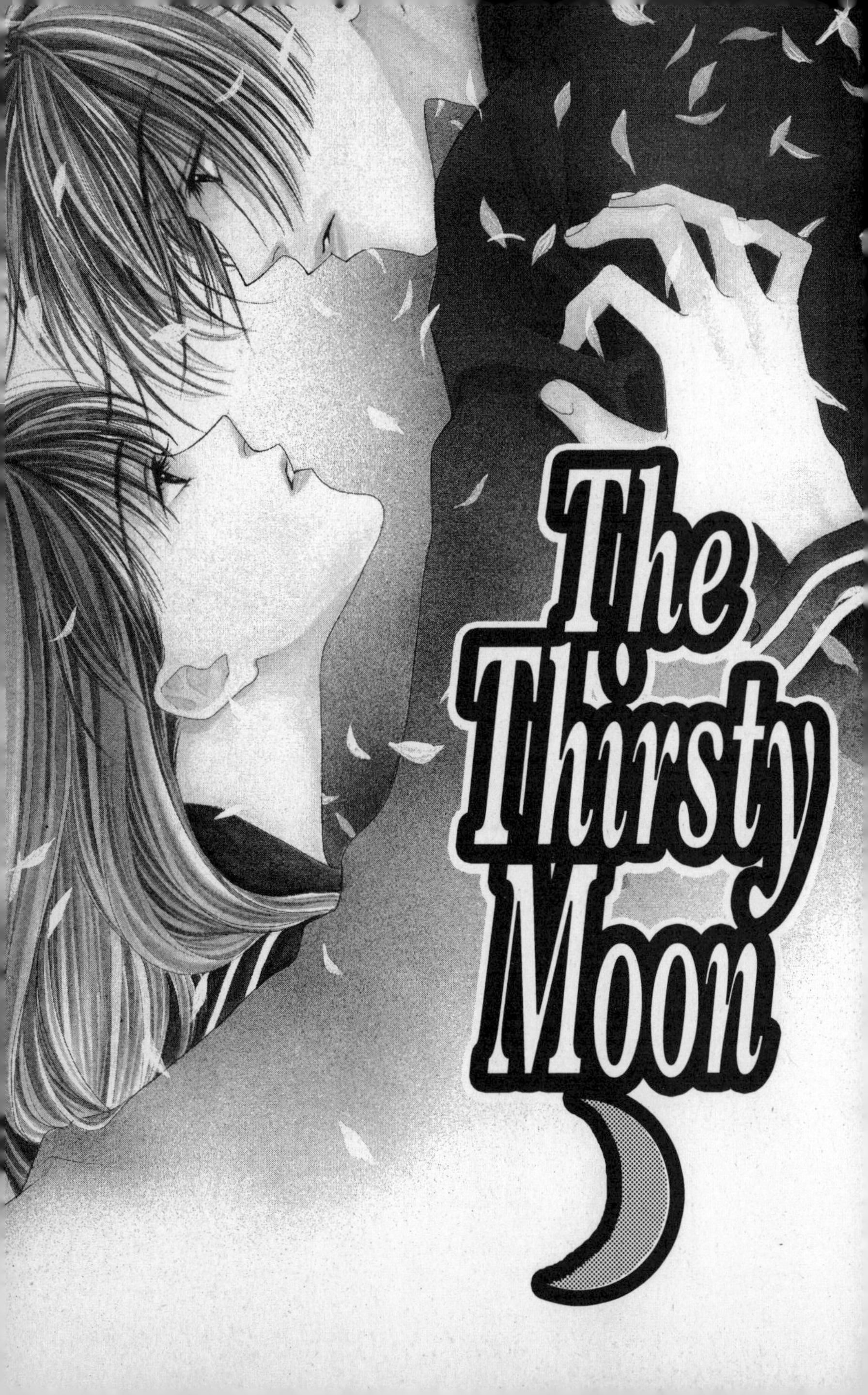
The Thirsty Moon

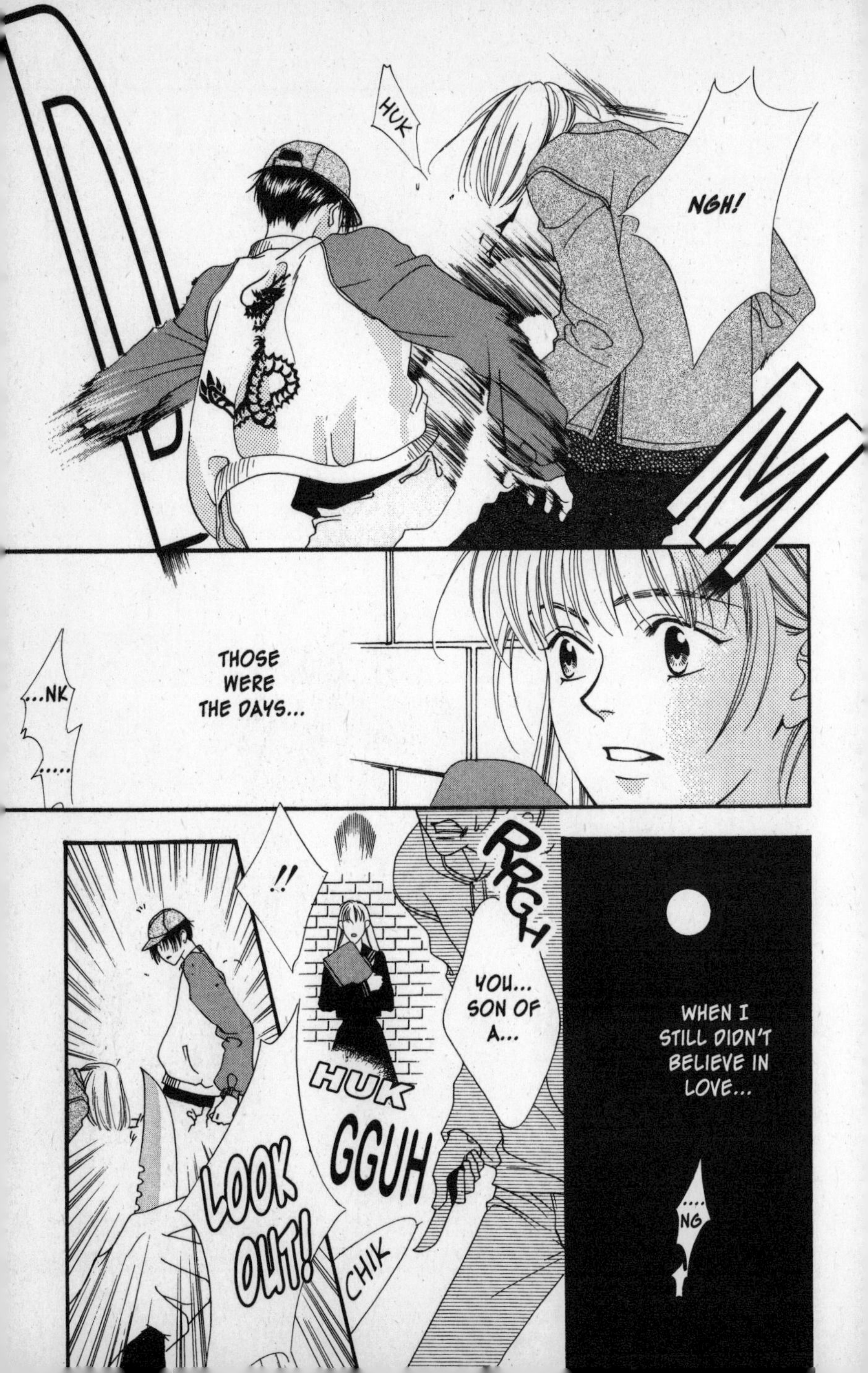
NGH!
HUK
THOSE WERE THE DAYS...
...NK
......
WHEN I STILL DIDN'T BELIEVE IN LOVE...
....NG
RRGH
YOU... SON OF A...
HUK
GGUH
CHIK
!!
LOOK OUT!

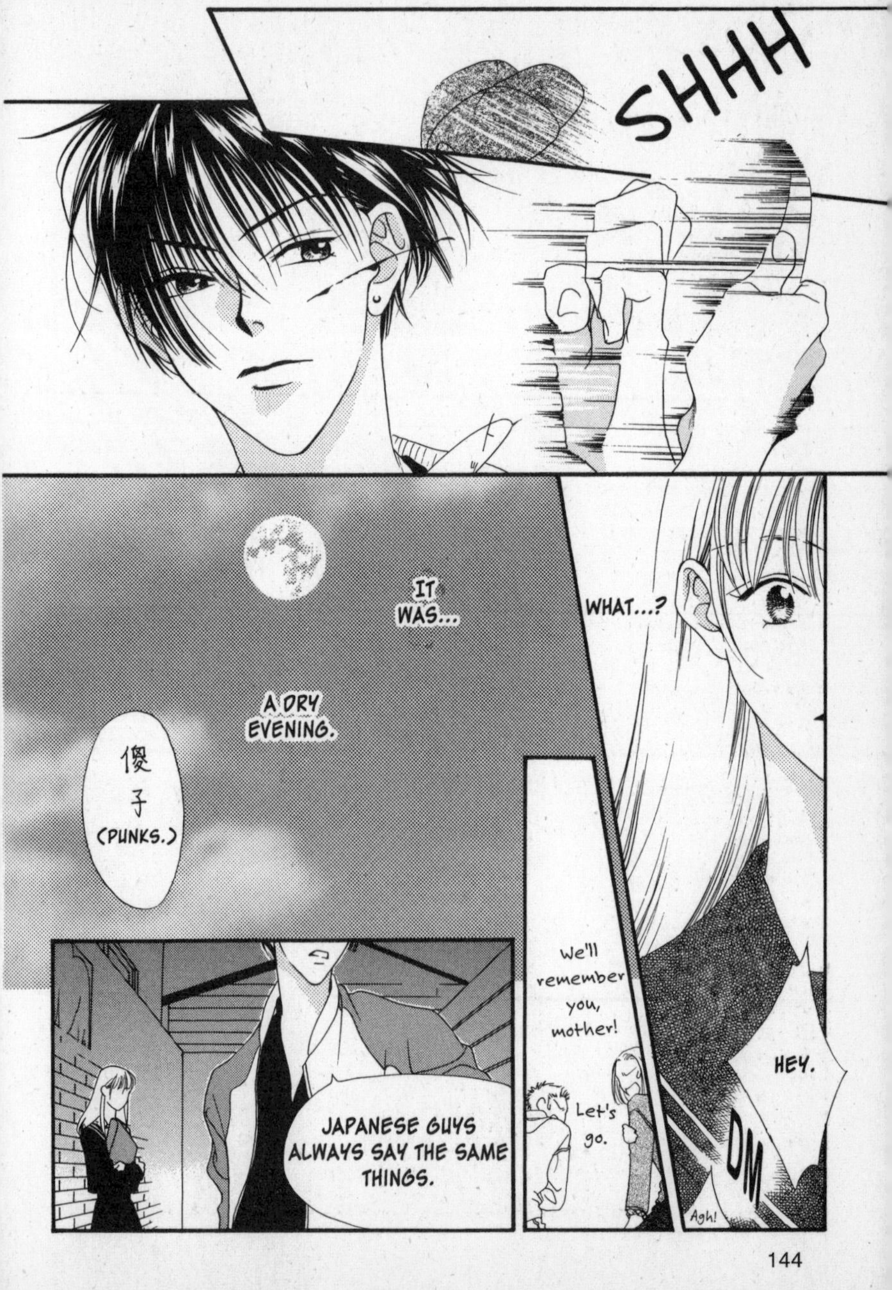

SHHH
WHAT...?
IT WAS...
A DRY EVENING.
傻子 (PUNKS.)
HEY.
DM
Agh!
We'll remember you, mother!
Let's go.
JAPANESE GUYS ALWAYS SAY THE SAME THINGS.

Whispered Secrets

Yue

I WROTE THIS QUITE A WHILE AGO, SO I KIND OF MISSED IT. I LIKED YUE'S NAME AND FACE.♡ WHEN I LOOK AT HIS HAIR NOW, IT LOOKS JUST LIKE THAT MUSICIAN "TM REVOLUTION"! YUE WAS MY FIRST CHINESE CHARACTER. CHINESE PRONUNCIATIONS OF KANJI ARE SO PRETTY! ♡ (TO FOREIGNERS JAPANESE SOUNDS SING-SONGY.) I'M GETTING SIDETRACKED HERE, BUT I'VE HEARD THAT THE CANTONESE UNDERSTAND OSAKA DIALECT. IS THAT POSSIBLE? ANYWAY, READING THIS STORY'S SAD ENDING AGAIN MAKES ME KIND OF MELANCHOLY. I RECOMMEND READING IT WHILE LISTENING TO STING'S "SHAPE OF MY HEART." I LISTENED TO IT THE WHOLE TIME I WAS WORKING ON THIS STORY. THAT SONG WILL MAKE YOU CRY. ♡ IT'S THE END THEME FROM THE FILM "THE PROFESSIONAL."

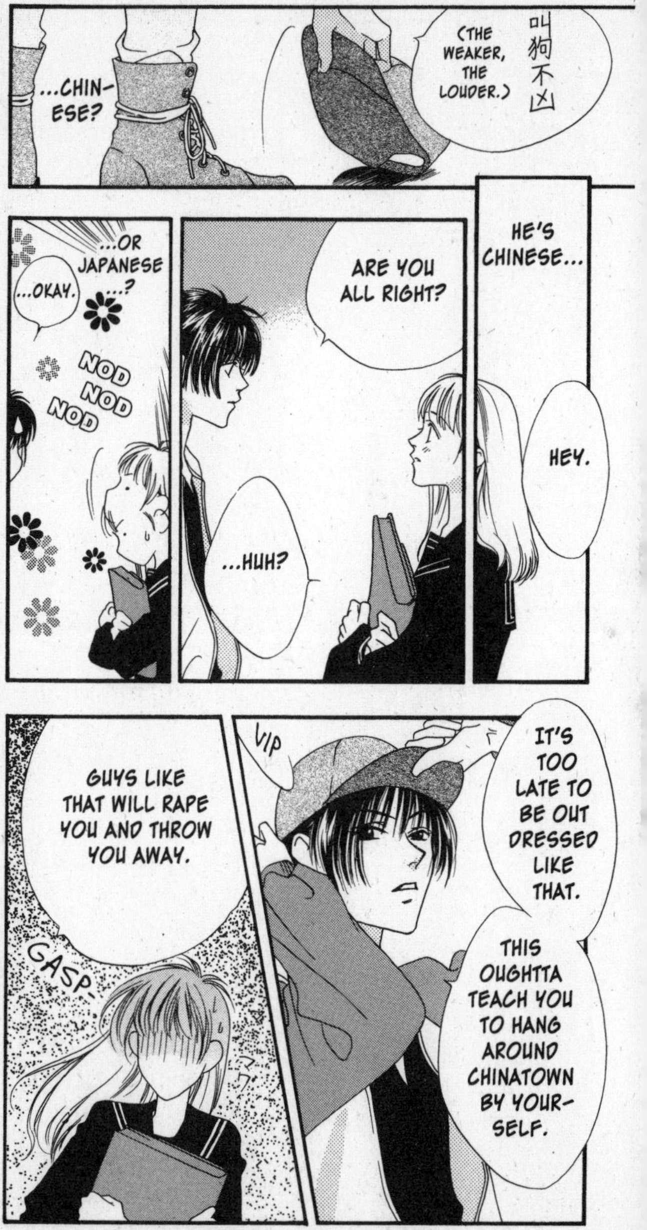

叫狗不凶
(THE WEAKER, THE LOUDER.)
...CHIN-ESE?
HE'S CHINESE...
HEY.
ARE YOU ALL RIGHT?
...HUH?
...OR JAPANESE ...?
...OKAY.
NOD NOD NOD
IT'S TOO LATE TO BE OUT DRESSED LIKE THAT.
THIS OUGHTTA TEACH YOU TO HANG AROUND CHINATOWN BY YOURSELF.
GUYS LIKE THAT WILL RAPE YOU AND THROW YOU AWAY.
GASP

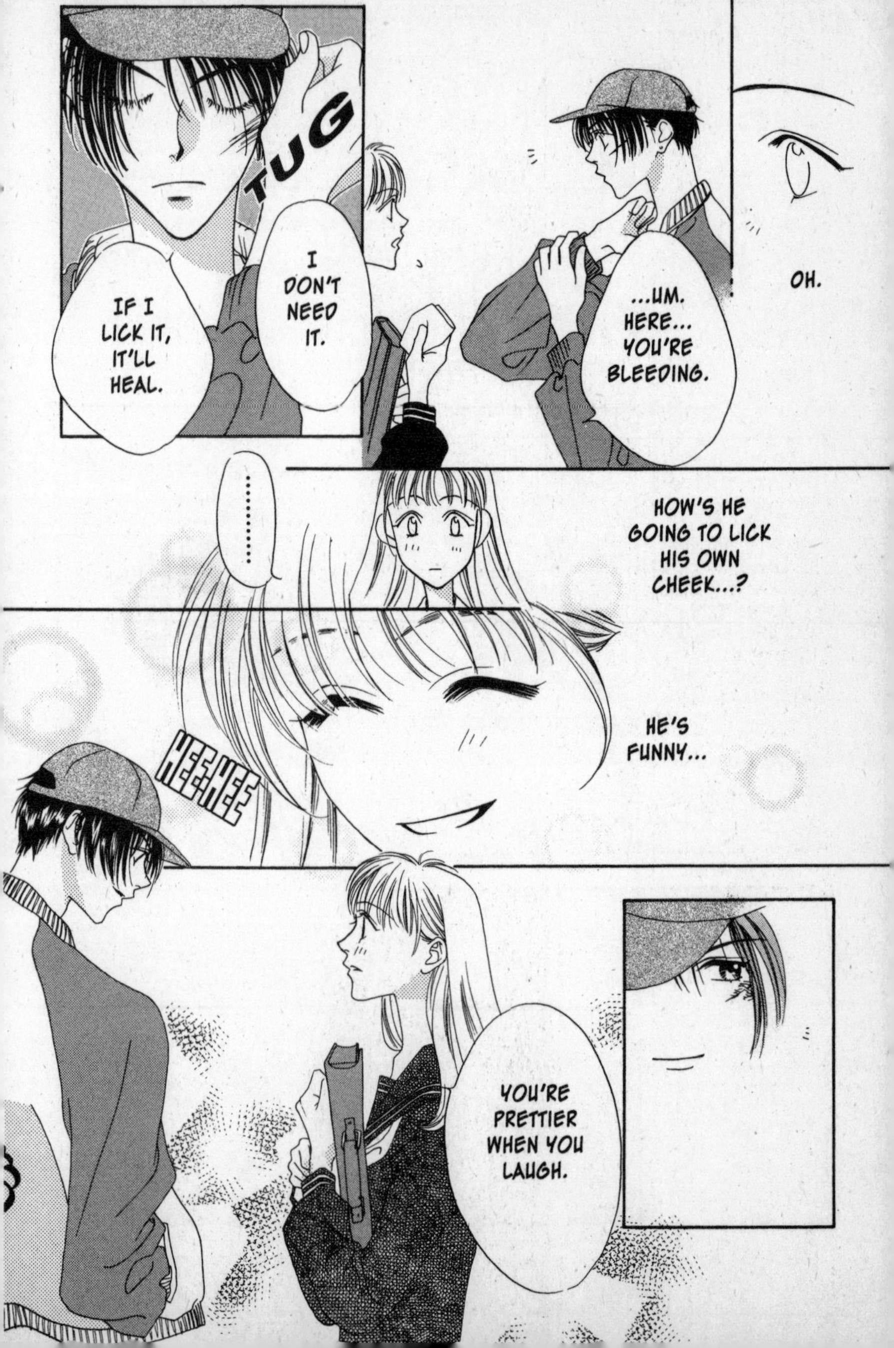
OH.
...UM. HERE... YOU'RE BLEEDING.
TUG
I DON'T NEED IT.
IF I LICK IT, IT'LL HEAL.
HOW'S HE GOING TO LICK HIS OWN CHEEK...?
......
HE'S FUNNY...
HEE HEE
YOU'RE PRETTIER WHEN YOU LAUGH.

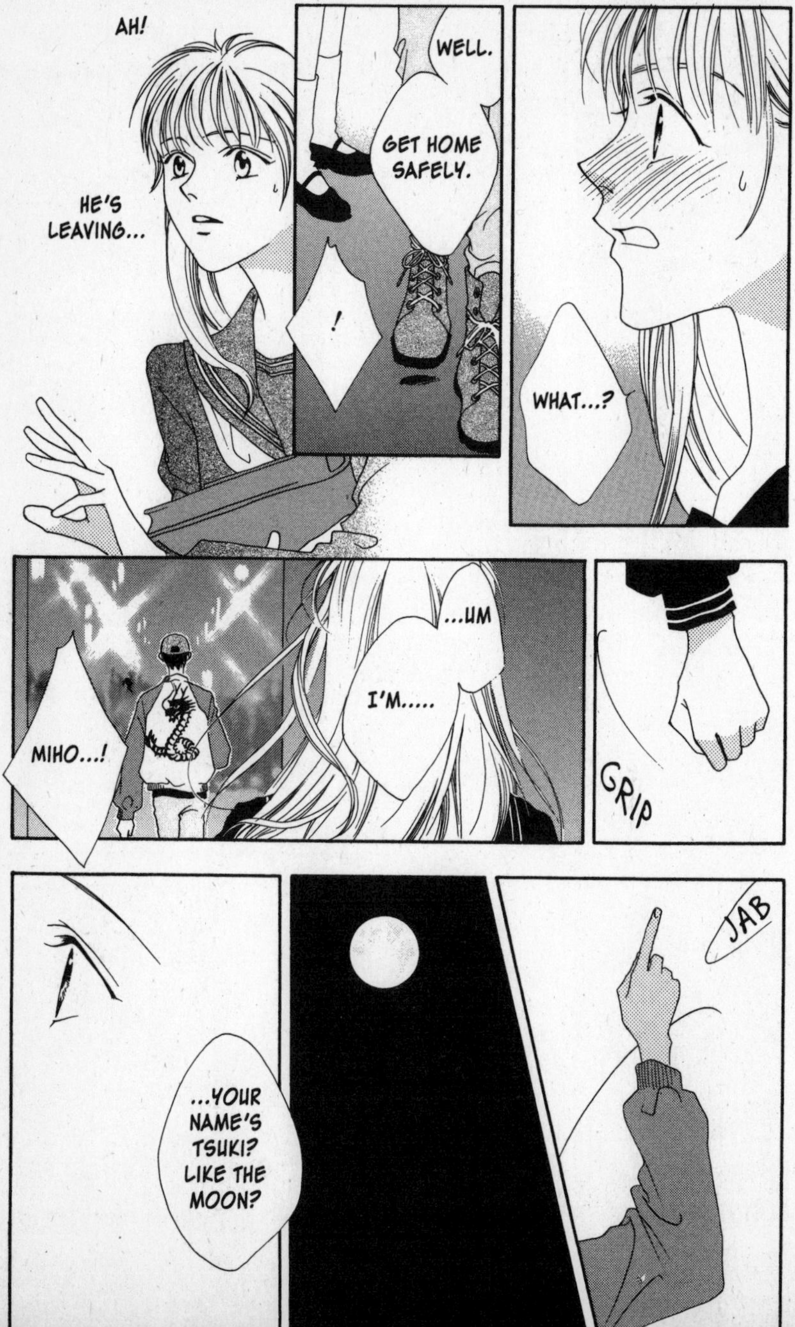
WHAT...?
WELL.
GET HOME SAFELY.
!
AH!
HE'S LEAVING...
GRIP
...UM
I'M.....
MIHO...!
JAB
...YOUR NAME'S TSUKI? LIKE THE MOON?

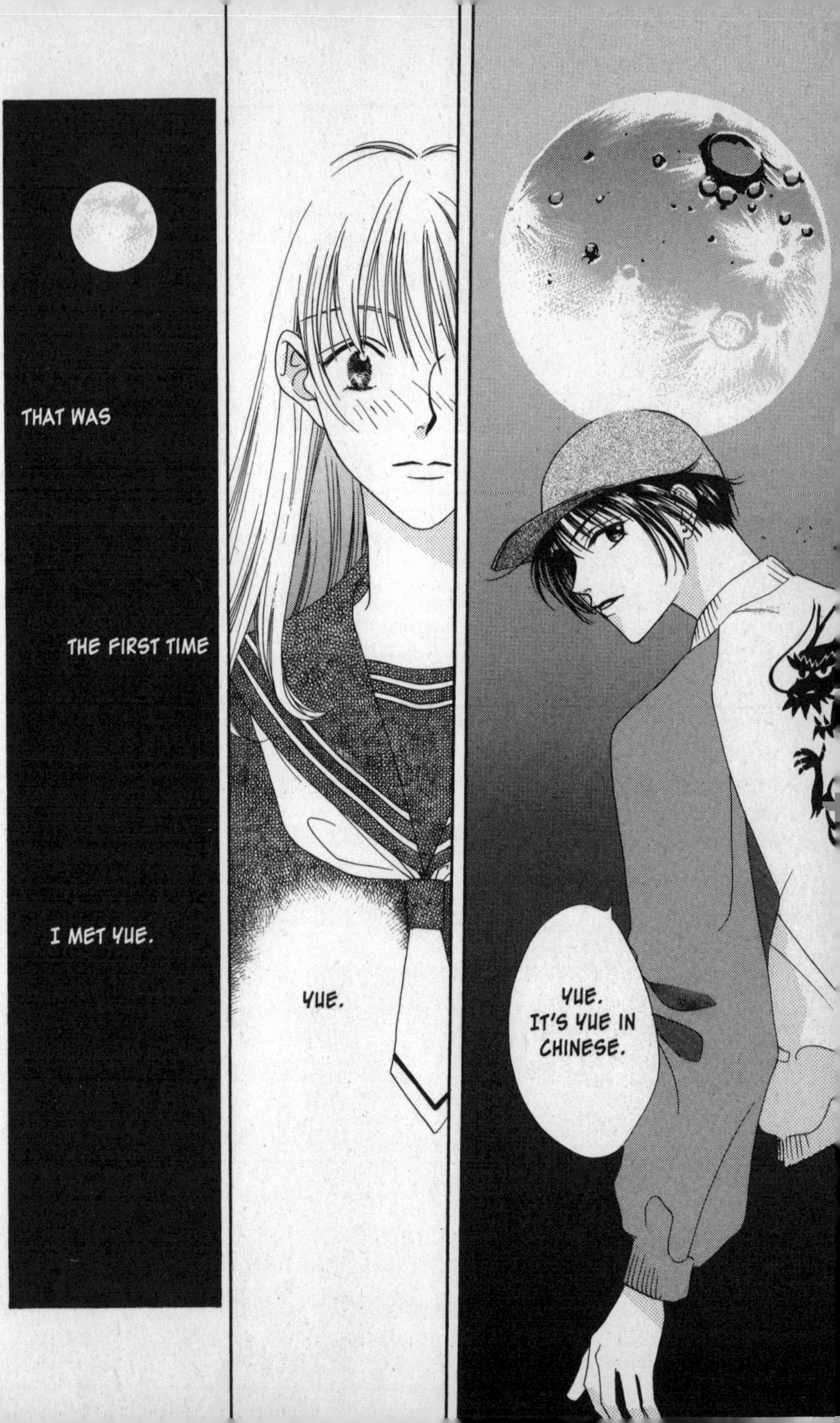
YUE.
IT'S YUE IN CHINESE.
YUE.
THAT WAS
THE FIRST TIME
I MET YUE.

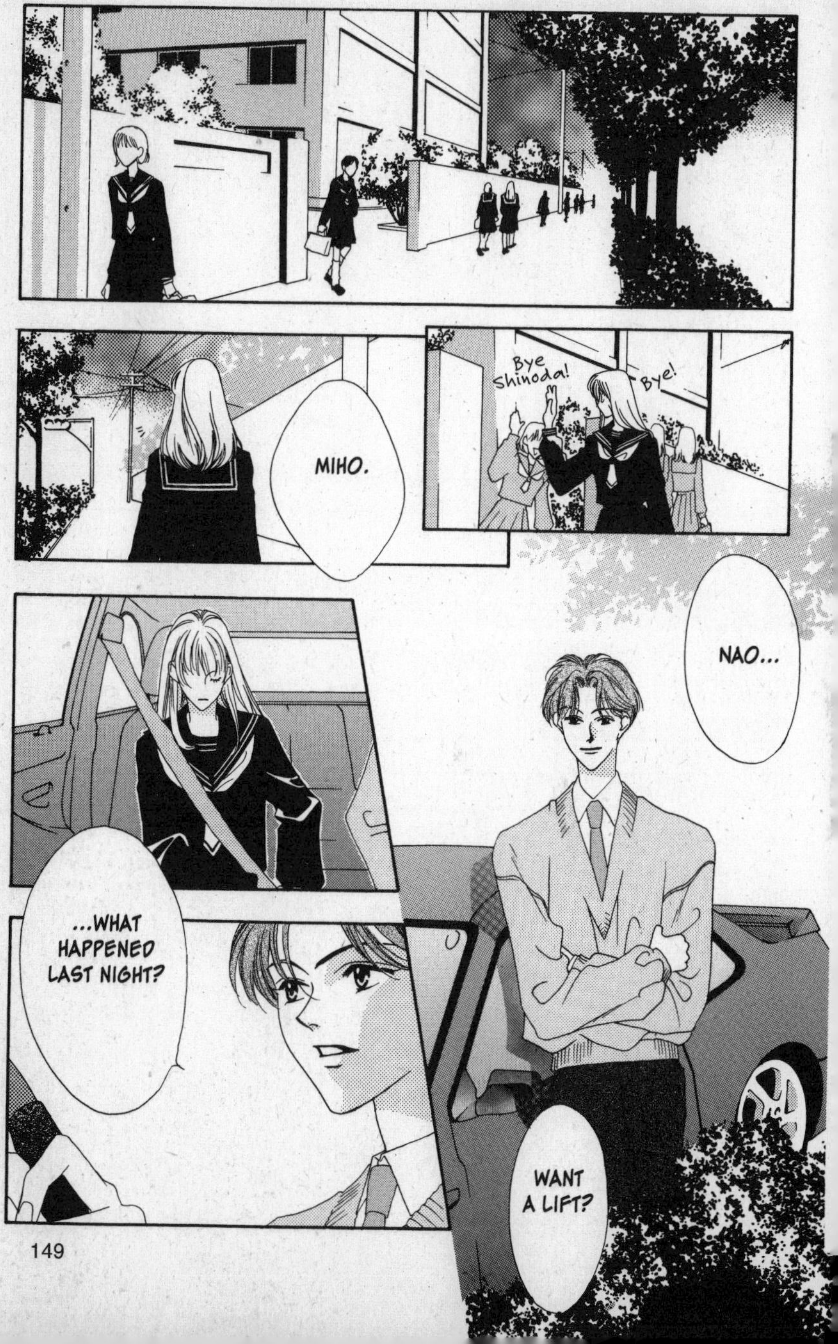
Bye!
Bye Shinoda!
MIHO.
NAO...
WANT A LIFT?
...WHAT HAPPENED LAST NIGHT?

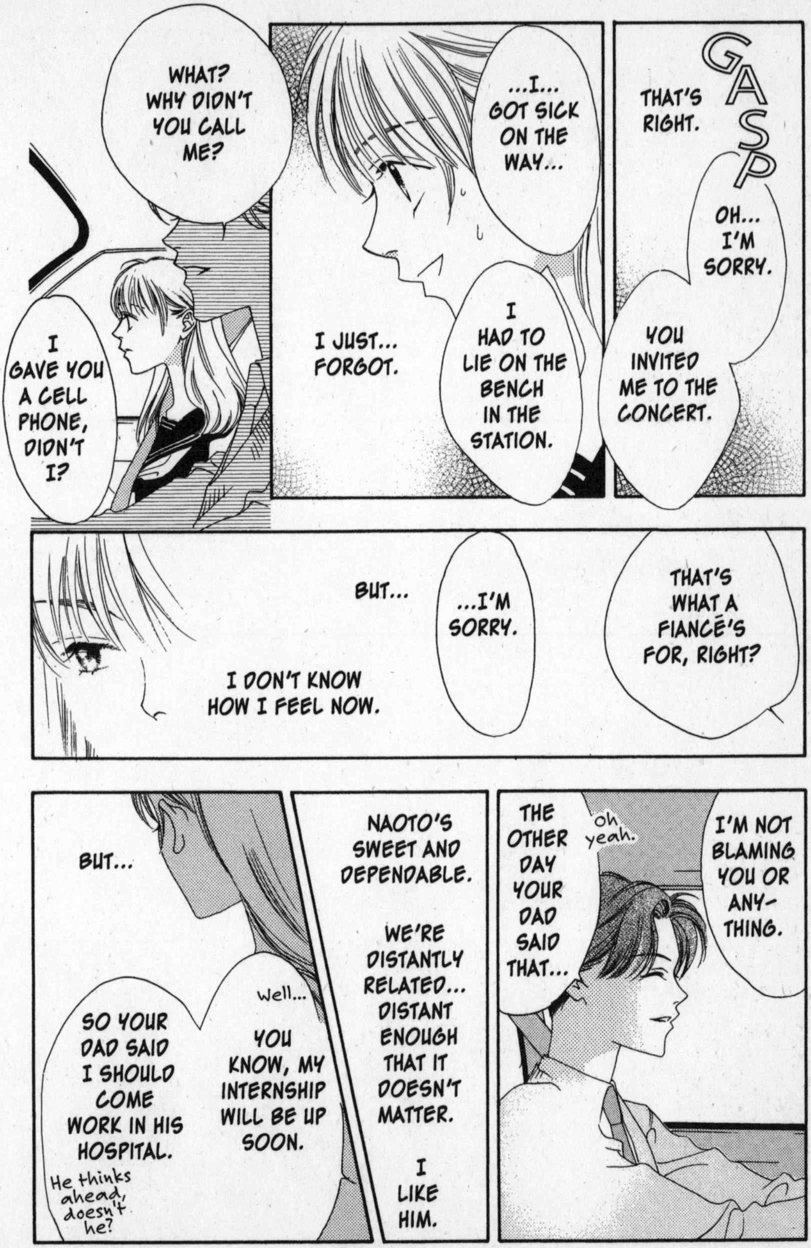
GASP
THAT'S RIGHT.
OH... I'M SORRY.
YOU INVITED ME TO THE CONCERT.
...I... GOT SICK ON THE WAY...
I HAD TO LIE ON THE BENCH IN THE STATION.
I JUST... FORGOT.
WHAT? WHY DIDN'T YOU CALL ME?
I GAVE YOU A CELL PHONE, DIDN'T I?
THAT'S WHAT A FIANCÉ'S FOR, RIGHT?
...I'M SORRY.
BUT...
I DON'T KNOW HOW I FEEL NOW.
I'M NOT BLAMING YOU OR ANY-THING.
Oh yeah.
THE OTHER DAY YOUR DAD SAID THAT...
NAOTO'S SWEET AND DEPENDABLE.
WE'RE DISTANTLY RELATED... DISTANT ENOUGH THAT IT DOESN'T MATTER.
I LIKE HIM.
BUT...
Well...
YOU KNOW, MY INTERNSHIP WILL BE UP SOON.
SO YOUR DAD SAID I SHOULD COME WORK IN HIS HOSPITAL.
He thinks ahead, doesn't he?

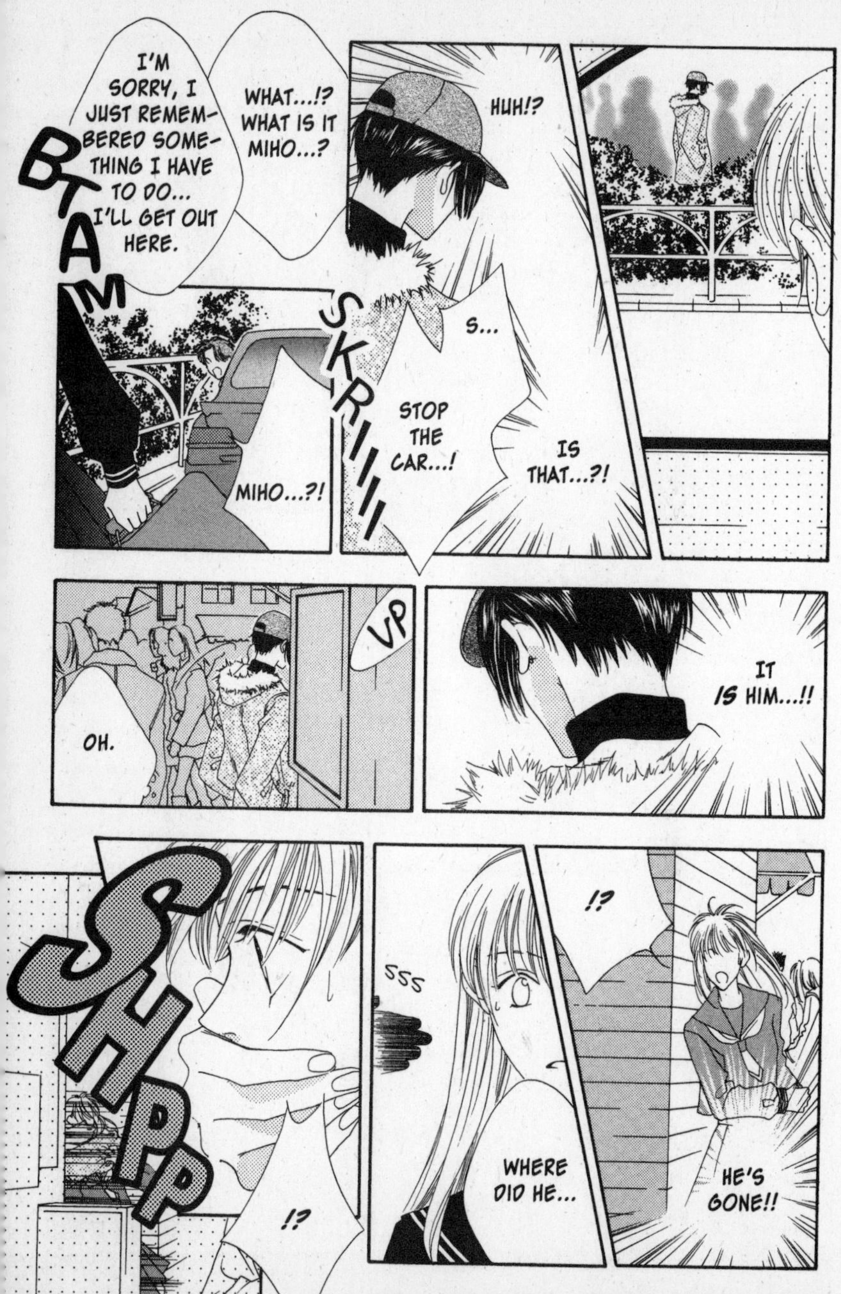
HUH!?
S...
STOP THE CAR...!
IS THAT...?!
SKRIIIII
WHAT...!? WHAT IS IT MIHO...?
I'M SORRY, I JUST REMEMBERED SOMETHING I HAVE TO DO... I'LL GET OUT HERE.
BTAM
MIHO...?!
IT IS HIM...!!
VP
OH.
!?
HE'S GONE!!
SSS
WHERE DID HE...
SHPP
!?

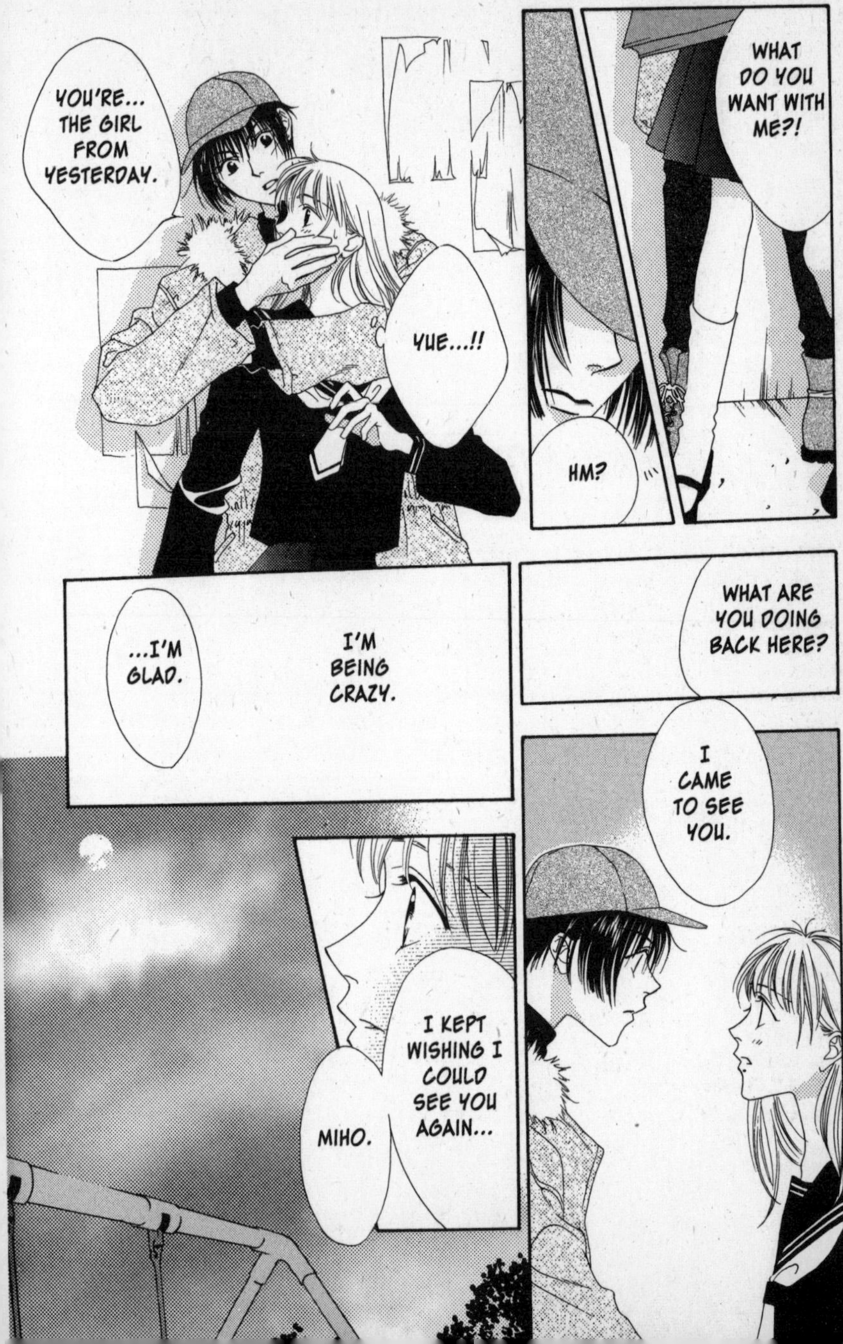
WHAT DO YOU WANT WITH ME?!
HM?
YUE...!!
YOU'RE... THE GIRL FROM YESTERDAY.
WHAT ARE YOU DOING BACK HERE?
I'M BEING CRAZY.
...I'M GLAD.
I CAME TO SEE YOU.
I KEPT WISHING I COULD SEE YOU AGAIN...
MIHO.

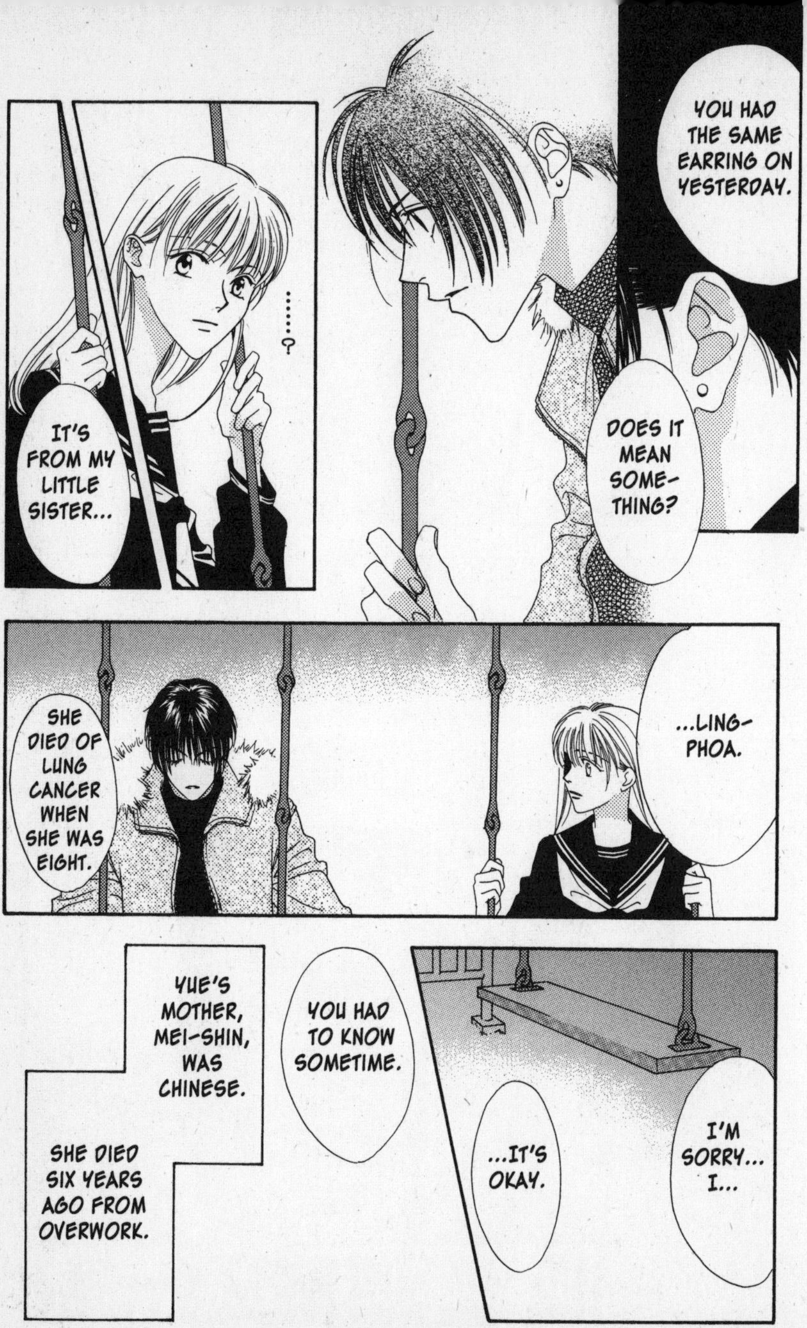
YOU HAD THE SAME EARRING ON YESTERDAY.
DOES IT MEAN SOMETHING?
......?
IT'S FROM MY LITTLE SISTER...
...LING-PHOA.
SHE DIED OF LUNG CANCER WHEN SHE WAS EIGHT.
I'M SORRY... I...
...IT'S OKAY.
YOU HAD TO KNOW SOMETIME.
YUE'S MOTHER, MEI-SHIN, WAS CHINESE.
SHE DIED SIX YEARS AGO FROM OVERWORK.

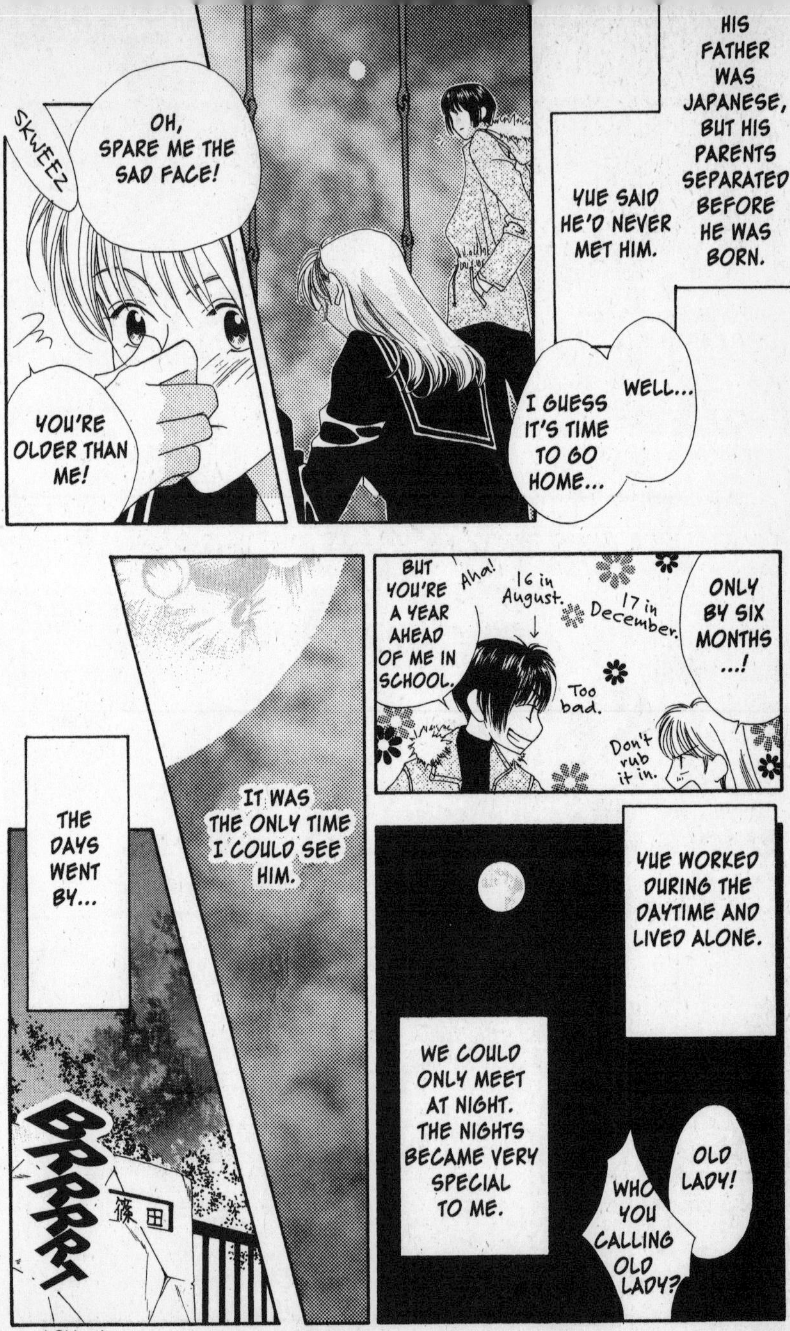
HIS FATHER WAS JAPANESE, BUT HIS PARENTS SEPARATED BEFORE HE WAS BORN.
YUE SAID HE'D NEVER MET HIM.
WELL...
I GUESS IT'S TIME TO GO HOME...
OH, SPARE ME THE SAD FACE!
SKWEEZ
YOU'RE OLDER THAN ME!
ONLY BY SIX MONTHS ...!
17 in December.
16 in August.
Aha!
BUT YOU'RE A YEAR AHEAD OF ME IN SCHOOL.
Too bad.
Don't rub it in.
YUE WORKED DURING THE DAYTIME AND LIVED ALONE.
OLD LADY!
WHO YOU CALLING OLD LADY?
WE COULD ONLY MEET AT NIGHT. THE NIGHTS BECAME VERY SPECIAL TO ME.
IT WAS THE ONLY TIME I COULD SEE HIM.
THE DAYS WENT BY...
BRRRRT
篠田

* Shinoda

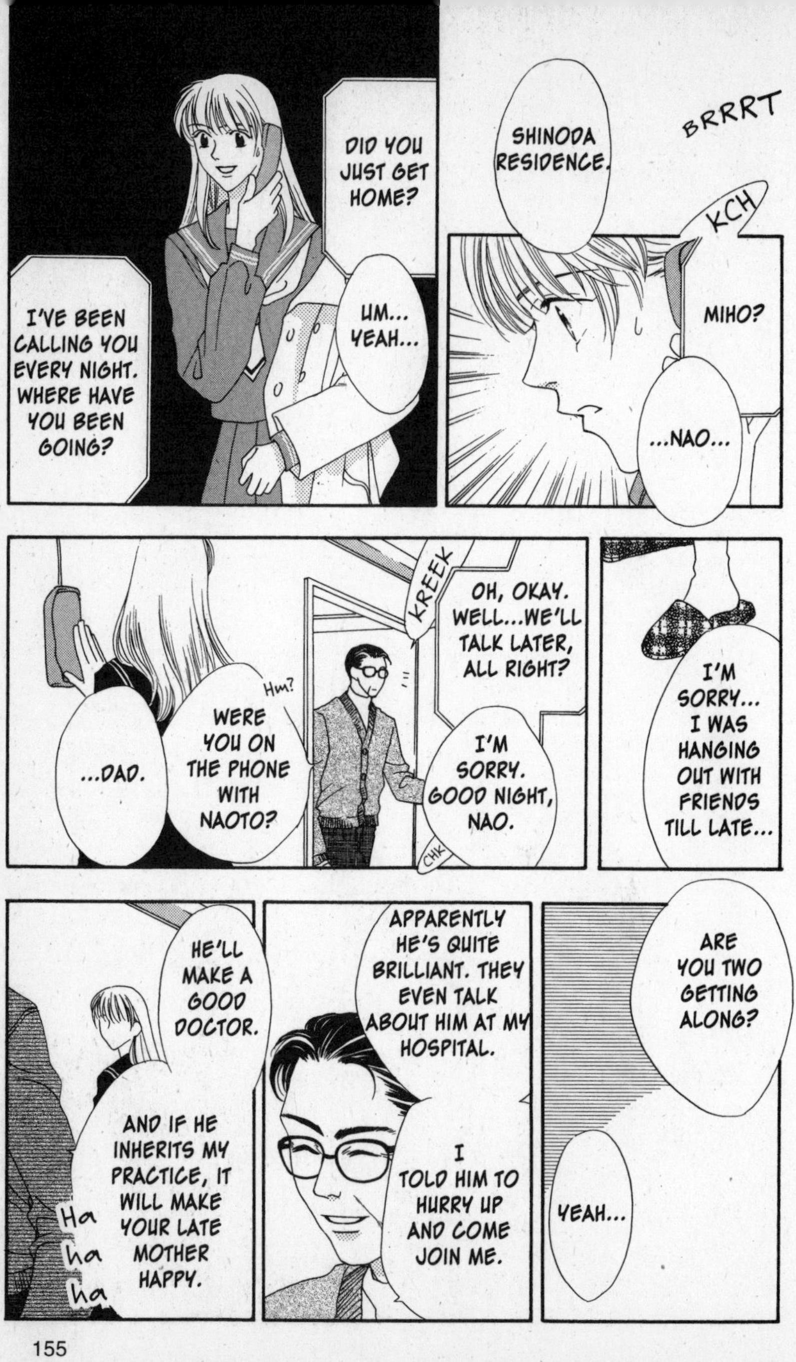

BRRRT
SHINODA RESIDENCE.
KCH
MIHO?
...NAO...
DID YOU JUST GET HOME?
UM... YEAH...
I'VE BEEN CALLING YOU EVERY NIGHT. WHERE HAVE YOU BEEN GOING?
I'M SORRY... I WAS HANGING OUT WITH FRIENDS TILL LATE...
OH, OKAY. WELL...WE'LL TALK LATER, ALL RIGHT?
KREEK
I'M SORRY. GOOD NIGHT, NAO.
CHK
Hm?
WERE YOU ON THE PHONE WITH NAOTO?
...DAD.
ARE YOU TWO GETTING ALONG?
YEAH...
APPARENTLY HE'S QUITE BRILLIANT. THEY EVEN TALK ABOUT HIM AT MY HOSPITAL.
I TOLD HIM TO HURRY UP AND COME JOIN ME.
HE'LL MAKE A GOOD DOCTOR.
AND IF HE INHERITS MY PRACTICE, IT WILL MAKE YOUR LATE MOTHER HAPPY.
Ha ha ha

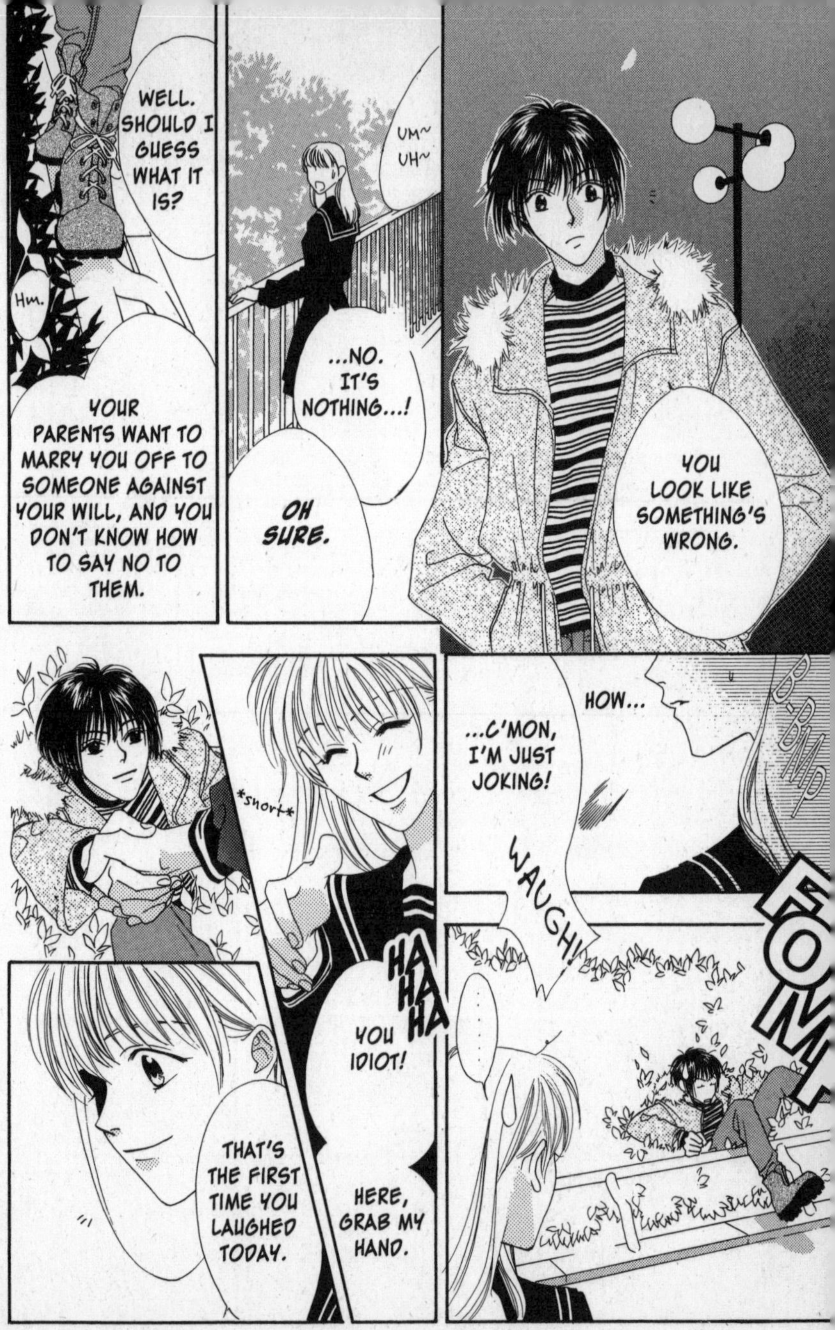
YOU LOOK LIKE SOMETHING'S WRONG.
UM~ UH~
...NO. IT'S NOTHING...!
OH SURE.
WELL. SHOULD I GUESS WHAT IT IS?
Hm.
YOUR PARENTS WANT TO MARRY YOU OFF TO SOMEONE AGAINST YOUR WILL, AND YOU DON'T KNOW HOW TO SAY NO TO THEM.
HOW...
...C'MON, I'M JUST JOKING!
B-BMP
WAUGH!
FOMP!
...
snort
HAHAHAHA
YOU IDIOT!
HERE, GRAB MY HAND.
THAT'S THE FIRST TIME YOU LAUGHED TODAY.

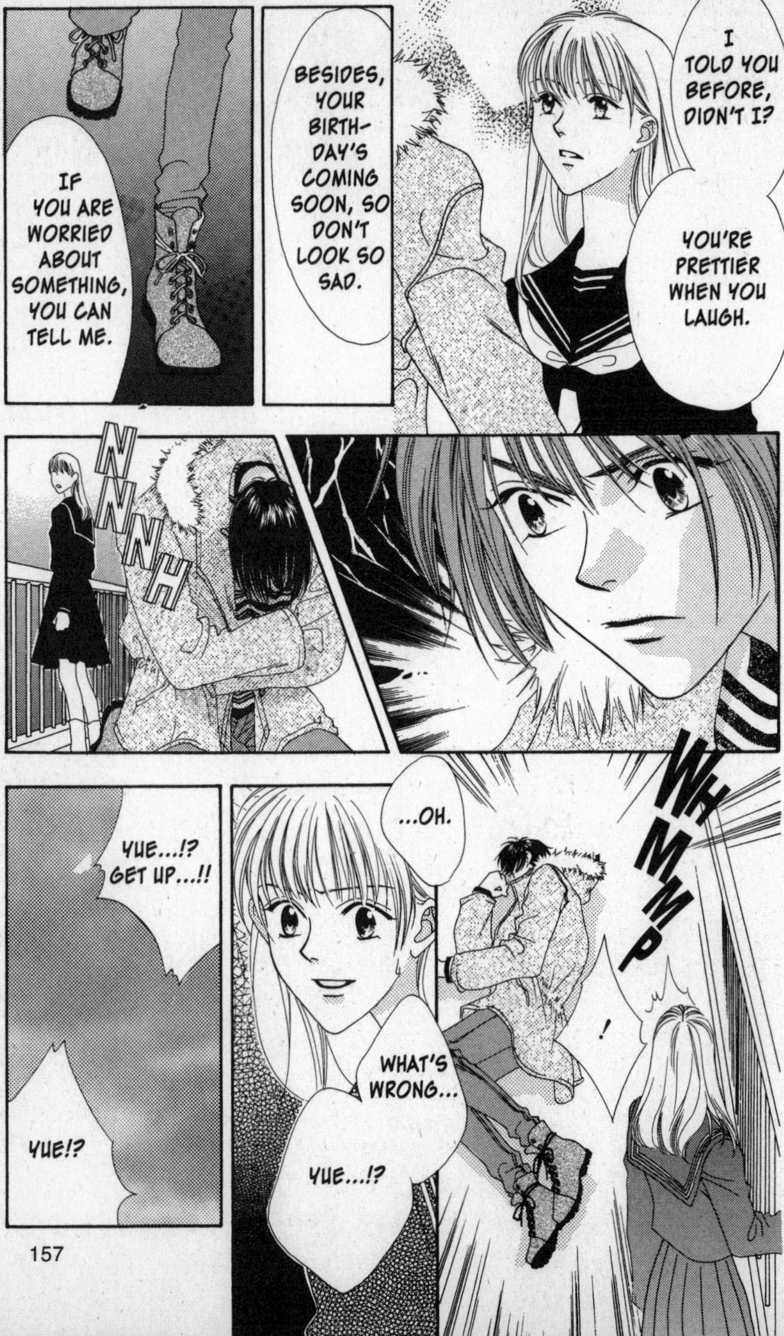

I TOLD YOU BEFORE, DIDN'T I?
YOU'RE PRETTIER WHEN YOU LAUGH.
BESIDES, YOUR BIRTH-DAY'S COMING SOON, SO DON'T LOOK SO SAD.
IF YOU ARE WORRIED ABOUT SOMETHING, YOU CAN TELL ME.
NNNNH
WHMMP
!
...OH.
WHAT'S WRONG...
YUE...!?
YUE...!? GET UP...!!
YUE!?

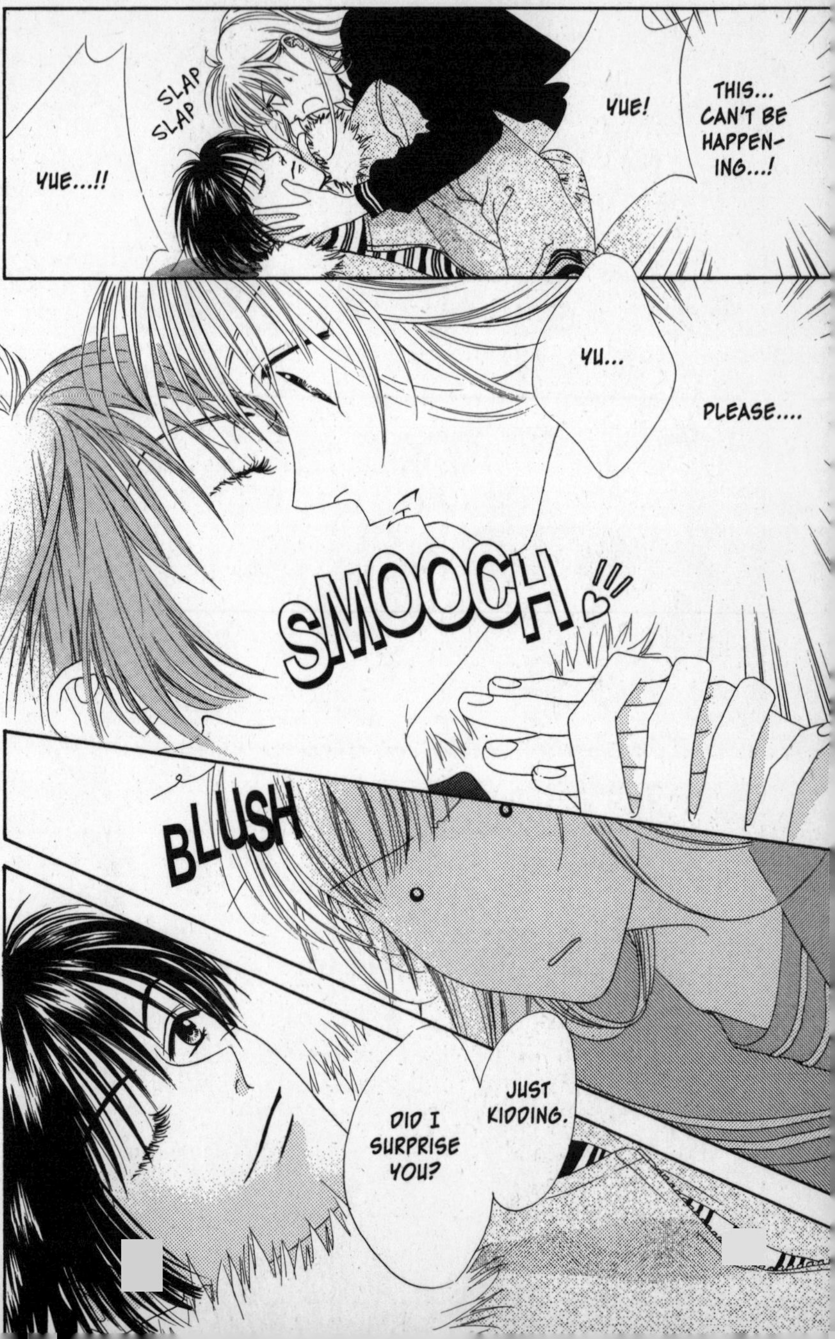
THIS... CAN'T BE HAPPEN-ING...!
YUE!
SLAP SLAP
YUE...!!
PLEASE....
YU...
SMOOCH!!!
BLUSH
JUST KIDDING.
DID I SURPRISE YOU?

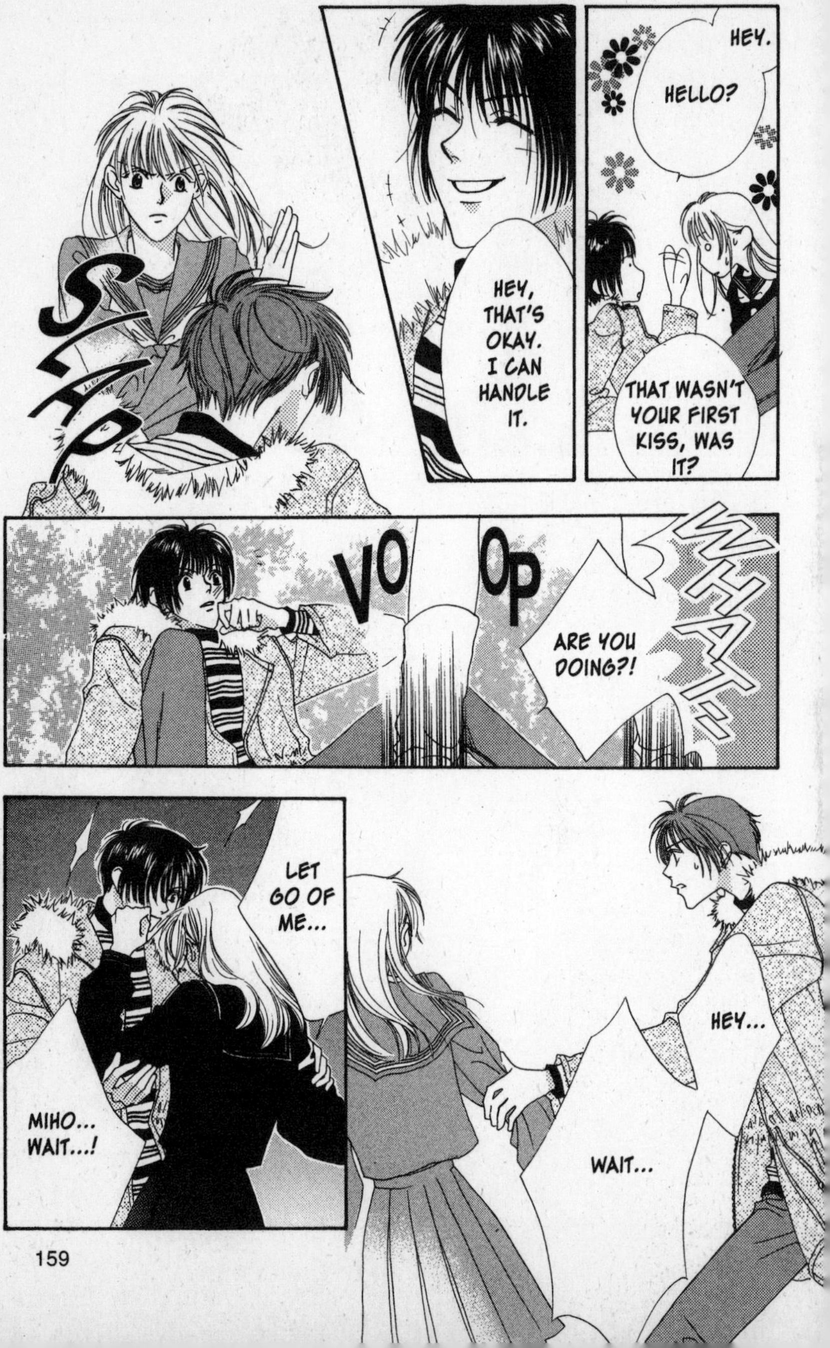
HEY.
HELLO?
THAT WASN'T YOUR FIRST KISS, WAS IT?
HEY, THAT'S OKAY. I CAN HANDLE IT.
SLAP
WHAT!!
ARE YOU DOING?!
VOOP
HEY...
WAIT...
LET GO OF ME...
MIHO... WAIT...!

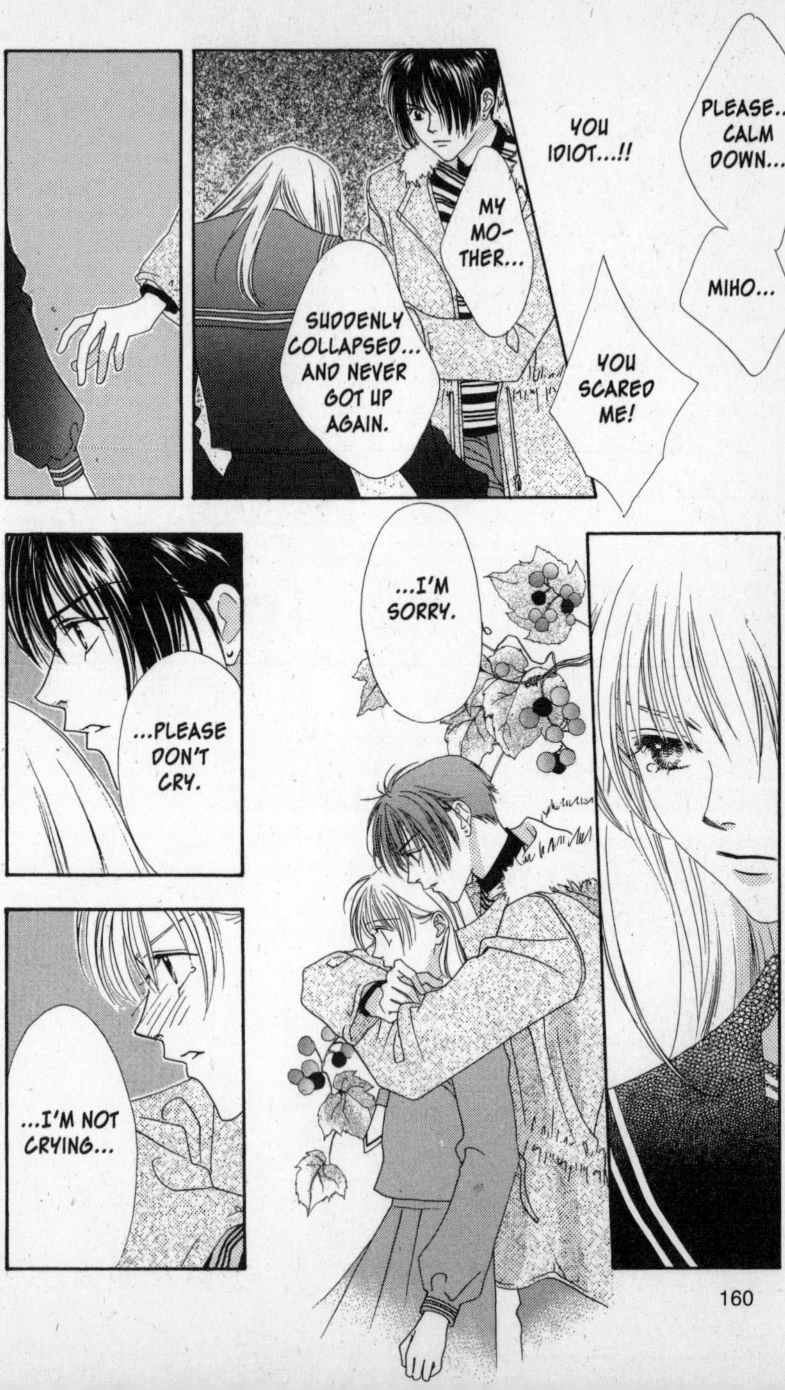
PLEASE... CALM DOWN...
MIHO...
YOU IDIOT...!!
YOU SCARED ME!
MY MO-THER...
SUDDENLY COLLAPSED... AND NEVER GOT UP AGAIN.
...I'M SORRY.
...PLEASE DON'T CRY.
...I'M NOT CRYING...

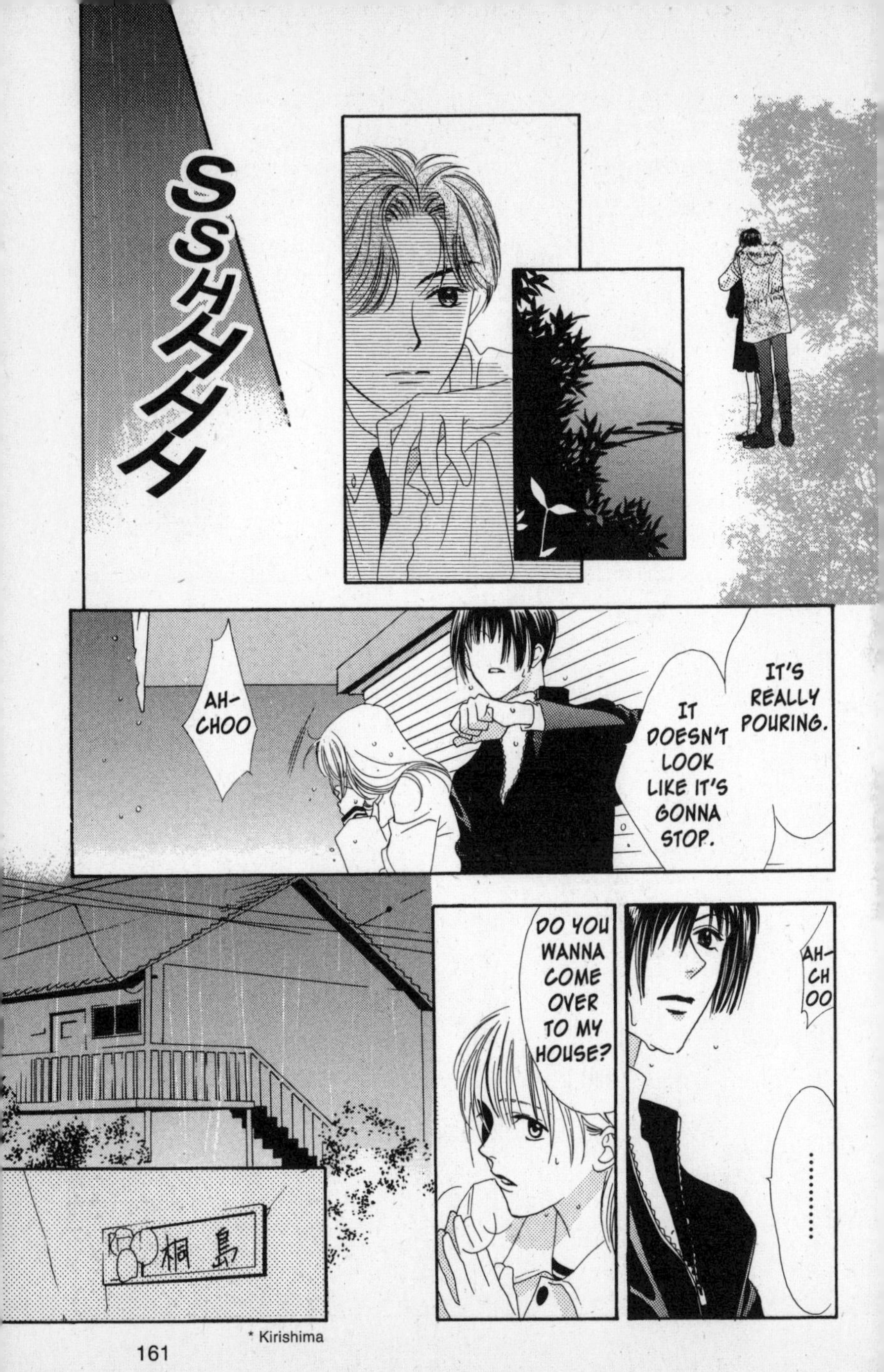
SSHHHH
IT'S REALLY POURING.
IT DOESN'T LOOK LIKE IT'S GONNA STOP.
AH-CHOO
AH-CHOO
......
DO YOU WANNA COME OVER TO MY HOUSE?
桐島

* Kirishima

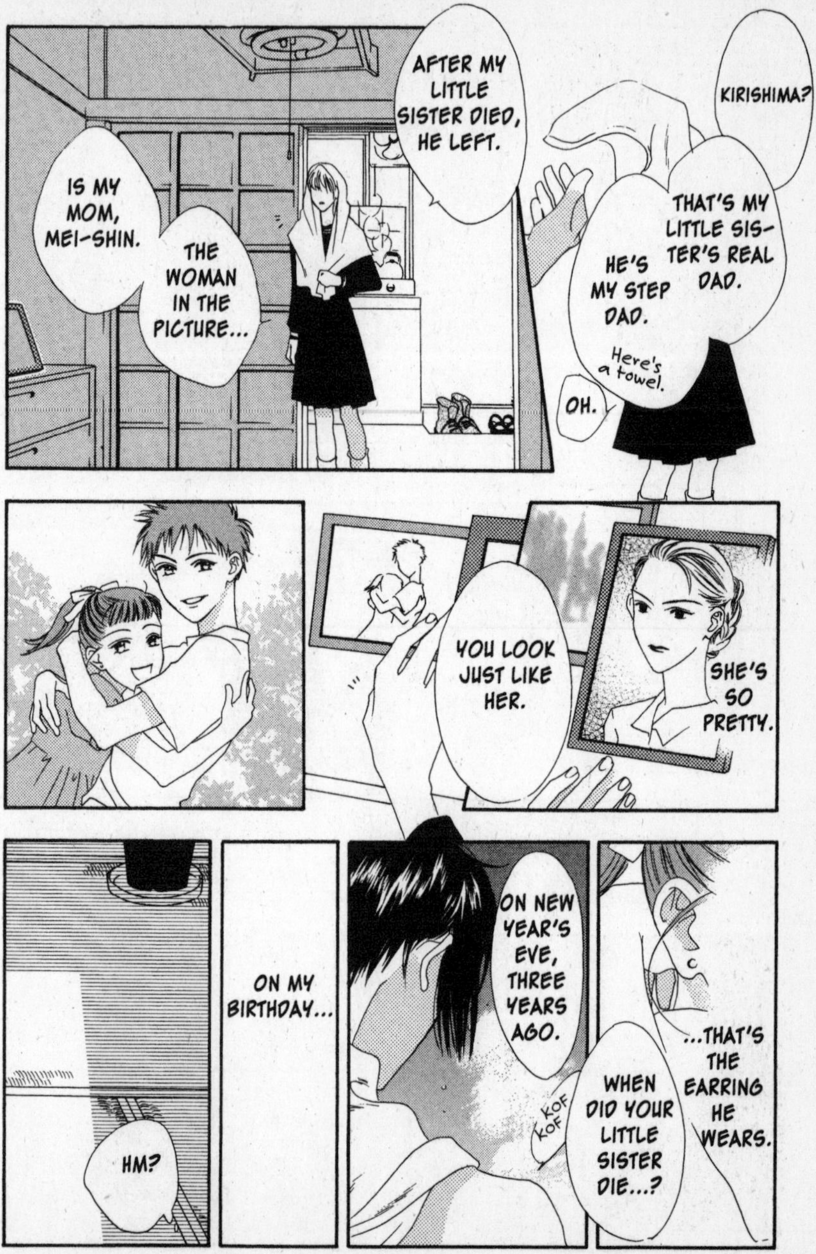
KIRISHIMA?
THAT'S MY LITTLE SISTER'S REAL DAD.
HE'S MY STEP DAD.
Here's a towel.
OH.
AFTER MY LITTLE SISTER DIED, HE LEFT.
THE WOMAN IN THE PICTURE...
IS MY MOM, MEI-SHIN.
SHE'S SO PRETTY.
YOU LOOK JUST LIKE HER.
...THAT'S THE EARRING HE WEARS.
WHEN DID YOUR LITTLE SISTER DIE...?
KOF KOF
ON NEW YEAR'S EVE, THREE YEARS AGO.
ON MY BIRTHDAY...
HM?

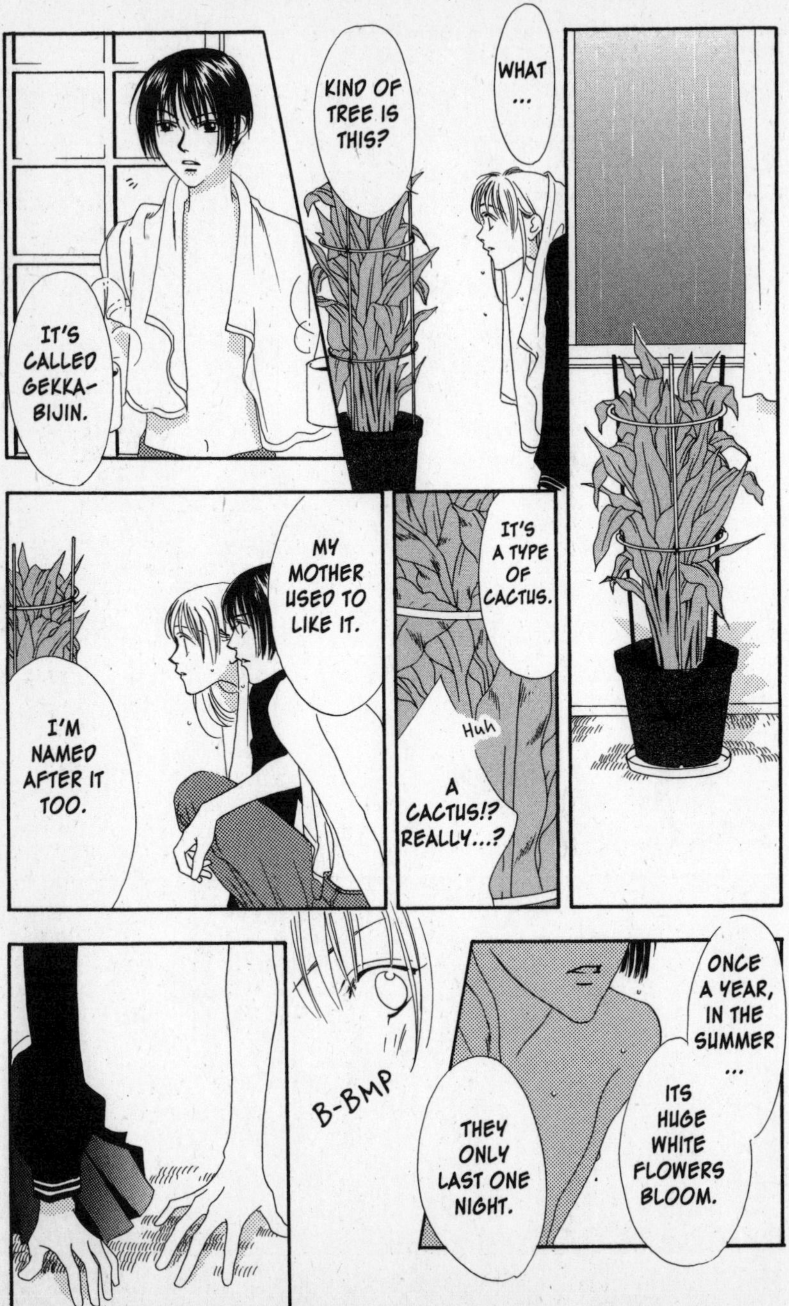
WHAT ...
KIND OF TREE IS THIS?
IT'S CALLED GEKKA-BIJIN.
IT'S A TYPE OF CACTUS.
Huh
A CACTUS!? REALLY...?
MY MOTHER USED TO LIKE IT.
I'M NAMED AFTER IT TOO.
ONCE A YEAR, IN THE SUMMER ...
ITS HUGE WHITE FLOWERS BLOOM.
THEY ONLY LAST ONE NIGHT.
B-BMP

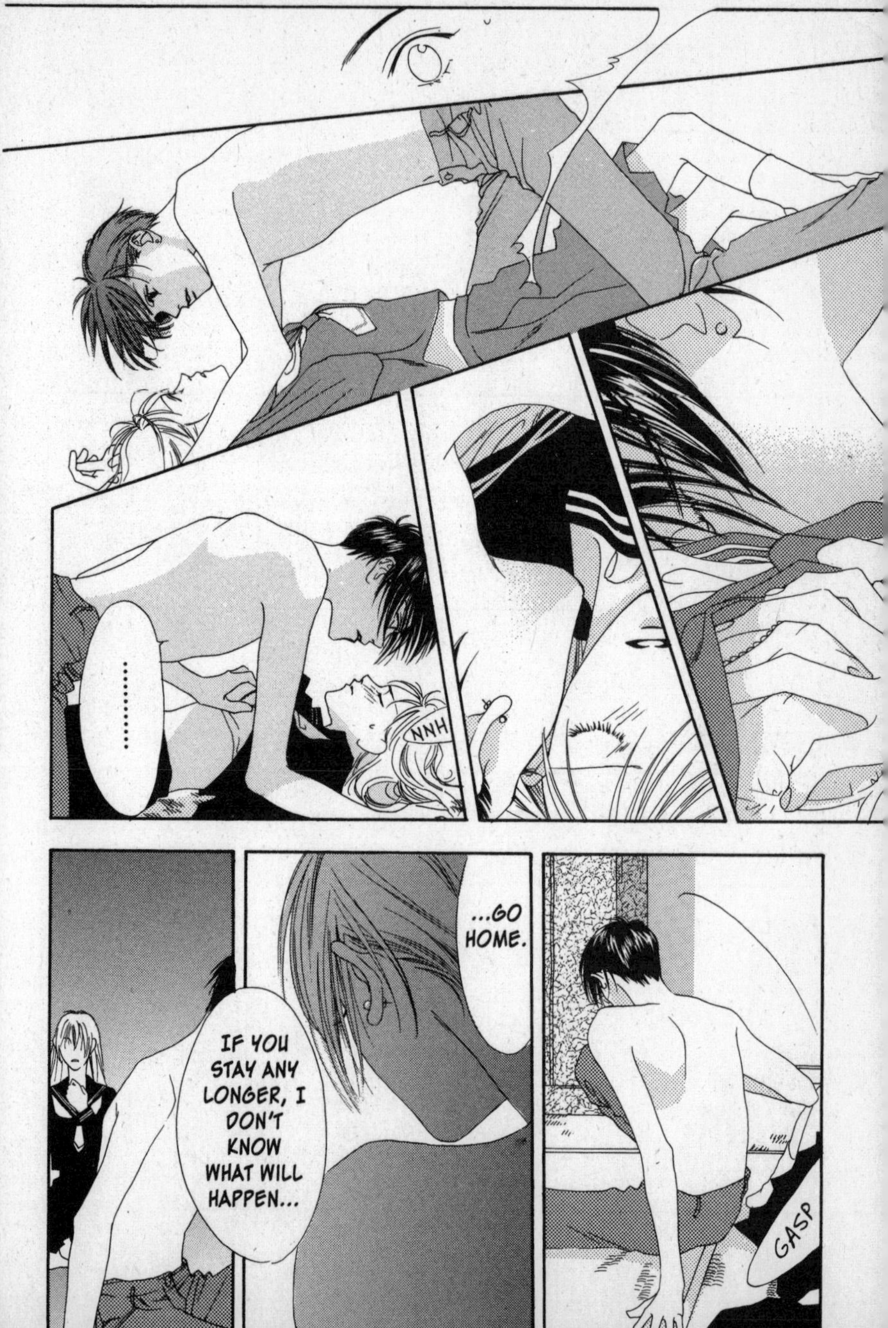
NNH
......
GASP
...GO HOME.
IF YOU STAY ANY LONGER, I DON'T KNOW WHAT WILL HAPPEN...

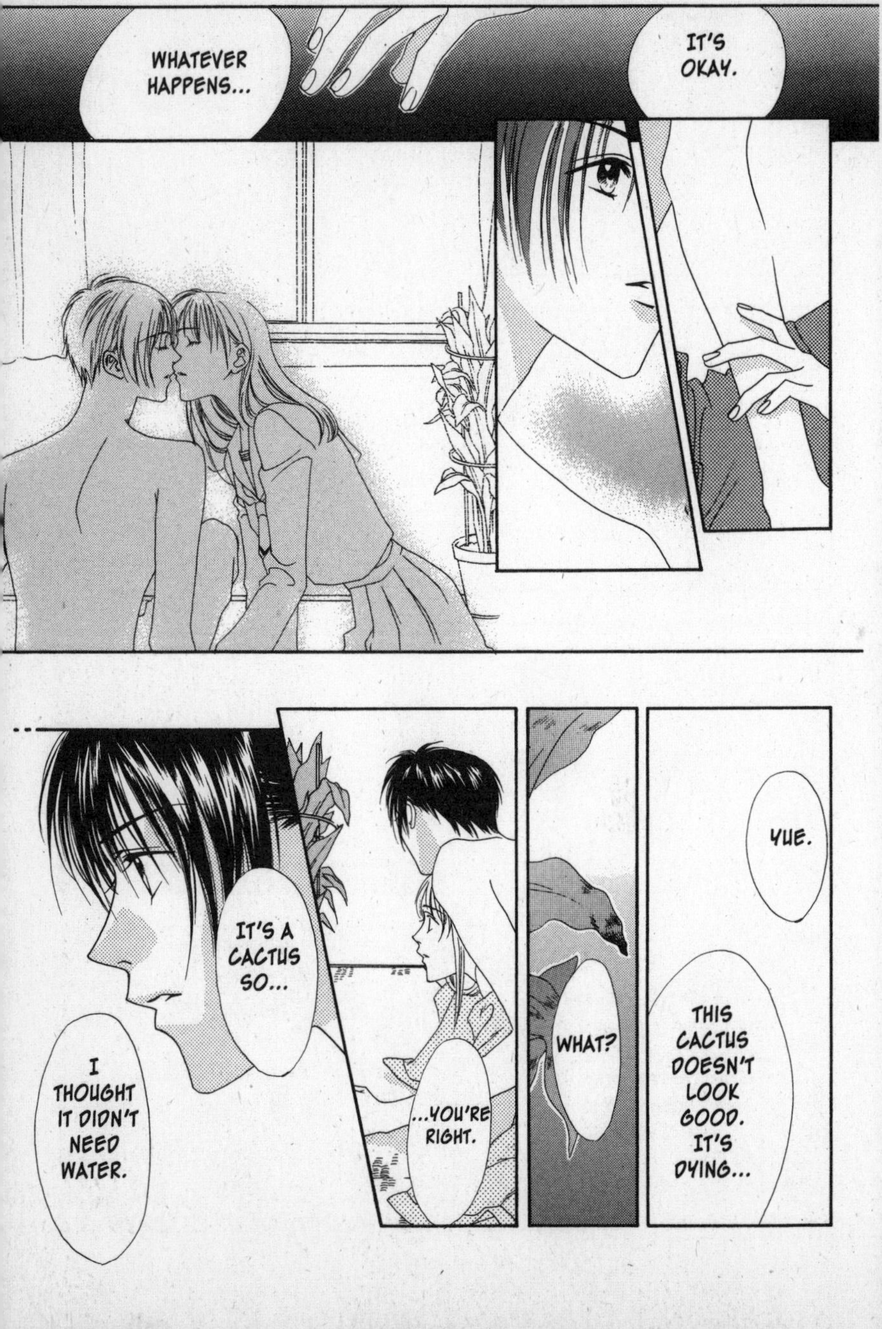
IT'S OKAY.
WHATEVER HAPPENS...
YUE.
THIS CACTUS DOESN'T LOOK GOOD. IT'S DYING...
WHAT?
...YOU'RE RIGHT.
IT'S A CACTUS SO...
I THOUGHT IT DIDN'T NEED WATER.

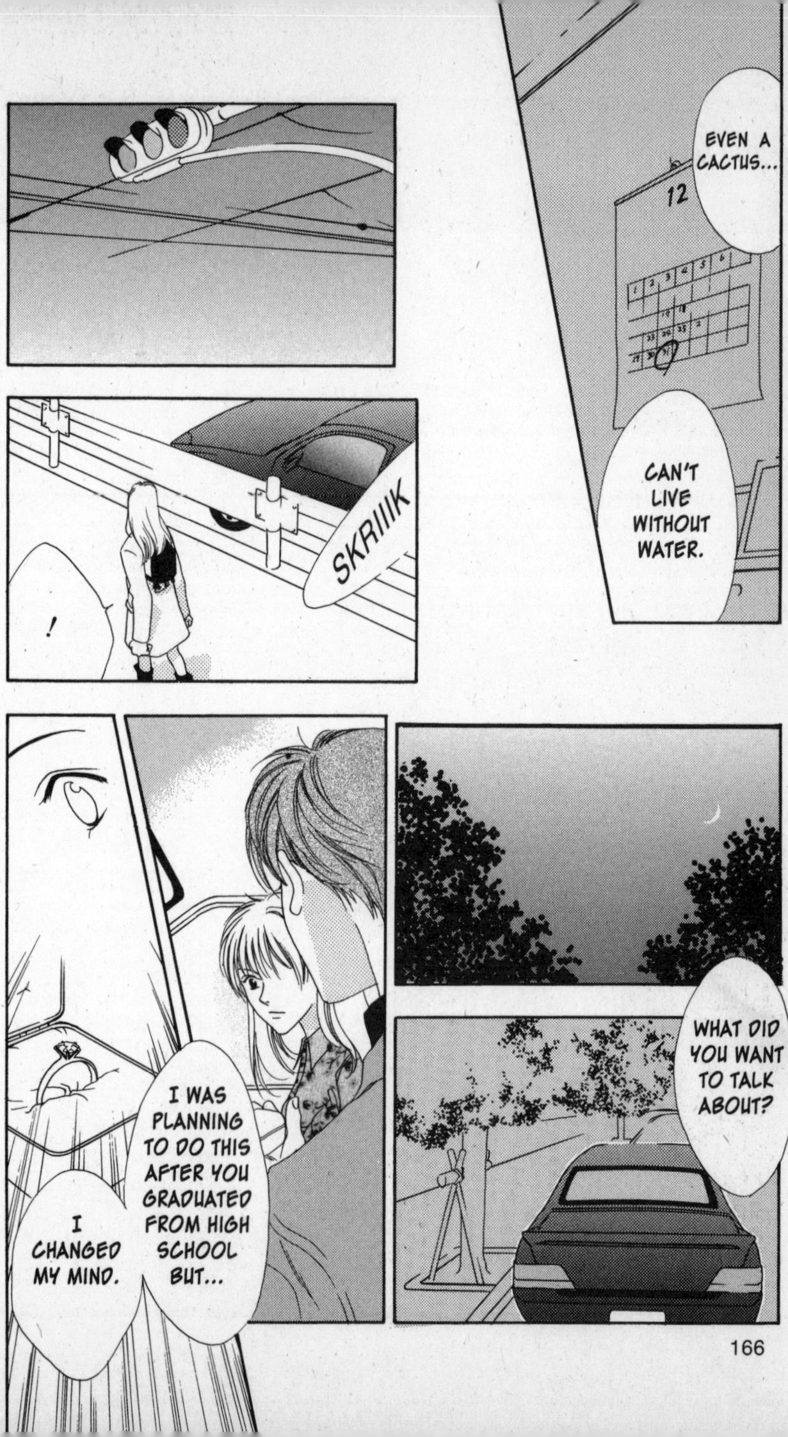
EVEN A CACTUS...
12
CAN'T LIVE WITHOUT WATER.
SKRIIIK
!
WHAT DID YOU WANT TO TALK ABOUT?
I WAS PLANNING TO DO THIS AFTER YOU GRADUATED FROM HIGH SCHOOL BUT...
I CHANGED MY MIND.

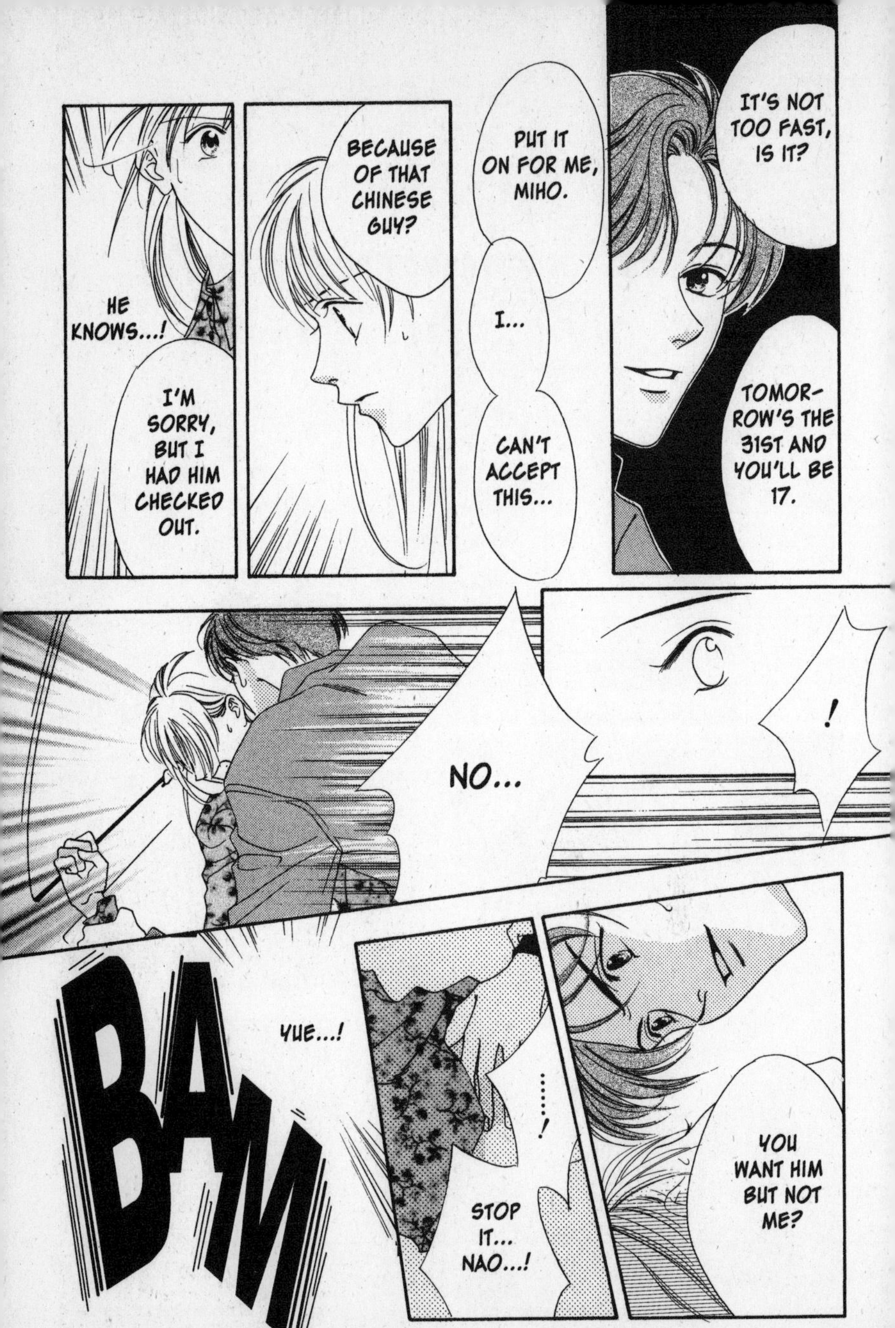
IT'S NOT TOO FAST, IS IT?
TOMOR-ROW'S THE 31ST AND YOU'LL BE 17.
PUT IT ON FOR ME, MIHO.
I...
CAN'T ACCEPT THIS...
BECAUSE OF THAT CHINESE GUY?
HE KNOWS...!
I'M SORRY, BUT I HAD HIM CHECKED OUT.
!
NO...
YOU WANT HIM BUT NOT ME?
......!
STOP IT... NAO...!
YUE...!
BAM

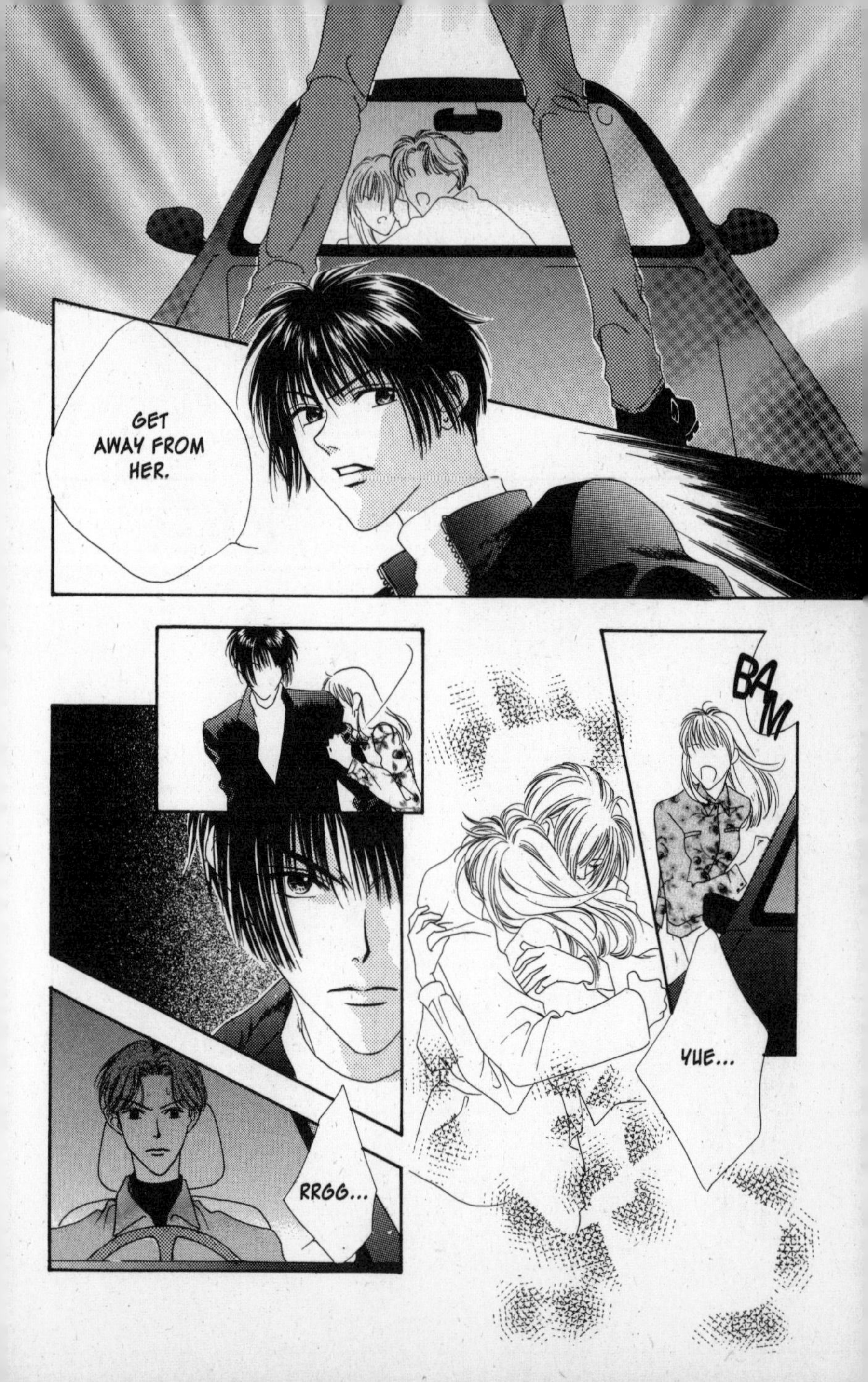
GET AWAY FROM HER.
BAM
YUE...
RRGG...

* Kirishima

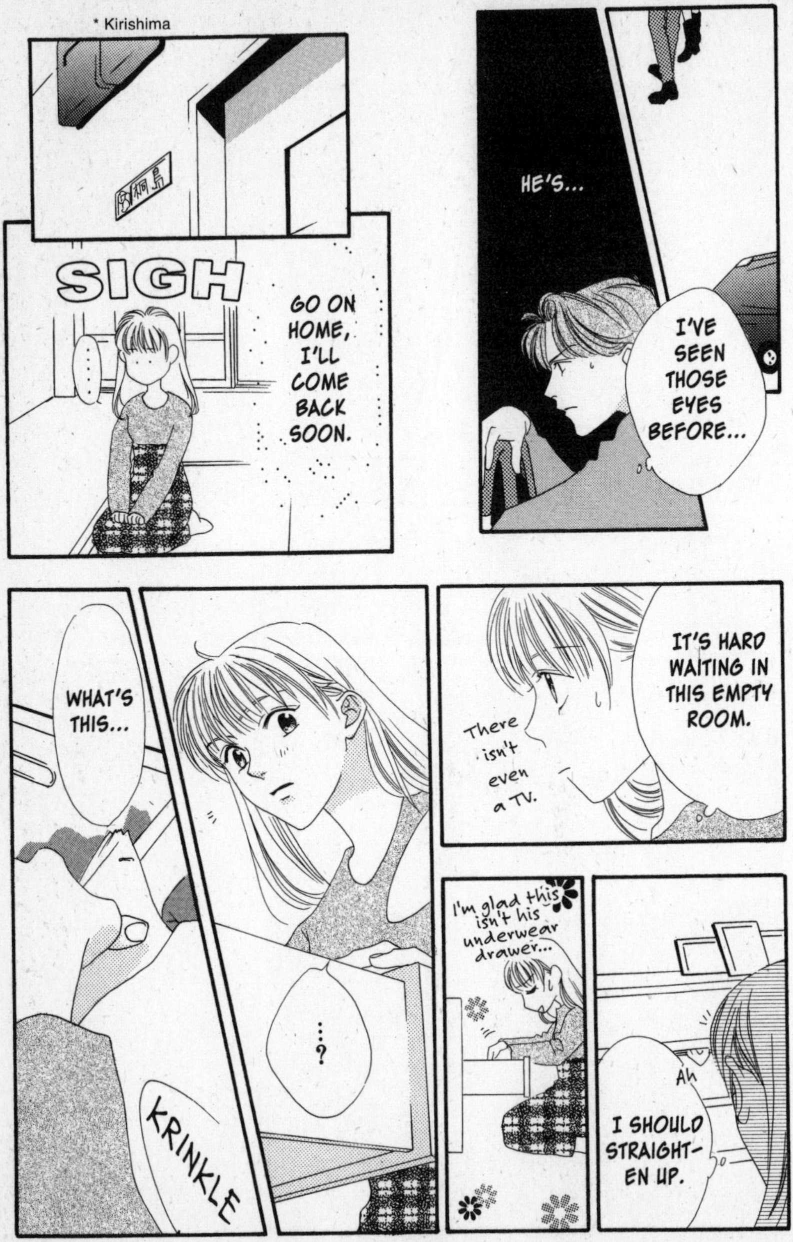
HE'S...
I'VE SEEN THOSE EYES BEFORE...
桐島
GO ON HOME, I'LL COME BACK SOON.
SIGH
...
IT'S HARD WAITING IN THIS EMPTY ROOM.
There isn't even a TV.
Ah
I SHOULD STRAIGHT-EN UP.
I'm glad this isn't his underwear drawer...
...?
WHAT'S THIS...
KRINKLE

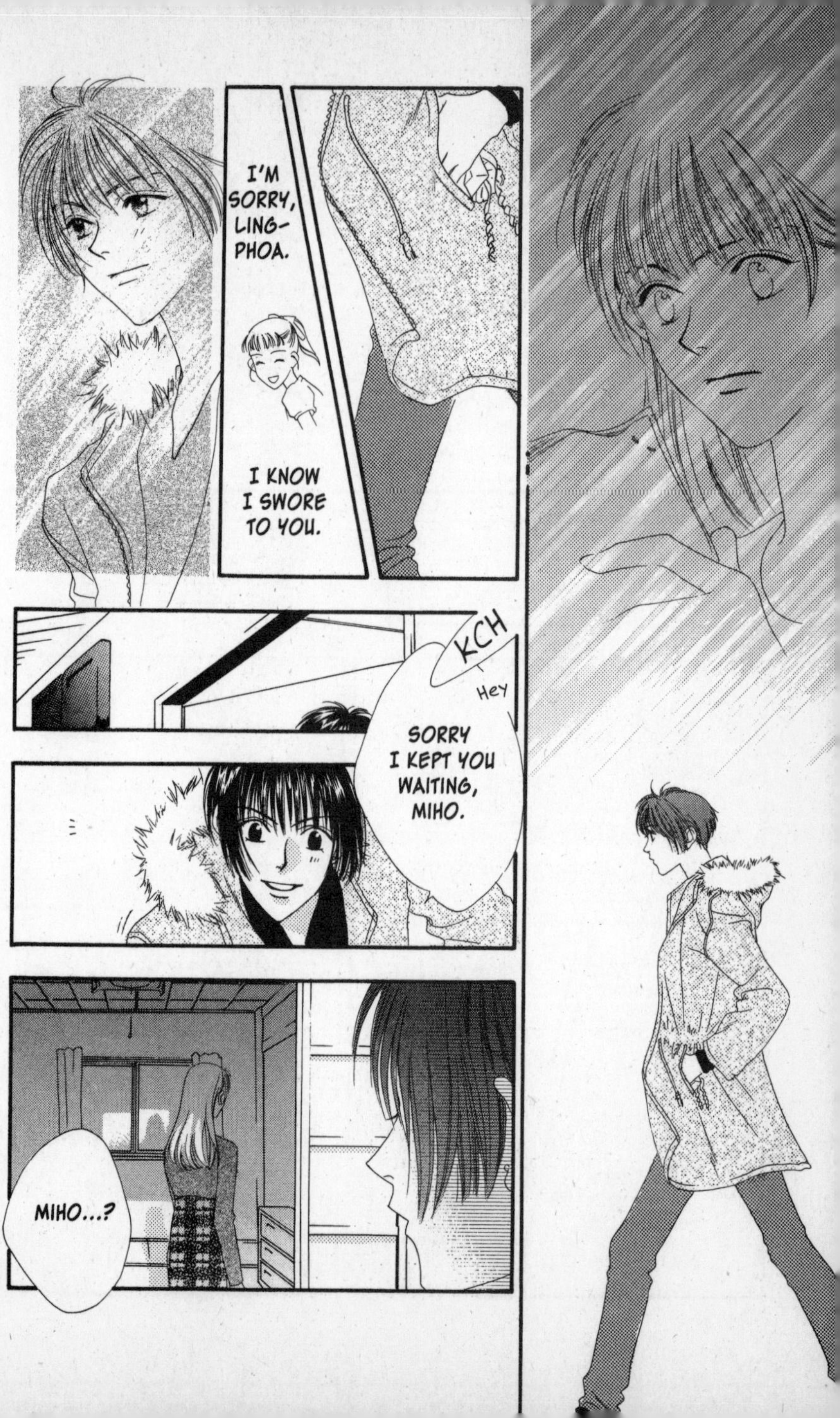
I'M SORRY, LING-PHOA.
I KNOW I SWORE TO YOU.
KCH
Hey
SORRY I KEPT YOU WAITING, MIHO.
MIHO...?

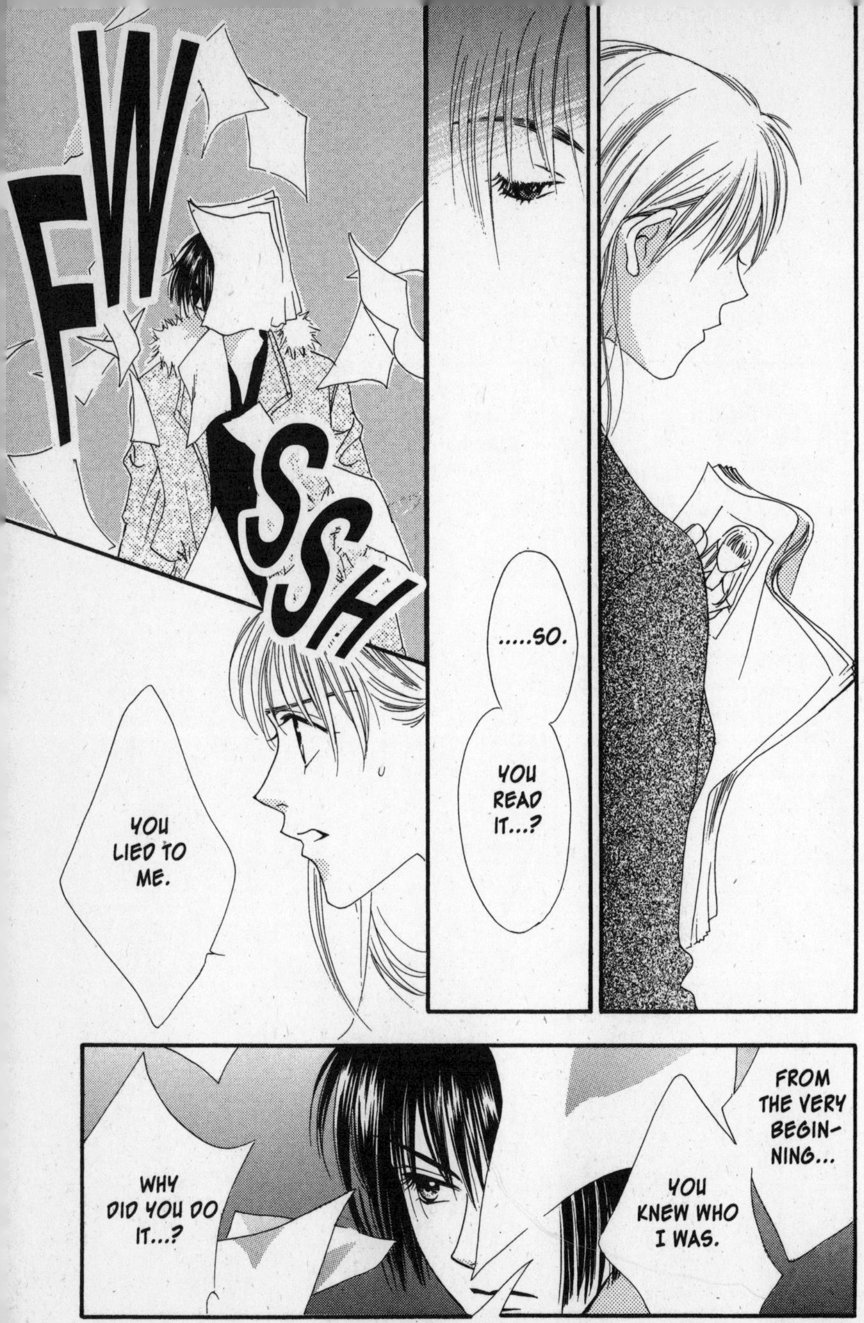
.....SO.
YOU READ IT...?
FWSSH
YOU LIED TO ME.
FROM THE VERY BEGINNING...
YOU KNEW WHO I WAS.
WHY DID YOU DO IT...?

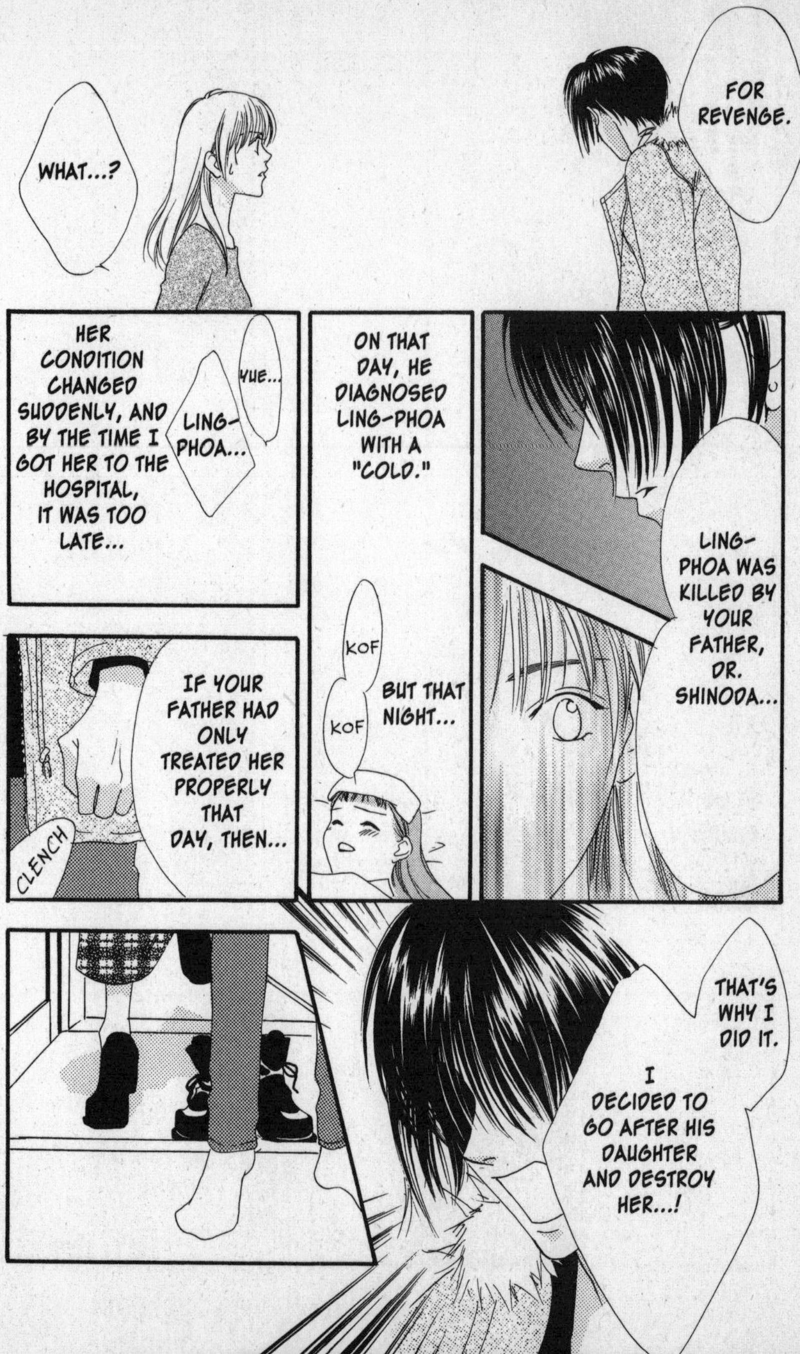
FOR REVENGE.
WHAT...?
LING-PHOA WAS KILLED BY YOUR FATHER, DR. SHINODA...
ON THAT DAY, HE DIAGNOSED LING-PHOA WITH A "COLD."
KOF
BUT THAT NIGHT...
KOF
YUE...
LING-PHOA...
HER CONDITION CHANGED SUDDENLY, AND BY THE TIME I GOT HER TO THE HOSPITAL, IT WAS TOO LATE...
IF YOUR FATHER HAD ONLY TREATED HER PROPERLY THAT DAY, THEN...
CLENCH
THAT'S WHY I DID IT.
I DECIDED TO GO AFTER HIS DAUGHTER AND DESTROY HER...!

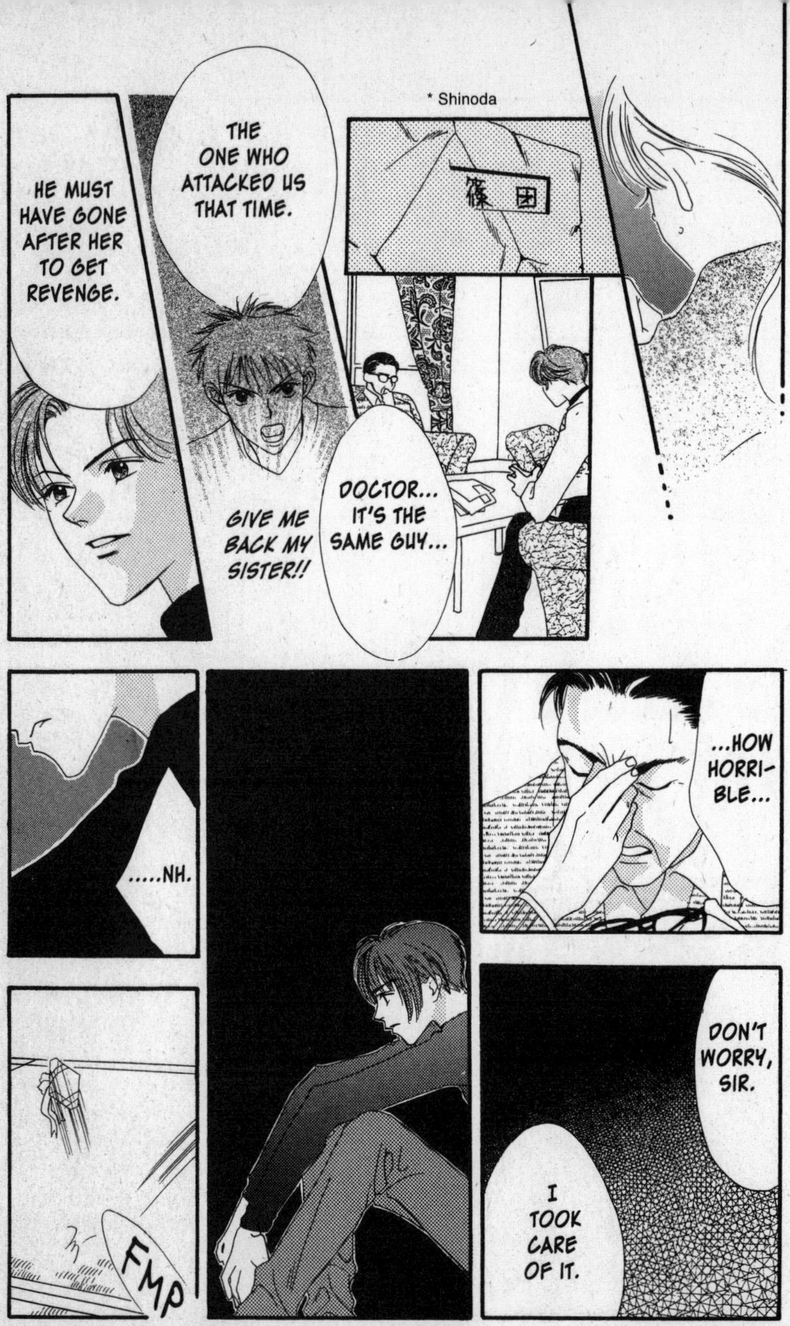
* Shinoda
篠田
DOCTOR... IT'S THE SAME GUY...
THE ONE WHO ATTACKED US THAT TIME.
GIVE ME BACK MY SISTER!!
HE MUST HAVE GONE AFTER HER TO GET REVENGE.
...HOW HORRI-BLE...
DON'T WORRY, SIR.
I TOOK CARE OF IT.
.....NH.
FMP

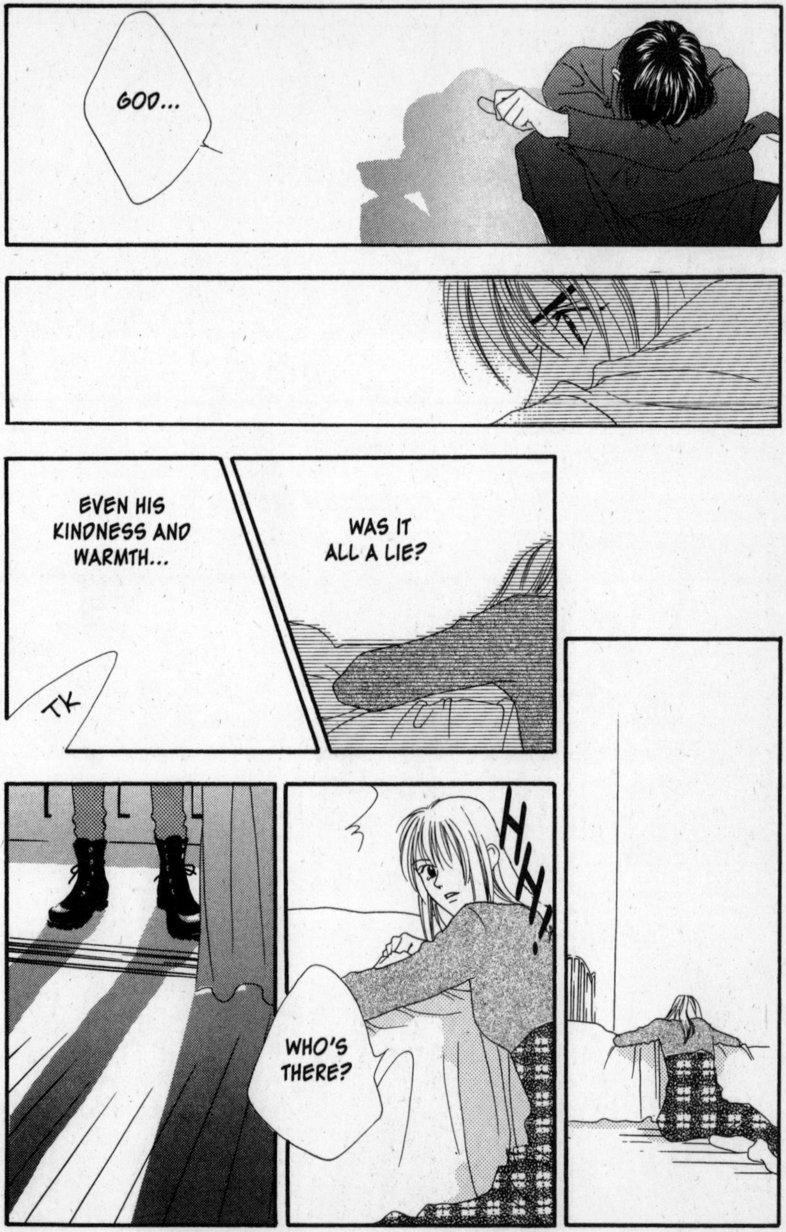
GOD...
WAS IT ALL A LIE?
EVEN HIS KINDNESS AND WARMTH...
TK
HH!
WHO'S THERE?

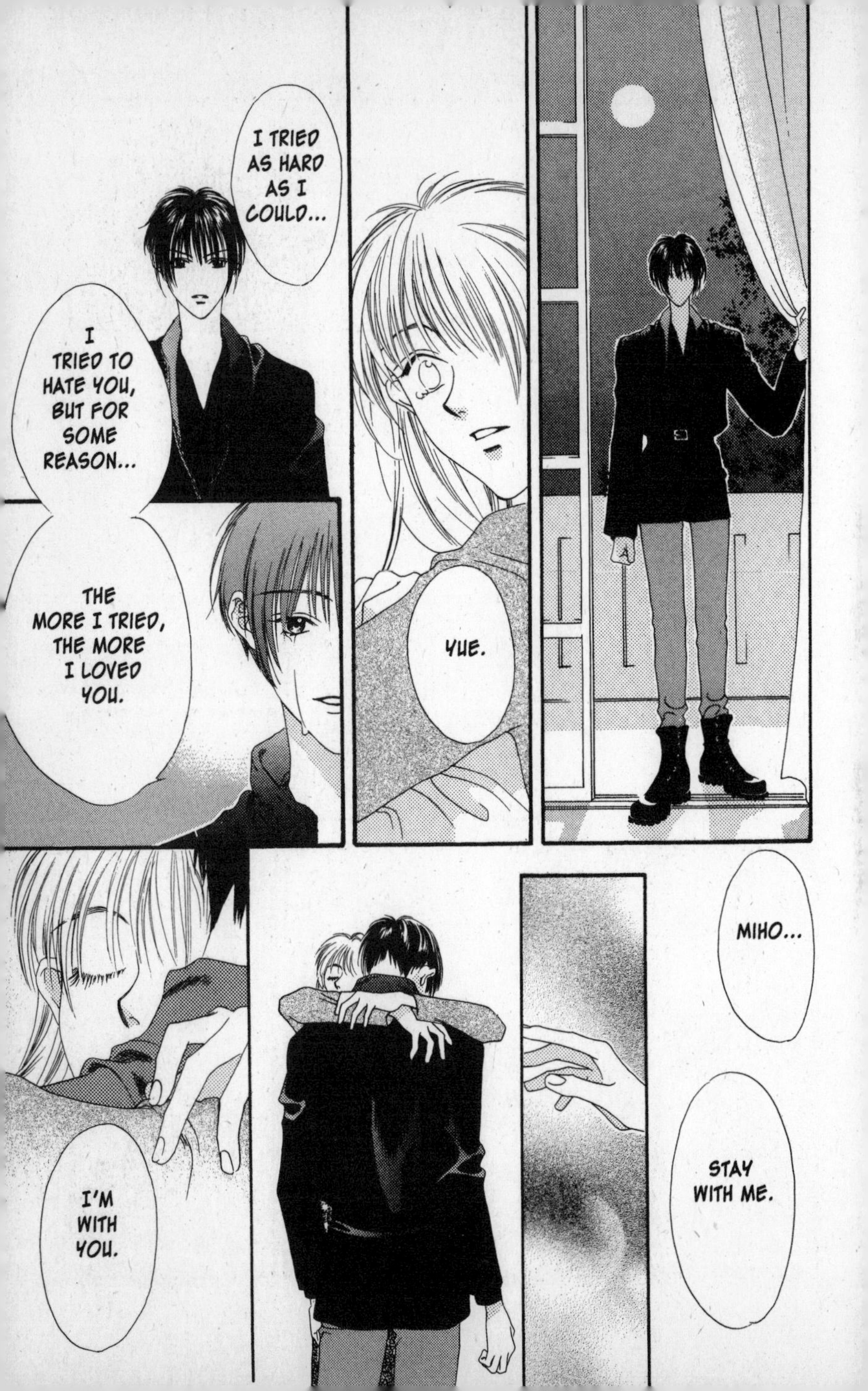
YUE.
I TRIED AS HARD AS I COULD...
I TRIED TO HATE YOU, BUT FOR SOME REASON...
THE MORE I TRIED, THE MORE I LOVED YOU.
MIHO...
STAY WITH ME.
I'M WITH YOU.

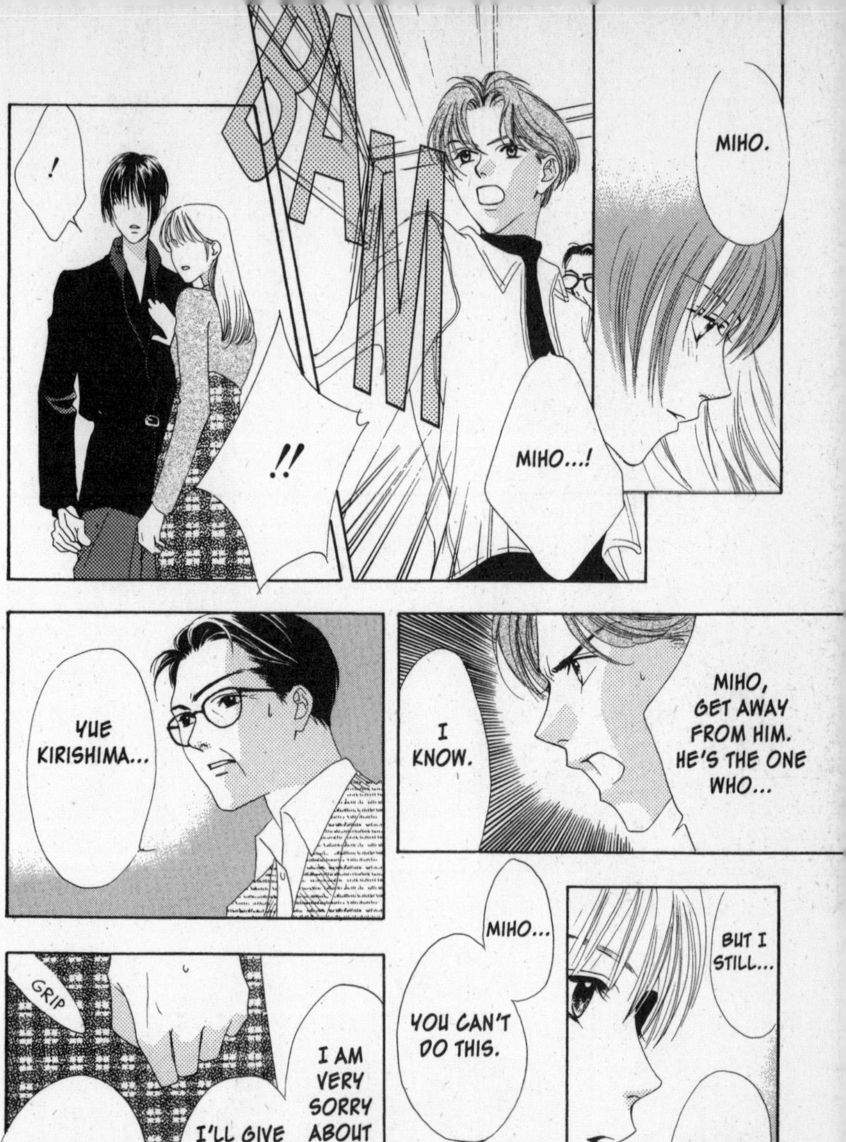
MIHO.
SPAM
MIHO...!
!!
!
MIHO, GET AWAY FROM HIM. HE'S THE ONE WHO...
I KNOW.
YUE KIRISHIMA...
BUT I STILL...
LOVE HIM.
MIHO...
YOU CAN'T DO THIS.
I AM VERY SORRY ABOUT YOUR LITTLE SISTER.
I'LL GIVE YOU THE APOLOGY THAT YOU ARE ASKING FOR.
GRIP
SO FORGET ABOUT MIHO...

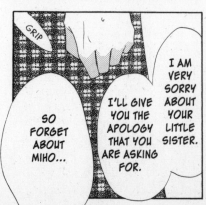

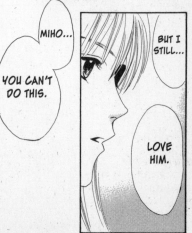

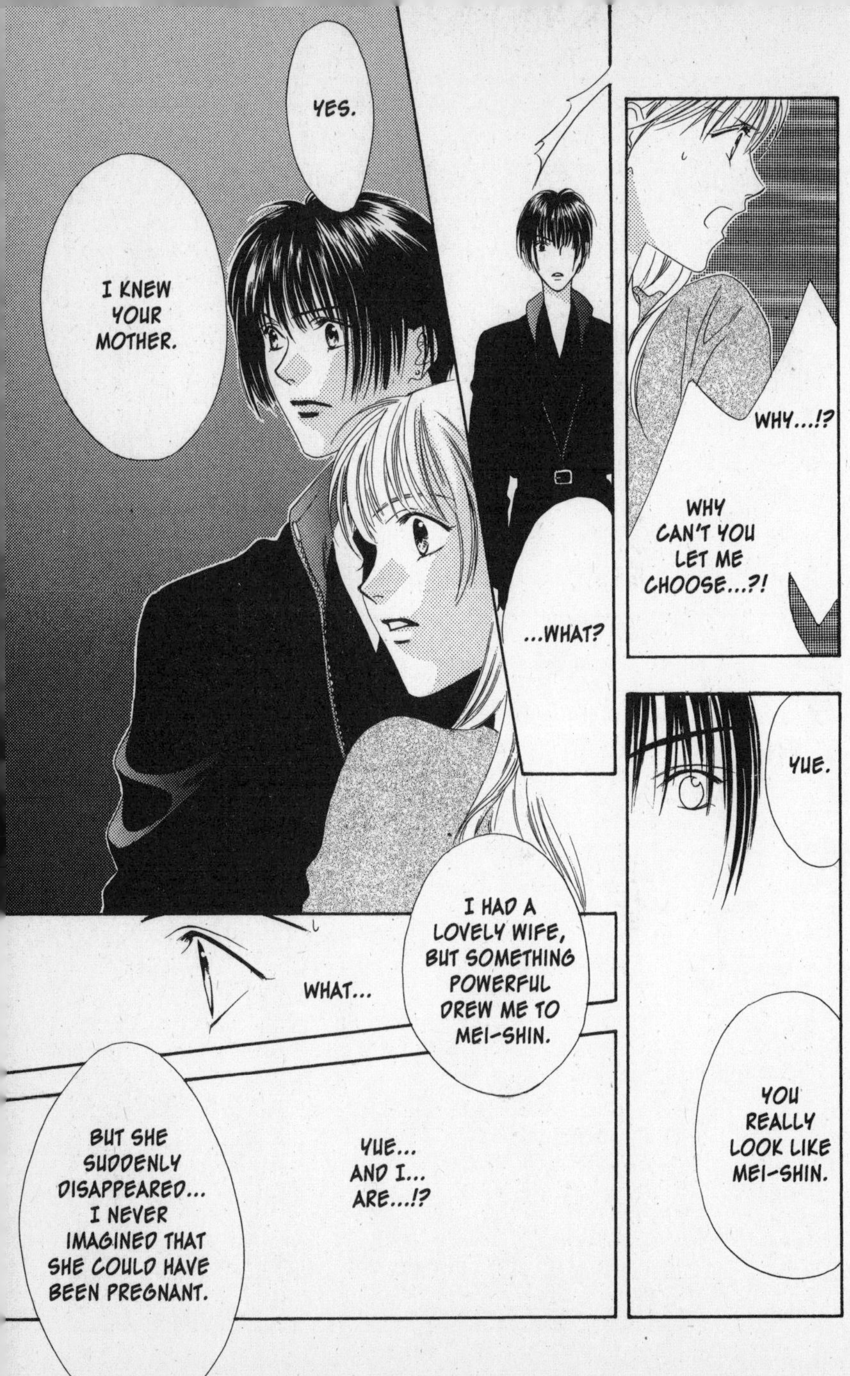
WHY...!?
WHY CAN'T YOU LET ME CHOOSE...?!
...WHAT?
YES.
I KNEW YOUR MOTHER.
YUE.
YOU REALLY LOOK LIKE MEI-SHIN.
I HAD A LOVELY WIFE, BUT SOMETHING POWERFUL DREW ME TO MEI-SHIN.
WHAT...
YUE... AND I... ARE...!?
BUT SHE SUDDENLY DISAPPEARED... I NEVER IMAGINED THAT SHE COULD HAVE BEEN PREGNANT.

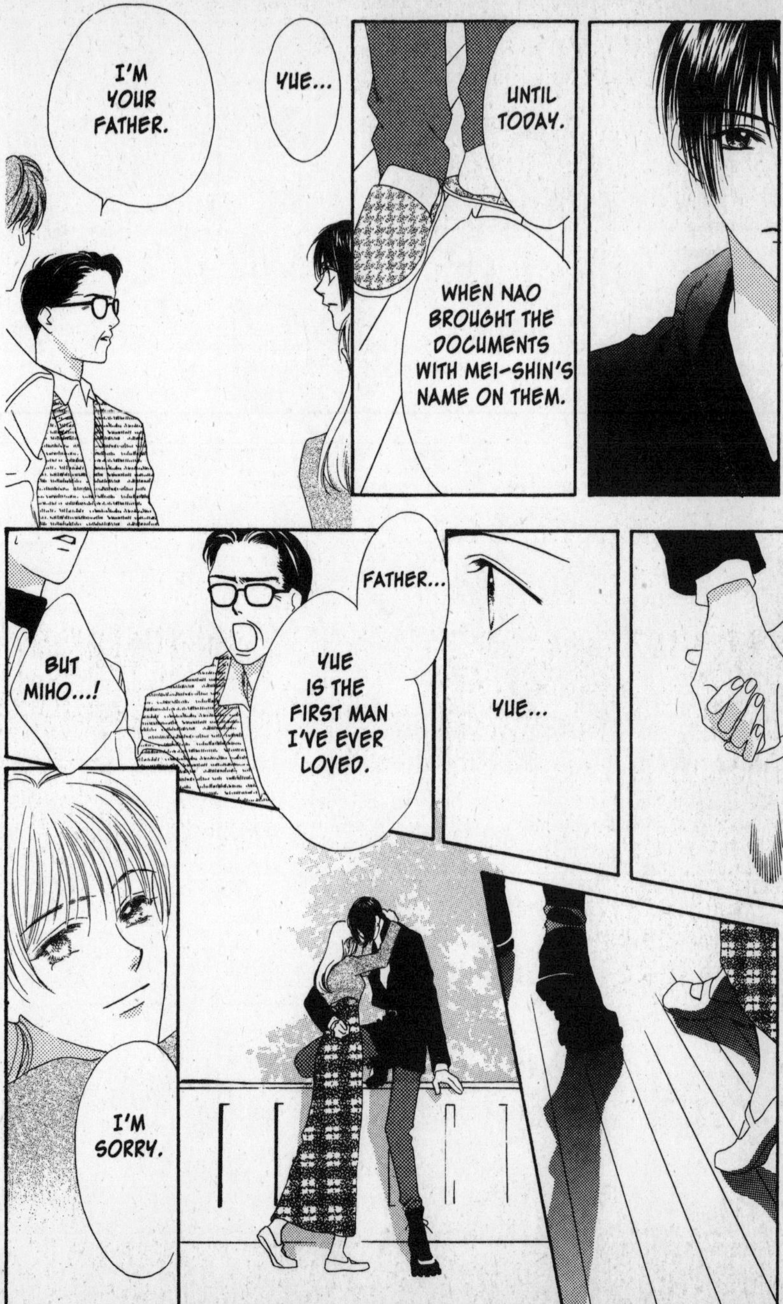
UNTIL TODAY.
WHEN NAO BROUGHT THE DOCUMENTS WITH MEI-SHIN'S NAME ON THEM.
YUE...
I'M YOUR FATHER.
YUE...
FATHER...
YUE IS THE FIRST MAN I'VE EVER LOVED.
BUT MIHO...!
I'M SORRY.

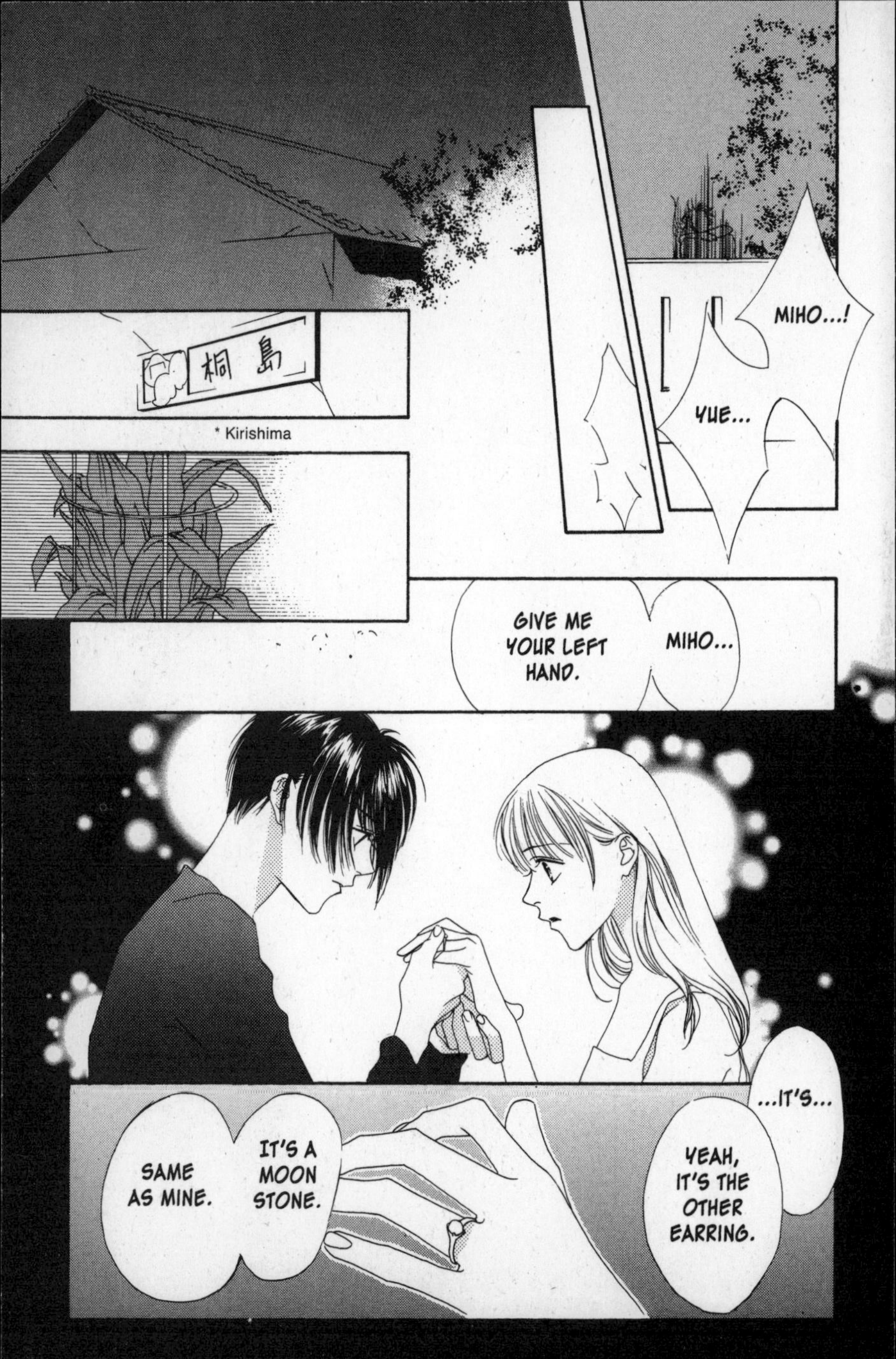
MIHO...!
YUE...
桐島
* Kirishima
MIHO...
GIVE ME YOUR LEFT HAND.
...IT'S...
YEAH, IT'S THE OTHER EARRING.
IT'S A MOON STONE.
SAME AS MINE.

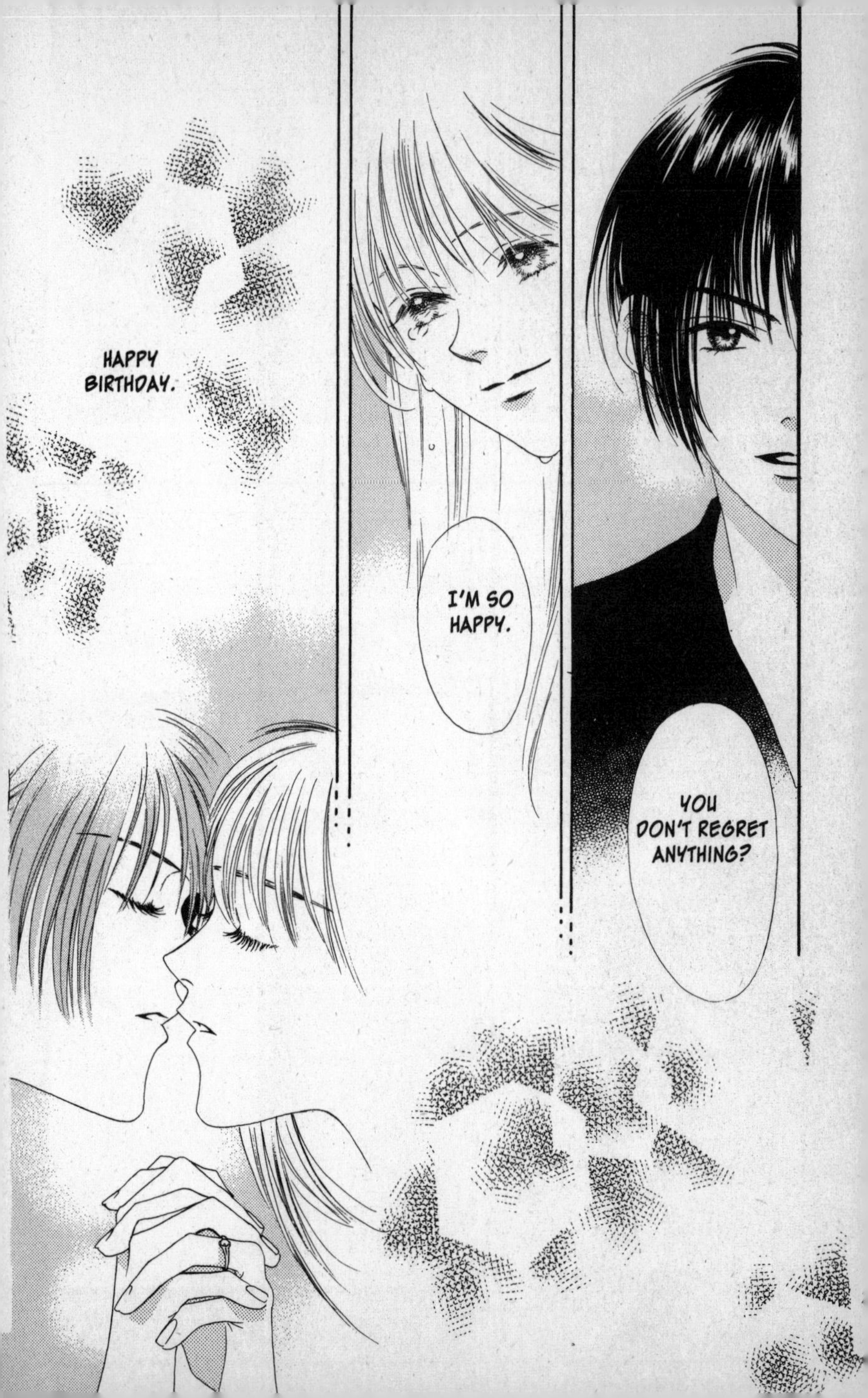
YOU DON'T REGRET ANYTHING?
I'M SO HAPPY.
HAPPY BIRTHDAY.

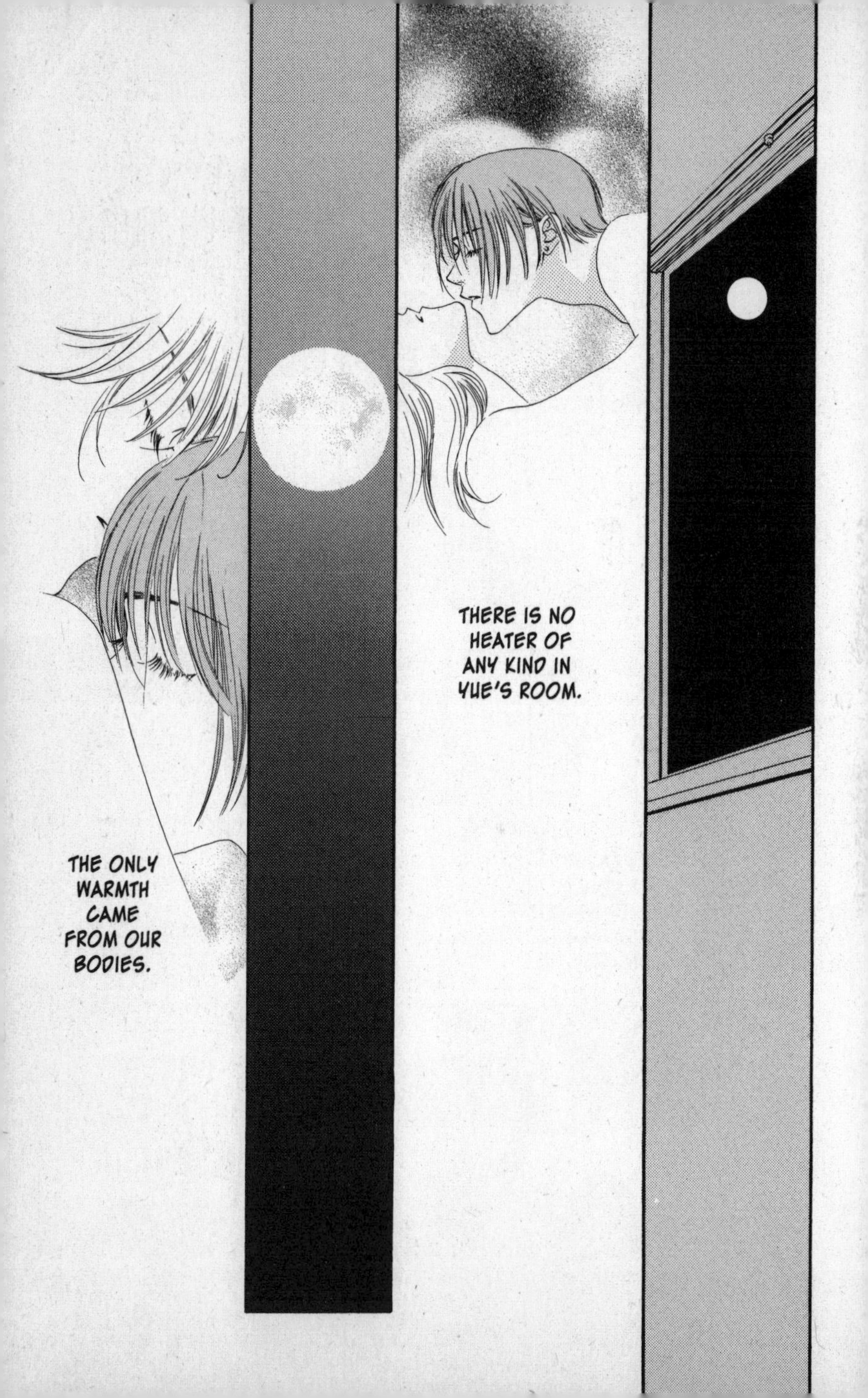
THERE IS NO HEATER OF ANY KIND IN YUE'S ROOM.
THE ONLY WARMTH CAME FROM OUR BODIES.

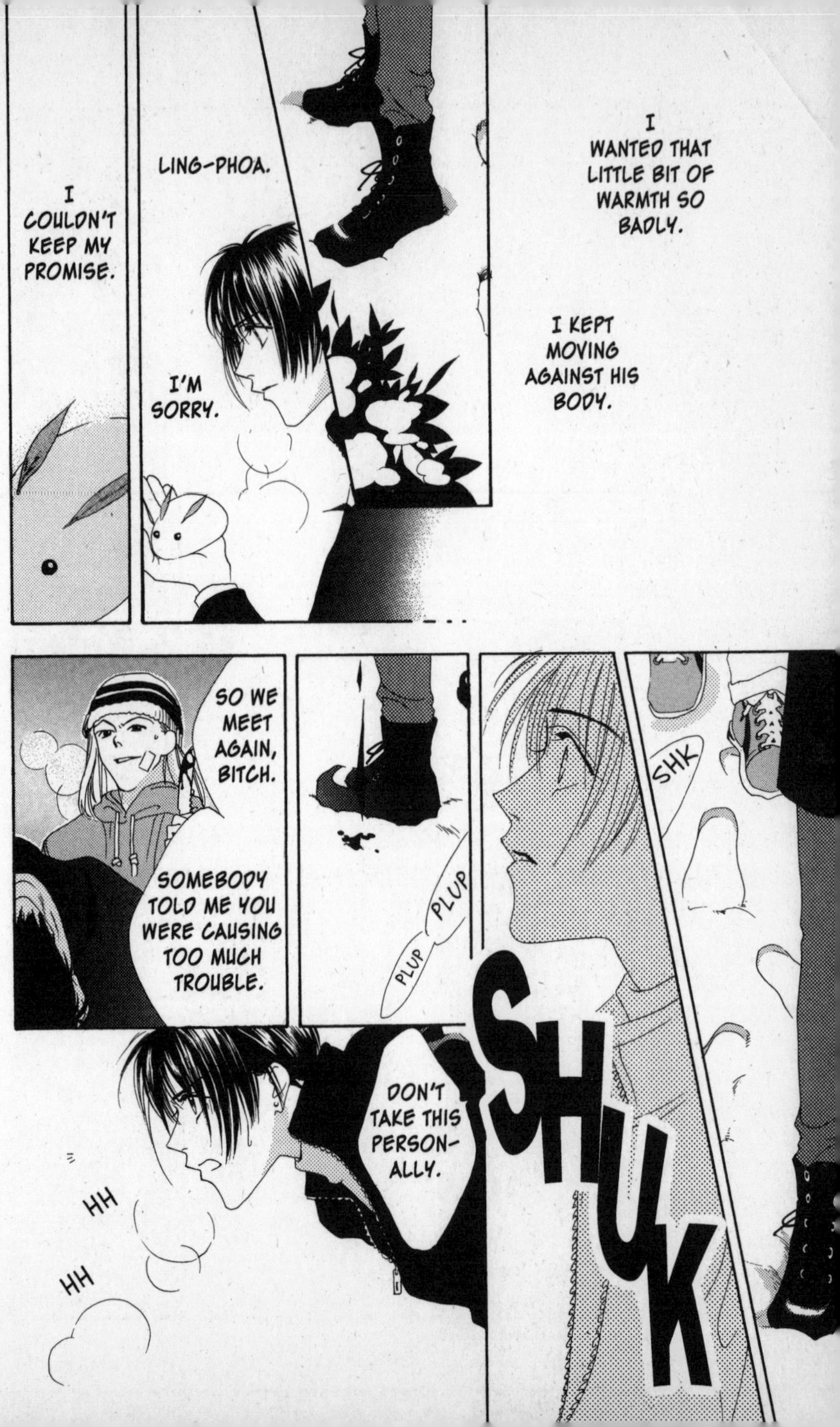
I WANTED THAT LITTLE BIT OF WARMTH SO BADLY.
I KEPT MOVING AGAINST HIS BODY.
LING-PHOA.
I'M SORRY.
I COULDN'T KEEP MY PROMISE.
SHK
PLUP
PLUP
PLUP
SO WE MEET AGAIN, BITCH.
SOMEBODY TOLD ME YOU WERE CAUSING TOO MUCH TROUBLE.
SHUK
DON'T TAKE THIS PERSON-ALLY.
HH
HH

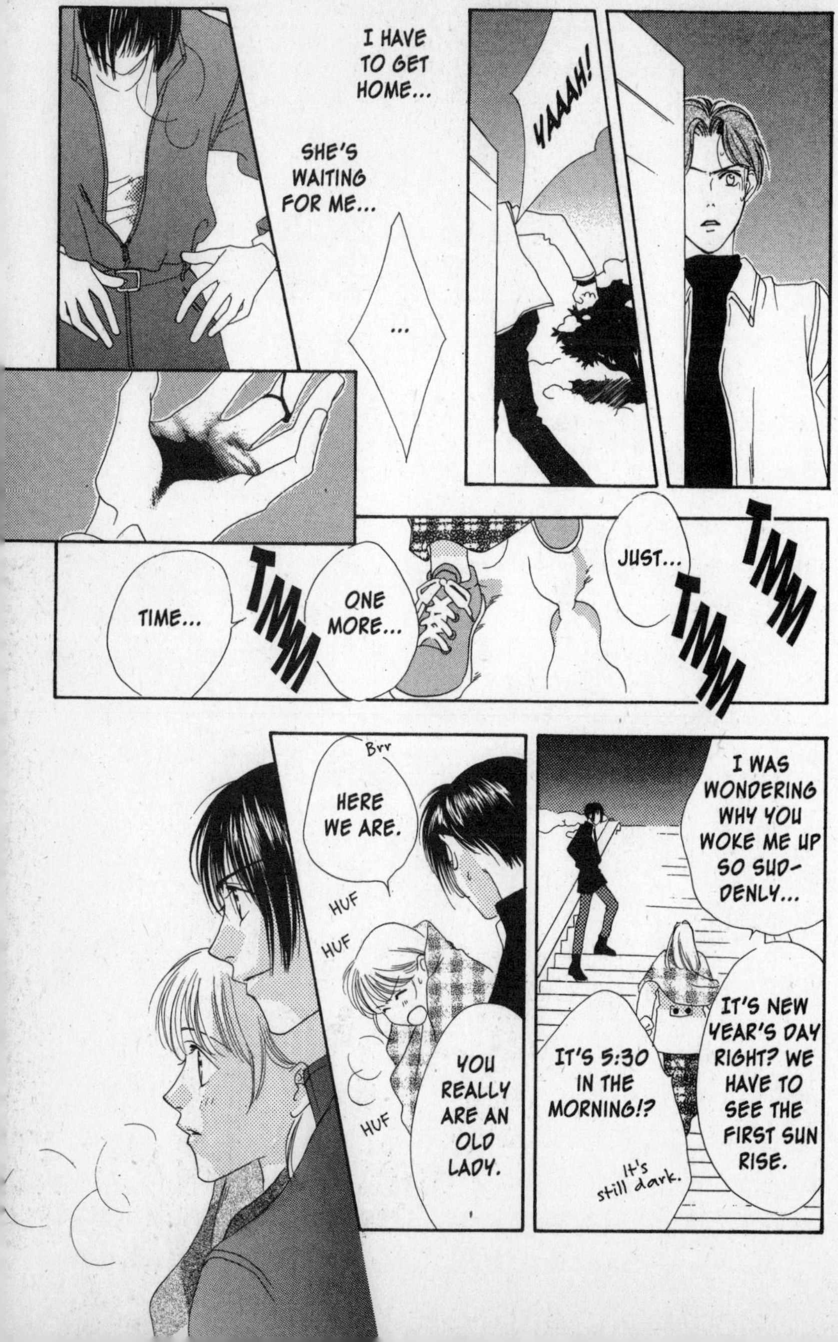
YAAAH!
I HAVE TO GET HOME...
SHE'S WAITING FOR ME...
...
TMM
TMM
JUST...
ONE MORE...
TIME...
TMM
I WAS WONDERING WHY YOU WOKE ME UP SO SUD-DENLY...
IT'S NEW YEAR'S DAY RIGHT? WE HAVE TO SEE THE FIRST SUN RISE.
IT'S 5:30 IN THE MORNING!?
It's still dark.
Brr
HERE WE ARE.
HUF
HUF
YOU REALLY ARE AN OLD LADY.
HUF

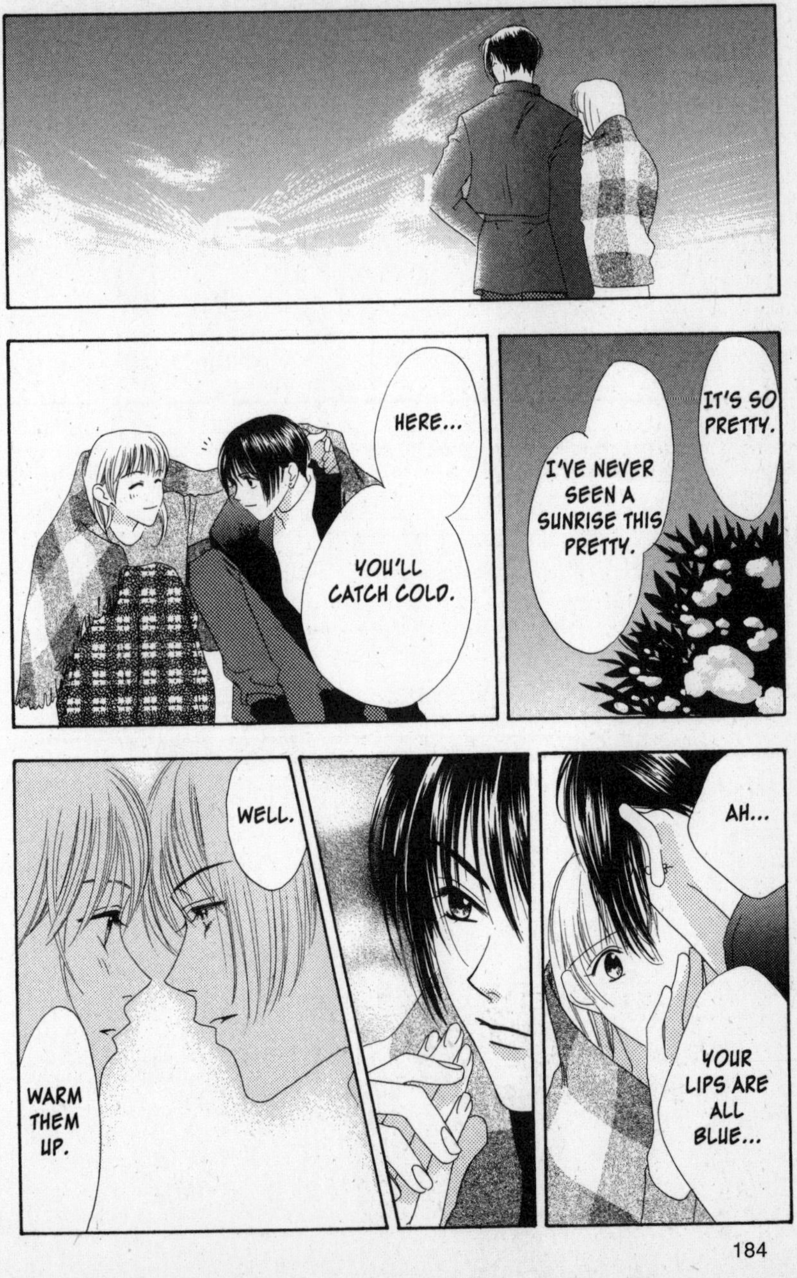
IT'S SO PRETTY.
I'VE NEVER SEEN A SUNRISE THIS PRETTY.
HERE...
YOU'LL CATCH COLD.
AH...
YOUR LIPS ARE ALL BLUE...
WELL.
WARM THEM UP.

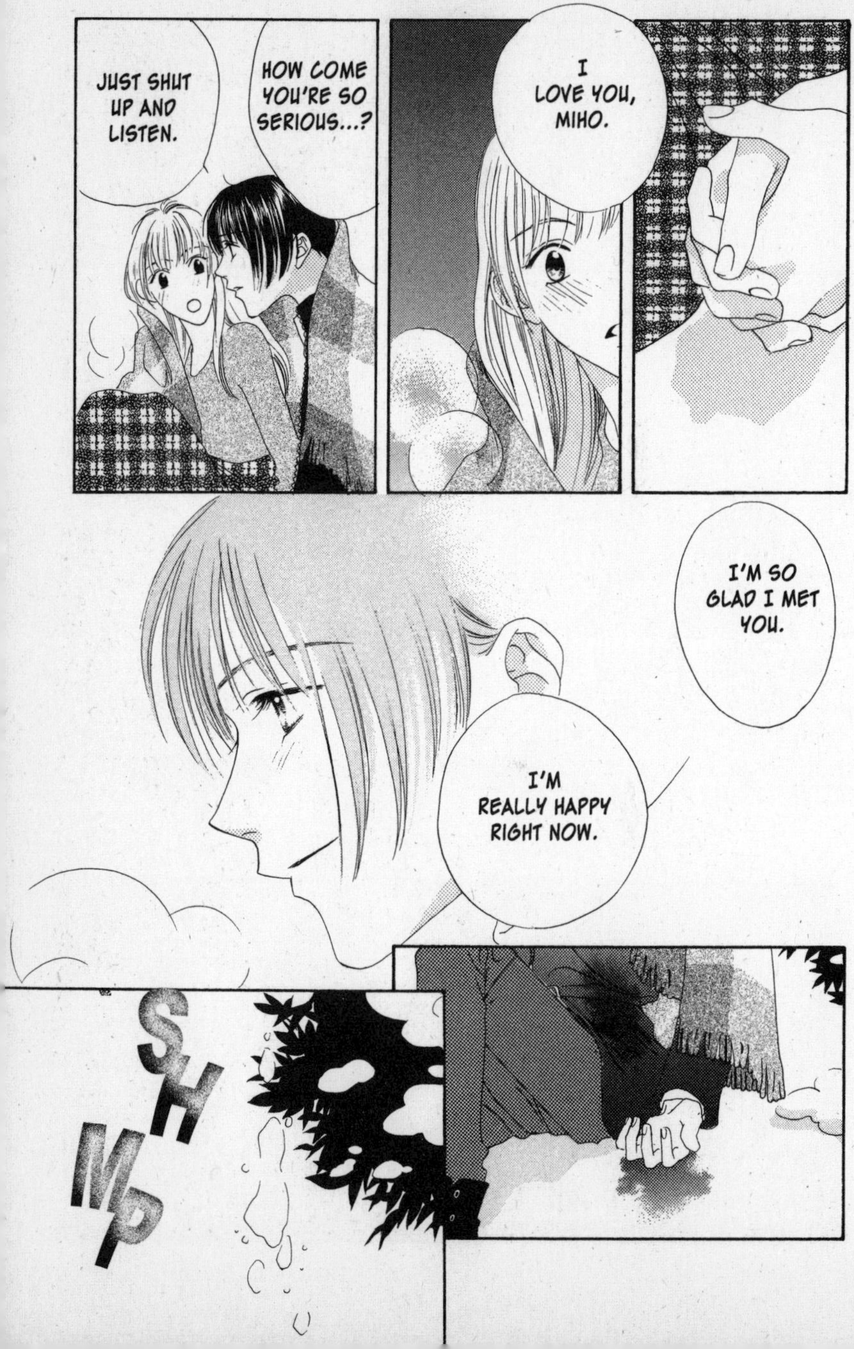
I LOVE YOU, MIHO.
HOW COME YOU'RE SO SERIOUS...?
JUST SHUT UP AND LISTEN.
I'M SO GLAD I MET YOU.
I'M REALLY HAPPY RIGHT NOW.
SHMP

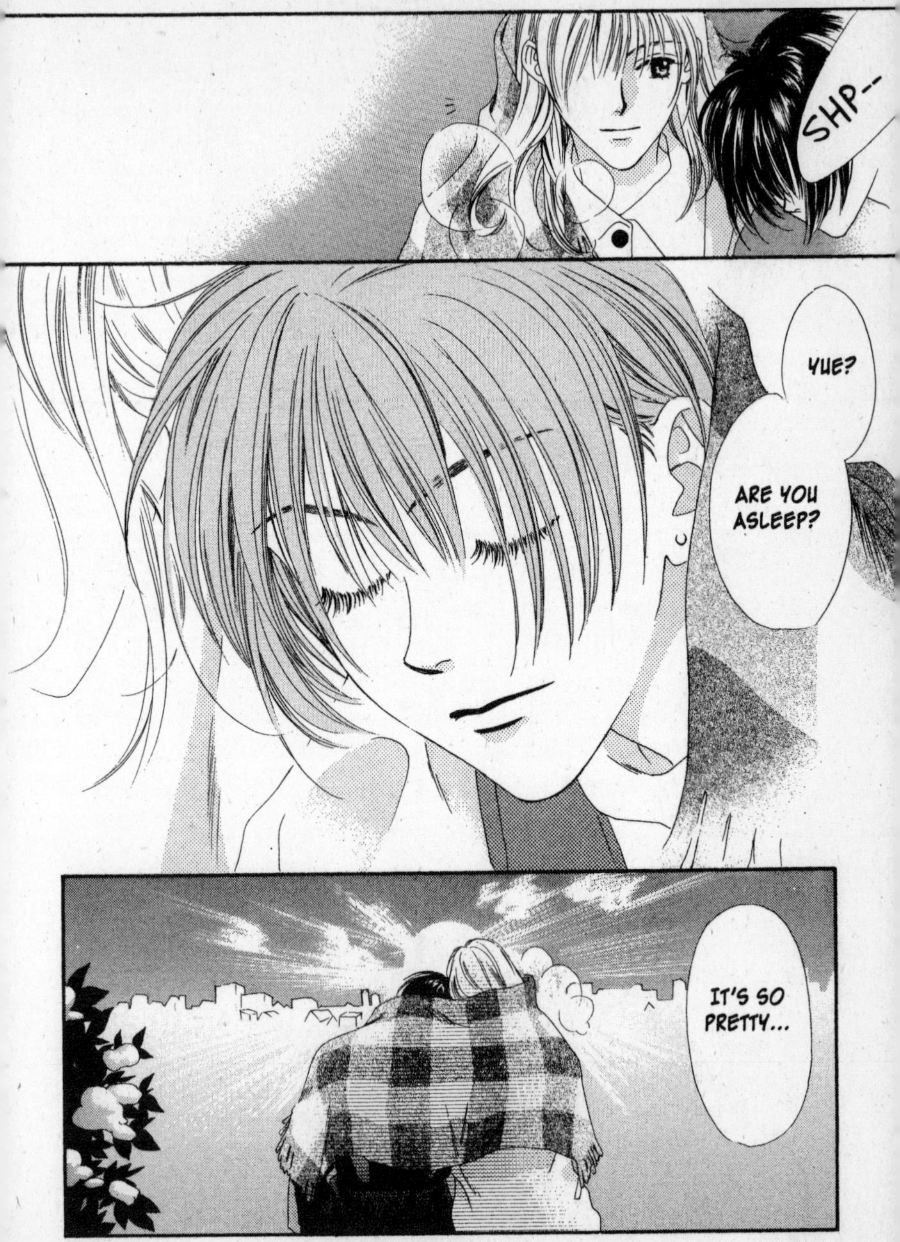
SHP--
YUE?
ARE YOU ASLEEP?
IT'S SO PRETTY...

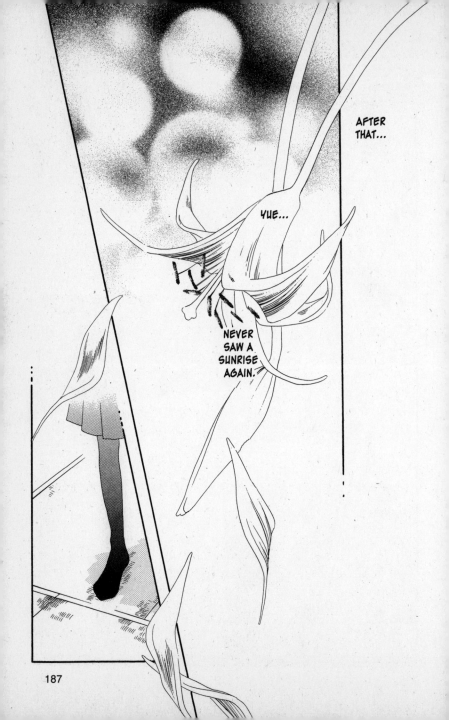

AFTER THAT...

YUE...

NEVER SAW A SUNRISE AGAIN.

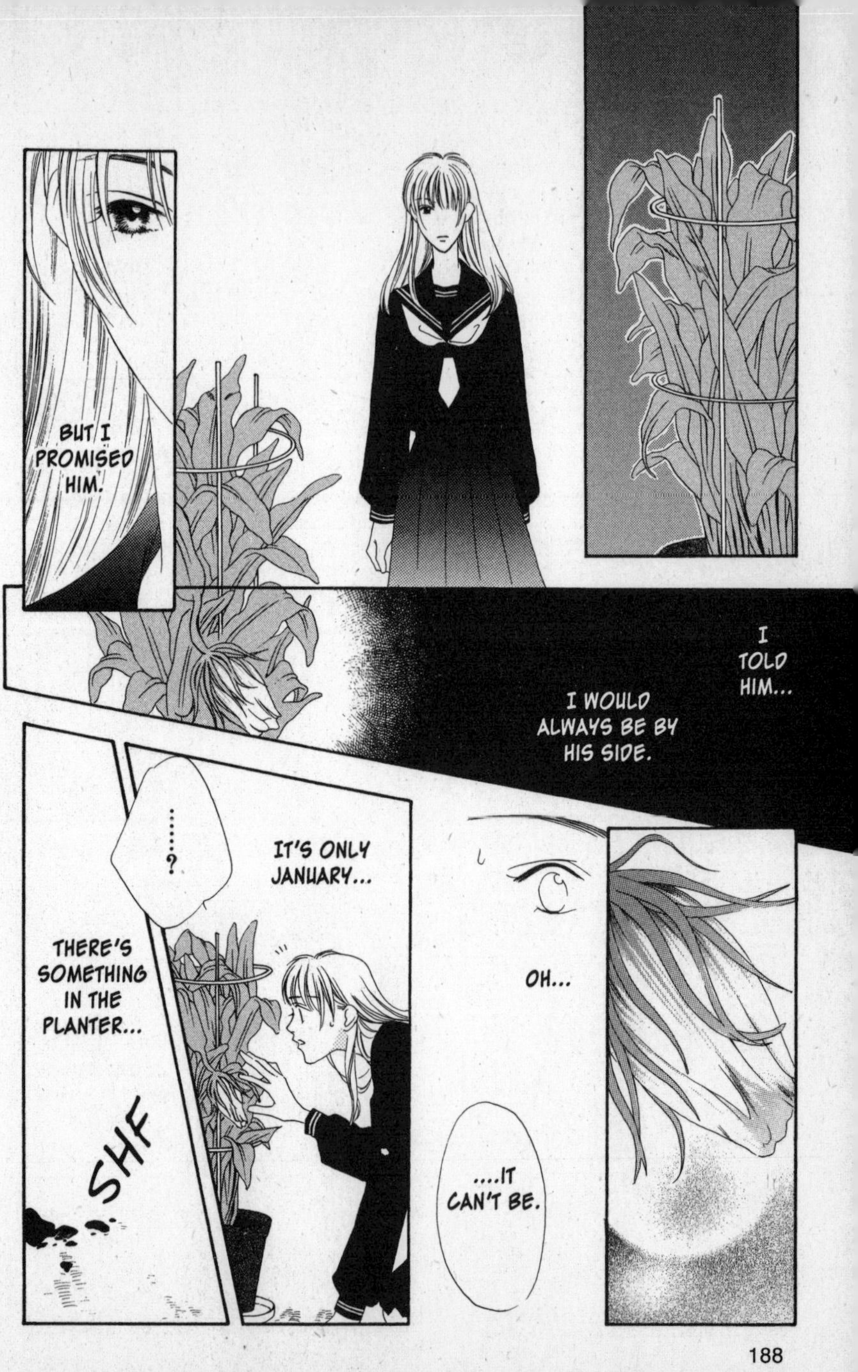
BUT I PROMISED HIM.
I TOLD HIM...
I WOULD ALWAYS BE BY HIS SIDE.
OH...
....IT CAN'T BE.
.....?
IT'S ONLY JANUARY...
THERE'S SOMETHING IN THE PLANTER...
SHF

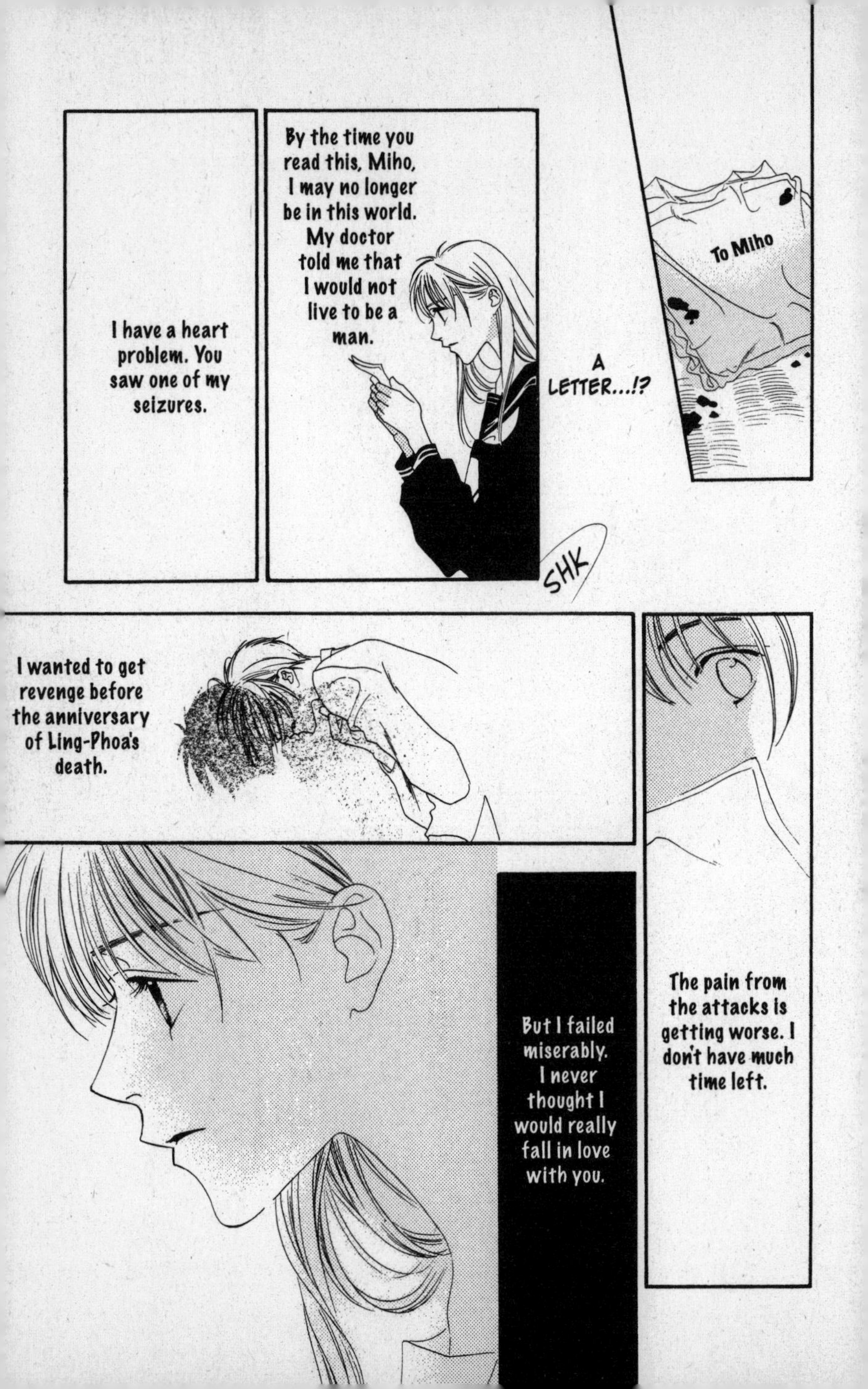
To Miho
A LETTER...!?
SHK
By the time you read this, Miho, I may no longer be in this world. My doctor told me that I would not live to be a man.
I have a heart problem. You saw one of my seizures.
The pain from the attacks is getting worse. I don't have much time left.
I wanted to get revenge before the anniversary of Ling-Phoa's death.
But I failed miserably. I never thought I would really fall in love with you.

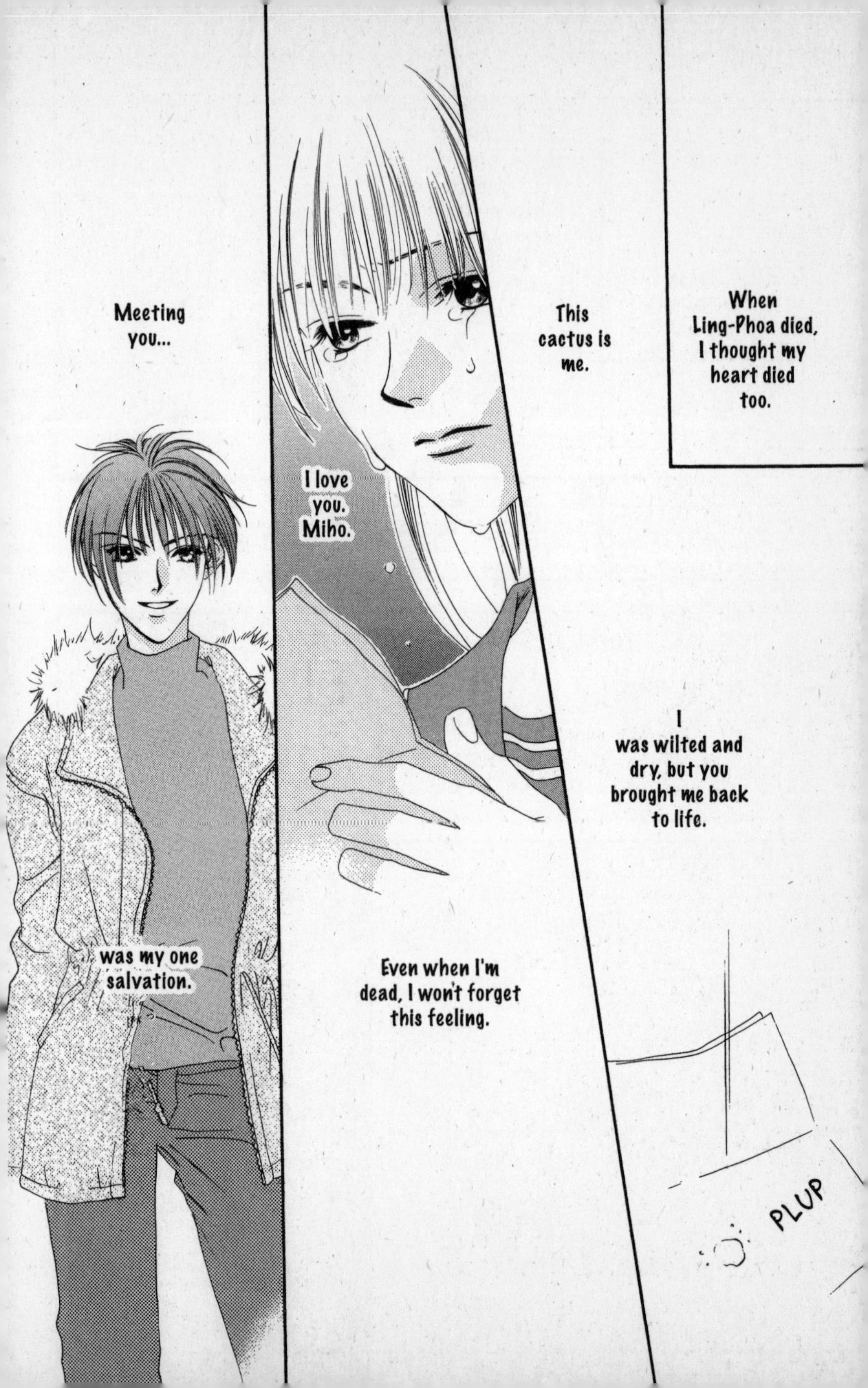
When Ling-Phoa died, I thought my heart died too.
This cactus is me.
I was wilted and dry, but you brought me back to life.
PLUP
I love you. Miho.
Even when I'm dead, I won't forget this feeling.
Meeting you...
was my one salvation.

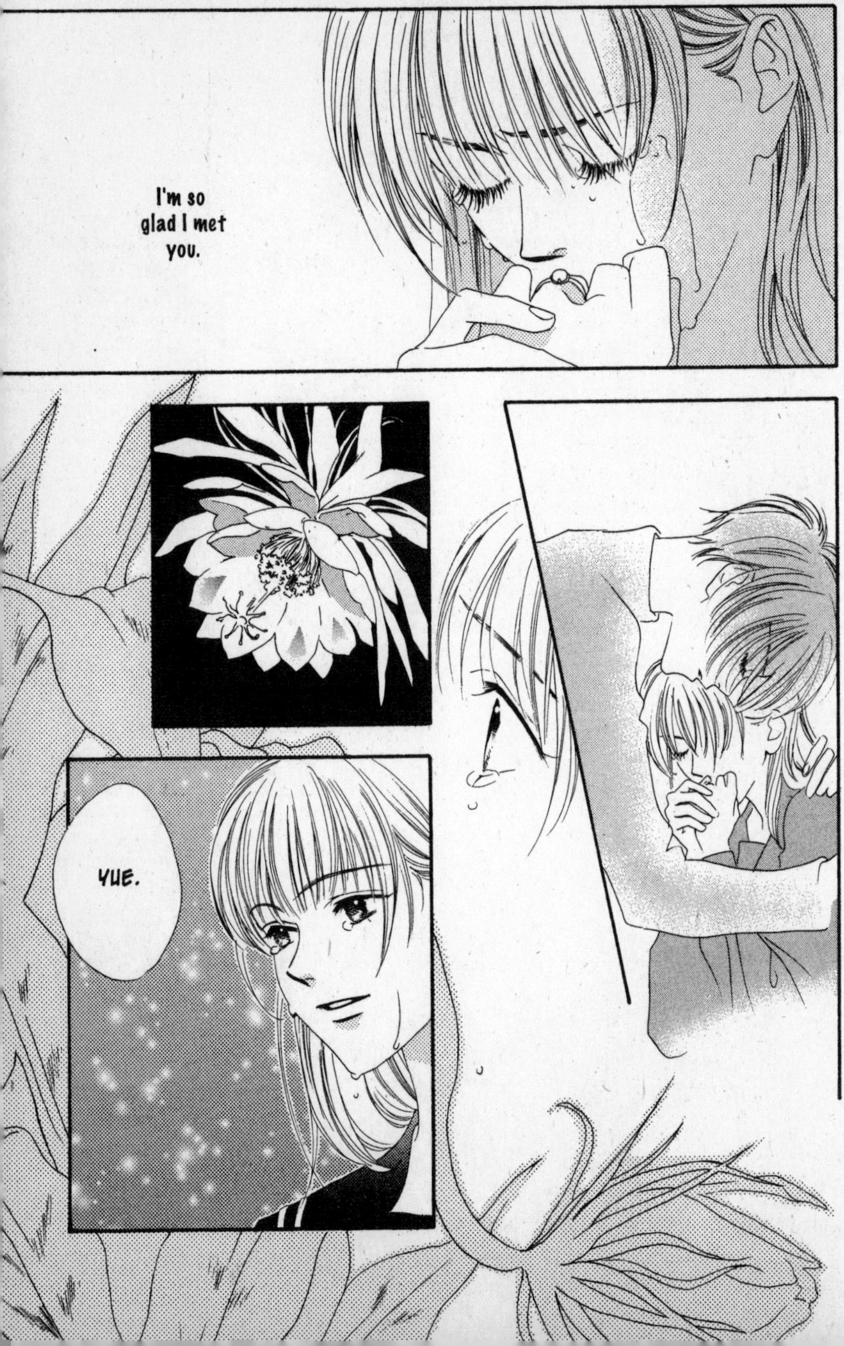
I'm so glad I met you.
YUE.

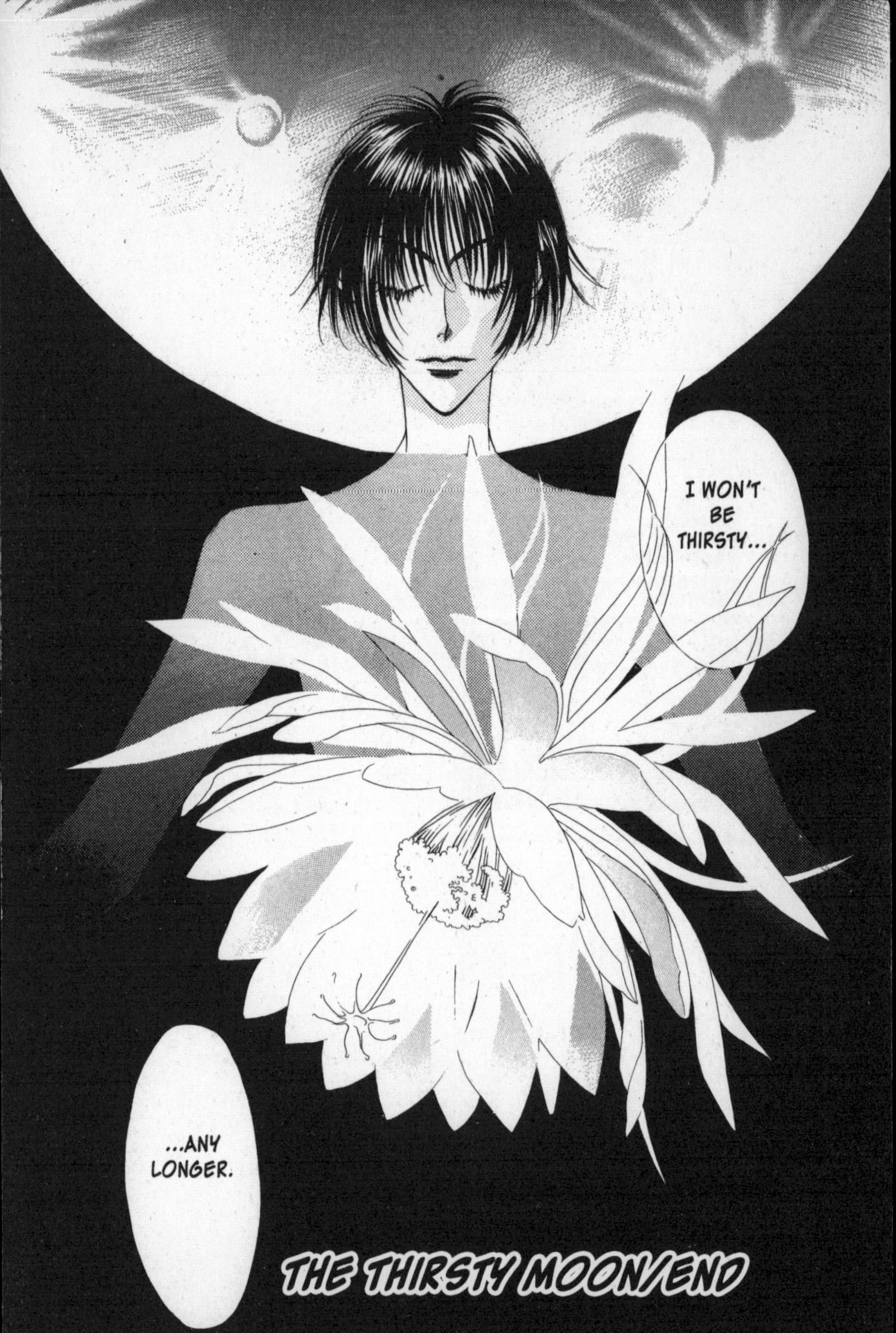
I WON'T BE THIRSTY...
...ANY LONGER.
THE THIRSTY MOON/END

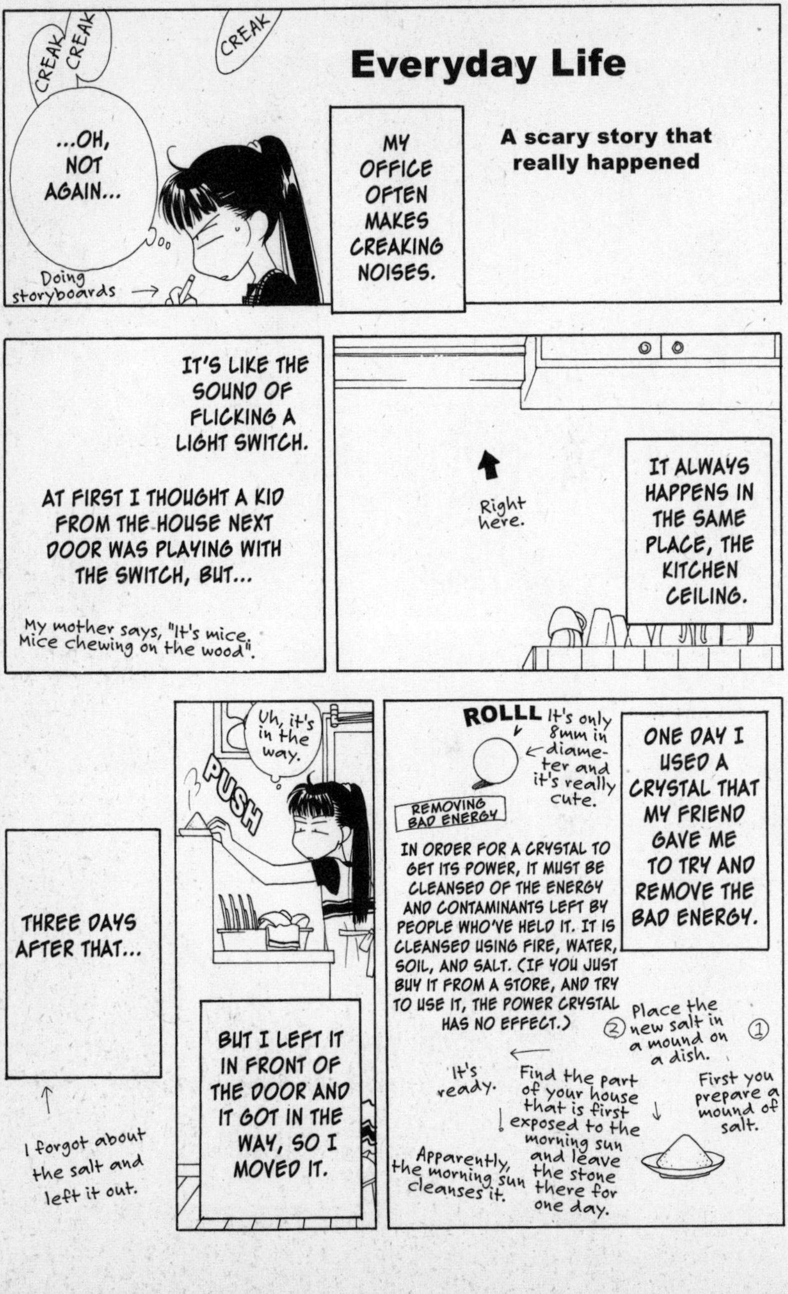
Everyday Life
A scary story that really happened
MY OFFICE OFTEN MAKES CREAKING NOISES.
CREAK
CREAK CREAK
...OH, NOT AGAIN...
Doing storyboards
IT ALWAYS HAPPENS IN THE SAME PLACE, THE KITCHEN CEILING.
Right here.
IT'S LIKE THE SOUND OF FLICKING A LIGHT SWITCH.
AT FIRST I THOUGHT A KID FROM THE HOUSE NEXT DOOR WAS PLAYING WITH THE SWITCH, BUT...
My mother says, "It's mice. Mice chewing on the wood".
ONE DAY I USED A CRYSTAL THAT MY FRIEND GAVE ME TO TRY AND REMOVE THE BAD ENERGY.
ROLLL
It's only 8mm in diameter and it's really cute.
REMOVING BAD ENERGY
IN ORDER FOR A CRYSTAL TO GET ITS POWER, IT MUST BE CLEANSED OF THE ENERGY AND CONTAMINANTS LEFT BY PEOPLE WHO'VE HELD IT. IT IS CLEANSED USING FIRE, WATER, SOIL, AND SALT. (IF YOU JUST BUY IT FROM A STORE, AND TRY TO USE IT, THE POWER CRYSTAL HAS NO EFFECT.)
① First you prepare a mound of salt.
② Place the new salt in a mound on a dish.
Find the part of your house that is first exposed to the morning sun and leave the stone there for one day.
It's ready.
Apparently, the morning sun cleanses it.
Uh, it's in the way.
PUSH
BUT I LEFT IT IN FRONT OF THE DOOR AND IT GOT IN THE WAY, SO I MOVED IT.
THREE DAYS AFTER THAT...
I forgot about the salt and left it out.

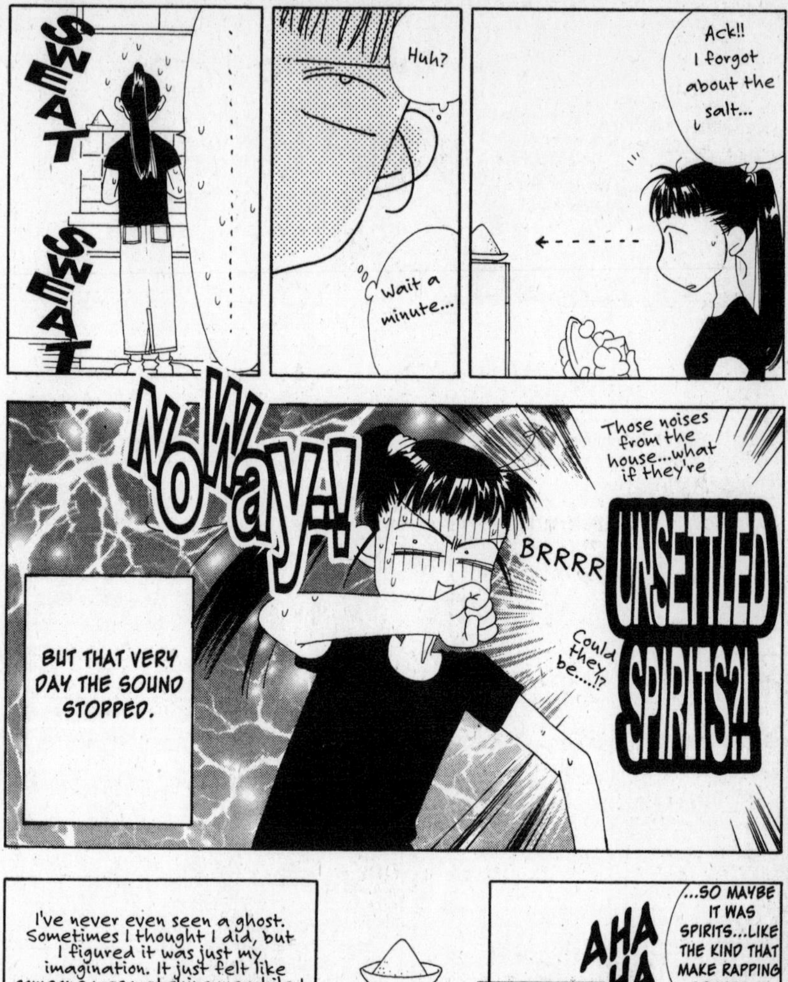
Ack!! I forgot about the salt...
Huh?
Wait a minute...
SWEAT
SWEAT
Those noises from the house...what if they're
UNSETTLED SPIRITS?!
BRRRR
Could they be....!?
NO WAY..!
BUT THAT VERY DAY THE SOUND STOPPED.
...SO MAYBE IT WAS SPIRITS...LIKE THE KIND THAT MAKE RAPPING SOUNDS AT SEANCES!
AHAHAHAHA
Ha ha ha
I TOLD PEOPLE ABOUT IT, BUT I NEVER REALLY THOUGHT IT COULD BE TRUE.
THAT'S RIGHT, THE ACTUAL USE FOR "PROTECTIVE SALT" IS TO KEEP AWAY BAD SPIRITS.
I've never even seen a ghost. Sometimes I thought I did, but I figured it was just my imagination. It just felt like someone was watching me while I worked. But my body type isn't supposed to attract evil spirits. Maybe I have a guardian angel...?
A fortune teller once told me that I have a strong connection with spirits, but I don't believe it!!
Maybe that's why I avoid places that give me a bad feeling?

WELL, I MAY NOT HAVE A CONNECTION TO SPIRITS, BUT I KNOW I'M SENSITIVE.

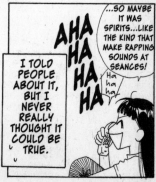

*"UNSETTLED SPIRITS" ARE SAID TO MAKE NOISES SO THAT THEIR PRESENCE IS KNOWN. THEY'RE SAID TO SOUND LIKE A LIVE TREE BEING PULLED FROM THE GROUND.

AFTER ALL, LIVING PEOPLE ARE MUCH STRONGER THAN SPIRITS. WE'VE GOT BREATH! WE'VE GOT POWER!

LOTS OF PEOPLE SAY THEY SAW SPIRITS WHO ONLY THINK THEY SAW THEM. ESPECIALLY YOUNG PEOPLE.

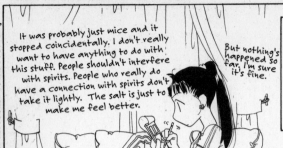

NOTHING GOOD COMES FROM THAT KIND OF STUFF, SO I TRY TO STAY AWAY FROM IT. (HEH)
But nothing's happened so far. I'm sure it's fine.
It was probably just mice and it stopped coincidentally. I don't really want to have anything to do with this stuff. People shouldn't interfere with spirits. People who really do have a connection with spirits don't take it lightly. The salt is just to make me feel better.
I KNEW MY ASSISTANTS WOULD GET SCARED SO I DIDN'T TELL THEM. HEH.
Yes, I'm evil.
Hagi, my hard working assistant.
scribble scribble
Shibachi, a huge fan of the star "Hyde."
draw draw
THIS IS OFF THE SUBJECT, BUT HANA-KIMI'S KAYASHIMA, THE BOY WITH THE SPIRIT CONNECTION, IS NAMED AFTER KAYASHIMA STATION ON OSAKA'S KEIHAN TRAIN LINE. THERE'S A LARGE TREE IN THE MIDDLE OF THAT STATION.
They say that, long ago, it was a tree god.
EVERY TIME THE WORKERS TRIED TO CUT THE TREE DOWN THEY GOT HURT. EVENTUALLY, FEARING THE TREE'S CURSE, THEY BUILT THE STATION AROUND IT. IT'S STILL THERE.
That's why my name is Taiki ("big tree") Kayashima.
Simple, isn't it?
HAUNTED SPOTS
OH YEAH, OH YEAH, THEN THERE'S THAT DEPARTMENT STORE. WHEN I GO ABOVE THE 6TH FLOOR, IT GETS REALLY HARD TO BREATHE, AND WHEN I GET OUT OF THE BUILDING, MY THROAT IS ALL DRY. (I'VE EXPERIENCED THIS MYSELF.)
Later I heard that the department store was rebuilt on the ruins of a store that burnt down. I always felt like my throat got dry when I was there, but I didn't think about it. Maybe that's why....
AND THERE'S A HOTEL IN OSAKA THAT'S FAMOUS FOR HAVING GHOSTS.
I said shut up!
KICK
Scared of ghosts, but likes ghost stories.

TO BE CONTINUED...

Everyday Life/End

IT'S FAMOUS.

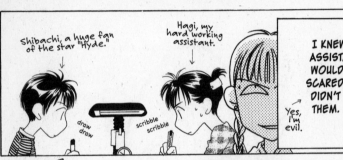

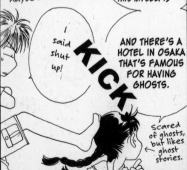

ABOUT THE AUTHOR

Hisaya Nakajo's manga series **Hanazakari no Kimitachi he** ("For You in Full Blossom," casually known as **Hana-Kimi**) has been a hit since it first appeared in 1997 in the shôjo manga magazine **Hana to Yume** ("Flowers and Dreams"). In Japan, a **Hana-Kimi** art book and several "drama CDs" have been released. Her other manga series include **Missing Piece** (2 volumes) and **Yumemiru Happa** ("The Dreaming Leaf," 1 volume).

Hisaya Nakajo's website:
www.wild-vanilla.com

IN THE NEXT VOLUME ...

It's the final day of the Osaka High School Festival, and the relay race and the "Miss Osaka" pageant are still up in the air! You'd think Mizuki, being an actual girl, would have an advantage over her classmates, but things are never so easy—and what if winning the contest blows her cover? That might be a relief for Nakatsu, who doesn't know that Mizuki's a girl. But Nakatsu's love life is about to get even *more* complicated...

ON SALE NOW!

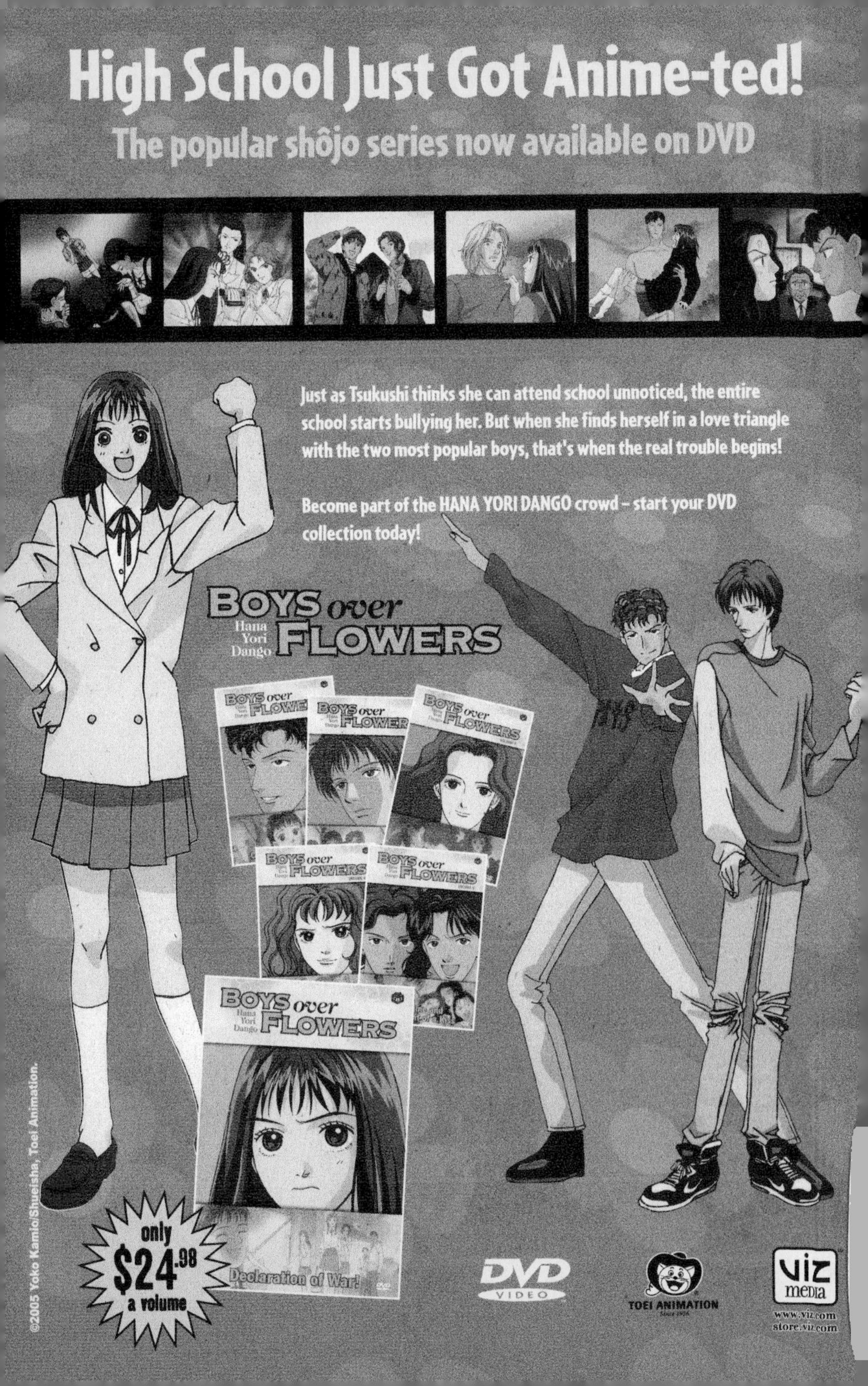
High School Just Got Anime-ted!
The popular shôjo series now available on DVD
Just as Tsukushi thinks she can attend school unnoticed, the entire school starts bullying her. But when she finds herself in a love triangle with the two most popular boys, that's when the real trouble begins!
Become part of the HANA YORI DANGO crowd – start your DVD collection today!
BOYS over FLOWERS
Hana Yori Dango
Declaration of War!
only $24.98 a volume
DVD VIDEO
TOEI ANIMATION
VIZ media
www.viz.com
store.viz.com
©2005 Yoko Kamio/Shueisha, Toei Animation.